COTTAGE PR...

Primary
Source Reader

FOR AMERICAN CULTURE

ACKNOWLEDGEMENTS

Many hands make light work! Several folks contributed to this reader. Thanks to Mr. Andrew Banbrick for his help in choosing and gathering selections, sources, and background information. Thanks to Dr. Stephen Davis for his help in choosing excerpts from "Heaven is a World of Love." Many thanks also to Grace Weitz for her help in compiling and editing those sources, and in writing introductions. Thanks to Rick Weitz and Kimberlynn Curles for their work on introductions also. The cover art is entitled "Washington Crossing the Delaware," a nineteenth century painting by Emanuel Gottlieb Leutze. (Source: wikimedia.org)

kpw

PRIMARY SOURCE READER

American Culture

Archbishop of Canterbury 13
THE MAGNA CHARTA

Christopher Columbus 30
JOURNAL, 1492

William Bradford 42
THE MAYFLOWER COMPACT

Richard Mather... 44
THE BAY PSALM BOOK

John Winthrop... 53
A MODEL OF CHRISTIAN CHARITY

Jonathan Edwards...74
SINNERS IN THE HANDS OF AN ANGRY GOD

Jonathan Edwards..97
HEAVEN IS A WORLD OF LOVE

James Otis, Jr. 110
WRITS OF ASSISTANCE

Samuel Davies 116
GREAT GOD OF WONDERS

Benjamin Franklin 119
SILENCE DOGOOD LETTERS

George Whitefield 134
THE METHOD OF GRACE

Patrick Henry 156
LIBERTY OR DEATH

John Dickinson 160
LETTERS FROM A FARMER IN PENNSYLVANIA TO THE INHABITANTS OF
THE BRITISH COLONIES

Continental Congress 166
THE OLIVE BRANCH PETITION

Second Continental Congress 173
DECLARATION OF INDEPENDENCE

Second Continental Congress 181
ARTICLES OF CONFEDERATION

Congress Of The Confederation 194
NORTHWEST ORDINANCE

Constitutional Convention 205
CONSTITUTION OF THE UNITED STATES

Alexander Hamilton 224
FEDERALIST 1, 2, & 84

John Jay 250
FEDERALIST 2

James Madison.. 257

FEDERALIST 10 & 51

Patrick Henry 274

ANTI-FEDERALIST WRITINGS

James Madison.. 287

BILL OF RIGHTS

United States Congress.. 290

AMENDMENTS TO THE CONSTITUTION

Francis Hopkinson 302

HAIL, COLUMBIA!

George Washington 304

FAREWELL ADDRESS

Presbyterian United Synod.. 326

REVISIONS TO THE WESTMINSTER CONFESSION

Episcopal Church In America.. 331

REVISIONS TO THE THIRTY-NINE ARTICLES

Francis Scott Key...335

THE STAR-SPANGLED BANNER

16th United States Congress... 337

MISSOURI COMPROMISE

John Quincy Adams.. 344

MONROE DOCTRINE

Congress of the United States... 348
             INDIAN REMOVAL ACT

Samuel Francis Smith... 351
             MY COUNTRY, 'TIS OF THEE

Alexis de Toqueville 353
             DEMOCRACY IN AMERICA

Daniel Webster 374
             SECOND REPLY TO HAYNE

Roger B. Taney... 385
             DRED SCOTT V. SANFORD

African-American Slaves 392
             NEGRO SPIRITUALS

Alexander Stephens 396
             CORNERSTONE SPEECH

Jefferson Davis... 411
             SECESSION SPEECH

Confederate States... 418
             CONFEDERATE CONSTITUTION

Robert E. Lee 441
             PERSONAL CORRESPONDENCE

Joshua Chamberlain... 448
             GETTYSBURG ACCOUNT

Abraham Lincoln...455
GETTYSBURG ADDRESS

Abraham Lincoln...457
EMANCIPATION PROCLAMATION

Abraham Lincoln...461
SECOND INAUGURAL ADDRESS

Philip Bliss 464
MAN OF SORROWS

Horatio Spafford... 466
IT IS WELL

Fanny Crosby 468
BLESSED ASSURANCE

Elizabeth Cady Stanton.. 470
DECLARATION OF SENTIMENTS

William Jennings Bryan...475
CROSS OF GOLD SPEECH

Katharine Lee Bates 486
AMERICA, THE BEAUTIFUL

Theodore Roosevelt.. 488
THE MAN WITH THE MUCK RAKE

Proclaim Liberty

. . . proclaim liberty throughout the land and to all the inhabitants
thereof.   — Leviticus 25:10

If a hope of freedom is to endure, it will endure as the fruits of
the gospel, for only the gospel proclaims liberty to mankind.
— Cotton Mather, "a father to the Founding Fathers"

Resistance to tyranny becomes the Christian and social
duty of each individual . . . Continue steadfast and, with a
proper sense of your dependence on God, nobly defend those
rights which heaven gave, and no man ought to take from us.
— John Hancock, First Signer of the Declaration of Independence

Honour thy father and thy mother: that thy days may be long upon
the land which the Lord thy God giveth thee.—Exodus 20:12

L iberty is often misunderstood as freedom from any kind of constraint. A moment's reflection, however, reveals that the unlimited and absolute freedom of one person could well annihilate the freedom, to say nothing of the life, of another. There are two main contexts, and therefore two types of liberty: spiritual and political. Both of these find expression in the City of God as well as the City of Man; at many points, the conception of freedom in both Athens and Jerusalem are in agreement.

In the Hebrew, the word rendered liberty is *d'ror*; it refers to the release of captives, or slaves. In Leviticus 25, it is connected with the year of Jubilee, a Sabbath of Sabbaths. Thus, God, through Moses, points His people both backward to Creation (Genesis 1), and forward to the ultimate and everlasting Sabbath rest (Hebrews 4). Israel, however, failed to obey, resulting in Yahweh's covenant lawsuit against them, proclaiming against them: "liberty to the sword, to pestilence, and to famine, declares the LORD" (Jeremiah 34:17). Thus, liberty has both positive and negative connotations and results for the people of God. In His steadfast kindness and mercy, God does not leave His people there, as we see in the words of the prophet Isaiah, speaking also of *d'ror*: "The Spirit of the Lord God is upon me, because the Lord has anointed me to bring good news to the poor; he has sent me to bind up the captives, to proclaim liberty to the captives, and the opening of the prison to those who are bound." (Isaiah 61:1). This is the very Scripture with which Jesus opens his earthly ministry. (Luke 4:18-19) The Hebrew *d'ror* is a beautifully poetic word, literally meaning *free flowing*. Furthermore, the Hebrew word is also translated in some places as the *swallow*: "Even the sparrow finds a home, and the *swallow* a nest, where she may lay her young, at your altars, O Lord of hosts, my King and my God." (Psalm 84:3) This psalm extols the loveliness of the Lord's dwelling place, His temple, the place of His worship. Thus, the Hebrew conception of liberty is intimately and ultimately connected with the acts of worship and obedience, which are commanded by God; this is clearly seen in the descriptive reason for the prescriptive norms of the Ten Commandments: "I am the Lord your God, who brought you out of the land of Egypt, out of the house of slavery." (Exodus 20:1) Thus, liberty is a paradox: God's people are set free to worship and obey.

The paradox of freedom has both spiritual and political/social implications. Limits are imposed in both spheres. Before the fall, Adam had perfect freedom that was to find expression in his worship and obedience. After the fall, liberty remains, but it is bound by and enslaved to sin, so that worship and obedience are hindered and even rendered impossible. In Christ, we are freed from the penalty of sin, but not immediately from its effects or influence (Romans 7).

In the City of Man, the concept of freedom also appears, and in many ways mirrors the biblical understanding. In Athens, the concept of freedom was a matter of constant philosophical pondering. The ancients understood that political freedom is not absolute; it always comes with limits of some sort. Plato and Aristotle recognized the civil war that rages wthin man's soul, and the political implications, inherent dangers, and limits of political systems from democracy to tyranny.

The Puritans, inheritors of both of these traditions, came to America seeking freedom, but they had no delusions of unhindered freedom. They sought the Hebrew understanding of freedom, desiring to worship and obey God with liberty of conscience.

As gospel-saturated believers, they understood that that man's fallen nature hinders both the spiritual and social/political aspects of freedom. Limits must be imposed in order for freedom to flower. The American experiment in liberty is the direct heir of this wisdom. Our founding founding fathers enshrined this understanding in the the great republic they created, and then defended with their own "lives, liberty, and sacred honor."

History has shown that the outworking of these ideals has fallen woefully short. The founders themselves, deeply flawed men, did not live up to the ideals which they so eloquently set forth. The injustices they countenanced would eventually bring a bloody civil war on the fledgling nation, and its bitter legacy continues to this day. Still, we must commend the noble aspirations and the accompanying wise actions, however imperfectly executed, undertaken to bequeath liberty to those who would come after. For without their wisdom and their work, the injustices that persist to our day would not even be recognized, let alone addressed. As God commands us in His law, we are to honor our fathers and our mothers; we, who would live long and well in the land, dare not disobey.

Future generations will stand in judgement over us. Our blind spots and flaws will be open for all to see. Just as we would hope for clear-eyed, yet grateful charity towards us, we must offer the same to the the men and women who founded and built this nation. Let us read the history of our nation with a hermeneutic of humility.

ARCHBISHOP OF CANTERBURY

The Magna Charta

The Magna Carta Libertatum (Medieval Latin for "the Great Charter of the Liberties") is commonly called Magna Carta (also Magna Charta; "(the) Great Charter"). Written in 1215 by the Archbishop of Canterbury, this document was designed to broker peace between the English King John and a group of dissenting barons. The charter called for protection of the church, protection for the barons from false imprisonment, prompt and fair trials, and limitiations on payments to the Crown. The unpopular King John reluctantly signed the charter at Runnytmeade, forced by the angry barons. It went through a series of rejections and refinements for the next 80 years, with King Edward I declaring the Magna Charta as settled English law in 1297.

John, by the grace of God, king of England, lord of Ireland, duke of Normandy and Aquitaine, and count of Anjou, to the archbishop, bishops, abbots, earls, barons, justiciaries, foresters, sheriffs, stewards, servants, and to all his bailiffs and liege subjects, greetings. Know that, having regard to God and for the salvation of our soul, and those of all our ancestors and heirs, and unto the honor of God and the advancement of his holy Church and for the rectifying of our realm, we have granted as underwritten by advice of our venerable fathers, Stephen, archbishop of Canterbury, primate of all England and cardinal of the holy Roman Church, Henry, archbishop of Dublin, William of London, Peter of Winchester, Jocelyn of Bath and Glastonbury, Hugh of Lincoln, Walter of Worcester, William of Coventry, Benedict of Rochester, bishops; of Master Pandulf, subdeacon and member of the household

of our lord the Pope, of brother Aymeric (master of the Knights of
the Temple in England), and of the illustrious men William Marshal,
earl of Pembroke, William, earl of Salisbury, William, earl of
Warenne, William, earl of Arundel, Alan of Galloway (constable
of Scotland), Waren Fitz Gerold, Peter Fitz Herbert, Hubert
De Burgh (seneschal of Poitou), Hugh de Neville, Matthew Fitz
Herbert, Thomas Basset, Alan Basset, Philip d'Aubigny, Robert
of Roppesley, John Marshal, John Fitz Hugh, and others, our
liegemen.

1. In the first place we have granted to God, and by this our
present charter confirmed for us and our heirs forever that the
English Church shall be free, and shall have her rights entire,
and her liberties inviolate; and we will that it be thus observed;
which is apparent from this that the freedom of elections, which is
reckoned most important and very essential to the English Church,
we, of our pure and unconstrained will, did grant, and did by our
charter confirm and did obtain the ratification of the same from
our lord, Pope Innocent III, before the quarrel arose between us
and our barons: and this we will observe, and our will is that it be
observed in good faith by our heirs forever. We have also granted
to all freemen of our kingdom, for us and our heirs forever, all the
underwritten liberties, to be had and held by them and their heirs,
of us and our heirs forever.

2. If any of our earls or barons, or others holding of us in chief
by military service shall have died, and at the time of his death
his heir shall be full of age and owe "relief", he shall have his
inheritance by the old relief, to wit, the heir or heirs of an earl, for
the whole baroncy of an earl by L100; the heir or heirs of a baron,
L100 for a whole barony; the heir or heirs of a knight, 100s, at most,

and whoever owes less let him give less, according to the ancient custom of fees.

3. If, however, the heir of any one of the aforesaid has been under age and in wardship, let him have his inheritance without relief and without fine when he comes of age.

4. The guardian of the land of an heir who is thus under age, shall take from the land of the heir nothing but reasonable produce, reasonable customs, and reasonable services, and that without destruction or waste of men or goods; and if we have committed the wardship of the lands of any such minor to the sheriff, or to any other who is responsible to us for its issues, and he has made destruction or waster of what he holds in wardship, we will take of him amends, and the land shall be committed to two lawful and discreet men of that fee, who shall be responsible for the issues to us or to him to whom we shall assign them; and if we have given or sold the wardship of any such land to anyone and he has therein made destruction or waste, he shall lose that wardship, and it shall be transferred to two lawful and discreet men of that fief, who shall be responsible to us in like manner as aforesaid.

5. The guardian, moreover, so long as he has the wardship of the land, shall keep up the houses, parks, fishponds, stanks, mills, and other things pertaining to the land, out of the issues of the same land; and he shall restore to the heir, when he has come to full age, all his land, stocked with ploughs and wainage, according as the season of husbandry shall require, and the issues of the land can reasonable bear.

6. Heirs shall be married without disparagement, yet so that before the marriage takes place the nearest in blood to that heir shall

have notice.

7. A widow, after the death of her husband, shall forthwith and without difficulty have her marriage portion and inheritance; nor shall she give anything for her dower, or for her marriage portion, or for the inheritance which her husband and she held on the day of the death of that husband; and she may remain in the house of her husband for forty days after his death, within which time her dower shall be assigned to her.

8. No widow shall be compelled to marry, so long as she prefers to live without a husband; provided always that she gives security not to marry without our consent, if she holds of us, or without the consent of the lord of whom she holds, if she holds of another.

9. Neither we nor our bailiffs[1] will seize any land or rent for any debt, as long as the chattels[2] of the debtor are sufficient to repay the debt; nor shall the sureties[3] of the debtor be distrained so long as the principal debtor is able to satisfy the debt; and if the principal debtor shall fail to pay the debt, having nothing wherewith to pay it, then the sureties shall answer for the debt; and let them have the lands and rents of the debtor, if they desire them, until they are indemnified for the debt which they have paid for him, unless the principal debtor can show proof that he is discharged thereof as against the said sureties.

10. If one who has borrowed from the Jews any sum, great or small, die before that loan be repaid, the debt shall not bear interest while the heir is under age, of whomsoever he may hold; and if

---

1 *bailiff*: "general term for "king's officers . . . [such as]sheriffs, mayors, etc." (OED)
2 *chattel*: "property, goods, money" (OED)
3 *surety*: "pledge, bond, or security given as a guarantee of good conduct, the fulfillment of certain duties, etc." (OED)

the debt fall into our hands, we will not take anything except the principal sum contained in the bond.

11. And if anyone die indebted to the Jews, his wife shall have her dower and pay nothing of that debt; and if any children of the deceased are left under age, necessaries shall be provided for them in keeping with the holding of the deceased; and out of the residue the debt shall be paid, reserving, however, service due to feudal lords; in like manner let it be done touching debts due to others than Jews.

12. No scutage[4] nor aid shall be imposed on our kingdom, unless by common counsel of our kingdom, except for ransoming our person, for making our eldest son a knight, and for once marrying our eldest daughter; and for these there shall not be levied more than a reasonable aid. In like manner it shall be done concerning aids from the city of London.

13. And the city of London shall have all it ancient liberties and free customs, as well by land as by water; furthermore, we decree and grant that all other cities, boroughs, towns, and ports shall have all their liberties and free customs.

14. And for obtaining the common counsel of the kingdom anent the assessing of an aid (except in the three cases aforesaid) or of a scutage, we will cause to be summoned the archbishops, bishops, abbots, earls, and greater barons, severally by our letters; and we will moveover cause to be summoned generally, through our sheriffs and bailiffs, and others who hold of us in chief, for a fixed date, namely, after the expiry of at least forty days, and at a fixed place; and in all letters of such summons we will specify the reason of the summons. And when the summons has thus been made, the business

4   *scutage*: "tax levied on knight's fees . . . paid in lieu of military service" (OED)

shall proceed on the day appointed, according to the counsel of such as are present, although not all who were summoned have come.

15. We will not for the future grant to anyone license to take an aid from his own free tenants, except to ransom his person, to make his eldest son a knight, and once to marry his eldest daughter; and on each of these occasions there shall be levied only a reasonable aid.

16. No one shall be distrained for performance of greater service for a knight's fee, or for any other free tenement, than is due therefrom.

17. Common pleas shall not follow our court, but shall be held in some fixed place.

18. Inquests of *novel disseisin*, of *mort d'ancestor*, and of *darrein presentment*[5] shall not be held elsewhere than in their own county courts, and that in manner following; We, or, if we should be out of the realm, our chief justiciar,[6] will send two justiciaries through every county four times a year, who shall alone with four knights of the county chosen by the county, hold the said assizes[7] in the county court, on the day and in the place of meeting of that court.

19. And if any of the said assizes cannot be taken on the day of the county court, let there remain of the knights and freeholders, who were present at the county court on that day, as many as may be required for the efficient making of judgments, according as the business be more or less.

20. A freeman shall not be amerced[8] for a slight offense, except

5 *Novel disseisin, mort d'ancestor,* and *darrein presentment* all have to do with unlawful seizure or dispossession of lands (OED)
6 *justiciar:* "a person who adminsters justice" (OED)
7 *assizes:* "legislative sitting, statute, statutory measure or matter" (OED)
8 amerce: "to punish an offense" with a monetary penalty (OED)

in accordance with the degree of the offense; and for a grave offense he shall be amerced in accordance with the gravity of the offense, yet saving always his "contentment"; and a merchant in the same way, saving his "merchandise"; and a villein shall be amerced in the same way, saving his "wainage" if they have fallen into our mercy: and none of the aforesaid amercements shall be imposed except by the oath of honest men of the neighborhood.

21. Earls and barons shall not be amerced except through their peers, and only in accordance with the degree of the offense.

22. A clerk shall not be amerced in respect of his lay holding except after the manner of the others aforesaid; further, he shall not be amerced in accordance with the extent of his ecclesiastical benefice.

23. No village or individual shall be compelled to make bridges at river banks, except those who from of old were legally bound to do so.

24. No sheriff, constable, coroners, or others of our bailiffs, shall hold pleas of our Crown.

25. All counties, hundred, wapentakes, and trithings (except our demesne manors) shall remain at the old rents, and without any additional payment.

26. If anyone holding of us a lay fief[9] shall die, and our sheriff or bailiff shall exhibit our letters patent of summons for a debt which the deceased owed us, it shall be lawful for our sheriff or bailiff to attach and enroll the chattels of the deceased, found upon the lay fief, to the value of that debt, at the sight of law worthy men,

---

9 *fief*: "a feudal estate" (Merriam-Webster)

provided always that nothing whatever be thence removed until the debt which is evident shall be fully paid to us; and the residue shall be left to the executors to fulfill the will of the deceased; and if there be nothing due from him to us, all the chattels shall go to the deceased, saving to his wife and children their reasonable shares.

27. If any freeman shall die intestate,[10] his chattels shall be distributed by the hands of his nearest kinsfolk and friends, under supervision of the Church, saving to every one the debts which the deceased owed to him.

28. No constable or other bailiff of ours shall take corn or other provisions from anyone without immediately tendering money therefor, unless he can have postponement thereof by permission of the seller.

29. No constable shall compel any knight to give money in lieu of castle-guard, when he is willing to perform it in his own person, or (if he himself cannot do it from any reasonable cause) then by another responsible man. Further, if we have led or sent him upon military service, he shall be relieved from guard in proportion to the time during which he has been on service because of us.

30. No sheriff or bailiff of ours, or other person, shall take the horses or carts of any freeman for transport duty, against the will of the said freeman.

31. Neither we nor our bailiffs shall take, for our castles or for any other work of ours, wood which is not ours, against the will of the owner of that wood.

32. We will not retain beyond one year and one day, the lands

---

10 *intestate*: "not having made a will" (OED)

those who have been convicted of felony, and the lands shall thereafter be handed over to the lords of the fiefs.

33. All kydells[11] for the future shall be removed altogether from Thames and Medway, and throughout all England, except upon the seashore.

34. The writ which is called *praecipe*[12] shall not for the future be issued to anyone, regarding any tenement whereby a freeman may lose his court.

35. Let there be one measure of wine throughout our whole realm; and one measure of ale; and one measure of corn, to wit, "the London quarter"; and one width of cloth (whether dyed, or russet, or "halberget"), to wit, two ells within the selvedges; of weights also let it be as of measures.

36. Nothing in future shall be given or taken for a writ of inquisition of life or limbs, but freely it shall be granted, and never denied.

37. If anyone holds of us by fee-farm,[13] either by socage[14] or by burage,[15] or of any other land by knight's service, we will not (by reason of that fee-farm, socage, or burgage), have the wardship of the heir, or of such land of his as if of the fief of that other; nor shall we have wardship of that fee-farm, socage, or burgage, unless such fee-farm owes knight's service. We will not by reason of any small serjeancy[16] which anyone may hold of us by the service of rendering

---

11 *kydell*: "A dam, weir, or barrier in a river, having an opening in it fitted with nets or other appliances for catching fish" (OED)
12 *praecipe*: "demanding action or an explanation of non-action" (OED)
13 *fee-farm*: "land . . . held in fee-simple subject to a perpetual fixed rent" (OED)
14 *socage*: land held "by certain determinate services other than knight-service" (OED)
15 *burage (burgage)*: "lands or tenements in cities and towns . . . held of the king or other lord, for a certain yearly rent" (OED)
16 *serjeancy*: "the office of a sergeant" (OED)

to us knives, arrows, or the like, have wardship of his heir or of the land which he holds of another lord by knight's service.

38. No bailiff for the future shall, upon his own unsupported complaint, put anyone to his "law", without credible witnesses brought for this purposes.

39. No freemen shall be taken or imprisoned or disseised[17] or exiled or in any way destroyed, nor will we go upon him nor send upon him, except by the lawful judgment of his peers or by the law of the land.

40. To no one will we sell, to no one will we refuse or delay, right or justice.

41. All merchants shall have safe and secure exit from England, and entry to England, with the right to tarry there and to move about as well by land as by water, for buying and selling by the ancient and right customs, quit from all evil tolls, except (in time of war) such merchants as are of the land at war with us. And if such are found in our land at the beginning of the war, they shall be detained, without injury to their bodies or goods, until information be received by us, or by our chief justiciar, how the merchants of our land found in the land at war with us are treated; and if our men are safe there, the others shall be safe in our land.

42. It shall be lawful in future for anyone (excepting always those imprisoned or outlawed in accordance with the law of the kingdom, and natives of any country at war with us, and merchants, who shall be treated as if above provided) to leave our kingdom and to return, safe and secure by land and water, except for a short period in time of war, on grounds of public policy- reserving always

---

17 *disseised*: "to dispossess . . . of estates, etc, usually wrongfully or by force" (OED)

the allegiance due to us.

43. If anyone holding of some escheat[18] (such as the honor of Wallingford, Nottingham, Boulogne, Lancaster, or of other escheats which are in our hands and are baronies) shall die, his heir shall give no other relief, and perform no other service to us than he would have done to the baron if that barony had been in the baron's hand; and we shall hold it in the same manner in which the baron held it.

44. Men who dwell without the forest need not henceforth come before our justiciaries of the forest upon a general summons, unless they are in plea, or sureties of one or more, who are attached for the forest.

45. We will appoint as justices, constables, sheriffs, or bailiffs only such as know the law of the realm and mean to observe it well.

46. All barons who have founded abbeys, concerning which they hold charters from the kings of England, or of which they have long continued possession, shall have the wardship of them, when vacant, as they ought to have.

47. All forests that have been made such in our time shall forthwith be disafforsted;[19] and a similar course shall be followed with regard to river banks that have been placed "in defense" by us in our time.

48. All evil customs connected with forests and warrens, foresters and warreners, sheriffs and their officers, river banks and their wardens, shall immediately by inquired into in each county by twelve sworn knights of the same county chosen by the honest men of the same county, and shall, within forty days of the said inquest,

---

18 *escheat*: confiscated "property, real or personal" (OED)
19 *disafforsted*: "have no Ranger" (OED)

be utterly abolished, so as never to be restored, provided always that
we previously have intimation thereof, or our justiciar, if we should
not be in England.

49. We will immediately restore all hostages and charters
delivered to us by Englishmen, as sureties of the peace of faithful
service.

50. We will entirely remove from their bailiwicks,[20] the relations
of Gerard of Athee (so that in future they shall have no bailiwick in
England); namely, Engelard of Cigogne, Peter, Guy, and Andrew
of Chanceaux, Guy of Cigogne, Geoffrey of Martigny with his
brothers, Philip Mark with his brothers and his nephew Geoffrey,
and the whole brood of the same.

51. As soon as peace is restored, we will banish from the kingdom
all foreign born knights, crossbowmen, serjeants, and mercenary
soldiers who have come with horses and arms to the kingdom's hurt.

52. If anyone has been dispossessed or removed by us, without
the legal judgment of his peers, from his lands, castles, franchises,
or from his right, we will immediately restore them to him; and if a
dispute arise over this, then let it be decided by the five and twenty
barons of whom mention is made below in the clause for securing
the peace. Moreover, for all those possessions, from which anyone
has, without the lawful judgment of his peers, been disseised or
removed, by our father, King Henry, or by our brother, King
Richard, and which we retain in our hand (or which as possessed
by others, to whom we are bound to warrant them) we shall have
respite until the usual term of crusaders; excepting those things
about which a plea has been raised, or an inquest made by our

---

20 *bailiwick*: "a district or place under the jurisdiction of a bailiff" (OED)

order, before our taking of the cross; but as soon as we return from the expedition, we will immediately grant full justice therein.

53. We shall have, moreover, the same respite and in the same manner in rendering justice concerning the disafforestation or retention of those forests which Henry our father and Richard our brother afforested, and concerning the wardship of lands which are of the fief of another (namely, such wardships as we have hitherto had by reason of a fief which anyone held of us by knight's service), and concerning abbeys founded on other fiefs than our own, in which the lord of the fee claims to have right; and when we have returned, or if we desist from our expedition, we will immediately grant full justice to all who complain of such things.

54. No one shall be arrested or imprisoned upon the appeal of a woman, for the death of any other than her husband.

55. All fines made with us unjustly and against the law of the land, and all amercements, imposed unjustly and against the law of the land, shall be entirely remitted, or else it shall be done concerning them according to the decision of the five and twenty barons whom mention is made below in the clause for securing the pease, or according to the judgment of the majority of the same, along with the aforesaid Stephen, archbishop of Canterbury, if he can be present, and such others as he may wish to bring with him for this purpose, and if he cannot be present the business shall nevertheless proceed without him, provided always that if any one or more of the aforesaid five and twenty barons are in a similar suit, they shall be removed as far as concerns this particular judgment, others being substituted in their places after having been selected by the rest of the same five and twenty for this purpose only, and after having been sworn.

56. If we have disseised or removed Welshmen from lands or
liberties, or other things, without the legal judgment of their peers
in England or in Wales, they shall be immediately restored to them;
and if a dispute arise over this, then let it be decided in the marches[21]
by the judgment of their peers; for the tenements[22] in England
according to the law of England, for tenements in Wales according
to the law of Wales, and for tenements in the marches according to
the law of the marches. Welshmen shall do the same to us and ours.

57. Further, for all those possessions from which any Welshman
has, without the lawful judgment of his peers, been disseised or
removed by King Henry our father, or King Richard our brother,
and which we retain in our hand (or which are possessed by others,
and which we ought to warrant), we will have respite until the usual
term of crusaders; excepting those things about which a plea has
been raised or an inquest made by our order before we took the
cross; but as soon as we return (or if perchance we desist from our
expedition), we will immediately grant full justice in accordance
with the laws of the Welsh and in relation to the foresaid regions.

58. We will immediately give up the son of Llywelyn and all the
hostages of Wales, and the charters delivered to us as security for
the peace.

59. We will do towards Alexander, king of Scots, concerning the
return of his sisters and his hostages, and concerning his franchises,
and his right, in the same manner as we shall do towards our other
barons of England, unless it ought to be otherwise according to the
charters which we hold from William his father, formerly king of

---

21 *marches*: "a set of laws governing the relations between people on opposite sides of a
   boundary" (OED)
22 *tenement*: "land or real property which is held of another by any tenure; a holding"
   (OED)

Scots; and this shall be according to the judgment of his peers in our court.

60. Moreover, all these aforesaid customs and liberties, the observances of which we have granted in our kingdom as far as pertains to us towards our men, shall be observed by all of our kingdom, as well clergy as laymen, as far as pertains to them towards their men.

61. Since, moveover, for God and the amendment of our kingdom and for the better allaying of the quarrel that has arisen between us and our barons, we have granted all these concessions, desirous that they should enjoy them in complete and firm endurance forever, we give and grant to them the underwritten security, namely, that the barons choose five and twenty barons of the kingdom, whomsoever they will, who shall be bound with all their might, to observe and hold, and cause to be observed, the peace and liberties we have granted and confirmed to them by this our present Charter, so that if we, or our justiciar, or our bailiffs or any one of our officers, shall in anything be at fault towards anyone, or shall have broken any one of the articles of this peace or of this security, and the offense be notified to four barons of the foresaid five and twenty, the said four barons shall repair to us (or our justiciar, if we are out of the realm) and, laying the transgression before us, petition to have that transgression redressed without delay. And if we shall not have corrected the transgression (or, in the event of our being out of the realm, if our justiciar shall not have corrected it) within forty days, reckoning from the time it has been intimated to us (or to our justiciar, if we should be out of the realm), the four barons aforesaid shall refer that matter to the rest of the five and twenty barons, and those five and twenty barons shall, together with the community

of the whole realm, distrain and distress us in all possible ways, namely, by seizing our castles, lands, possessions, and in any other way they can, until redress has been obtained as they deem fit, saving harmless our own person, and the persons of our queen and children; and when redress has been obtained, they shall resume their old relations towards us. And let whoever in the country desires it, swear to obey the orders of the said five and twenty barons for the execution of all the aforesaid matters, and along with them, to molest us to the utmost of his power; and we publicly and freely grant leave to everyone who wishes to swear, and we shall never forbid anyone to swear.

All those, moveover, in the land who of themselves and of their own accord are unwilling to swear to the twenty five to help them in constraining and molesting us, we shall by our command compel the same to swear to the effect foresaid. And if any one of the five and twenty barons shall have died or departed from the land, or be incapacitated in any other manner which would prevent the foresaid provisions being carried out, those of the said twenty five barons who are left shall choose another in his place according to their own judgment, and he shall be sworn in the same way as the others. Further, in all matters, the execution of which is entrusted to these twenty five barons, if perchance these twenty five are present and disagree about anything, or if some of them, after being summoned, are unwilling or unable to be present, that which the majority of those present ordain or command shall be held as fixed and established, exactly as if the whole twenty five had concurred in this; and the said twenty five shall swear that they will faithfully observe all that is aforesaid, and cause it to be observed with all their might. And we shall procure nothing from anyone, directly or indirectly, whereby any part of these concessions and liberties might be revoked or diminished; and if any such things has been procured, let it be void and null, and we shall never use it personally or by another.

62. And all the will, hatreds, and bitterness that have arisen between us and our men, clergy and lay, from the date of the quarrel, we have completely remitted and pardoned to everyone. Moreover, all trespasses occasioned by the said quarrel, from Easter in the sixteenth year of our reign till the restoration of peace, we have fully remitted to all, both clergy and laymen, and completely forgiven, as far as pertains to us. And on this head, we have caused to be made for them letters testimonial patent of the lord Stephen, archbishop of Canterbury, of the lord Henry, archbishop of Dublin, of the bishops aforesaid, and of Master Pandulf as touching this security and the concessions aforesaid.

63. Wherefore we will and firmly order that the English Church be free, and that the men in our kingdom have and hold all the aforesaid liberties, rights, and concessions, well and peaceably, freely and quietly, fully and wholly, for themselves and their heirs, of us and our heirs, in all respects and in all places forever, as is aforesaid. An oath, moreover, has been taken, as well on our part as on the part of the barons, that all these conditions aforesaid shall be kept in good faith and without evil intent. Given under our hand - the above named and many others being witnesses - in the meadow which is called Runnymede, between Windsor and Staines, on the fifteenth day of June, in the seventeenth year of our reign.

CHRISTOPHER COLUMBUS
Journal, 1492

*Christopher Columbus (1451-1506), that most famous of sea explorers,
undertook four transcontinental voyages sponsored by Queen Isabel and
King Ferdinand of Aragon and Castille, now part of Spain. Columbus
convinced the King and Queen that he could find a new and faster route
to India. He paved the way for the European conquest and colonization of
the Americas. Although the Vikings, and possibly the Celts, had traveled
to the Americas prior to Columbus, he gets the credit for "discovering"
the new world. This excerpt was translated by Sir Clements R. Markham,
and published in 1906 as part of Original Narratives Of Early American
History. Oddly, Columbus sometimes refers to himself in the third person.*

*In the final entry included here Columbus states one of his purposes for
this trip. This is one reason why Dr. George Grant calls Columbus "The
Last Crusader."[1]*

IN THE NAME OF OUR LORD JESUS CHRIST

Because, O most Christian, and very high, very excellent,
and puissant Princes, King and Queen of the Spains and
of the islands of the Sea, our Lords, in this present year
of 1492, after your Highnesses had given an end to the war with the
Moors who reigned in Europe, and had finished it in the very great
city of Granada, where in this present year, on the second day of the
month of January, by force of arms, I saw the royal banners of your
Highnesses placed on the towers of Alfambra, which is the fortress
of that city, and I saw the Moorish King come forth from the gates
of the city and kiss the royal hands of your Highnesses, and of the

---

[1] Read Dr. Grant's narrative history of Columbus and his journeys in *The Last Crusader
— The Untold Story of Christopher Columbus*, published by Crossway Books in 1992.

Prince my Lord, and presently in that same month, acting on the
information that I had given to your Highnesses touching the lands
of India, and respecting a Prince who is called Gran Can, which
means in our language King of Kings, how he and his ancestors had
sent to Rome many times to ask for learned men of our holy faith to
teach him, and how the Holy Father had never complied, insomuch
that many people believing in idolatries were lost by receiving
doctrine of perdition: your Highnesses, as Catholic Christians and
Princes who love the holy Christian faith, and the propagation of
it, and who are enemies to the sect of Mahoma and to all idolatries
and heresies, resolved to send me, Cristobal Colon, to the said parts
of India to see the said princes, and the cities and lands, and their
disposition, with a view that they might be converted to our holy
faith; and ordered that I should not go by land to the eastward,
as had been customary, but that I should go by way of the west,
whither up to this day, we do not know for certain that any one has
gone.

Thus, after having turned out all the Jews from all your
kingdoms and lordships, in the same month of January, your
Highnesses gave orders to me that with a sufficient fleet I should go
to the said parts of India, and for this they made great concessions to
me, and ennobled me, so that henceforward I should be called Don,
and should be Chief Admiral of the Ocean Sea, perpetual Viceroy
and Governor of all the islands and continents that I should discover
and gain, and that I might hereafter discover and gain in the
Ocean Sea, and that my eldest son should succeed, and so on from
generation to generation for ever.

I left the city of Granada on the 12th day of May, in the same
year of 1492, being Saturday, and came to the town of Palos, which

is a seaport; where I equipped three vessels well suited for such
service; and departed from that port, well supplied with provisions
and with many sailors, on the 3d day of August of the same year,
being Friday, half an hour before sunrise, taking the route to the
islands of Canaria, belonging to your Highnesses, which are in
the said Ocean Sea, that I might thence take my departure for
navigating until I should arrive at the Indies, and give the letters of
your Highnesses to those princes, so as to comply with my orders.
As part of my duty I thought it well to write an account of all the
voyage very punctually, noting from day to day all that I should do
and see, and that should happen, as will be seen further on. Also,
Lords Princes, I resolved to describe each night what passed in the
day, and to note each day how I navigated at night. I propose to
construct a new chart for navigating, on which I shall delineate all
the sea and lands of the Ocean in their proper positions under their
bearings; and further, I propose to prepare a book, and to put down
all as it were in a picture, by latitude from the equator, and western
longitude. Above all, I shall have accomplished much, for I shall
forget sleep, and shall work at the business of navigation, that so the
service may be performed; all which will entail great labor.

FRIDAY, 3D OF AUGUST

We departed on Friday, the 3d of August, in the year 1492,
from the bar of Saltes, at 8 o'clock, and proceeded with a strong
sea breeze until sunset, towards the south, for 60 miles, equal to 15
leagues; afterwards S.W. and W.S.W., which was the course for
the Canaries.

TUESDAY, 25TH OF SEPTEMBER

This day began with a calm, and afterwards there was wind.

They were on their west course until night. The Admiral conversed with Martin Alonso Pinzon, captain of the other caravel Pinta, respecting a chart which he had sent to the caravel three days before, on which, as it would appear, the Admiral had certainis lands depicted in that sea. Martin Alonso said that the ships were in the position on which the islands were placed, and the Admiral replied that so it appeared to him: but it might be that they had not fallen in with them, owing to the currents which had always set the ships to the N.E., and that they had not made so much as the pilots reported. The Admiral then asked for the chart to be returned, and it was sent back on a line. The Admiral then began to plot the position on it, with the pilot and mariners. At sunset Martin Alonso went up on the poop of his ship, and with much joy called to the Admiral, claiming the reward as he had sighted land. When the Admiral heard this positively declared, he says that he gave thanks to the Lord on his knees while Martin Alonso said the Gloria in excelsis with his people. The Admiral's crew did the same. Those of the Niña all went up on the mast and into the rigging, and declared that it was land. It so seemed to the Admiral, and that it was distant 25 leagues. They all continued to declare it was land until night. The Admiral ordered the course to be altered from W. to S.W., in which direction the land had appeared. That day they made 4 leagues on a west course, and 17 S.W. during the night, in all 21; but the people were told that 13 was the distance made good: for it was always feigned to them that the distances were less, so that the voyage might not appear so long. Thus two reckonings were kept on this voyage, the shorter being feigned, and the longer being the true one. The sea was very smooth, so that many sailors bathed alongside. They saw many dorados and other fish.

TUESDAY, 2ND OF OCTOBER

Course west, and during the day and night 39 leagues were made good, counted for the crew as 30. The sea always smooth. Many thanks be given to God, says the Admiral, that the weed is coming from east to west, contrary to its usual course. Many fish were seen, and one was killed. A white bird was also seen that appeared to be a gull.

WEDNESDAY, 3RD OF OCTOBER

They navigated on the usual course, and made good 47 leagues, counted as 40. Sandpipers appeared, and much weed, some of it very old and some quite fresh and having fruit. They saw no birds. The Admiral, therefore, thought that they had left the islands behind them which were depicted on the charts. The Admiral here says that he did not wish to keep the ships beating about during the last week, and in the last few days when there were so many signs of land, although he had information of certain islands in this region. For he wished to avoid delay, his object being to reach the Indies. He says that to delay would not be wise.

THURSDAY, 11TH OF OCTOBER

The course was W.S.W., and there was more sea than there had been during the whole of the voyage. They saw sandpipers, and a green reed near the ship. Those of the caravel Pinta saw a cane and a pole, and they took up another small pole which appeared to have been worked with iron; also another bit of cane, a land-plant, and a small board. The crew of the caravel Niña also saw signs of land, and a small branch covered with berries. Every one breathed afresh and rejoiced at these signs. The run until sunset was 27 leagues.

After sunset the Admiral returned to his original west course, and they went along at the rate of 12 miles an hour. Up to two hours after midnight they had gone 90 miles, equal to 221/2 leagues. As the caravel Pinta was a better sailer, and went ahead of the Admiral, she found the land, and made the signals ordered by the Admiral. The land was first seen by a sailor named Rodrigo de Triana. But the Admiral, at ten o'clock, being on the castle of the poop, saw a light, though it was so uncertain that he could not affirm it was land. He called Pero Gutierrez, a gentleman of the King's bedchamber, and said that there seemed to be a light, and that he should look at it. He did so, and saw it. The Admiral said the same to Rodrigo Sanchez of Segovia, whom the King and Queen had sent with the fleet as inspector, but he could see nothing, because he was not in a place whence anything could be seen. After the Admiral had spoken he saw the light once or twice, and it was like a wax candle rising and falling. It seemed to few to be an indication of land; but the Admiral made certain that land was close. When they said the Salve, which all the sailors were accustomed to sing in their way, the Admiral asked and admonished the men to keep a good look-out on the forecastle, and to watch well for land; and to him who should first cry out that he saw land, he would give a silk doublet, besides the other rewards promised by the Sovereigns, which were 10,000 maravedis to him who should first see it.109-4 At two hours after midnight the land was sighted at a distance of[110] two leagues. They shortened sail, and lay by under the mainsail without the bonnets.

[FRIDAY, 12TH OF OCTOBER]

The vessels were hove to, waiting for daylight; and on Friday they arrived at a small island of the Lucayos, called in the language

of the Indians, Guanahani. Presently they saw naked people. The
Admiral went on shore in the armed boat, and Martin Alonso
Pinzon, and Vicente Yañez, his brother, who was captain of the
Niña. The Admiral took the royal standard, and the captains went
with two banners of the green cross, which the Admiral took in all
the ships as a sign, with an F and a Y and a crown over each letter,
one on one side of the cross and the other on the other. Having
landed, they saw trees very green, and much water, and fruits of
diverse kinds. The Admiral called to the two captains, and to the
others who leaped on shore, and to Rodrigo Escovedo, secretary of
the whole fleet, and to Rodrigo Sanchez of Segovia, and said that
they should bear faithful testimony that he, in presence of all, had
taken, as he now took, possession of the said island for the King and
for the Queen his Lords, making the declarations that are required,
as is now largely set forth in the testimonies which were then made
in writing.

Presently many inhabitants of the island assembled. What
follows is in the actual words of the Admiral in his book of the
first navigation and discovery of the Indies. "I," he says, "that we
might form great friendship, for I knew that they were a people who
could be more easily freed and converted to our holy faith by love
than by force, gave to some of them red caps, and glass beads to
put round their necks, and many other things of little value, which
gave them great pleasure, and made them so much our friends that
it was a marvel to see. They afterwards came to the ship's boats
where we were, swimming and bringing us parrots, cotton threads
in skeins, darts, and many other things; and we exchanged them
for other things that we gave them, such as glass beads and small
bells. In fine, they took all, and gave what they had with good will.

It appeared to me to be a race of people very poor in everything. They go as naked as when their mothers bore them, and so do the women, although I did not see more than one young girl. All I saw were youths, none more than thirty years of age. They are very well made, with very handsome bodies, and very good countenances. Their hair is short and coarse, almost like the hairs of a horse's tail. They wear the hairs brought down to the eyebrows, except a few locks behind, which they wear long and never cut. They paint themselves black, and they are the color of the Canarians, neither black nor white. Some paint themselves white, others red, and others of what color they find. Some paint their faces, others the whole body, some only round the eyes, others only on the nose. They neither carry nor know anything of arms, for I showed them swords, and they took them by the blade and cut themselves through ignorance. They have no iron, their darts being wands without iron, some of them having a fish's tooth at the end, and others being pointed in various ways. They are all of fair stature and size, with good faces, and well made. I saw some with marks of wounds on their bodies, and I made signs to ask what it was, and they gave me to understand that people from other adjacent islands came with the intention of seizing them, and that they defended themselves. I believed, and still believe, that they come here from the mainland to take them prisoners. They should be good servants and intelligent, for I observed that they quickly took in what was said to them, and I believe that they would easily be made Christians, as it appeared to me that they had no religion. I, our Lord being pleased, will take hence, at the time of my departure, six natives for your Highnesses, that they may learn to speak. I saw no beast of any kind except parrots, on this island." The above is in the words of the Admiral.

SATURDAY, 13TH OF OCTOBER

"As soon as dawn broke many of these people came to the beach, all youths, as I have said, and all of good stature, a very handsome people. Their hair is not curly, but loose and coarse, like horse hair. In all the forehead is broad, more so than in any other people I have hitherto seen. Their eyes are very beautiful and not small, and themselves far from black, but the color of the Canarians. Nor should anything else be expected, as this island is in a line east and west from the island of Hierro in the Canaries. Their legs are very straight, all in one line, and no belly, but very well formed. They came to the ship in small canoes, made out of the trunk of a tree like a long boat, and all of one piece, and wonderfully worked, considering the country. They are large, some of them holding 40 to 45 men, others smaller, and some only large enough to hold one man. They are propelled with a paddle like a baker's shovel, and go at a marvellous rate. If the canoe capsizes, they all promptly begin to swim, and to bale it out with calabashes that they take with them. They brought skeins of cotton thread, parrots, darts, and other small things which it would be tedious to recount, and they give all in exchange for anything that may be given to them. I was attentive, and took trouble to ascertain if there was gold. I saw that some of them had a small piece fastened in a hole they have in the nose, and by signs I was able to make out that to the south, or going from the island to the south, there was a king who had great cups full, and who possessed a great quantity. I tried to get them to go there, but afterwards I saw that they had no inclination. I resolved to wait until to-morrow in the afternoon and then to depart, shaping a course to the S.W., for, according to what many of them told me,[113] there was land to the S., to the S.W., and N.W., and that the natives from the N.W. often came to attack them, and went on to the S.W. in search of gold and precious stones.

"This island is rather large and very flat, with bright green trees, much water, and a very large lake in the centre, without any mountain, and the whole land so green that it is a pleasure to look on it. The people are very docile, and for the longing to possess our things, and not having anything to give in return, they take what they can get, and presently swim away. Still, they give away all they have got, for whatever may be given to them, down to broken bits of crockery and glass. I saw one give 16 skeins of cotton for three ceotis113-1 of Portugal, equal to one blanca of Spain, the skeins being as much as an arroba of cotton thread. I shall keep it, and shall allow no one to take it, preserving it all for your Highnesses, for it may be obtained in abundance. It is grown in this island, though the short time did not admit of my ascertaining this for a certainty. Here also is found the gold they wear fastened in their noses. But, in order not to lose time, I intend to go and see if I can find the island of Cipango. Now, as it is night, all the natives have gone on shore with their canoes."

SUNDAY, 14TH OF OCTOBER

"At dawn I ordered the ship's boat and the boats of the caravels to be got ready, and I went along the coast of the island and to the N.N.E., to see the other side, which was on the other side to the east, and also to see the villages. Presently I saw two or three, and the people all came to the shore, calling out and giving thanks to God. Some of them brought us water, others came with food, and when they saw that I did want to land, they got into the sea, and came swimming to us. We understood that they asked us if we had come from heaven. One old man came into the boat, and others cried out, in loud voices, to all the men and women, to come and see the men who had come from heaven, and to bring them to eat and drink. Many came, including women, each bringing something, giving thanks to God, throwing themselves on the ground and shouting to us to come on shore. But I was afraid to land, seeing an extensive reef of rocks which surrounded the island, with deep water between it and the shore forming a port large enough for as many ships as there are in Christendom, but with a very narrow entrance. It is true that within this reef there are some sunken rocks, but the sea has no more motion than the water in a well. In order to see all this I went this morning, that I might be able to give a full account to your Highnesses, and also where a fortress might be established. I saw a piece of land which appeared like an island, although it is not one, and on it there were six houses. It might be converted into an island in two days, though I do not see that it would be necessary, for these people are very simple as regards the use of arms, as your Highnesses will see from the seven that I caused to be taken, to bring home and learn our language and return; unless your Highnesses should order them all to be brought to Castile, or to be kept as captives on the same island; for with fifty men they can all be subjugated and made to do what is required of them. Close to the above peninsula there are gardens of the most beautiful trees I ever saw, and with leaves as green as those of Castile in the month of April and May, and much water. I examined all that port, and afterwards I returned to the ship and made sail. I saw so many islands that I hardly knew how to determine to which I should go first. Those natives I had with me said, by signs, that there were so many that they could not be numbered, and they gave the names of more than a hundred. At last I looked out for the largest, and resolved to shape a course for it, and so I did. It will be distant five leagues from this of San Salvador, and the others some more, some less. All are very flat, and all are inhabited. The natives make war on each other, although these are very simple-minded and handsomely-formed people."

WEDNESDAY, 26TH OF DECEMBER

. . . He trusted in God that, when he returned from Spain, according to his intention, he would find a tun of gold collected by barter by those he was to leave behind, and that they would have found the mine, and spices in such quantities that the Sovereigns would, in three years, be able to undertake and fit out an expedition to go and conquer the Holy Sepulchre. "With this in view," he says, "I protested to your Highnesses that all the profits of this my enterprise should be spent in the conquest of Jerusalem, and your Highnesses laughed and said that it pleased them, and that, without this, they entertained that desire."

WILLIAM BRADFORD

The Mayflower Compact

On September 6, 1620, a small band of men and women set sail from
Plymouth, England. They were bound for Virginia in the New World,
seeking freedom to worshp according to the dictates of conscience. The
passage was stormy and perilous, but on November 11, 1620, as William
Bradford writes in his History of Plimouth Plantation: *"Being thus arived
in a good harbor and brought safe to land, they fell upon their knees &
blessed ye God of heaven, who had brought them over ye vast & furious
ocean, and delivered them from all ye periles & miseries therof, againe
to set their feete on ye firme and stable earth, their proper elemente . . .
Before they came ashore, being ye first foundation of their govermente in
this place; occasioned partly by ye discontented & mutinous speeches that
some of the strangers amongst them had let fall from them in ye ship—That
when they came a shore they would use their owne libertie; for none had
power to comand them, the patente they had being for Virginia, and not
for New-england, which belonged to an other Goverment, with which ye
Virginia Company had nothing to doe. And partly that shuch an acte
by them done (this their condition considered) might be as firme as any
patent, and in some respects more sure."* Thus the Mayflower Compact
laid the framework and declared the purpose for the Massachusetts Bay, or
Plymouth, Colony.

In the name of God, Amen. We whose names are
underwritten, the loyal subjects of our dread Sovereign Lord
King James, by the Grace of God of Great Britain, France,
and Ireland King, Defender of the Faith, etc. Having undertaken
for the Glory of God and advancement of the Christian Faith and
Honour of our King and Country, a Voyage to plant the First

Colony in the Northern Parts of Virginia, do by these presents
solemnly and mutually in the presence of God and one of another,
Covenant and Combine ourselves together in a Civil Body Politic, for
our better ordering and preservation and furtherance of the ends
aforesaid; and by virtue hereof to enact, constitute and frame such
just and equal Laws, Ordinances, Acts, Constitutions and Offices
from time to time, as shall be thought most meet and convenient
for the general good of the Colony, unto which we promise all due
submission and obedience. In witness whereof we have hereunder
subscribed our names at Cape Cod, the 11th of November, in the
year of the reign of our Sovereign Lord King James, of England,
France and Ireland the eighteenth, and of Scotland the fifty-fourth.
Anno Domini 1620.

John Carver	Edward Tilly	Digery Priest
William Bradford	John Tilly	Thomas Williams
Edward Winslow	Francis Cooke	Gilbert Winslow
William Brewster	Thomas Rogers	Edmund Margeson
Isaac Allerton	Thomas Tinker	Peter Brown
Miles Standish	John Rigdale	Richard Bitteridge
John Alden	Edward Fuller	George Soule
Samuel Fuller	John Turner	Richard Clark
Christopher Martin	Francis Eaton	Richard Gardiner
William Mullins	James Chilton	John Allerton
William White	John Craxton	Thomas English
Richard Warren	John Billington	Edward Doten
John Howland	Moses Fletcher	dward Leister
E Stephen Hopkins	John Goodman	

RICHARD MATHER

The Bay Psalm Book

Richard Mather, a Massachusets Puritan, produced the first book printed
in the United States in 1640. The title page for The Bay Psalm Book *reads,*

The Whole Booke of Psalmes
Faithfully
TRANSLATED into ENGLISH
Metre.
Whereunto is prefixed a discourse
declaring not only the lawfullnes, but also
the necessity of the heavenly Ordinance
of singing Scripture Psalmes in
the Churches of God.
Imprinted, 1640

PREFACE

The singing of Psalms, though it breath forth nothing but holy harmony, and melody: yet such is the subtlety of the enemy, and enmity of our nature against the Lord, and his ways, that our hearts can find matter of discord in this harmony, and crotchets [i.e., whimsical notions] of division in this holy melody.—for.—There have been three questions especially stirring concerning singing. First, what psalms are to be sung in churches? whether David's and other scripture psalms, or the psalms invented by the gifts of godly men in every age of the church. Secondly, if scripture psalms, whether in their own words, or in such metre as English poetry is wont to run in? Thirdly, by whom are they to be sung? whether by the whole churches together with their voices? or by one man singing alone and the rest joining in silence, and in the close saying amen.

. . . Obj. 1. If it be said that the Saints in the primitive Church did compile spiritual songs of their own inditing [i.e., composition], and sing them before the Church. 1 Cor. 14:15,16.

Ans. We answer first, that those Saints compiled these spiritual songs by the extraordinary gifts of the Spirit (common in those days) whereby they were enabled to praise the Lord in strange tongues, wherein learned Paraeus proves those psalms were uttered, in his Comment[ary] on that place vers 14 which extraordinary gifts, if they were still in the Churches, we should allow them the like liberty now. Secondly, suppose those psalms were sung by an ordinary gift (which we suppose cannot be evicted [i.e., evidenced]) does it therefore follow that they did not, and that we ought not to sing David's psalms, must the ordinary gifts of a private man quench the Spirit still speaking to us by the extraordinary gifts of his servant David. There is not the least foot-step of example, or precept, or color reason for such bold practice.

Obj. 2. Ministers are allowed to pray conceived prayers, and why not to sing conceived psalms? must we not sing in the Spirit as well as pray in the Spirit?

Ans. First because every good minister has not the gift of spiritual poetry to compose extemporaneous psalms as he has of prayer. Secondly, suppose he had, yet seeing psalms are to be sung by a joint consent and harmony of all the

Church in heart and voice (as we shall prove) this cannot
be done except he that composes a psalm, brings into the
Church set forms of psalms of his own invention; for which
we find no warrant or precedent in any ordinary officers of
the Church throughout the scriptures. Thirdly, because the
book of psalms is so complete a system of psalms, which the
Holy Ghost himself in infinite wisdom has made to suit all
conditions, necessities, temptations, affections, etc. of men in
all ages . . .

Question. But why may not one compose a psalm and
sing it alone with a loud voice and the rest join with him in
silence and in the end say amen.

Ans. If such a practice was found in the Church
of Corinth, when any had a psalm suggested by an
extraordinary gift; yet in singing ordinary psalms the whole
Church is to join together in heart and voice to praise the
Lord. —for—

First, David's psalms as has been shown, were sung in
heart and voice together by the twenty-four orders of the
musicians of the Temple, who typed out the twenty-four
Elders all the members especially of Christian Churches
Rev. 5:8. who are made Kings and Priests to God to praise
him as they did: for if they were any other order of singing
Choristers beside the body of the people to succeed those, the
Lord would doubtless have given direction in the gospel for
their qualification, election, maintenance etc. as he did for
the musicians of the Temple, and as his faithfulness had done
for all other church officers in the New Testament.

Secondly, others beside the Levites (the chief singers) in the Jewish Church did also sing the Lord's songs; else why are they commanded frequently to sing: as in Ps. 100:1,2,3. Ps. 95:1,2,3. Ps. 102. title with verse 18. and Ex. 15:1. not only Moses but all Israel sang that song, they spake saying (as it is in the orig[inal language]) all as well as Moses, the women also as well as the men. v. 20,21. and Deut. 32. (whereto some think, John had reference as well as to Ex. 15:1. when he brings in the Protestant Churches getting the victory over the Beast with harps in their hands and singing the song of Moses. Rev. 15:3.) this song Moses is commanded not only to put it into their hearts but into their mouths also: Deut. 31:19. which argues, that they were with their mouths to sing together as well as with their hearts.

Thirdly, Isaiah foretells in the days of the New Testament that God's watchmen and desolate lost souls, (signified by waste places) should with their voices sing together, Isa. 52:8,9. and Rev. 7:9,10. the song of the Lamb was by many together, and the Apostle expressly commands the singing of psalms, hymns, etc. not to any select Christians, but to the whole Church. Eph. 5:19. Col. 3:16. Paul and Silas sang together in private Acts 16:25 and must the public hear only one man sing? to all these we may add the practice of the primitive Churches; the testimony of ancient and holy Basil is instead of many Epist. 63 [letter 207; sec. 3].

. . . As for the scruple that some take at the translation of the Book of Psalms into metre, because David's psalms were sung in his own words without metre: we answer— First, there are many verses together in several psalms of

David which run in rhythms (as those that know Hebrew and as Buxtorf shows Thesau. pa. 629.) which shows at least the lawfulness of singing psalms in English rhythms.

Secondly, the psalms are penned in such verses as are suitable to the poetry of the Hebrew language, and not in the common style of such other books of the Old Testament as are not poetical; now no Protestant doubts but that all the books of scripture should by God's ordinance be extant in the mother tongue of each nation, that they may be understood of all, hence the psalms are to be translated into our English tongue; and in it our English tongue we are to sing them, then as all our English songs (according to the course of our English poetry) do run in metre, so ought David's psalms to be translated into metre, that so we may sing the Lord's songs, as in our English tongue so in such verses as are familiar to an English ear which are commonly metrical: and as it can be no just offense to any good conscience to sing David's Hebrew songs in English words, so neither to sing his poetical verses in English poetical metre: men might as well stumble at singing the Hebrew psalms in our English tunes (and not in the Hebrew tunes) as at singing them in English metre, (which are our verses) and not in such verses as are generally used by David according to the poetry of the Hebrew language: but the truth is, as the Lord has hid from us the Hebrew tunes, lest we should think ourselves bound to imitate them; so also the course and frame (for the most part) of their Hebrew poetry, that we might not think ourselves bound to imitate that, but that every nation without scruple might follow as

the grave sort of tunes of their own country songs, so the
graver sort of verses of their own country poetry.

. . . As for other objections taken from the difficulty
of Ainsworth's tunes, and the corruptions in our common
psalm books, we hope they are answered in this new
edition of psalms; which we here present to God and his
Churches. For although we have cause to bless God in many
respects for the religious endeavours of the translators of
the psalms into metre usually annexed to our Bibles, yet it
is not unknown to the godly learned that they have rather
presented a paraphrase than the words of David translated
according to the rule 2 Chron. 29:30. and that their addition
to the words, detractions from the words are not seldom and
rare, but very frequent and many times needless, (which
we suppose would not be approved of if the Psalms were
so translated into prose) and that their variations of the
sense, and alterations to the sacred text too frequently,
may justly minister matter of offense to them that are able
to compare the translation with the text; of which failings,
some judicious have often complained, others have been
grieved, whereupon it has been generally desired, that as we
do enjoy other, so (if it were the Lord's will) we might enjoy
this ordinance also in its native purity: we have therefore
done our endeavour to make a plain and familiar translation
of the psalms and words of David into English metre, and
have not so much as presumed to paraphrase to give the
sense of his meaning in other words; we have therefore
attended herein as our chief guide the original, shunning all
additions, except such as even the best translators of them in

prose supply, avoiding all material detractions from words or sense. The word v which we translate and as it is redundant sometimes in the Hebrew, so sometimes (though not very often) it has been left out and yet not then, if the sense were not fair without it.

As for our translations, we have with our English Bibles (to which next to the original we have had respect) used the idioms of our own tongue instead of hebraisms, lest they might seem English barbarisms.

. . . If therefore the verses are not always so smooth and elegant as some may desire or expect; let them consider that God's altar needs not our polishings: Ex. 20. for we have respected rather a plain translation, than to smooth our verses with the sweetness of any paraphrases, and so have attended conscience rather than elegance, fidelity rather than poetry, in translating the Hebrew words into English language, and David's poetry into English metre; that so we may sing in Sion the Lord's songs of praise according to his own will; until he take us from hence, and wipe away all out tears, and bid us enter into our Master's joy to sing eternal hallelujahs.

PSALM 23 (COMMON METER)

The Lord to me a shepherd is,
    Want therefore I shall not,
    He in the folds of tender grass
  Doth make me down to lie

  To waters calm he gently leads
  Restore my soul doth he

He doth in paths of righteousness
   For his names sake lead me.

Yea though in valley of death's shade
   I walk none ill I'll fear,
Because thou art with me, thy rod,
   and staff my comfort are.

For me a table thou hast spread
   In presence of my foes;
Thou dost annoint my head with oil
   My cup it over-flows.

Goodness and mercy surely shall
   All my days follow me;
And in the Lord's house I shall dwell
   So long as days shall be.

PSALM 100 (LONG METER)

Make ye a joyful sounding noise
   unto Jehovah, all the earth:
   Serve ye Jehovah with gladness:
   before his presence come with mirth.

Know, that Jehovah he is God,
   who hath us formed it is he,
   and not ourselves: his own people
   and sheep of his pasture are we.

Enter into his gates with praise,
   into His courts with thankfulness:
   make ye confession unto him,
   and his name reverently bless.

Because Jehovah he is good,
    for evermore is his mercy:
and unto generations all
    continue doth his verity.

PSALM 100 (COMMON METER)

Make ye a joyful noise unto
        Jehovah all the earth:
        Serve ye Jehovah with gladness:
    before him come with mirth.

Know, that Jehovah he is God,
    not we ourselves, but he
hath made us: his people, and sheep
    of his pasture are we.

O enter ye into his gates
    with praise, and thankfulness
into his Courts: confess to him,
    and his Name do ye bless.

Because Jehovah he is good,
    his bounteous mercy
is everlasting: and his truth
    is to eternity.

JOHN WINTHROP

A Model of Christian Charity

John Winthrop gave the sermon "A Model of Christian Charity" to passengers bound for the Massachusetts Bay Colony aboard the Arabella in 1630. Here, he sets forth a vision for a new society that would be "a city upon a hill." Thus, Winthrop laid the foundation for American exceptionalism. We include here the introduction from The Winthrop Society website:

> "Redacted and introduced by John Beardsley.
>
> This is Winthrop's most famous thesis, written on board the Arabella, 1630. We love to imagine the occasion when he personally spoke this oration to some large portion of the Winthrop fleet passengers during or just before their passage.
>
> In an age not long past, when the Puritan founders were still respected by the educational establishment, this was required reading in many courses of American history and literature. However, it was often abridged to just the first and last few paragraphs. This left the overture of the piece sounding unkind and fatalistic, and the finale rather sternly zealous. A common misrepresentation of the Puritan character.
>
> Winthrop's genius was logical reasoning combined with a sympathetic nature. To remove this work's central arguments about love and relationships is to completely lose the sense of the whole. Therefore we present it here in its well-balanced entirety. The biblical quotations are as Winthrop wrote them, and remain sometimes at slight variance from the King

James version. This editor has corrected the chapter and verse
citations to correspond to the King James text, assuming that
the modern reader will wish to conveniently refer to that most
popular English version of the Bible, as the Governor lays out
his argument for charity and decent human behavior in the
community.

Winthrop's intent was to prepare the people for planting a new
society in a perilous environment, but his practical wisdom is
timeless."[1]

God Almighty in his most holy and wise providence hath so disposed of the condition of mankind, as in all times some must be rich, some poor, some high and eminent in power and dignity; others mean and in subjection.

THE REASON HEREOF:1ST REASON.

First to hold conformity with the rest of His world, being delighted to show forth the glory of his wisdom in the variety and difference of the creatures, and the glory of His power in ordering all these differences for the preservation and good of the whole, and the glory of His greatness, that as it is the glory of princes to have many officers, so this great king will have many stewards, counting himself more honored in dispensing his gifts to man by man, than if he did it by his own immediate hands.

2ND REASON.

Secondly, that He might have the more occasion to manifest the work of his Spirit: first upon the wicked in moderating and restraining them, so that the rich and mighty should not eat up the poor, nor the poor and despised rise up against and shake off their

---

1 "A Model of Christian Charity." The Winthrop Society: Descendants of the Great Migration. Accessed August 11, 2017. *http://winthropsociety.com/doc_charity.php.*

yoke. Secondly, in the regenerate, in exercising His graces in them, as in the great ones, their love, mercy, gentleness, temperance etc., and in the poor and inferior sort, their faith, patience, obedience etc.

3RD REASON.

Thirdly, that every man might have need of others, and from hence they might be all knit more nearly together in the bonds of brotherly affection. From hence it appears plainly that no man is made more honorable than another or more wealthy etc., out of any particular and singular respect to himself, but for the glory of his Creator and the common good of the creature, Man. Therefore God still reserves the property of these gifts to Himself as Ezek. 16:17, He there calls wealth, His gold and His silver, and Prov. 3:9, He claims their service as His due, "Honor the Lord with thy riches," etc. — All men being thus (by divine providence) ranked into two sorts, rich and poor; under the first are comprehended all such as are able to live comfortably by their own means duly improved; and all others are poor according to the former distribution.

There are two rules whereby we are to walk one towards another: Justice and Mercy. These are always distinguished in their act and in their object, yet may they both concur in the same subject in each respect; as sometimes there may be an occasion of showing mercy to a rich man in some sudden danger or distress, and also doing of mere justice to a poor man in regard of some particular contract, etc.

There is likewise a double Law by which we are regulated in our conversation towards another. In both the former respects, the Law of Nature and the Law of Grace (that is, the moral law or the law of the gospel) to omit the rule of justice as not properly belonging to this purpose otherwise than it may fall into consideration in some particular cases. By the first of these laws, Man as he was enabled so withal is commanded to love his neighbor as himself. Upon this ground stands all the precepts of the moral law, which concerns our dealings with men. To apply this to the works of mercy, this law requires two things. First, that every man afford his help to another in every want or distress.

Secondly, that he perform this out of the same affection which makes him careful of his own goods, according to the words of our Savior (from Matthew 7:12), whatsoever ye would that men should do to you. This was practiced by Abraham and Lot in entertaining the angels and the old man of Gibea. The law of Grace or of the Gospel hath some difference from the former (the law of nature), as in these respects: First, the law of nature was given to Man in the estate of innocence. This of the Gospel in the estate of regeneracy. Secondly, the former propounds one man to another, as the same flesh and image of God. This as a brother in Christ also, and in the communion of the same Spirit, and so teacheth to put a difference between Christians and others. Do good to all, especially to the household of faith. Upon this ground the Israelites were to put a difference between the brethren of such as were strangers, though not of the Canaanites.

Thirdly, the Law of Nature would give no rules for dealing with enemies, for all are to be considered as friends in the state of innocence, but the Gospel commands love to an enemy. Proof: If thine enemy hunger, feed him; "Love your enemies... Do good to them that hate you" (Matt. 5:44).

This law of the Gospel propounds likewise a difference of seasons and occasions. There is a time when a Christian must sell all and give to the poor, as they did in the Apostles' times. There is a time also when Christians (though they give not all yet) must give beyond their ability, as they of Macedonia (2 Cor. 8). Likewise, community of perils calls for extraordinary liberality, and so doth community in some special service for the church.

Lastly, when there is no other means whereby our Christian brother may be relieved in his distress, we must help him beyond our ability rather than tempt God in putting him upon help by miraculous or extraordinary means. This duty of mercy is exercised in the kinds: giving, lending and forgiving (of a debt).

QUESTION: What rule shall a man observe in giving in respect of the measure?

ANSWER: If the time and occasion be ordinary he is to give out of his abundance. Let him lay aside as God hath blessed him. If the time and occasion be extraordinary, he must be ruled by them; taking this withal, that then a man cannot likely do too much, especially if he may leave himself and his family under probable means of comfortable subsistence.

OBJECTION: A man must lay up for posterity, the fathers lay up for posterity and children, and he is worse than an infidel that provideth not for his own.

ANSWER: For the first, it is plain that it being spoken by way of comparison, it must be meant of the ordinary and usual course of fathers, and cannot extend to times and occasions extraordinary. For the other place the Apostle speaks against such as walked inordinately, and it is without question, that he is worse than an infidel who through his own sloth and voluptuousness shall neglect to provide for his family.

OBJECTION: "The wise man's eyes are in his head," saith Solomon, "and foreseeth the plague;" therefore he must forecast and lay up against evil times when he or his may stand in need of all he can gather.

ANSWER: This very Argument Solomon useth to persuade to liberality (Eccle. 11), "Cast thy bread upon the waters...for thou knowest not what evil may come upon the land." Luke 16:9, "Make you friends of the riches of iniquity..." You will ask how this shall be? Very well. For first he that gives to the poor, lends to the Lord and He will repay him even in this life an hundredfold to him or his. The righteous is ever merciful and lendeth, and his seed enjoyeth the blessing; and besides we know what advantage it will be to us in the day of account when many such witnesses shall stand forth for us to witness the improvement of our talent. And I would know of those who plead so much for laying up for time to come, whether they hold that to be Gospel Matthew 6:19, "Lay not up for yourselves treasures upon earth," etc. If they acknowledge it, what extent will they allow it? If only to those primitive times, let them consider the reason whereupon our Savior grounds it. The first is that they are subject to the moth, the rust, the thief. Secondly, they will steal away the heart: "where the treasure is there will your heart be also."

The reasons are of like force at all times. Therefore the exhortation must be general and perpetual, with always in respect of the love and affection to riches and in regard of the things themselves when any special service for the church or particular distress of our brother do call for the use of them; otherwise it is not only lawful but necessary to lay up as Joseph did to have ready upon such occasions, as the Lord (whose stewards we are of them) shall call for them from us. Christ gives us an instance of the first, when he sent his disciples for the donkey, and bids them answer the owner thus, "the Lord hath need of him." So when the Tabernacle was to be built, He sends to His people to call for their silver and gold, etc., and yields no other reason but that it was for His work. When Elisha comes to the widow of Sareptah and finds her preparing to make ready her pittance for herself and family, he bids her first provide for him, he challenges first God's part which she must first give before she must serve her own family. All these teach us that the Lord looks that when He is pleased to call for His right in any thing we have, our own interest we have must stand aside till His turn be served. For the other, we need look no further then to that of 1 John 3:17, "He who hath this world's goods and seeth his brother to need and shuts up his compassion from him, how dwelleth the love of God in him?" Which comes punctually to this conclusion: If thy brother be in want and thou canst help him, thou needst not make doubt of what thou shouldst do; if thou lovest God thou must help him.

QUESTION: What rule must we observe in lending?

ANSWER: Thou must observe whether thy brother hath present or probable or possible means of repaying thee, if there be none of those, thou must give him according to his necessity, rather then lend him as he requires (requests). If he hath present means of repaying thee, thou art to look at him not as an act of mercy, but by way of commerce, wherein thou art to walk by the rule of justice; but if his means of repaying thee be only probable or possible, then he is an object of thy mercy, thou must lend him, though there be

danger of losing it. (Deut. 15:7-8): "If any of thy brethren be poor
... thou shalt lend him sufficient." That men might not shift off this
duty by the apparent hazard, He tells them that though the year
of Jubilee were at hand (when he must remit it, if he were not able
to repay it before), yet he must lend him, and that cheerfully. It
may not grieve thee to give him, saith He. And because some might
object, why so I should soon impoverish myself and my family, he
adds, with all thy work, etc., for our Savior said (Matt. 5:42), "From
him that would borrow of thee turn not away."

QUESTION: What rule must we observe in forgiving (a debt)?

ANSWER: Whether thou didst lend by way of commerce or in
mercy, if he hath nothing to pay thee, thou must forgive, (except
in cause where thou hast a surety or a lawful pledge). Deut. 15:1-2
--- Every seventh year the creditor was to quit that which he lent to
his brother if he were poor, as appears in verse 4. "Save when there
shall be no poor with thee." In all these and like cases, Christ gives
a general rule (Matt. 7:12), "Whatsoever ye would that men should
do to you, do ye the same to them."

QUESTION: What rule must we observe and walk by in cause
of community of peril?

ANSWER: The same as before, but with more enlargement
towards others and less respect towards ourselves and our own
right. Hence it was that in the primitive Church they sold all,
had all things in common, neither did any man say that which he
possessed was his own. Likewise in their return out of the captivity,
because the work was great for the restoring of the church and the
danger of enemies was common to all, Nehemiah directs the Jews to
liberality and readiness in remitting their debts to their brethren,

and disposing liberally to such as wanted, and stand not upon their
own dues which they might have demanded of them. Thus did
some of our forefathers in times of persecution in England, and
so did many of the faithful of other churches, whereof we keep an
honorable remembrance of them; and it is to be observed that both
in Scriptures and latter stories of the churches that such as have been
most bountiful to the poor saints, especially in those extraordinary
times and occasions, God hath left them highly commended to
posterity, as Zaccheus, Cornelius, Dorcas, Bishop Hooper, the Cutler
of Brussels and divers others. Observe again that the Scripture
gives no caution to restrain any from being over liberal this way;
but all men to the liberal and cheerful practice hereof by the sweeter
promises; as to instance one for many (Isaiah 58:6-9) "Is not this
the fast I have chosen to loose the bonds of wickedness, to take off
the heavy burdens, to let the oppressed go free and to break every
yoke ... to deal thy bread to the hungry and to bring the poor that
wander into thy house, when thou seest the naked to cover them ...
and then shall thy light brake forth as the morning and thy health
shall grow speedily, thy righteousness shall go before God, and
the glory of the Lord shalt embrace thee; then thou shall call and
the Lord shall answer thee," etc. And from Ch. 2:10 (??) "If thou
pour out thy soul to the hungry, then shall thy light spring out in
darkness, and the Lord shall guide thee continually, and satisfy thy
soul in draught, and make fat thy bones, thou shalt be like a watered
garden, and they shalt be of thee that shall build the old waste
places," etc. On the contrary most heavy curses are laid upon such
as are straightened towards the Lord and his people (Judg. 5:23),
"Curse ye Meroshe ... because they came not to help the Lord." He
who shutteth his ears from hearing the cry of the poor, he shall cry
and shall not be heard." (Matt. 25) "Go ye cursed into everlasting

fire," etc. "I was hungry and ye fed me not." (2 Cor. 9:6) "He that
soweth sparingly shall reap sparingly."

Having already set forth the practice of mercy according to the rule
of God's law, it will be useful to lay open the grounds of it also,
being the other part of the Commandment and that is the affection
from which this exercise of mercy must arise, the Apostle tells us
that this love is the fulfilling of the law, not that it is enough to love
our brother and so no further; but in regard of the excellency of his
parts giving any motion to the other as the soul to the body and the
power it hath to set all the faculties at work in the outward exercise
of this duty; as when we bid one make the clock strike, he doth not
lay hand on the hammer, which is the immediate instrument of the
sound, but sets on work the first mover or main wheel; knowing that
will certainly produce the sound which he intends. So the way to
draw men to the works of mercy, is not by force of Argument from
the goodness or necessity of the work; for though this cause may
enforce, a rational mind to some present act of mercy, as is frequent
in experience, yet it cannot work such a habit in a soul, as shall
make it prompt upon all occasions to produce the same effect, but by
framing these affections of love in the heart which will as naturally
bring forth the other, as any cause doth produce the effect.

The definition which the Scripture gives us of love is this: Love
is the bond of perfection. First it is a bond or ligament. Secondly, it
makes the work perfect. There is no body but consists of parts and
that which knits these parts together, gives the body its perfection,
because it makes each part so contiguous to others as thereby they
do mutually participate with each other, both in strength and
infirmity, in pleasure and pain. To instance in the most perfect
of all bodies: Christ and his Church make one body. The several

parts of this body considered a part before they were united, were
as disproportionate and as much disordering as so many contrary
qualities or elements, but when Christ comes, and by his spirit and
love knits all these parts to himself and each to other, it is become
the most perfect and best proportioned body in the world (Eph. 4:15-
16). Christ, by whom all the body being knit together by every joint
for the furniture thereof, according to the effectual power which is
in the measure of every perfection of parts, a glorious body without
spot or wrinkle; the ligaments hereof being Christ, or his love, for
Christ is love (1 John 4:8). So this definition is right. Love is the
bond of perfection.

From hence we may frame these conclusions:

First of all, true Christians are of one body in Christ (1 Cor. 12).
Ye are the body of Christ and members of their part. All the parts
of this body being thus united are made so contiguous in a special
relation as they must needs partake of each other's strength and
infirmity; joy and sorrow, weal and woe. If one member suffers, all
suffer with it, if one be in honor, all rejoice with it.

Secondly, the ligaments of this body which knit together are
love.

Thirdly, no body can be perfect which wants its proper ligament.

Fourthly, All the parts of this body being thus united are made
so contiguous in a special relation as they must needs partake of
each other's strength and infirmity, joy and sorrow, weal and woe.
(1 Cor. 12:26) If one member suffers, all suffer with it; if one be in
honor, all rejoice with it.

Fifthly, this sensitivity and sympathy of each other's conditions

will necessarily infuse into each part a native desire and endeavor,
to strengthen, defend, preserve and comfort the other. To insist a
little on this conclusion being the product of all the former, the truth
hereof will appear both by precept and pattern. 1 John 3:16, "We
ought to lay down our lives for the brethren." Gal. 6:2, "Bear ye one
another's burden's and so fulfill the law of Christ."

For patterns we have that first of our Savior who, out of his good
will in obedience to his father, becoming a part of this body and
being knit with it in the bond of love, found such a native sensitivity
of our infirmities and sorrows as he willingly yielded himself to
death to ease the infirmities of the rest of his body, and so healed
their sorrows. From the like sympathy of parts did the Apostles
and many thousands of the Saints lay down their lives for Christ.
Again the like we may see in the members of this body among
themselves. Rom. 9 --- Paul could have been contented to have been
separated from Christ, that the Jews might not be cut off from the
body. It is very observable what he professeth of his affectionate
partaking with every member; "Who is weak (saith he) and I am
not weak? Who is offended and I burn not?" And again (2 Cor.
7:13), "Therefore we are comforted because ye were comforted."
Of Epaphroditus he speaketh (Phil. 2:25-30) that he regarded not
his own life to do him service. So Phoebe and others are called the
servants of the church. Now it is apparent that they served not for
wages, or by constraint, but out of love. The like we shall find in the
histories of the church, in all ages; the sweet sympathy of affections
which was in the members of this body one towards another; their
cheerfulness in serving and suffering together; how liberal they
were without repining, harborers without grudging, and helpful
without reproaching; and all from hence, because they had fervent
love amongst them; which only makes the practice of mercy constant

and easy.

The next consideration is how this love comes to be wrought. Adam in his first estate was a perfect model of mankind in all their generations, and in him this love was perfected in regard of the habit. But Adam, himself rent from his Creator, rent all his posterity also one from another; whence it comes that every man is born with this principle in him to love and seek himself only, and thus a Man continueth till Christ comes and takes possession of the soul and infuseth another principle, love to God and our brother, and this latter having continual supply from Christ, as the head and root by which he is united, gets predominant in the soul, so by little and little expels the former. 1 John 4:7 --- Love cometh of God and every one that loveth is born of God, so that this love is the fruit of the new birth, and none can have it but the new creature. Now when this quality is thus formed in the souls of men, it works like the Spirit upon the dry bones. Ezek. 37:7 --- "Bone came to bone." It gathers together the scattered bones, or perfect old man Adam, and knits them into one body again in Christ, whereby a man is become again a living soul.

The third consideration is concerning the exercise of this love, which is twofold, inward or outward. The outward hath been handled in the former preface of this discourse. From unfolding the other we must take in our way that maxim of philosophy, "simile simili gaudet," or like will to like; for as of things which are turned with disaffection to each other, the ground of it is from a dissimilitude or arising from the contrary or different nature of the things themselves; for the ground of love is an apprehension of some resemblance in the things loved to that which affects it. This is the cause why the Lord loves the creature, so far as it hath any of

his Image in it; He loves his elect because they are like Himself, He
beholds them in His beloved son.

So a mother loves her child, because she thoroughly conceives
a resemblance of herself in it. Thus it is between the members of
Christ; each discerns, by the work of the Spirit, his own Image
and resemblance in another, and therefore cannot but love him as
he loves himself. Now when the soul, which is of a sociable nature,
finds anything like to itself, it is like Adam when Eve was brought
to him. She must be one with himself. This is flesh of my flesh
(saith he) and bone of my bone. So the soul conceives a great delight
in it; therefore she desires nearness and familiarity with it. She
hath a great propensity to do it good and receives such content in
it, as fearing the miscarriage of her beloved, she bestows it in the
inmost closet of her heart. She will not endure that it shall want
any good which she can give it. If by occasion she be withdrawn
from the company of it, she is still looking towards the place where
she left her beloved. If she heard it groan, she is with it presently.
If she find it sad and disconsolate, she sighs and moans with it.
She hath no such joy as to see her beloved merry and thriving. If
she see it wronged, she cannot hear it without passion. She sets no
bounds to her affections, nor hath any thought of reward. She finds
recompense enough in the exercise of her love towards it.

We may see this acted to life in Jonathan and David. Jonathan a
valiant man endued with the spirit of love, so soon as he discovered
the same spirit in David had presently his heart knit to him by this
ligament of love; so that it is said he loved him as his own soul, he
takes so great pleasure in him, that he strips himself to adorn his
beloved. His father's kingdom was not so precious to him as his
beloved David, David shall have it with all his heart. Himself desires

no more but that he may be near to him to rejoice in his good. He chooseth to converse with him in the wilderness even to the hazard of his own life, rather than with the great Courtiers in his father's Palace. When he sees danger towards him, he spares neither rare pains nor peril to direct it. When injury was offered his beloved David, he would not bear it, though from his own father. And when they must part for a season only, they thought their hearts would have broke for sorrow, had not their affections found vent by abundance of tears. Other instances might be brought to show the nature of this affection; as of Ruth and Naomi, and many others; but this truth is cleared enough. If any shall object that it is not possible that love shall be bred or upheld without hope of requital, it is granted; but that is not our cause; for this love is always under reward. It never gives, but it always receives with advantage:

First in regard that among the members of the same body, love and affection are reciprocal in a most equal and sweet kind of commerce.

Secondly, in regard of the pleasure and content that the exercise of love carries with it, as we may see in the natural body. The mouth is at all the pains to receive and mince the food which serves for the nourishment of all the other parts of the body; yet it hath no cause to complain; for first the other parts send back, by several passages, a due proportion of the same nourishment, in a better form for the strengthening and comforting the mouth. Secondly, the labor of the mouth is accompanied with such pleasure and content as far exceeds the pains it takes. So is it in all the labor of love among Christians. The party loving, reaps love again, as was showed before, which the soul covets more then all the wealth in the world.

Thirdly, nothing yields more pleasure and content to the soul
then when it finds that which it may love fervently; for to love and
live beloved is the soul's paradise both here and in heaven. In the
State of wedlock there be many comforts to learn out of the troubles
of that condition; but let such as have tried the most, say if there be
any sweetness in that condition comparable to the exercise of mutual
love.

From the former considerations arise these conclusions:

First, this love among Christians is a real thing, not imaginary.

Secondly, this love is as absolutely necessary to the being of the
body of Christ, as the sinews and other ligaments of a natural body
are to the being of that body.

Thirdly, this love is a divine, spiritual, nature; free, active,
strong, courageous, permanent; undervaluing all things beneath its
proper object and of all the graces, this makes us nearer to resemble
the virtues of our heavenly father.

Fourthly, it rests in the love and welfare of its beloved. For the
full certain knowledge of those truths concerning the nature, use,
and excellency of this grace, that which the holy ghost hath left
recorded, 1 Cor. 13, may give full satisfaction, which is needful for
every true member of this lovely body of the Lord Jesus, to work
upon their hearts by prayer, meditation continual exercise at least of
the special influence of this grace, till Christ be formed in them and
they in him, all in each other, knit together by this bond of love.

It rests now to make some application of this discourse, by the
present design, which gave the occasion of writing of it. Herein are
four things to be propounded; first the persons, secondly, the work,

thirdly the end, fourthly the means.

First, for the persons. We are a company professing ourselves
fellow members of Christ, in which respect only, though we were
absent from each other many miles, and had our employments as far
distant, yet we ought to account ourselves knit together by this bond
of love and live in the exercise of it, if we would have comfort of our
being in Christ. This was notorious in the practice of the Christians
in former times; as is testified of the Waldenses, from the mouth of
one of the adversaries Aeneas Sylvius "mutuo ament pene antequam
norunt" --- they use to love any of their own religion even before
they were acquainted with them.

Secondly for the work we have in hand. It is by a mutual consent,
through a special overvaluing providence and a more than an
ordinary approbation of the churches of Christ, to seek out a place of
cohabitation and consortship under a due form of government both
civil and ecclesiastical. In such cases as this, the care of the public
must oversway all private respects, by which, not only conscience,
but mere civil policy, doth bind us. For it is a true rule that
particular estates cannot subsist in the ruin of the public.

Thirdly, the end is to improve our lives to do more service to
the Lord; the comfort and increase of the body of Christ, whereof
we are members, that ourselves and posterity may be the better
preserved from the common corruptions of this evil world, to serve
the Lord and work out our salvation under the power and purity of
his holy ordinances.

Fourthly, for the means whereby this must be effected. They
are twofold, a conformity with the work and end we aim at. These
we see are extraordinary, therefore we must not content ourselves

with usual ordinary means. Whatsoever we did, or ought to have done, when we lived in England, the same must we do, and more also, where we go. That which the most in their churches maintain as truth in profession only, we must bring into familiar and constant practice; as in this duty of love, we must love brotherly without dissimulation, we must love one another with a pure heart fervently. We must bear one another's burdens. We must not look only on our own things, but also on the things of our brethren.

Neither must we think that the Lord will bear with such failings at our hands as he doth from those among whom we have lived; and that for these three reasons:

First, in regard of the more near bond of marriage between Him and us, wherein He hath taken us to be His, after a most strict and peculiar manner, which will make Him the more jealous of our love and obedience. So He tells the people of Israel, you only have I known of all the families of the earth, therefore will I punish you for your transgressions.

Secondly, because the Lord will be sanctified in them that come near Him. We know that there were many that corrupted the service of the Lord; some setting up altars before his own; others offering both strange fire and strange sacrifices also; yet there came no fire from heaven, or other sudden judgment upon them, as did upon Nadab and Abihu, whom yet we may think did not sin presumptuously.

Thirdly, when God gives a special commission He looks to have it strictly observed in every article; When He gave Saul a commission to destroy Amaleck, He indented with him upon certain articles, and because he failed in one of the least, and that upon a fair pretense, it lost him the kingdom, which should have been his reward, if he had observed his commission.

Thus stands the cause between God and us. We are entered into covenant with Him for this work. We have taken out a commission. The Lord hath given us leave to draw our own articles. We have professed to enterprise these and those accounts, upon these and those ends. We have hereupon besought Him of favor and blessing. Now if the Lord shall please to hear us, and bring us in peace to the place we desire, then hath He ratified this covenant and sealed our commission, and will expect a strict performance of the articles contained in it; but if we shall neglect the observation of these articles which are the ends we have propounded, and, dissembling with our God, shall fall to embrace this present world and prosecute our carnal intentions, seeking great things for ourselves and our posterity, the Lord will surely break out in wrath against us, and be revenged of such a people, and make us know the price of the breach of such a covenant.

Now the only way to avoid this shipwreck, and to provide for our posterity, is to follow the counsel of Micah, to do justly, to love mercy, to walk humbly with our God. For this end, we must be knit together, in this work, as one man. We must entertain each other in brotherly affection. We must be willing to abridge ourselves of our superfluities, for the supply of others' necessities. We must uphold a familiar commerce together in all meekness, gentleness, patience and liberality. We must delight in each other; make others' conditions our own; rejoice together, mourn together, labor and suffer together, always having before our eyes our commission and community in the work, as members of the same body. So shall we keep the unity of the spirit in the bond of peace. The Lord will be our God, and delight to dwell among us, as His own people, and will command a blessing upon us in all our ways, so that we shall see much more of His wisdom, power, goodness and truth, than formerly we have been acquainted with. We shall find that the God of Israel is among us, when ten of us shall be able to resist a thousand of our enemies; when He shall make us a praise and glory that men shall say of succeeding plantations, "may the Lord make it like that of New England." For we must consider that we shall be as a city upon a hill. The eyes of all people are upon us. So that if we shall deal falsely with our God in this work we have undertaken, and so cause Him to withdraw His present help from us, we shall be made a story and a by-word through the world. We shall open the mouths of enemies to speak evil of the ways of God, and all professors for God's sake. We shall shame the faces of many of God's worthy servants, and cause their prayers to be turned into curses upon us till we be consumed out of the good land whither we are going.

And to shut this discourse with that exhortation of Moses, that faithful servant of the Lord, in his last farewell to Israel, Deut. 30. "Beloved, there is now set before us life and death, good and evil," in that we are commanded this day to love the Lord our God, and to love one another, to walk in his ways and to keep his Commandments and his ordinance and his laws, and the articles of our Covenant with Him, that we may live and be multiplied, and that the Lord our God may bless us in the land whither we go to possess it. But if our hearts shall turn away, so that we will not obey, but shall be seduced, and worship other Gods, our pleasure and profits, and serve them; it is propounded unto us this day, we shall surely perish out of the good land whither we pass over this vast sea to possess it.

Therefore let us choose life,

that we and our seed may live,

by obeying His voice and cleaving to Him,

for He is our life and our prosperity.

JONATHAN EDWARDS

Sinners in the Hands of an Angry God

"Jonathan Edwards, often called America's greatest theologian and philosopher and the last Puritan, was a powerful force behind the First Great Awakening, as well as a champion of Christian zeal and spirituality. Both Christian and secular scholarship concur on his importance in American history. The treasures from Edwards's pen have been mined, pondered, and evaluated to the present day. His famous sermon, 'Sinners in the Hands of an Angry God,' is still being read and studied in America's public schools as a specimen of eighteenth-century literature. Students of American history pay much attention to Edwards's scientific, philosophical, and psychological writings; theologians and church historians regard Edwards's work on revivals as unexcelled in analysis and scope. Christians continue to read his sermons with great appreciation for their rich doctrine, clear and forceful style, and powerful depiction of the majesty of God, the sinfulness of sin, and Christ's power to save." — Dr. Joel Beeke, Meet the Puritans

Jonathan Edwards was a steady, measured preacher. He read his sermons with conviction but without theatrics. He did not shout or raise his voice. He first preached "Sinners in the Hands of an Angry God" to his congregation in Northampton, Massachusetts to no remarkable effect. Later, he preached it again in Enfield, Connecticut, with a very different effect. The Reverend Stephen Williams, who was present, wrote in his diary, "We went over to Enfield where we met dear Mr. E. of N.H., who preached a most awakening sermon from Deut 32,35, and before sermon was done there was a great moaning and crying through ye whole House, what Shall I do to be Sav'd—oh, I am going to Hell—oh, what shall I do *for Christ., &c., &c., so that ye minister was obliged to desist, ye shrieks and crys were piercing and amazing—after Some time of waiting, the congregation were still, so yt a prayer was made by Mr. W. and after that we descendd from the pulpitt and discoursed with the people—Some in one place and Some in another—and Amazing and Astonishing ye power of God was Seen—and Several Souls were hopefully wrought upon yt night, and oh ye cheerfulness and pleasantness of their countenances yt received comfort—oh yt God wd strengthen and confirm—we sung a hymn and pray'd and dismiss'd ye Assembly."*

Mr. Edwards's SERMON On the Danger of the UNCONVERTED.

Preached at Enfield, July 8th 1741.
At a Time of great Awakenings ; and attended with
remarkable Impressions on many of the Hearers.
By Jonathan Edwards, A.M.
Pastor of the Church of Christ in Northampton.

SERMON TEXT: Amos ix. 2, 3.

Though they dig into Hell, thence shall mine Hand take them; though they climb up to Heaven, thence will I bring them down. And though they hide themselves in the Top of Carmel, I will search and take them out thence; and though they be hid from my Sight in the Bottom of the Sea, thence I will command the Serpent, and he shall bite them.

In this verse is threatened the vengeance of God on the wicked unbelieving Israelites, that were God's visible people, and lived under means of grace; and that notwithstanding all God's wonderful works that he had wrought towards that people, yet remained, as is expressed verse 28, void of counsel, having no understanding in them; and that, under all the cultivations of heaven, brought forth bitter and poisonous fruit; as in the two verses next preceding the text.

The expression that I have chosen for my text, their foot shall slide in due time, seems to imply the following things relating to the punishment and destruction that these wicked Israelites were exposed to.

1. That they were always exposed to destruction; as one that stands or walks in slippery places is always exposed to fall. This is implied in the manner of their destruction's coming upon them, being represented by their foot's sliding. The same is expressed, Psalm lxxiii. 18: "Surely thou didst set them in slippery places; thou castedst them down into destruction."

2. It implies that they were always exposed to sudden, unexpected destruction; as he that walks in slippery places is every moment liable to fall, he can't foresee one moment whether he shall stand or fall the next; and when he does fall, he falls at once, without warning, which is also expressed in that Psalm lxxiii. 18, 19: "Surely thou didst set them in slippery places: thou castedst them down into destruction. How are they brought into desolation, as in a moment!"

3. Another thing implied is, that they are liable to fall of themselves, without being thrown down by the hand of another; as he that stands or walks on slippery ground needs nothing but his own weight to throw him down.

4. That the reason why they are not fallen already, and don't fall now, is only that God's appointed time is not come. For it is said that when that due time, or appointed time comes, their foot shall slide. Then they shall be left to fall, as they are inclined by their own

weight. God won't hold them up in these slippery places any longer, but will let them go; and then, at that very instant, they shall fall to destruction; as he that stands in such slippery declining ground on the edge of a pit that he can't stand alone, when he is let go he immediately falls and is lost.

The observation from the words that I would now insist upon is this,

There is nothing that keeps wicked men at any one moment out of hell, but the mere pleasure of God.

By the mere pleasure of God, I mean his sovereign pleasure, his arbitrary will, restrained by no obligation, hindered by no manner of difficulty, any more than if nothing else but God's mere will had in the least degree or in any respect whatsoever any hand in the preservation of wicked men one moment.

The truth of this observation may appear by the following considerations.

1. There is no want of power in God to cast wicked men into hell at any moment. Men's hands can't be strong when God rises up: the strongest have no power to resist him, nor can any deliver out of his hands.

He is not only able to cast wicked men into hell, but he can most easily do it. Sometimes an earthly prince meets with a great deal of difficulty to subdue a rebel that has found means to fortify himself, and has made himself strong by the number of his followers. But it is not so with God. There is no fortress that is any defence against the power of God. Though hand join in hand, and vast multitudes of God's enemies combine and associate themselves, they are easily broken in pieces: they are as great heaps of light chaff before the whirlwind; or large quantities of dry stubble before devouring flames. We find it easy to tread on and crush a worm that we see crawling on the earth; so 'tis easy for us to cut or singe a slender thread that any thing hangs by; thus easy is it for God, when he pleases, to cast his enemies down to hell. What are we, that we should think to stand before him, at whose rebuke the earth trembles, and before whom the rocks are thrown down!

2. They deserve to be cast into hell; so that divine justice never stands in the way, it makes no objection against God's using his power at any moment to destroy them. Yea, on the contrary, justice calls aloud for an infinite punishment of their sins. Divine justice says of the tree that brings forth such grapes of Sodom, "Cut it down, why cumbereth it the ground?" Luke xiii. 7. The sword of divine justice is every moment brandished over their heads, and 'tis nothing but the hand of arbitrary mercy, and God's mere will, that holds it back.

3. They are already under a sentence of condemnation to hell. They don't only justly deserve to be cast down thither, but the sentence of the law of God, that eternal and immutable rule of righteousness that God has fixed between him and mankind, is gone out against them, and stands against them; so that they are bound over already to hell: John iii. 18, "He that believeth not is condemned already." So that every unconverted man properly belongs to hell; that is his place; from thence he is: John viii. 23, "Ye are from beneath:" and thither he is bound; 'tis the place that justice, and God's word, and the sentence of his unchangeable law, assigns to him.

4. They are now the objects of that very same anger and wrath of God, that is expressed in the torments of hell: and the reason why they don't go down to hell at each moment is not because God, in whose power they are, is not then very angry with them; as angry as he is with many of those miserable creatures that he is now tormenting in hell, and do there feel and bear the fierceness of his wrath. Yea, God is a great deal more angry with great numbers that are now on earth, yea, doubtless, with many that are now in this congregation, that, it may be, are at ease and quiet, than he is with many of those that are now in the flames of hell.

So that it is not because God is unmindful of their wickedness, and don't resent it, that he don't let loose his hand and cut them off. God is not altogether such a one as themselves, though they may imagine him to be so. The wrath of God burns against them; their damnation don't slumber; the pit is prepared; the fire is made ready; the furnace is now hot, ready to receive them; the flames do now rage and glow. The glittering sword is whet, and held over them, and the pit hath opened her mouth under them.

5. The devil stands ready to fall upon them, and seize them as his own, at what moment God shall permit him. They belong to him; he has their souls in his possession, and under his dominion. The Scripture represents them as his goods, Luke xi. 21. The devils watch them; they are ever by them, at their right hand; they stand waiting for them, like greedy hungry lions that see their prey, and expect to have it, but are for the present kept back; if God should withdraw his hand by which they are restrained, they would in one moment fly upon their poor souls. The old serpent is gaping for them; hell opens its mouth wide to receive them; and if God should permit it, they would be hastily swallowed up and lost.

6. There are in the souls of wicked men those hellish principles reigning, that would presently kindle and flame out into hell-fire, if it were not for God's restraints. There is laid in the very nature of carnal men a foundation for the torments of hell: there are those corrupt principles, in reigning power in them, and in full possession of them, that are seeds of hell-fire. These principles are active and powerful, exceeding violent in their nature, and if it were not for the restraining hand of God upon them, they would soon break out, they would flame out after the same manner as the same corruptions, the same enmity does in the heart of damned souls, and would beget the same torments in 'em as they do in them. The souls of the wicked are in Scripture compared to the troubled sea, Isaiah lvii. 20. For the present God restrains their wickedness by his mighty power, as he does the raging waves of the troubled sea, saying, "Hitherto shalt thou come, and no further;" but if God should withdraw that restraining power, it would soon carry all afore it. Sin is the ruin and misery of the soul; it is destructive in its nature; and if God should leave it without restraint, there would need nothing else to make the soul perfectly miserable. The corruption of the heart of man is a thing that is immoderate and boundless in its fury; and while wicked men live here, it is like fire pent up by God's restraints, whenas if it were let loose, it would set on fire the course of nature; and as the heart is now a sink of sin, so, if sin was not restrained, it would immediately turn the soul into a fiery oven, or a furnace of fire and brimstone.

7. It is no security to wicked men for one moment, that there are no visible means of death at hand. 'Tis no security to a natural man, that he is now in health, and that he don't see which way he should now immediately go out of the world by any accident, and that

there is no visible danger in any respect in his circumstances. The manifold and continual experience of the world in all ages shows that this is no evidence that a man is not on the very brink of eternity, and that the next step won't be into another world. The unseen, unthought of ways and means of persons' going suddenly out of the world are innumerable and inconceivable. Unconverted men walk over the pit of hell on a rotten covering, and there are innumerable places in this covering so weak that they won't bear their weight, and these places are not seen. The arrows of death fly unseen at noonday; the sharpest sight can't discern them. God has so many different, unsearchable ways of taking wicked men out of the world and sending 'em to hell, that there is nothing to make it appear that God had need to be at the expense of a miracle, or go out of the ordinary course of his providence, to destroy any wicked man, at any moment. All the means that there are of sinners' going out of the world are so in God's hands, and so absolutely subject to his power and determination, that it don't depend at all less on the mere will of God, whether sinners shall at any moment go to hell, than if means were never made use of, or at all concerned in the case.

8. Natural men's prudence and care to preserve their own lives, or the care of others to preserve them, don't secure 'em a moment. This, divine providence and universal experience does also bear testimony to. There is this clear evidence that men's own wisdom is no security to them from death; that if it were otherwise we should see some difference between the wise and politic men of the world and others, with regard to their liableness to early and unexpected death; but how is it in fact? Eccles. ii. 16, "How dieth the wise man? As the fool."

9. All wicked men's pains and contrivance they use to escape

hell, while they continue to reject Christ, and so remain wicked men, don't secure 'em from hell one moment. Almost every natural man that hears of hell flatters himself that he shall escape it; he depends upon himself for his own security, he flatters himself in what he has done, in what he is now doing, or what he intends to do; every one lays out matters in his own mind how he shall avoid damnation, and flatters himself that he contrives well for himself, and that his schemes won't fail. They hear indeed that there are but few saved, and that the bigger part of men that have died heretofore are gone to hell; but each one imagines that he lays out matters better for his own escape than others have done: he don't intend to come to that place of torment; he says within himself, that he intends to take care that shall be effectual, and to order matters so for himself as not to fail.

But the foolish children of men do miserably delude themselves in their own schemes, and in their confidence in their own strength and wisdom; they trust to nothing but a shadow. The bigger part of those that heretofore have lived under the same means of grace, and are now dead, are undoubtedly gone to hell; and it was not because they were not as wise as those that are now alive; it was not because they did not lay out matters as well for themselves to secure their own escape. If it were so that we could come to speak with them, and could inquire of them, one by one, whether they expected, when alive, and when they used to hear about hell, ever to be subjects of that misery, we, doubtless, should hear one and another reply, "No, I never intended to come here: I had laid out matters otherwise in my mind; I thought I should contrive well for myself: I thought my scheme good: I intended to take effectual care; but it came upon me unexpected; I did not look for it at that time, and in that manner; it came as a thief: death outwitted me: God's wrath was too quick for me. O my cursed foolishness! I was flattering myself, and pleasing myself with vain dreams of what I would do hereafter; and when I was saying peace and safety, then sudden destruction came upon me."

10. God has laid himself under no obligation, by any promise, to keep any natural man out of hell one moment. God certainly has made no promises either of eternal life, or of any deliverance or preservation from eternal death, but what are contained in the covenant of grace, the promises that are given in Christ, in whom all the promises are yea and amen. But surely they have no interest in the promises of the covenant of grace that are not the children of the covenant, and that do not believe in any of the promises of the covenant, and have no interest in the Mediator of the covenant.

So that, whatever some have imagined and pretended about promises made to natural men's earnest seeking and knocking, 'tis plain and manifest, that whatever pains a natural man takes in religion, whatever prayers he makes, till he believes in Christ, God is under no manner of obligation to keep him a moment from eternal destruction.

So that thus it is, that natural men are held in the hand of God over the pit of hell; they have deserved the fiery pit, and are already sentenced to it; and God is dreadfully provoked, his anger is as great towards them as to those that are actually suffering the executions of the fierceness of his wrath in hell, and they have done nothing in the least to appease or abate that anger, neither is God in the least bound by any promise to hold 'em up one moment; the devil is waiting for them, hell is gaping for them, the flames gather and flash about them, and would fain lay hold on them and swallow them up; the fire pent up in their own hearts is struggling to break out; and they have no interest in any Mediator, there are no means within reach that can be any security to them. In short they have no refuge, nothing to take hold of; all that preserves them every moment is the mere arbitrary will, and uncovenanted, unobliged forbearance of an incensed God.

APPLICATION

The use may be of awakening to unconverted persons in this congregation. This that you have heard is the case of every one of you that are out of Christ. That world of misery, that lake of burning brimstone, is extended abroad under you. There is the dreadful pit of the glowing flames of the wrath of God; there is hell's wide gaping mouth open; and you have nothing to stand upon, nor any thing to take hold of. There is nothing between you and hell but the air; 'tis only the power and mere pleasure of God that holds you up.

You probably are not sensible of this; you find you are kept out of hell, but don't see the hand of God in it, but look at other things, as the good state of your bodily constitution, your care of your own life, and the means you use for your own preservation. But indeed these things are nothing; if God should withdraw his hand, they would avail no more to keep you from falling than the thin air to hold up a person that is suspended in it.

Your wickedness makes you as it were heavy as lead, and to tend downwards with great weight and pressure towards hell; and if God should let you go, you would immediately sink and swiftly descend and plunge into the bottomless gulf, and your healthy constitution, and your own care and prudence, and best contrivance, and all your righteousness, would have no more influence to uphold you and keep you out of hell than a spider's web would have to stop a falling rock. Were it not that so is the sovereign pleasure of God, the earth would not bear you one moment; for you are a burden to it; the creation groans with you; the creature is made subject to the bondage of your corruption, not willingly; the sun don't willingly shine upon you to give you light to serve sin and Satan; the earth don't willingly yield her increase to satisfy your lusts; nor is it willingly a stage for your wickedness to be acted upon; the air don't willingly serve you for breath to maintain the flame of life in your vitals, while you spend your life in the service of God's enemies. God's creatures are good, and were made for men to serve God with, and don't willingly subserve to any other purpose, and groan when they are abused to purposes so directly contrary to their nature and end. And the world would spew you out, were it not for the sovereign hand of him who hath subjected it in hope. There are the black clouds of God's wrath now hanging directly over your heads, full of the dreadful storm, and big with thunder; and were it not for the restraining hand of God, it would immediately burst forth upon you. The sovereign pleasure of God, for the present, stays his rough wind; otherwise it would come with fury, and your destruction would come like a whirlwind, and you would be like the chaff of the summer threshing floor.

The wrath of God is like great waters that are dammed for the present; they increase more and more, and rise higher and higher, till an outlet is given; and the longer the stream is stopped, the more rapid and mighty is its course, when once it is let loose. 'Tis true, that judgment against your evil work has not been executed

hitherto; the floods of God's vengeance have been withheld; but your
guilt in the mean time is constantly increasing, and you are every
day treasuring up more wrath; the waters are continually rising, and
waxing more and more mighty; and there is nothing but the mere
pleasure of God that holds the waters back, that are unwilling to be
stopped, and press hard to go forward. If God should only withdraw
his hand from the floodgate, it would immediately fly open, and the
fiery floods of the fierceness and wrath of God would rush forth
with inconceivable fury, and would come upon you with omnipotent
power; and if your strength were ten thousand times greater than it
is, yea, ten thousand times greater than the strength of the stoutest,
sturdiest devil in hell, it would be nothing to withstand or endure it.

The bow of God's wrath is bent, and the arrow made ready on
the string, and justice bends the arrow at your heart, and strains the
bow, and it is nothing but the mere pleasure of God, and that of an
angry God, without any promise or obligation at all, that keeps the
arrow one moment from being made drunk with your blood.

Thus are all you that never passed under a great change of
heart by the mighty power of the Spirit of God upon your souls; all
that were never born again, and made new creatures, and raised
from being dead in sin to a state of new and before altogether
unexperienced light and life, (however you may have reformed your
life in many things, and may have had religious affections, and may
keep up a form of religion in your families and closets, and in the
house of God, and may be strict in it), you are thus in the hands
of an angry God; 'tis nothing but his mere pleasure that keeps you
from being this moment swallowed up in everlasting destruction.

However unconvinced you may now be of the truth of what you
hear, by and by you will be fully convinced of it. Those that are

gone from being in the like circumstances with you see that it was so with them; for destruction came suddenly upon most of them; when they expected nothing of it, and while they were saying, Peace and safety: now they see, that those things that they depended on for peace and safety were nothing but thin air and empty shadows.

The God that holds you over the pit of hell, much as one holds a spider or some loathsome insect over the fire, abhors you, and is dreadfully provoked; his wrath towards you burns like fire; he looks upon you as worthy of nothing else, but to be cast into the fire; he is of purer eyes than to bear to have you in his sight; you are ten thousand times so abominable in his eyes, as the most hateful and venomous serpent is in ours. You have offended him infinitely more than ever a stubborn rebel did his prince: and yet it is nothing but his hand that holds you from falling into the fire every moment. 'Tis ascribed to nothing else, that you did not go to hell the last night; that you was suffered to awake again in this world after you closed your eyes to sleep; and there is no other reason to be given why you have not dropped into hell since you arose in the morning, but that God's hand has held you up. There is no other reason to be given why you han't gone to hell since you have sat here in the house of God, provoking his pure eyes by your sinful wicked manner of attending his solemn worship. Yea, there is nothing else that is to be given as a reason why you don't this very moment drop down into hell.°

O sinner! consider the fearful danger you are in. 'Tis a great furnace of wrath, a wide and bottomless pit, full of the fire of wrath, that you are held over in the hand of that God whose wrath is provoked and incensed as much against you as against many of the damned in hell. You hang by a slender thread, with the flames of divine wrath flashing about it, and ready every moment to singe it and burn it asunder; and you have no interest in any Mediator, and nothing to lay hold of to save yourself, nothing to keep off the flames of wrath, nothing of your own, nothing that you ever have done, nothing that you can do, to induce God to spare you one moment.

And consider here more particularly several things concerning that wrath that you are in such danger of.

1. Whose wrath it is. It is the wrath of the infinite God. If it were only the wrath of man, though it were of the most potent prince, it would be comparatively little to be regarded. The wrath of kings is very much dreaded, especially of absolute monarchs, that have the possessions and lives of their subjects wholly in their power, to be disposed of at their mere will. Prov. xx. 2, "The fear of a king is as the roaring of a lion: whoso provoketh him to anger sinneth against his own soul." The subject that very much enrages an arbitrary prince is liable to suffer the most extreme torments that human art can invent, or human power can inflict. But the greatest earthly potentates, in their greatest majesty and strength, and when clothed in their greatest terrors, are but feeble, despicable worms of the dust, in comparison of the great and almighty Creator and King of heaven and earth: it is but little that they can do when most enraged, and when they have exerted the utmost of their fury. All the kings of the earth before God are as grasshoppers; they are nothing, and less than nothing: both their love and their hatred is to be despised. The wrath of the great King of kings is as much more terrible than theirs, as his majesty is greater. Luke xii. 4, 5, "And I say unto you my friends, Be not afraid of them that kill the body, and after that have no more that they can do. But I will forewarn

you whom you shall fear: Fear him, which after he hath killed hath power to cast into hell; yea, I say unto you, Fear him."

2. 'Tis the fierceness of his wrath that you are exposed to. We often read of the fury of God; as in Isaiah lix. 18: "According to their deeds, accordingly he will repay fury to his adversaries." So Isaiah lxvi. 15, "For, behold, the Lord will come with fire, and with his chariots like a whirlwind, to render his anger with fury, and his rebuke with flames of fire." And so in many other places. So we read of God's fierceness, Rev. xix. 15. There we read of "the wine-press of the fierceness and wrath of Almighty God." The words are exceeding terrible: if it had only been said, "the wrath of God," the words would have implied that which is infinitely dreadful: but 'tis not only said so, but "the fierceness and wrath of God." The fury of God! The fierceness of Jehovah! Oh, how dreadful must that be! Who can utter or conceive what such expressions carry in them! But it is not only said so, but "the fierceness and wrath of Almighty God." As though there would be a very great manifestation of his almighty power in what the fierceness of his wrath should inflict, as though omnipotence should be as it were enraged, and exerted, as men are wont to exert their strength in the fierceness of their wrath. Oh! then, what will be the consequence! What will become of the poor worm that shall suffer it! Whose hands can be strong! And whose heart endure! To what a dreadful, inexpressible, inconceivable depth of misery must the poor creature be sunk who shall be the subject of this!

Consider this, you that are here present, that yet remain in an unregenerate state. That God will execute the fierceness of his anger implies that he will inflict wrath without any pity. When God beholds the ineffable extremity of your case, and sees your torment so vastly disproportioned to your strength, and sees how your poor soul is crushed, and sinks down, as it were, into an infinite gloom; he will have no compassion upon you, he will not forbear the executions of his wrath, or in the least lighten his hand; there shall be no moderation or mercy, nor will God then at all stay his rough wind; he will have no regard to your welfare, nor be at all careful lest you should suffer too much in any other sense, than only that you should not suffer beyond what strict justice requires: nothing shall be withheld because it is so hard for you to bear. Ezek. viii. 18, "Therefore will I also deal in fury: mine eye shall not spare, neither will I have pity: and though they cry in mine ears with a loud voice, yet will I not hear them." Now God stands ready to pity you; this is a day of mercy; you may cry now with some encouragement of obtaining mercy: but when once the day of mercy is past, your most lamentable and dolorous cries and shrieks will be in vain; you will be wholly lost and thrown away of God, as to any regard to your welfare; God will have no other use to put you to, but only to suffer misery; you shall be continued in being to no other end; for you will be a vessel of wrath fitted to destruction; and there will be no other use of this vessel, but only to be filled full of wrath: God will be so far from pitying you when you cry to him, that 'tis said he will only "laugh and mock," Prov. i. 25, 26, &c.

How awful are those words, Isaiah lxiii. 3, which are the words of the great God: "I will tread them in mine anger, and trample them in my fury; and their blood shall be sprinkled upon my garments, and I will stain all my raiment." 'Tis perhaps impossible to conceive of words that carry in them greater manifestations of these three things, viz., contempt and hatred and fierceness of indignation. If you cry to God to pity you, he will be so far from

pitying you in your doleful case, or showing you the least regard
or favor, that instead of that he'll only tread you under foot: and
though he will know that you can't bear the weight of omnipotence
treading upon you, yet he won't regard that, but he will crush you
under his feet without mercy; he'll crush out your blood, and make
it fly, and it shall be sprinkled on his garments, so as to stain all
his raiment. He will not only hate you, but he will have you in the
utmost contempt; no place shall be thought fit for you but under his
feet, to be trodden down as the mire of the streets.

3. The misery you are exposed to is that which God will inflict
to that end, that he might show what that wrath of Jehovah is.
God hath had it on his heart to show to angels and men, both how
excellent his love is, and also how terrible his wrath is. Sometimes
earthly kings have a mind to show how terrible their wrath is, by
the extreme punishments they would execute on those that provoke
'em. Nebuchadnezzar, that mighty and haughty monarch of the
Chaldean empire, was willing to show his wrath when enraged with
Shadrach, Meshech, and Abednego; and accordingly gave order
that the burning fiery furnace should be heated seven times hotter
than it was before; doubtless, it was raised to the utmost degree of
fierceness that human art could raise it; but the great God is also
willing to show his wrath, and magnify his awful Majesty and
mighty power in the extreme sufferings of his enemies. Rom. ix.
22, "What if God, willing to show his wrath, and to make his power
known, endured with much long-suffering the vessels of wrath
fitted to destruction?" And seeing this is his design, and what he
has determined, to show how terrible the unmixed, unrestrained
wrath, the fury and fierceness of Jehovah is, he will do it to effect.
There will be something accomplished and brought to pass that will

be dreadful with a witness. When the great and angry God hath
risen up and executed his awful vengeance on the poor sinner, and
the wretch is actually suffering the infinite weight and power of his
indignation, then will God call upon the whole universe to behold
that awful majesty and mighty power that is to be seen in it. Isa.
xxxiii. 12, 13, 14, "And the people shall be as the burnings of lime,
as thorns cut up shall they be burnt in the fire. Hear, ye that are
far off, what I have done; and ye that are near, acknowledge my
might. The sinners in Zion are afraid; fearfulness hath surprised the
hypocrites," &c.

Thus it will be with you that are in an unconverted state, if you
continue in it; the infinite might, and majesty, and terribleness, of
the Omnipotent God shall be magnified upon you in the ineffable
strength of your torments. You shall be tormented in the presence of
the holy angels, and in the presence of the Lamb; and when you shall
be in this state of suffering, the glorious inhabitants of heaven shall
go forth and look on the awful spectacle, that they may see what the
wrath and fierceness of the Almighty is; and when they have seen
it, they will fall down and adore that great power and majesty. Isa.
lxvi. 23, 24, "And it shall come to pass, that from one new moon to
another, and from one sabbath to another, shall all flesh come to
worship before me, saith the Lord. And they shall go forth, and look
upon the carcasses of the men that have transgressed against me:
for their worm shall not die, neither shall their fire be quenched; and
they shall be an abhorring unto all flesh."

4. It is everlasting wrath. It would be dreadful to suffer this
fierceness and wrath of Almighty God one moment; but you must
suffer it to all eternity: there will be no end to this exquisite, horrible
misery. When you look forward, you shall see a long forever,

a boundless duration before you, which will swallow up your
thoughts, and amaze your soul; and you will absolutely despair
of ever having any deliverance, any end, any mitigation, any rest
at all; you will know certainly that you must wear out long ages,
millions of millions of ages, in wrestling and conflicting with this
almighty, merciless vengeance; and then when you have so done,
when so many ages have actually been spent by you in this manner,
you will know that all is but a point to what remains. So that your
punishment will indeed be infinite. Oh, who can express what the
state of a soul in such circumstances is! All that we can possibly
say about it gives but a very feeble, faint representation of it; it is
inexpressible and inconceivable: for "who knows the power of God's
anger?"

How dreadful is the state of those that are daily and hourly in
danger of this great wrath and infinite misery! But this is the dismal
case of every soul in this congregation that has not been born again,
however moral and strict, sober and religious, they may otherwise
be. Oh, that you would consider it, whether you be young or old!
There is reason to think that there are many in this congregation
now hearing this discourse, that will actually be the subjects of this
very misery to all eternity. We know not who they are, or in what
seats they sit, or what thoughts they now have. It may be they are
now at ease, and hear all these things without much disturbance,
and are now flattering themselves that they are not the persons,
promising themselves that they shall escape. If we knew that there
was one person, and but one, in the whole congregation, that was
to be the subject of this misery, what an awful thing it would be to
think of! If we knew who it was, what an awful sight would it be to
see such a person! How might all the rest of the congregation lift up

a lamentable and bitter cry over him! But alas! instead of one, how many is it likely will remember this discourse in hell! And it would be a wonder, if some that are now present should not be in hell in a very short time, before this year is out. And it would be no wonder if some persons that now sit here in some seats of this meeting-house in health, and quiet and secure, should be there before to-morrow morning. Those of you that finally continue in a natural condition, that shall keep out of hell longest, will be there in a little time! Your damnation don't slumber; it will come swiftly and, in all probability, very suddenly upon many of you. You have reason to wonder that you are not already in hell. 'Tis doubtless the case of some that heretofore you have seen and known, that never deserved hell more than you and that heretofore appeared as likely to have been now alive as you. Their case is past all hope; they are crying in extreme misery and perfect despair. But here you are in the land of the living and in the house of God, and have an opportunity to obtain salvation. What would not those poor, damned, hopeless souls give for one day's such opportunity as you now enjoy!

And now you have an extraordinary opportunity, a day wherein Christ has flung the door of mercy wide open, and stands in the door calling and crying with a loud voice to poor sinners; a day wherein many are flocking to him and pressing into the Kingdom of God. Many are daily coming from the east, west, north and south; many that were very likely in the same miserable condition that you are in are in now a happy state, with their hearts filled with love to him that has loved them and washed them from their sins in his own blood, and rejoicing in hope of the glory of God. How awful is it to be left behind at such a day! To see so many others feasting, while you are pining and perishing! To see so many rejoicing and singing for joy of heart, while you have cause to mourn for sorrow of heart and howl for vexation of spirit! How can you rest for one moment in such a condition? Are not your souls as precious as the souls of the people at Suffield, where they are flocking from day to day to Christ?

Are there not many here that have lived long in the world that are not to this day born again, and so are aliens from the commonwealth of Israel and have done nothing ever since they have lived but treasure up wrath against the day of wrath? Oh, sirs, your case in an especial manner is extremely dangerous; your guilt and hardness of heart is extremely great. Don't you see how generally persons of your years are passed over and left in the present remarkable and wonderful dispensation of God's mercy? You had need to consider yourselves and wake thoroughly out of sleep; you cannot bear the fierceness and the wrath of the infinite God.

And you that are young men and young women, will you neglect this precious season that you now enjoy, when so many others of your age are renouncing all youthful vanities and flocking to Christ? You especially have now an extraordinary opportunity; but if you neglect it, it will soon be with you as it is with those persons that spent away all the precious days of youth in sin and are now come to such a dreadful pass in blindness and hardness.

And you children that are unconverted, don't you know that you are going down to hell to bear the dreadful wrath of that God that is now angry with you every day and every night? Will you be content to be the children of the devil, when so many other children in the land are converted and are become the holy and happy children of the King of kings?

And let every one that is yet out of Christ and hanging over the pit of hell, whether they be old men and women or middle-aged or young people or little children, now hearken to the loud calls of God's word and providence. This acceptable year of the Lord that is a day of such great favor to some will doubtless be a day of as remarkable vengeance to others. Men's hearts harden and their guilt increases apace at such a day as this, if they neglect their souls. And never was there so great danger of such persons being given up to hardness of heart and blindness of mind. God seems now to be hastily gathering in his elect in all parts of the land; and probably the bigger part of adult persons that ever shall be saved will be brought in now in a little time, and that it will be as it was on that great outpouring of the Spirit upon the Jews in the Apostles' days, the election will obtain and the rest will be blinded. If this should be the case with you, you will eternally curse this day, and will curse the day that ever you was born to see such a season of the pouring out of God's Spirit, and will wish that you had died and gone to hell before you had seen it. Now undoubtedly it is as it was in the days of John the Baptist, the axe is in an extraordinary manner laid at the root of the trees, that every tree that bringeth not forth good fruit may be hewn down and cast into the fire.

Therefore let every one that is out of Christ now awake and fly from the wrath to come. The wrath of Almighty God is now undoubtedly hanging over great part of this congregation. Let every one fly out of Sodom. "Haste and escape for your lives, look not behind you, escape to the mountain, lest ye be consumed."

JONATHAN EDWARDS

Heaven Is a World of Love

*Jonathan Edwards is best known as the fire-and-brimstone preacher
of "Sinners in the Hands of an Angry God," but this lesser-known
sermon shows his pastoral love and tenderness as well. From the Editor's
Introduction to* Charity and Its Fruits: *The rhetorical power of this last
sermon ["Heaven Is a World of Love"] is rivaled only by his other "virtuoso
performance," "Sinners in the Hands of an Angry God."*

SERMON TEXT: 1 CORINTHIANS 13:8-10

*Charity never faileth; but whether there be prophecies, they shall
fail; whether there be tongues, they shall cease; whether there be
knowledge, it shall vanish away. For we know in part, and we
prophesy in part. But when that which is perfect is come, then that
which is in part shall be done away.*

The Apostle in the text speaks of a state of the church which is
perfect, and therefore a state in which the Holy Spirit shall more
perfectly and abundantly be given to the church than it now is. But
the way in which it shall be given, when it is so abundantly poured
forth, will be in that great fruit of the Spirit, holy and divine love
in the hearts of all the blessed inhabitants of that world. So that the
heavenly state of the church is a state which is distinguished from its
earthly state, as it is that state which God has designed especially
for such a communication of his Holy Spirit, and in which it shall be
given perfectly; whereas in the present state of the church, it is given
with such great imperfection; and also a state in which this shall
be, as it were, the only gift or fruit of the Spirit, as being the most
perfect and glorious, and which being brought to perfection renders

others, which God was wont to communicate to his church on earth, needless.

. . . Heaven is a part of the creation which God has built for this end, to be the place of his glorious presence. And it is his abode forever. Here he will dwell and gloriously manifest himself to eternity. And this renders heaven a world of love; for God is the fountain of love, as the sun is the fountain of light. And therefore the glorious presence of God in heaven fills heaven with love, as the sun placed in the midst of the hemisphere in a clear day fills the world with light. The Apostle tells us that God is love, 1 John 4:8. And therefore seeing he is an infinite Being, it follows that he is an infinite fountain of love. Seeing he is an all-sufficient Being, it follows that he is a full and overflowing and an inexhaustible fountain of love. Seeing he is an unchangeable and eternal Being, he is an unchangeable and eternal source of love. There even in heaven dwells that God from whom every stream of holy love, yea, every drop that is or ever was proceeds . . . There in heaven this fountain of love, this eternal three in one, is set open without any obstacle to hinder access to it. There this glorious God is manifested and shines forth in full glory, in beams of love; there the fountain overflows in streams and rivers of love and delight, enough for all to drink at, and to swim in, yea, so as to overflow the world as it were with a deluge of love.

. . . There are none but lovely objects in heaven . . . Everything which is to be beheld there is amiable. The God, who dwells and gloriously manifests himself there, is infinitely lovely. There is to be seen a glorious heavenly Father, a glorious Redeemer; there is to be felt and possessed a glorious Sanctifier. All the persons who belong to that blessed society are lovely. The Father of the family is so, and so are all his children. The Head of the body is so, and so are all the members. Concerning the angels, there are none who are unlovely. There are no evil angels suffered to infest heaven as they do this world. They are not suffered to come near, but are kept at a distance with a great gulf between them. In the church of saints there are no unlovely persons; there are no false professors, none who pretend to be saints, who are persons of an unchristian, hateful spirit and behavior, as is often the case in this world. There is no one object there to give offense, or at any time to give any occasion for any passion or motion of hatred; but every object shall draw forth love.

. . . Not only shall all objects there be lovely, but each shall be perfectly lovely. There are many things in this world which in general are lovely, but yet are not perfectly free from that which is the contrary. Many men are amiable and worthy to be loved, but yet they are not without those things which are very disagreeable. But it is not so in heaven. There shall be no pollution or deformity of any kind seen in any one person or thing. Everyone is perfectly pure, all over lovely; everything shall be perfectly pleasant. That world is perfectly bright without darkness, perfectly clear without spot. There shall be none appearing with any defects, either natural or moral. There is nothing seen there which is sinful, nothing weak or foolish. Nothing shall appear to which nature is averse, nothing which shall offend the most delicate eye. There shall be no string out of tune to cause any jar in the harmony of that world, no unpleasant note to cause any discord.

. . . In that world, wherever the inhabitants turn their eyes they shall see nothing but beauty and glory. In the most stately cities on earth, however magnificent the buildings are, yet the streets are filthy and defiled, being made to be trodden under foot. But the very street of this heavenly city is represented as being as pure gold, like unto transparent glass, Revelation 21:21. That it should be like pure gold only does not sufficiently represent the purity of them; but they are also like the transparent glass or crystal.

. . .Their love shall be without any remains of a contrary principle. Having no pride or selfishness to interrupt or hinder its exercises, their hearts shall be full of love. That which was in the heart as but a grain of mustard seed in this world shall there be as a great tree. The soul which only had a little spark of divine love in it in this world shall be, as it were, wholly turned into love; and be like the sun, not having a spot in it, but being wholly a bright, ardent flame. There shall be no remaining enmity, distaste, coldness and deadness of heart towards God and Christ; not the least remainder of any principle of envy to be exercised towards any angels or saints who are superior in glory, no contempt or slight towards any who are inferior.

. . . Those who have a lower station in glory than others suffer no diminution of their own happiness by seeing others above them in glory. On the contrary they rejoice in it. All that whole society rejoice in each other's happiness; for the love of benevolence is perfect in them. Everyone has not only a sincere but a perfect good will to every other. Sincere and strong love is greatly gratified and delighted in the prosperity of the beloved. And if the love be perfect, the greater the prosperity of the beloved is, the more is the lover pleased and delighted. For the prosperity of the beloved is, as it were, the food of love; and therefore the greater that prosperity is, the more richly is love feasted. The love of benevolence is delighted in beholding the prosperity of another, as the love of complacence is delighted in viewing the beauty of another. So that the superior prosperity of those who are higher in glory is so far from being any damp to the happiness of saints of lower degree that it is an addition to it, or a part of it. There is undoubtedly an inconceivably pure, sweet and fervent love between the saints in glory; and their love is in proportion to the perfection and amiableness of the objects beloved. And therefore it must necessarily cause delight in them when they see others' happiness and glory to be in proportion to their amiableness, and so in proportion to their love of them. Those who are highest in glory are those who are highest in holiness, and therefore are those who are most beloved by all the saints. For they love those most who are most holy, and so they will all rejoice in it that they are most happy. And it will be a damp to none of the saints to see them who have higher degrees of holiness and likeness to God to be more loved than themselves; for all shall have as much love as they desire, and as great manifestations of love as they can bear; all shall be fully satisfied.

. . .And when there is perfect satisfaction, there is no room for envy. And they will have no temptation to envy those who are above them in glory from their superiors being lifted up with pride. We are apt to conceive that those who are more holy, and more happy than others in heaven, will be elated and lifted up in their spirit above others. Whereas their being above them in holiness implies their being superior to them in humility; for their superior humility is part of their superior holiness. Though all are perfectly free from pride, yet as some will have greater degrees of divine knowledge than others, will have larger capacities to see more of the divine perfections, so they will see more of their own comparative littleness and nothingness, and therefore will be lowest abased in humility. And besides, the inferior in glory will have no temptation to envy those who are higher. For those who are highest will not only be more beloved by the lower saints for their higher holiness, but they will also have more of a spirit of love to others. They will love those who are below them more than other saints of less capacity. They who are in highest degrees of glory will be of largest capacity, and so of greatest knowledge, and will see most of God's loveliness, and consequently will have love to God and love to saints most abounding in their hearts. So that those who are lower in glory will not envy those who are above them. They will be most beloved of those who are highest in glory, and the superior in glory will be so far from slighting those who are inferior, that they will have more abundant love to them, greater degrees of love in proportion to their superior knowledge and happiness; the higher in glory, the more like Christ in this respect. So that they will love them more than those who are their equals. And what puts it beyond doubt that seeing the superior happiness of others will be no damp to their happiness is this, that the superior happiness which they have consists in their greater humility, and their greater love to them, and to God and Christ, whom they will look upon as themselves. Such a sweet and perfect harmony will there be in the heavenly society, and perfect love reigning in every heart towards everyone without control, and without alloy, or any interruption. And no envy, or malice, or revenge, or contempt, or selfishness shall enter there, but shall be kept as far off as earth and hell are from heaven.

. . . They shall enjoy each other's love in perfect and undisturbed prosperity. What oftentimes diminishes the pleasure and sweetness of earthly friendship is that though they live in love, yet they live in poverty, and meet with great difficulties and sore afflictions whereby they are grieved for themselves, and for one another.

For love and friendship in such cases, though in some respects lightens each other's burdens, yet in other respects adds to persons' afflictions, because it makes them sharers in others' afflictions. So that they have not only their afflictions to bear, but also those of their afflicted friends. But there shall be no adversity in heaven to give occasion for a pitiful grief of spirit, or to molest those heavenly friends in the enjoyment of each other's friendship. But they shall enjoy one another's love in the greatest prosperity, in glorious riches, having the possession of all things . . . And so all the saints enjoy each other's love in glory and prosperity in comparison with which the wealth and honor of the greatest earthly princes is sordid beggary. So that as they love one another, they have not only their own but each other's prosperity to rejoice in, and are by love made partakers of each other's glory. Such is every saint's love to other saints that it, as it were, makes that glory, which he sees other saints enjoy, his own. He so rejoices in it that they enjoy such glory, that it is in some respects to him as if he, himself, enjoyed it.

. . . They shall know that they shall forever be continued in the perfect enjoyment of each other's love. They shall know that God and Christ will be forever, and that their love will be continued and be fully manifested forever, and that all their beloved fellow saints shall live forever in glory with the same love in their hearts. And they shall know that they themselves shall ever live to love God, and love the saints, and enjoy their love. They shall be in no fear of any end of this happiness, nor shall they be in any fear or danger of any abatement of it through a weariness of the exercises and expressions of love, or cloyed with the enjoyment of it, or the beloved objects becoming old or decayed, or stale or tasteless. All things shall flourish there in an eternal youth. Age will not diminish anyone's beauty or vigor, and there love shall flourish in everyone's breast, as a living spring perpetually springing, or as a flame which never decays. And the holy pleasure shall be as a river which ever runs, and is always clear and full. The paradise of love shall always be continued as in a perpetual spring. There shall be no autumn or winter; every plant there shall be in perpetual bloom with the same undecaying pleasantness and fragrancy, always springing forth, always blossoming, and always bearing fruit.

. . . Those are principles contrary to love which make this world so much like a tempestuous sea. It is selfishness, and revenge, and envy, and such things which keep this world in a constant tumult, and make it a scene of confusion and uproar, where no quiet rest is to be enjoyed, unless it be in renouncing the world, and looking to another world. But what rest is there in that world which the God of love and peace fills with his glorious presence, where the Lamb of God lives and reigns, and fills that world with the pleasant beams of his love; where is nothing to give any offense, no object to be seen but what has perfect sweetness and amiableness; where the saints shall find and enjoy all which they love, and so be perfectly satisfied; where there is no enemy and no enmity in any heart, but perfect love in all to everyone; where there is a perfect harmony between the higher and the lower ranks of inhabitants of that world, none envying another, but everyone resting and rejoicing in the happiness of every other. All their love is holy, humble, and perfectly Christian, without the least impurity or carnality; where love is always mutual, where the love of the beloved is answerable to the love of the lovers; where there is no hypocrisy or dissembling, but perfect simplicity and sincerity; where is no treachery, unfaithfulness or inconstancy, nor any such thing as jealousy. And no clog or hindrance to the exercises and expressions of love, nor imprudence or indecency in the manner of expressing love, no instance of folly or indiscretion in any word or deed; where there is no separation wall, no misunderstanding or strangeness, but full acquaintance and perfect intimacy in all; no division through different opinions or interests, where all that glorious loving society shall be most nearly and divinely related, and all shall be one another's, having given themselves one to another. And all shall enjoy one another in perfect prosperity, riches, and honor, without any sickness, pain, or persecution, or any enemy to molest them, any talebearer, or busybody to create jealousies and misunderstandings.

And all this in a garden of love, the Paradise of God, where everything has a cast of holy love, and everything conspires to promote and stir up love, and nothing to interrupt its exercises; where everything is fitted by an all-wise God for the enjoyment of love under the greatest advantages. And all this shall be without any fading of the beauty of the objects beloved, or any decaying of love in the lover, and any satiety in the faculty which enjoys love. O! what tranquility may we conclude there is in such a world as this! Who can express the sweetness of this peace? What a calm is this, what a heaven of rest is here to arrive at after persons have gone through a world of storms and tempests, a world of pride, and selfishness, and envy, and malice, and scorn, and contempt, and contention and war? What a Canaan of rest, a land flowing with milk and honey to come to after one has gone through a great and terrible wilderness, full of spiteful and poisonous serpents, where no rest could3 be found? What joy may we conclude springs up in the hearts of the saints after they have passed their wearisome pilgrimage to be brought to such a paradise?

. . . Hence we may learn how happy those persons are who are entitled to heaven. There are some such persons living on earth to whom the happiness of this world belongs, as much and much more than a man's estate belongs to him. They have a part and interest in this world of love; they have proper right and title to it. Revelation 22:14, "Blessed are they that do his commandments, that they may have right to the tree of life, and may enter in through the gates into the city." And doubtless there are such persons among us. How happy are they who are entitled to an inheritance in such a world as this! Surely they are the blessed of the earth.

. . . They are those who have freely chosen that happiness which is to be had in the exercise and enjoyment of such love as is in heaven above all other conceivable happiness. They see and understand so much of this as to know that this is the best good. They do not merely assent that it is so from rational arguments which may be offered for it, but they have seen that it is so; they know it is so from what little they have tasted. It is the happiness of love, and the happiness of a life of such love, heavenly love, holy and humble and divine love; love to God, and love to Christ, and love to saints for God's and Christ's sake, and the enjoyment of the fruits of God's love, holy communion with God and Christ and with holy persons. This is what they have a relish for. They feel within them such a nature that such a happiness suits their disposition and relish and appetite above all others; not only above what they have, but above all that they can conceive they might have. The world does not afford anything like it. They have chosen this before any other. Their souls go out after it more than any other, and their hearts are more in pursuit of it than any other. They have chosen it freely, not merely because they have met with such sorrow, and are in such low and afflicted circumstances, that they do not expect much from the world. But their hearts are so captivated by this good that they choose it for its own sake beyond all worldly good, if they had ever so much of it, and could enjoy it ever so long. Canticles 1:2, "Thy love is better than wine."

. . . Let the consideration of what has been said of heaven stir you up earnestly to seek after it. If heaven be such a blessed world, then let this be our chosen country, and the inheritance we seek. Let us turn our course this way. It is not impossible that this glorious world may be obtained by us. It is offered to us. Though it be so excellent and blessed a country, yet God stands ready to give us an inheritance there, if this be the country we choose, and upon which we set our hearts, and spend our time chiefly in seeking it. God gives men their choice. They may have their inheritance where they choose it, and may obtain heaven if they will seek it by patient continuance in well-doing, Romans 2:7. We are all of us, as it were, set here in this world as in a large wilderness with divers countries about it, with several ways or paths leading to those different countries, and we are left to our choice what course we will take. If we heartily choose heaven, and set our hearts chiefly on that blessed Canaan, that land of love, and love the path which leads to it, we may walk in it; and if we continue so to do, it will certainly lead us to heaven at last. Let what we have heard of the land of love excite us all to turn our faces towards that land, and bend our course thitherward. Is not what we have heard of the happy state of that country and the many delights which are in it enough to make us thirst after it, and to cause us with the greatest earnestness and steadfastness of resolution to press towards, and to spend our whole lives in traveling in the way which leads thither? What joyful news might it well be to us when we hear of such a world of perfect peace and holy love, to hear that there is an opportunity for us to come, that we may spend an eternity in such a world.

. . . Is not what we have heard of that blessed world enough to make us weary of this world of pride and malice and contention and perpetual jarring and strife, a world of confusion, a wilderness of hissing serpents, a tempestuous ocean where there is no quiet rest, where all are for themselves, and self-interest governs, and all are striving to set themselves up, and little regarding what becomes of others; all together seeking worldly good which is the bone of contention among them, where men are continually envying and calumniating and reproaching one another and multitudes otherwise injuring and abusing one another, a world full of injustice, where there is abundance of opposition and cruelty without any remedy? A world where there is so much falsehood and treachery, fickleness and inconstancy, hypocrisy and deceit; where there is so little trust to be had in men, and where even good men have so many failings which tend to render them unlovely and uncomfortable. Truly this is an evil world, and so it is like to be. It is in vain for us to expect that this world will be any other than a world of pride and enmity and strife, and so a restless world. The times may hereafter be mended, yet those things will always be found in the world as long as it stands. Who would content himself with a portion in such a world? What man acting wisely and considerately would concern himself much about laying up a store in such a world as this, and would not rather neglect the world, apply all his heart and all his strength to lay up treasure in heaven, and to press towards that world of love? What will it signify for us to hoard up great quantities here in this world? How may the thought of having our portion here in such a world as this be sinking to a man when there is an interest in such a glorious world offered? and especially when if we have our portion here, when we have done with this world, we have our eternal portion in hell, that world of hatred, a world of the wrath of God, and cruelty and malice of devils and damned spirits.

We all of us naturally desire rest and quietness; and if we would obtain, let us seek that world of peace and love of which we have heard. Here is doubtless a sweet rest to be had. Hebrews 4:9, "There remaineth therefore a rest to the people of God." If we obtain an interest in that world, then when we have done with this we shall leave all our cares and troubles, our fatigues and perplexities and disappointments forever. We shall rest from those storms, we shall rest from our wearisome travel. Revelation 14:13, "Blessed are the dead which die in the Lord from henceforth; yea, saith the Spirit, that they may rest from their labors."

JAMES OTIS, JR.

Writs of Assistance

The Writs of Assistance are a little known document of great importance to the American experiment in liberty. The Writs were a general search warrant; they specified neither persons nor goods to be searched, and were used to enforce trade and navigation laws. Attorney James Otis Jr. was enlisted to defend several business owners in New England against the Writs. This opening speech by Otis was heard by future founding father John Adams who would call this speech, "The Spark which originated the American Revolution."

May it please your Honours: I was desired by one of the court to look into the (law) books, and consider the question now before them concerning Writs of Assistance. I have accordingly considered it, and now appear not only in obedience to your order, but likewise in behalf of the inhabitants of this town, who have presented another petition, and out of regard to the liberties of the subject. And I take this opportunity to declare that whether under a fee or not (for in such a cause as this I despise a fee) I will to my dying day oppose, with all the powers and faculties God has given me, all such instruments of slavery on the one hand and villainy on the other, as this Writ of Assistance is.

It appears to me the worst instrument of arbitrary power, the most destructive of English liberty and the fundamental principles of law that ever was found in an English lawbook. I must therefore beg your Honours' patience and attention to the whole range of an argument that may perhaps appear uncommon in many things, as well as to points of learning that are more remote and unusual, that the whole tendency of my design may the more easily be perceived, the conclusions better descend, and the force of them be better felt. I shall not think much of my pains in this cause, as I engaged in it from principle.

I was solicited to argue this case as Advocate-General; and, because I would not, I have been charged with desertion from my office. To this charge I can give a very sufficient answer. I renounced that office and I argue this cause from the same principle; and I argue it with the greatest pleasure, as it is in favour of British liberty, at a time when we hear the greatest monarch upon earth declaring from his throne that he glories in the name of Briton and that the privileges of his people are dearer to him than the most valuable prerogatives of his crown; and as it is in opposition to a kind of power, the exercise of which in former periods of history cost one king of England his head and another his crown, I have taken more pains in this cause than I ever will take again, although my engaging in this and another popular cause has raised much resentment.

But I think I can sincerely declare that I cheerfully submit myself to every odious name for conscience' sake; and from my soul I despise all those whose guilt, malice, or folly has made them my foes. Let the consequences be what they will, I am determined to proceed. The only principles of public conduct that are worthy of a gentleman or a man are to sacrifice estate, ease, health, and applause, and even life, to the sacred calls of his country. These manly sentiments, in private life, make good citizens; in public life, the patriot and the hero. I do not say that, when brought to the test, I shall be invincible. I pray God I may never be brought to the melancholy trial; but if ever I should, it will then be known how far

I can reduce to practice principles which I know to be founded in truth. In the meantime, I will proceed to the subject of this writ.

In the first place, may it please your honours, I will admit that writs of one kind may be legal; that is, special writs, directed to special officers, and to search certain houses, etc., specially set forth in the writ, may be granted by the Court of Exchequer at home, upon oath made before the Lord Treasurer by the person who asks it, that he suspects such goods to be concealed in those very places he desires to search. The Act of 14 Charles II., which Mr. Gridley mentions, proves this. And in this light the writ appears like a warrant from a Justice of the Peace to search for stolen goods. Your honours will find in the old books concerning the office of a Justice of the Peace, precedents of general warrants to search suspected houses. But in more modern books you will find only special warrants to search such and such houses, specially named, in which the complainant has before sworn that he suspects his goods are concealed; and will find it adjudged that special warrants only are legal.

In the same manner I rely on it, that the writ prayed for in this petition is illegal. It is a power that places the liberty of every man in the hands of every petty officer. I say, I admit that special Writs of Assistance, to search special places, may be granted to certain persons on oath; but I deny that the writ now prayed for can be granted, for I beg leave to make some observations on the writ itself, before I proceed to other Acts of Parliament.

In the first place, the writ is universal, being directed "to all and singular justices, sheriffs, constables, and all other officers and subjects"; so that, in short, it is directed to every subject in the

King's domains. Every one with this writ may be a tyrant; if this commission be legal, a tyrant in a legal manner, also, may control, imprison, or murder any one within the realm. In the next place, it is perpetual; there is no return.

A man is accountable to no person for his doings. Every man may reign secure in his petty tyranny, and spread terror and desolation around him [until the trump of the Archangel shall excite different emotions in his soul].

In the third place, a person with this writ, in the daytime, may enter all houses, shops, etc., at will, and command all to assist him. Fourthly, by this writ not only deputies, etc., but even their menial servants, are allowed to lord it over us. [What is this but to have the curse of Canaan with a witness on us: to be the servants of servants, the most despicable of God's creation?] Now one of the most essential branches of English liberty is the freedom of one's house.

A man's house is his castle; and whilst he is quiet, he is as well guarded as a prince in his castle. This writ, if it should be declared legal, would totally annihilate this privilege. Custom-house officers may enter our houses when they please; we are commanded to permit their entry. Their menial servants may enter, may break locks, bars, and everything in their way; and whether they break through malice or revenge, no man, no court can inquire. Bare suspicion without oath is sufficient.

This wanton exercise of this power is not a chimerical suggestion of a heated brain. I will mention some facts. Mr. Pew had one of these writs, and when Mr. Ware succeeded him, he endorsed this writ over to Mr. Ware, so that these writs are negotiable from one officer to another; and so your Honours have no opportunity of judging the persons to whom this vast power is delegated.

Another instance is this: Mr. Justice Walley had called this same Mr. Ware before him, by a constable, for a breach of the Sabbath-day Acts, or that of profane swearing. As soon as he had finished, Mr. Ware asked him if he had done. He replied, "Yes." "Well, then," said Mr. Ware, "I will show you a little of my power. I command you to permit me to search your house for uncustomed goods," and went on to search the house from garret to cellar; and then served the constable in the same manner!

But to show another absurdity in this writ, if it should be established, I insist upon it every person, by the 14 Charles II., has this power as well as the Custom-house officers. The words are, "it shall be lawful for any person or persons authorized, etc." What a scene does this open! Every man prompted by revenge, ill-humor or wantonness to inspect the inside of his neighbour's house, may get a Writ of Assistance. Others will ask it from self defence; one arbitrary exertion will provoke another, until society be involved in tumult and in blood!

Again, these writs are not returned. Writs, in their nature, are temporary things. When the purposes for which they are issued are answered, they exist no more; but these live forever; no one can be called to account. Thus reason and the constitution are both against this writ. Let us see what authority there is for it. Not more than one instance can be found of it in all our law-books; and that was in the zenith of arbitrary power, namely, in the reign of Charles II., when star-chamber powers were pushed to extremity by some ignorant clerk of the exchequer. But had this writ been in any book whatever, it would have been illegal. All precedents are under the control of the principles of law. Lord Talbot (the Earl of Shrewsbury, an English peer of the era of William and Mary) says it is better to observe these than any precedents, though in the House of Lords the last resort of the subject.

No Acts of Parliament can establish such a writ; though it should be made in the very words of the petition, it would be void. An act against the constitution is void. But this proves no more than what I before observed, that special writs may be granted on oath and probable suspicion. The act of 7 and 8 William III. that the officers of the plantations shall have the same powers, etc., is confined to this sense; that an officer should show probable ground; should take his oath of it; should do this before a magistrate; and that such magistrate, if he think proper, should issue a special warrant to a constable to search the places. That of 6 Anne can prove no more.

SAMUEL DAVIES

Great God of Wonders

Along with creeds, catechisms, and sermons, hymns give us important insights into the doctrinal and theological understanding of each generation. Church historian Philip Schaff says, "Christ is the centre of sacred art as well as of theology and religion. The noblest works of the master-painters are attempts to portray His 'human face divine,' now in the charm of childhood, now in the agony of the cross, now in the glory of the resurrrection, now in His majesty as the jndge of the world. From Him music has drawn its highest inspiration, and Handel transcended himself when he made "Messiah" his theme. The sweetest lyrics of Zion in all ages celebrate the events of His life and the bonndless wealth of mercy and peace that is treasured up in His person and work for every believer. The hymns of Jesus are the Holy of holies in the temple of sacred poetry . . . here the hymnists of ancient, medieval, and modem times, from every section of Christendom — profound divines, stately bishops, humble monks, faithful pastors, devout laymen, holy women — unite with one voice in the common adoration of a common Saviour. He is the theme of all ages, tongues, and creeds, the divine harmony of all human discords, the solution of all the dark problems of life."[1]

Samuel Davis (1723-1761) was one of the first Presbyterian ministers in Virginia, where a majority of churches were affiliated with the Church of England. He was a tireless advocate for religious liberty, and served as the fourth president of the College of New Jersey, later known as Princeton. He was a poet as well as a preacher, and wrote several hymns. "Great God of Wonders" is still in the Presbyterain Trinity Hymnal today.

---

1 Schaff, Philip, *Christ in Song*, (New York: Anson D. F. Randolph & Company, 1870), Preface.

Great God of wonders! All Thy ways
    Are matchless, Godlike and divine;
    But the fair glories of Thy grace
    More Godlike and unrivaled shine,
    More Godlike and unrivaled shine.

    Crimes of such horror to forgive,
    Such guilty, daring worms to spare;
    This is Thy grand prerogative,
    And none shall in the honor share,
    And none shall in the honor share

    Angels and men, resign your claim
    To pity, mercy, love and grace:
    These glories crown Jehovah's Name
    With an incomparable glaze
    With an incomparable glaze.

    In wonder lost, with trembling joy,
    We take the pardon of our God:
    Pardon for crimes of deepest dye,
    A pardon bought with Jesus' blood,
    A pardon bought with Jesus' blood.

    O may this strange, this matchless grace,
    This Godlike miracle of love,
    Fill the whole earth with grateful praise,
    And all th'angelic choirs above,
    And all th'angelic choirs above.

Who is a pardoning God like Thee?
Or who has grace so rich and free?
Or who has grace so rich and free?

BENJAMIN FRANKLIN

Silence Dogood Letters

"My brother had, in 1720 or 1721, begun to print a newspaper. It was
the second that appeared in America, and was called the New England
Courant . . . after having worked in composing the types and printing
off the sheets, I was employed to carry the papers thro' the streets to the
customers.

He had some ingenious men among his friends, who amus'd themselves
by writing little pieces for this paper, which gain'd it credit and made
it more in demand, and these gentlemen often visited us. Hearing their
conversations, and their accounts of the approbation their papers were
received with, I was excited to try my hand among them; but, being still a
boy, and suspecting that my brother would object to printing anything of
mine in his paper if he knew it to be mine, I contrived to disguise my hand,
and, writing an anonymous paper, I put it in at night under the door of
the printing-house. It was found in the morning, and communicated to his
writing friends when they call'd in as usual. They read it, commented on it
in my hearing, and I had the exquisite pleasure of finding it met with their
approbation, and that, in their different guesses at the author, none were
named but men of some character among us for learning and ingenuity.
I suppose now that I was rather lucky in my judges, and that perhaps
they were not really so very good ones as I then esteem'd them." —Ben
Franklin, in his Autobiography

Among the "little pieces" that young Ben Franklin wrote were the Silence
Dogood letters. In a total of fourteen letters penned between April and
October of 1722, Franklin, in the guise of a clergyman's widow, poked
fun at the follies and foibles of the folks around him. James Franklin was

delighted with the letters, and published them on the front page of the
Courant. Silence Dogood, a.k.a. Ben Franklin, received a fair number of
marriage proposals from men who admired her strength of character.

When Franklin quit writing the letters, his brother placed an ad in the
Courant to try to find Silence Dogood. Ben finally confessed; his brother
was furious. Finally, after a few other run-ins with his irate brother,
Franklin left Boston for Philadephia, and the rest is history.

SILENCE DOGOOD NO. I

April 2, 1722
To the Author of the New-England Courant.
Sir,

I t may not be improper in the first place to inform your
Readers, that I intend once a Fortnight to present them, by the
Help of this Paper, with a short Epistle, which I presume will
add somewhat to their Entertainment.

And since it is observed, that the Generality of People, now a
days, are unwilling either to commend or dispraise what they read,
until they are in some measure informed who or what the Author
of it is, whether he be poor or rich, old or young, a Schollar or a
Leather Apron Man, &c. and give their Opinion of the Performance,
according to the Knowledge which they have of the Author's
Circumstances, it may not be amiss to begin with a short Account of
my past Life and present Condition, that the Reader may not be at a
Loss to judge whether or no my Lucubrations are worth his reading.

At the time of my Birth, my Parents were on Ship-board in
their Way from London to N. England. My Entrance into this
troublesome World was attended with the Death of my Father, a

Misfortune, which tho' I was not then capable of knowing, I shall
never be able to forget; for as he, poor Man, stood upon the Deck
rejoycing at my Birth, a merciless Wave entred the Ship, and in
one Moment carry'd him beyond Reprieve. Thus, was the first Day
which I saw, the last that was seen by my Father; and thus was my
disconsolate Mother at once made both a Parent and a Widow.

When we arrived at Boston (which was not long after) I was put
to Nurse in a Country Place, at a small Distance from the Town,
where I went to School, and past my Infancy and Childhood in
Vanity and Idleness, until I was bound out Apprentice, that I might
no longer be a Charge to my Indigent Mother, who was put to hard
Shifts for a Living.

My Master was a Country Minister, a pious good-natur'd
young Man, and a Batchelor: he labour'd with all his Might to
instil vertuous and godly Principles into my tender Soul, well
knowing that it was the most suitable Time to make deep and lasting
Impressions on the Mind, while it was yet untainted with Vice,
free and unbiass'd. He endeavour'd that I might be instructed in
all that Knowledge and Learning which is necessary for our Sex,
and deny'd me no Accomplishment that could possibly be attained
in a Country Place; such as all Sorts of Needle-Work, Writing,
Arithmetick, &c. and observing that I took a more than ordinary
Delight in reading ingenious Books, he gave me the free Use of his
Library, which tho' it was but small, yet it was well chose, to inform
the Understanding rightly, and enable the Mind to frame great and
noble Ideas.

Before I had liv'd quite two Years with this Reverend Gentleman,
my indulgent Mother departed this Life, leaving me as it were by my

self, having no Relation on Earth within my Knowledge.

I will not abuse your Patience with a tedious Recital of all the frivolous Accidents of my Life, that happened from this Time until I arrived to Years of Discretion, only inform you that I liv'd a chearful Country Life, spending my leisure Time either in some innocent Diversion with the neighbouring Females, or in some shady Retirement, with the best of Company, Books. Thus I past away the Time with a Mixture of Profit and Pleasure, having no affliction but what was imaginary, and created in my own Fancy; as nothing is more common with us Women, than to be grieving for nothing, when we have nothing else to grieve for.

As I would not engross too much of your Paper at once, I will defer the Remainder of my Story until my next Letter; in the mean time desiring your Readers to exercise their Patience, and bear with my Humours now and then, because I shall trouble them but seldom. I am not insensible of the Impossibility of pleasing all, but I would not willingly displease any; and for those who will take Offence were none is intended, they are beneath the Notice of Your Humble Servant,

Silence Dogood.

SILENCE DOGOOD NO. II

April 16, 1722

To the Author of the New-England Courant.

Sir,

Histories of Lives are seldom entertaining, unless they contain something either admirable or exemplar: And since there is little or nothing of this Nature in my own Adventures, I will not tire your Readers with tedious Particulars of no Consequence, but will briefly, and in as few Words as possible, relate the most material Occurrences of my Life, and according to my Promise, confine all to this Letter.

My Reverend master who had hitherto remained a Batchelor, (after much meditation on the Eighteenth verse of the Second Chapter of Genesis,) took up a Resolution to marry; and having made several unsuccessful fruitless Attempts on the more topping Sort of our Sex, and being tir'd with making troublesome Journeys and Visits to no Purpose, he began unexpectedly to cast a loving Eye upon Me, whom he had brought up cleverly to his Hand.

There is certainly scarce any Part of a Man's Life in which he appears more silly and ridiculous, than when he makes his first Onset in Courtship. The aukward Manner in which my Master first discover'd his Intentions, made me, in spite of my Reverence to his Person, burst out into an unmannerly Laughter: However, having ask'd his Pardon, and with much ado compos'd my Countenance, I promis'd him I would take his Proposal into serious Consideration, and speedily give him an Answer.

As he had been a great Benefactor (and in a Manner a Father to me) I could not well deny his Request, when I once perceived he was

in earnest. Whether it was Love, or Gratitude, or Pride, or all Three
that made me consent, I know not; but it is certain, he found it no
hard Matter, by the Help of his Rhetorick, to conquer my Heart,
and perswade me to marry him.

This unexpected Match was very astonishing to all the Country
round about, and served to furnish them with Discourse for a long
Time after; some approving it, others disliking it, as they were led by
their various Fancies and Inclinations.

We lived happily together in the Heighth of conjugal Love and
mutual Endearments, for near Seven Years, in which Time we added
Two likely Girls and a Boy to the Family of the Dogoods: But alas!
When my Sun was in its meridian Altitude, inexorable unrelenting
Death, as if he had envy'd my Happiness and Tranquility, and
resolv'd to make me entirely miserable by the Loss of so good an
Husband, hastened his Flight to the Heavenly World, by a sudden
unexpected Departure from this.

I have now remained in a State of Widowhood for several Years,
but it is a State I never much admir'd, and I am apt to fancy that
I could be easily perswaded to marry again, provided I was sure
of a good-humour'd, sober, agreeable Companion: But one, even
with these few good Qualities, being hard to find, I have lately
relinquish'd all Thoughts of that Nature.

At present I pass away my leisure Hours in Conversation, either
with my honest Neighbour Rusticus and his Family, or with the
ingenious Minister of our Town, who now lodges at my House, and
by whose Assistance I intend now and then to beautify my Writings
with a Sentence or two in the learned Languages, which will not
only be fashionable, and pleasing to those who do not understand it,

but will likewise be very ornamental.

I shall conclude this with my own Character, which (one would think) I should be best able to give. Know then, That I am an Enemy to Vice, and a Friend to Vertue. I am one of an extensive Charity, and a great Forgiver of private Injuries: A hearty Lover of the Clergy and all good Men, and a mortal Enemy to arbitrary Government and unlimited Power. I am naturally very jealous for the Rights and Liberties of my Country; and the least appearance of an Incroachment on those invaluable Priviledges, is apt to make my Blood boil exceedingly. I have likewise a natural Inclination to observe and reprove the Faults of others, at which I have an excellent Faculty. I speak this by Way of Warning to all such whose Offences shall come under my Cognizance, for I never intend to wrap my Talent in a Napkin. To be brief; I am courteous and affable, good humour'd (unless I am first provok'd,) and handsome, and sometimes witty, but always, Sir, Your Friend and Humble Servant,

Silence Dogood.

SILENCE DOGOOD NO. III

   April 30, 1722

   To the Author of the New-England Courant. [No. 3

Sir,

I t is undoubtedly the Duty of all Persons to serve the Country
   they live in, according to their Abilities; yet I sincerely
   acknowledge, that I have hitherto been very deficient in this
Particular; whether it was for want of Will or Opportunity, I will
not at present stand to determine: Let it suffice, that I now take up
a Resolution, to do for the future all that lies in my Way for the
Service of my Countrymen.

   I have from my Youth been indefatigably studious to gain and
treasure up in my Mind all useful and desireable Knowledge,
especially such as tends to improve the Mind, and enlarge the
Understanding: And as I have found it very beneficial to me, I am
not without Hopes, that communicating my small Stock in this
Manner, by Peace-meal to the Publick, may be at least in some
Measure useful.

   I am very sensible that it is impossible for me, or indeed any one
Writer to please all Readers at once. Various Persons have different
Sentiments; and that which is pleasant and delightful to one, gives
another a Disgust. He that would (in this Way of Writing) please
all, is under a Necessity to make his Themes almost as numerous as
his Letters. He must one while be merry and diverting, then more
solid and serious; one while sharp and satyrical, then (to mollify
that) be sober and religious; at one Time let the Subject be Politicks,
then let the next Theme be Love: Thus will every one, one Time or

other find some thing agreeable to his own Fancy, and in his Turn
be delighted.

According to this Method I intend to proceed, bestowing now
and then a few gentle Reproofs on those who deserve them, not
forgetting at the same time to applaud those whose Actions merit
Commendation. And here I must not forget to invite the ingenious
Part of your Readers, particularly those of my own Sex to enter into
a Correspondence with me, assuring them, that their Condescension
in this Particular shall be received as a Favour, and accordingly
acknowledged.

I think I have now finish'd the Foundation, and I intend in my
next to begin to raise the Building. Having nothing more to write
at present, I must make the usual excuse in such Cases, of being in
haste, assuring you that I speak from my Heart when I call my self,
The most humble and obedient of all the Servants your Merits have
acquir'd,

Silence Dogood.

SILENCE DOGOOD NO. VI
June 11, 1722

*Quem Dies videt veniens Superbum, Hunc Dies vidit fugiens
jacentem. Seneca.*

    To the Author of the New-England Courant.
Sir,

    Among the many reigning Vices of the Town which may at
any Time come under my Consideration and Reprehension, there
is none which I am more inclin'd to expose than that of Pride. It is
acknowledg'd by all to be a Vice the most hateful to God and Man.
Even those who nourish it in themselves, hate to see it in others. The
proud Man aspires after Nothing less than an unlimited Superiority
over his Fellow-Creatures. He has made himself a King in Soliloquy;
fancies himself conquering the World; and the Inhabitants thereof
consulting on proper Methods to acknowledge his Merit. I speak
it to my Shame, I my self was a Queen from the Fourteenth to the
Eighteenth Year of my Age, and govern'd the World all the Time of
my being govern'd by my Master. But this speculative Pride may be
the Subject of another Letter: I shall at present confine my Thoughts
to what we call Pride of Apparel. This Sort of Pride has been
growing upon us ever since we parted with our Homespun Cloaths
for Fourteen Penny Stuffs, &c. And the Pride of Apparel has begot
and nourish'd in us a Pride of Heart, which portends the Ruin of
Church and State. Pride goeth before Destruction, and a haughty
Spirit before a Fall: And I remember my late Reverend Husband
would often say upon this Text, That a Fall was the natural
Consequence, as well as Punishment of Pride. Daily Experience
is sufficient to evince the Truth of this Observation. Persons of
small Fortune under the Dominion of this Vice, seldom consider
their Inability to maintain themselves in it, but strive to imitate
their Superiors in Estate, or Equals in Folly, until one Misfortune

comes upon the Neck of another, and every Step they take is a Step backwards. By striving to appear rich they become really poor, and deprive themselves of that Pity and Charity which is due to the humble poor Man, who is made so more immediately by Providence.

This Pride of Apparel will appear the more foolish, if we consider, that those airy Mortals, who have no other Way of making themselves considerable but by gorgeous Apparel, draw after them Crowds of Imitators, who hate each other while they endeavour after a Similitude of Manners. They destroy by Example, and envy one another's Destruction.

I cannot dismiss this Subject without some Observations on a particular Fashion now reigning among my own Sex, the most immodest and inconvenient of any the Art of Woman has invented, namely, that of Hoop-Petticoats. By these they are incommoded in their General and Particular Calling, and therefore they cannot answer the Ends of either necessary or ornamental Apparel. These monstrous topsy-turvy Mortar-Pieces, are neither fit for the Church, the Hall, or the Kitchen; and if a Number of them were well mounted on Noddles-Island, they would look more like Engines of War for bombarding the Town, than Ornaments of the Fair Sex. An honest Neighbour of mine, happening to be in Town some time since on a publick Day, inform'd me, that he saw four Gentlewomen with their Hoops half mounted in a Balcony, as they withdrew to the Wall, to the great Terror of the Militia, who (he thinks) might attribute their irregular Volleys to the formidable Appearance of the Ladies Petticoats.

I assure you, Sir, I have but little Hopes of perswading my Sex, by this Letter, utterly to relinquish the extravagant Foolery, and

Indication of Immodesty, in this monstrous Garb of their's; but
I would at least desire them to lessen the Circumference of their
Hoops, and leave it with them to consider, Whether they, who pay
no Rates or Taxes, ought to take up more Room in the King's High-
Way, than the Men, who yearly contribute to the Support of the
Government. I am, Sir, Your Humble Servant,

Silence Dogood.

SILENCE DOGOOD NO. 8

July 9, 1722

To the Author of the New-England Courant. [No. VIII.

Sir,

I prefer the following Abstract from the London Journal to
any Thing of my own, and therefore shall present it to your
Readers this week without any further Preface.

"Without Freedom of Thought, there can be no such Thing as
Wisdom; and no such Thing as publick Liberty, without Freedom of
Speech; which is the Right of every Man, as far as by it, he does not
hurt or controul the Right of another: And this is the only Check it
ought to suffer, and the only Bounds it ought to know.

"This sacred Privilege is so essential to free Goverments, that
the Security of Property, and the Freedom of Speech always go
together; and in those wretched Countries where a Man cannot
call his Tongue his own, he can scarce call any Thing else his own.
Whoever would overthrow the Liberty of a Nation, must begin
by subduing the Freeness of Speech; a Thing terrible to Publick
Traytors.

"This Secret was so well known to the Court of King Charles the First, that his wicked Ministry procured a Proclamation, to forbid the People to talk of Parliaments, which those Traytors had laid aside. To assert the undoubted Right of the Subject, and defend his Majesty's legal Prerogative, was called Disaffection, and punished as Sedition. Nay, People were forbid to talk of Religion in their Families: For the Priests had combined with the Ministers to cook up Tyranny, and suppress Truth and the Law, while the late King James, when Duke of York, went avowedly to Mass, Men were fined, imprisoned and undone, for saying he was a Papist: And that King Charles the Second might live more securely a Papist, there was an Act of Parliament made, declaring it Treason to say that he was one.

"That Men ought to speak well of their Governours is true, while their Governours deserve to be well spoken of; but to do publick Mischief, without hearing of it, is only the Prerogative and Felicity of Tyranny: A free People will be shewing that they are so, by their Freedom of Speech.

"The Administration of Government, is nothing else but the Attendance of the Trustees of the People upon the Interest and Affairs of the People: And as it is the Part and Business of the People, for whose Sake alone all publick Matters are, or ought to be transacted, to see whether they be well or ill transacted; so it is the Interest, and ought to be the Ambition, of all honest Magistrates, to have their Deeds openly examined, and publickly scann'd: Only the wicked Governours of Men dread what is said of them; *Audivit Tiberius probra queis lacerabitur, atque perculsus est.* The publick Censure was true, else he had not felt it bitter.

"Freedom of Speech is ever the Symptom, as well as the Effect

of a good Government. In old Rome, all was left to the Judgment
and Pleasure of the People, who examined the publick Proceedings
with such Discretion, and censured those who administred them
with such Equity and Mildness, that in the space of Three Hundred
Years, not five publick Ministers suffered unjustly. Indeed whenever
the Commons proceeded to Violence, the great Ones had been the
Agressors.

"Guilt only dreads Liberty of Speech, which drags it out of
its lurking Holes, and exposes its Deformity and Horrour to
Daylight. Horatius, Valerius, Cincinnatus, and other vertuous
and undesigning Magistrates of the Roman Commonwealth,
had nothing to fear from Liberty of Speech. Their virtuous
Administration, the more it was examin'd, the more it brightned
and gain'd by Enquiry. When Valerius in particular, was accused
upon some slight grounds of affecting the Diadem; he, who was the
first Minister of Rome, does not accuse the People for examining his
Conduct, but approved his Innocence in a Speech to them; and gave
such Satisfaction to them, and gained such Popularity to himself,
that they gave him a new Name; inde cognomen factum Publicolae
est; to denote that he was their Favourite and their Friend. *Latae
deinde leges — Ante omnes de provocatione Adversus Magistratus
Ad Populum*, Livii, lib. 2. Cap. 8.

"But Things afterwards took another Turn. Rome, with the
Loss of its Liberty, lost also its Freedom of Speech; then Mens
Words began to be feared and watched; and then first began
the poysonous Race of Informers, banished indeed under the
righteous Administration of Titus, Narva, Trajan, Aurelius, &c.
but encouraged and enriched under the vile Ministry of Sejanus,
Tigillinus, Pallas, and Cleander: Queri libet, quod in secreta nostra

non inquirant principes, nisi quos Odimus, says Pliny to Trajan.

"The best Princes have ever encouraged and promoted Freedom of Speech; they know that upright Measures would defend themselves, and that all upright Men would defend them. Tacitus, speaking of the Reign of some of the Princes abovemention'd, says with Extasy, Rara Temporum felicitate, ubi sentire quae velis, & quae sentias dicere licet: A blessed Time when you might think what you would, and speak what you thought.

"I doubt not but old Spencer and his Son, who were the Chief Ministers and Betrayers of Edward the Second, would have been very glad to have stopped the Mouths of all the honest Men in England. They dreaded to be called Traytors, because they were Traytors. And I dare say, Queen Elizabeth's Walsingham, who deserved no Reproaches, feared none. Misrepresentation of publick Measures is easily overthrown, by representing publick Measures truly; when they are honest, they ought to be publickly known, that they may be publickly commended; but if they are knavish or pernicious, they ought to be publickly exposed, in order to be publickly detested."

Yours, &c.,

Silence Dogood.

GEORGE WHITEFIELD

The Method of Grace

George Whitefield (1714-1770) was an English Purtian who had a large
hand in the Great Awakening in both Britain and America, along with
his acquaintance, Jonathan Edwards, and his college friends, Charles and
John Wesley. He was ordained by the Church of England, but not assigned
a pulpit, so he began his lifelong practice of preaching out of doors where
anyone could hear. Whitefield, along with the Wesley brothers, traveled to
the colony of Georgia the first time in 1738 for evangelistic endeavours, and
Whitefield traveled back and forth to North America several times before
his death in Massachusetts in 1770.

Benjamin Franklin reported, "In 1739 arriv'd among us from England
the Rev. Mr. Whitefield, who had made himself remarkable there as an
itinerant Preacher. He was at first permitted to preach in some of our
Churches; but the Clergy taking a Dislike to him, soon refus'd him their
Pulpits and he was oblig'd to preach in the Fields. The Multitudes of all
Sects and Denominations that attended his Sermons were enormous and
it was [a] matter of Speculation to me who was one of the Number, to
observe the extraordinary Influence of his Oratory on his Hearers, and
how much they admir'd and respected him, notwithstanding his common
Abuse of them, by assuring them they were naturally half Beasts and half
Devils. It was wonderful to see the Change soon made in the Manners
[behavior] of our Inhabitants; from being thoughtless or indifferent about
Religion, it seem'd as if all the World were growing Religious; so that one
could not walk thro' the Town in an Evening without Hearing Psalms sung
in different Families of every Street." Whitefield's "abuse of them" were
his gospel warnings, which were not to Franklin's taste. However, the two

struck up an unlikely friendship built on love for humanity and respect for one another.

Franklin went on to describe Whitefield's preaching: "He had a loud and clear Voice, and articulated his Words and Sentences so perfectly that he might be heard and understood at a great Distance, especially as his Auditors [audience], however numerous, observ'd the most exact Silence. He preach'd one Evening from the Top of the Court House Steps, which are in the middle of Market Street, and on the West Side of Second Street which crosses it at right angles. oth Streets were fill'd with his Hearers to a considerable Distance. Being among the hindmost in Market Street, I had the Curiosity to learn how far he could be heard, by retiring backwards down the Street towards the River; and I found his Voice distinct till I came near Front Street, when some Noise in that Street, obscur'd it. Imagining then a Semicircle, of which my Distance should be the Radius, and that it were fill'd with Auditors, to each of whom I allow'd two square feet, I computed that he might well be heard by more than Thirty Thousand. This reconcil'd me to the Newspaper Accounts of his having preach'd to 25,000 People in the Fields, and to the ancient Histories of Generals haranguing whole Armies, of which I had sometimes doubted."

Upon his death, Early American poet Phillis Wheatley penned "An Elegiac Poem On the Death of That Celebrated Divine, and Eminent Servant of Jesus Christ, the late Reverend, and Pious George Whitefield. She writes of his preaching:

> Thou didst, in strains of eloquence refin'd,
> Inflame the soul, and captivate the mind.

The sermon reproduced below is one of Whitefield's finest.

Jeremiah 6:14 — *"They have healed also the hurt of the daughter of my people slightly, saying, Peace, peace, when there is no peace.*

As God can send a nation or people no greater blessing than to give them faithful, sincere, and upright ministers, so the greatest curse that God can possibly send upon a people in this world, is to give them over to blind, unregenerate, carnal, lukewarm, and unskilled guides. And yet, in all ages, we find that there have been many wolves in sheep's clothing, many that daubed with untempered mortar, that prophesied smoother things than God did allow. As it was formerly, so it is now; there are many that corrupt the Word of God and deal deceitfully with it. It was so in a special manner in the prophet Jeremiah's time; and he, faithful to his Lord, faithful to that God who employed him, did not fail from time to time to open his mouth against them, and to bear a noble testimony to the honor of that God in whose name he from time to time spake. If you will read this prophecy, you will find that none spake more against such ministers than Jeremiah, and here especially in the chapter out of which the text is taken, he speaks very severely against them — he charges them with several crimes; particularly, he charges them with covetousness: says he in the 13th verse, 'from the least of them even to the greatest of them, every one is given to covetousness; and from the prophet even unto the priest, every one dealeth false.' And then, in the words of the text, in a more special manner, he exemplifies how they had dealt falsely, how they had behaved treacherously to poor souls: says he, 'They have healed also the hurt of the daughter of my people slightly, saying, Peace, peace, when there is no peace.' The prophet, in the name of God, had been denouncing war against the people, he had been telling them that their house should be left desolate, and that the Lord would certainly visit the land with war. 'Therefore,' says he, in the 11th verse, 'I am full of the fury of the Lord; I am weary with holding in; I will pour it out upon the children abroad, and upon the assembly of young men together; for even the husband with

the wife shall be taken, the aged with him that is full of days. And
their houses shall be turned unto others, with their fields and wives
together; for I will stretch out my hand upon the inhabitants of the
land, saith the Lord.' The prophet gives a thundering message, that
they might be terrified and have some convictions and inclinations
to repent; but it seems that the false prophets, the false priests, went
about stifling people's convictions, and when they were hurt or a
little terrified, they were for daubing over the wound, telling them
that Jeremiah was but an enthusiastic preacher, that there could
be no such thing as war among them, and saying to people, Peace,
peace, be still, when the prophet told them there was no peace. The
words, then, refer primarily unto outward things, but I verily believe
have also a further reference to the soul, and are to be referred to
those false teachers, who, when people were under conviction of
sin, when people were beginning to look towards heaven, were for
stifling their convictions and telling them they were good enough
before. And, indeed, people generally love to have it so; our hearts
are exceedingly deceitful, and desperately wicked; none but the
eternal God knows how treacherous they are. How many of us cry,
Peace, peace, to our souls, when there is no peace! How many are
there who are now settled upon their lees, that now think they are
Christians, that now flatter themselves that they have an interest in
Jesus Christ; whereas if we come to examine their experiences, we
shall find that their peace is but a peace of the devil's making — it is
not a peace of God's giving — it is not a peace that passeth human
understanding. It is matter, therefore, of great importance, my dear
hearers, to know whether we may speak peace to our hearts. We are
all desirous of peace; peace is an unspeakable blessing; how can we
live without peace? And, therefore, people from time to time must
be taught how far they must go, and what must be wrought in them,

before they can speak peace to their hearts. This is what I design
at present, that I may deliver my soul, that I may be free from the
blood of those to whom I preach — that I may not fail to declare the
whole counsel of God. I shall, from the words of the text, endeavor
to show you what you must undergo, and what must be wrought in
you before you can speak peace to your hearts.

But before I come directly to this, give me leave to premise a
caution or two. And the first is, that I take it for granted you believe
religion to be an inward thing; you believe it to be a work in the
heart, a work wrought in the soul by the power of the Spirit of God.
If you do not believe this, you do not believe your Bibles. If you do
not believe this, though you have got your Bibles in your hand, you
hate the Lord Jesus Christ in your heart; for religion is everywhere
represented in Scripture as the work of God in the heart. 'The
kingdom of God is within us,' says our Lord; and, 'He is not a
Christian who is one outwardly; but he is a Christian who is one
inwardly.' If any of you place religion in outward things, I shall not
perhaps please you this morning; you will understand me no more
when I speak of the work of God upon a poor sinner's heart, than
if I were talking in an unknown tongue. I would further premise a
caution, that I would by no means confine God to one way of acting.
I would by no means say, that all persons, before they come to have
a settled peace in their hearts, are obliged to undergo the same
degrees of conviction. No; God has various ways of bringing his
children home; his sacred Spirit bloweth when, and where, and how
it listeth. But, however, I will venture to affirm this, that before ever
you can speak peace to your heart, whether by shorter or longer
continuance of your convictions, whether in a more pungent or in a
more gentle way, you must undergo what I shall hereafter lay down
in the following discourse.

First, then, before you can speak peace to your hearts, you must be made to see, made to feel, made to weep over, made to bewail, your actual transgressions against the law of God. According to the covenant of works, 'The soul that sinneth it shall die;' cursed is that man, be he what he may, that continueth not in all things that are written in the book of the law to do them. We are not only to do some things, but we are to do all things, and we are to continue so to do; so that the least deviation from the moral law, according to the covenant of works, whether in thought, word, or deed, deserves eternal death at the hand of God. And if one evil thought, if one evil word, if one evil action, deserves eternal damnation, how many hells, my friends, do every one of us deserve, whose whole lives have been one continued rebellion against God! Before ever, therefore, you can speak peace to your hearts, you must be brought to see, brought to believe, what a dreadful thing it is to depart from the living God. And now, my dear friends, examine your hearts, for I hope you came hither with a design to have your souls made better. Give me leave to ask you, in the presence of God, whether you know the time, and if you do not know exactly the time, do you know there was a time, when God wrote bitter things against you, when the arrows of the Almighty were within you? Was ever the remembrance of your sins grievous to you? Was the burden of your sins intolerable to your thoughts? Did you ever see that God's wrath might justly fall upon you, on account of your actual transgressions against God? Were you ever in all your life sorry for your sins? Could you ever say, My sins are gone over my head as a burden too heavy for me to bear? Did you ever experience any such thing as this? Did ever any such thing as this pass between God and your soul? If not, for Jesus Christ's sake, do not call yourselves Christians; you may speak peace to your hearts, but there is no peace. May the

Lord awaken you, may the Lord convert you, may the Lord give you peace, if it be his will, before you go home!

But further: you may be convinced of your actual sins, so as to be made to tremble, and yet you may be strangers to Jesus Christ, you may have no true work of grace upon your hearts. Before ever, therefore, you can speak peace to your hearts, conviction must go deeper; you must not only be convinced of your actual transgressions against the law of God, but likewise of the foundation of all your transgressions. And what is that? I mean original sin, that original corruption each of us brings into the world with us, which renders us liable to God's wrath and damnation. There are many poor souls that think themselves fine reasoners, yet they pretend to say there is no such thing as original sin; they will charge God with injustice in imputing Adam's sin to us; although we have got the mark of the beast and of the devil upon us, yet they tell us we are not born in sin. Let them look abroad into the world and see the disorders in it, and think, if they can, if this is the paradise in which God did put man. No! everything in the world is out of order. I have often thought, when I was abroad, that if there were no other argument to prove original sin, the rising of wolves and tigers against man, nay, the barking of a dog against us, is a proof of original sin. Tigers and lions durst not rise against us, if it were not for Adam's first sin; for when the creatures rise up against us, it is as much as to say, You have sinned against God, and we take up our Master's quarrel. If we look inwardly, we shall see enough of lusts, and man's temper contrary to the temper of God. There is pride, malice, and revenge, in all our hearts; and this temper cannot come from God; it comes from our first parent, Adam, who, after he fell from God, fell out of God into the devil. However, therefore, some people may deny this, yet when conviction comes, all carnal

reasonings are battered down immediately and the poor soul begins
to feel and see the fountain from which all the polluted streams do
flow. When the sinner is first awakened, he begins to wonder —
How came I to be so wicked? The Spirit of God then strikes in, and
shows that he has no good thing in him by nature; then he sees that
he is altogether gone out of the way, that he is altogether become
abominable, and the poor creature is made to live down at the foot
of the throne of God, and to acknowledge that God would be just
to damn him, just to cut him off, though he never had committed
one actual sin in his life. Did you ever feel and experience this, any
of you — to justify God in your damnation — to own that you
are by nature children of wrath, and that God may justly cut you
off, though you never actually had offended him in all your life? If
you were ever truly convicted, if your hearts were ever truly cut, if
self were truly taken out of you, you would be made to see and feel
this. And if you have never felt the weight of original sin, do not
call yourselves Christians. I am verily persuaded original sin is the
greatest burden of a true convert; this ever grieves the regenerate
soul, the sanctified soul. The indwelling of sin in the heart is the
burden of a converted person; it is the burden of a true Christian.
He continually cries out, "O! who will deliver me from this body of
death,' this indwelling corruption in my heart? This is that which
disturbs a poor soul most. And, therefore, if you never felt this
inward corruption, if you never saw that God might justly curse you
for it, indeed, my dear friends, you may speak peace to your hearts,
but I fear, nay, I know, there is no true peace.

Further: before you can speak peace to your hearts, you must
not only be troubled for the sins of your life, the sin of your nature,
but likewise for the sins of your best duties and performances.

When a poor soul is somewhat awakened by the terrors of the
Lord, then the poor creature, being born under the covenant of
works, flies directly to a covenant of works again. And as Adam and
Eve hid themselves among the trees of the garden, and sewed fig
leaves together to cover their nakedness, so the poor sinner, when
awakened, flies to his duties and to his performances, to hide himself
from God, and goes to patch up a righteousness of his own. Says he,
I will be mighty good now — I will reform — I will do all I can;
and then certainly Jesus Christ will have mercy on me. But before
you can speak peace to your heart, you must be brought to see that
God may damn you for the best prayer you ever put up; you must
be brought to see that all your duties — all your righteousness —
as the prophet elegantly expresses it — put them all together, are
so far from recommending you to God, are so far from being any
motive and inducement to God to have mercy on your poor soul,
that he will see them to be filthy rags, a menstruous cloth — that
God hates them, and cannot away with them, if you bring them
to him in order to recommend you to his favor. My dear friends,
what is there in our performances to recommend us unto God?
Our persons are in an unjustified state by nature, we deserve to be
damned ten thousand times over; and what must our performances
be? We can do no good thing by nature: 'They that are in the flesh
cannot please God.' You may do many things materially good,
but you cannot do a thing formally and rightly good; because
nature cannot act above itself. It is impossible that a man who is
unconverted can act for the glory of God; he cannot do anything in
faith, and 'whatsoever is not of faith is sin.' After we are renewed,
yet we are renewed but in part, indwelling sin continues in us, there
is a mixture of corruption in every one of our duties; so that after
we are converted, were Jesus Christ only to accept us according to

our works, our works would damn us, for we cannot pt up a prayer but it is far from that perfection which the moral law requireth. I do not know what you may think, but I can say that I cannot pray but I sin — I cannot preach to you or any others but I sin — I can do nothing without sin; and, as one expresseth it, my repentance wants to be repented of, and my tears to be washed in the precious blood of my dear Redeemer. Our best duties are as so many splendid sins. Before you can speak peace in your heart, you must not only be made sick of your original and actual sin, but you must be made sick of your righteousness, of all your duties and performances. There must be a deep conviction before you can be brought out of your self-righteousness; it is the last idol taken out of our heart. The pride of our heart will not let us submit to the righteousness of Jesus Christ. But if you never felt that you had o righteousness of your own, if you never felt the deficiency of your own righteousness, you cannot come to Jesus Christ. There are a great many now who may say, Well, we believe all this; but there is a great difference betwixt talking and feeling. Did you ever feel the want of a dear Redeemer? Did you ever feel the want of Jesus Christ, upon the account of the deficiency of your own righteousness? And can you now say from your heart, Lord, thou mayst justly damn me for the best duties that ever I did perform? If you are not thus brought out of self, you may speak peace to yourselves, but yet there is no peace.

But then, before you can speak peace to your souls, there is one particular sin you must be greatly troubled for, and yet I fear there are few of you think what it is; it is the reigning, the damning sin of the Christian world, and yet the Christian world seldom or never think of it. And pray what is that? It is what most of you think you are not guilty of — and that is, the sin of unbelief. Before you can speak peace to your heart, you must be troubled for the unbelief of you heart. But, can it be supposed that any of you are unbelievers here in this church-yard, that are born in Scotland, in a reformed country, that go to church every Sabbath? Can any of you that receive the sacrament once a year — O that it were administered oftener! — can it be supposed that you who had tokens for the sacrament, that you who keep up family prayer, that any of you do not believe in the Lord Jesus Christ? I appeal to your own hearts, if you would not think me uncharitable, if I doubted whether any of you believed in Christ; and yet, I fear upon examination, we should find that most of you have not so much faith in the Lord Jesus Christ as the devil himself. I am persuaded the devil believes more of the Bible than most of us do. He believes the divinity of Jesus Christ; that is more than many who call themselves Christians do; nay, he believes and trembles, and that is more than thousands amongst us do. My friends, we mistake a historical faith for a true faith, wrought in the heart by the Spirit of God. You fancy you believe, because you believe there is such a book as we call the Bible — because you go to church; all this you may do, and have no true faith in Christ. Merely to believe there was such a person as Christ, merely to believe there is a book called the Bible, will do you no good, more than to believe there was such a man a Caesar or Alexander the Great. The Bible is a sacred depository. What thanks have we to give to God for these lively oracles! But yet we may have these, and not believe in the Lord Jesus Christ. My dear friends, there must be a principle wrought in the heart by the Spirit of the living God. Did I ask you how long it is since you believed in Jesus Christ, I suppose most of you would tell me, you believed in Jesus Christ as long as ever you remember — you never did misbelieve. Then, you could not give me a better proof that you never yet believed in Jesus Christ, unless you were sanctified early, as from the womb; for, they that otherwise believer in Christ know there was a time when they did not believe in Jesus Christ. You say you love God with all your heart, soul, and strength. If I were to ask you how long it is since you loved God, you would say, As long as you can remember; you never hated God, you know no time when there was enmity in your heart against God. Then, unless you were sanctified very early, you never loved God in your life. My dear friends, I am more particular in this, because it is a most deceitful delusion, whereby so many people are carried away, that they believe already. Therefore, it is remarked of Mr. Marshall, giving account of his experiences, that he had been working for life, and he had ranged all his sins under the ten commandments, and then coming to a minister, asked him the reason why he could not get peace. The minister looked at his catalogue, Away, says he, I do not find one word of the sin of unbelief in all your catalogue. It is the peculiar work of the Spirit of God to convince us of our unbelief — that we have got no faith. Says Jesus Christ, of the sin of unbelief; 'of sin,' says Christ, 'because they believe not on me.' Now, my dear friends, did God ever show you that you had no faith? Were you ever made to bewail a hard heart of unbelief? Was it ever the language of your heart, Lord, give me faith; Lord, enable me to lay hold on thee; Lord, enable me to call thee my Lord and my God? Did Jesus Christ ever convince you in this manner? Did he ever convince you of your inability to close with Christ, and make you to cry out to God to give you faith? If not, do not speak peace to your heart. May the Lord awaken you, and give you true, solid peace before you go hence and be no more!

Once more then: before you can speak peace to your heart, you must not only be convinced of your actual and original sin, the sins of your own righteousness, the sin of unbelief, but you must be enabled to lay hold upon the perfect righteousness, the all-sufficient righteousness, of the Lord Jesus Christ; you must lay hold by faith on the righteousness of Jesus Christ, and then you shall have peace. 'Come,' says Jesus, 'unto me, all ye that are weary and heavy laden, and I will give you rest.' This speaks encouragement to all that are weary and heavy laden; but the promise of rest is made to them only upon their coming and believing, and taking him to be their God and their all. Before we can ever have peace with God, we must be justified by faith through our Lord Jesus Christ, we must be enabled to apply Christ to our hearts, we must have Christ brought home to our souls, so as his righteousness may be made our righteousness, so as his merits may be imputed to our souls. My dear friends, were you ever married to Jesus Christ? Did Jesus Christ ever give himself to you? Did you ever close with Christ by a lively faith, so as to feel Christ in your hearts, so as to hear him speaking peace to your souls? Did peace ever flow in upon your hearts like a river? Did you ever feel that peace that Christ spoke to his disciples? I pray God he may come and speak peace to you. These things you must experience. I am not talking of the invisible realities of another world, of inward religion, of the work of God upon a poor sinner's heart. I am not talking of a matte of great importance, my dear hearers; you are all concerned in it, your souls are concerned in it, your eternal salvation is concerned in it. You may be all at peace, but perhaps the devil has lulled you asleep into a carnal lethargy and security, and will endeavor to keep you there, till he get you to hell, and there you will be awakened; but it will be dreadful to be awakened and find yourselves so fearfully mistaken, when the great gulf is fixed, when you will be calling to all eternity for a drop of water to cool your tongue, and shall not obtain it.

Give me leave, then, to address myself to several sorts of persons; and O may God, of his infinite mercy, bless the application! There are some of you perhaps can say, Through grace we can go along with you. Blessed be God, we have been convinced of our actual sins, we have been convinced of original sin, we have been convinced of self-righteousness, we have felt the bitterness of unbelief, and through grace we have closed with Jesus Christ; we can speak peace to our hearts, because God hath spoken peace to us. Can you say so? Then I will salute you, as the angels did the women the first day of the week, All hail! Fear not ye, my dear brethren, you are happy souls; you may lie down and be at peace indeed, for God hath given you peace; you may be content under all the dispensations of providence, for nothing can happen to you now, but what shall be the effect of God's love to your soul; you need not fear what sightings may be without, seeing there is peace within. Have you closed with Christ? Is God your friend? Is Christ your friend? Then, look up with comfort; all is yours, and you are Christ's, and Christ is God's. Everything shall work together for your good; the very hairs of your head are numbered; he that toucheth you, toucheth the apple of God's eye. But then, my dear friends, beware of resting on your first conversion. You that are young believers in Christ, you should be looking out for fresh discoveries of the Lord Jesus Christ every moment; you must not build upon your past experiences, you must not build upon a work within you, but always come out of yourselves to the righteousness of Jesus Christ without you; you must be always coming as poor sinners to draw water out of the wells of salvation; you must be forgetting the things that are behind, and be continually pressing forward to the things that are before. My dear

friends, you must keep u a tender, close walk with the Lord Jesus
Christ. There are many of us who lose our peace by our untender
walk; something or other gets in betwixt Christ and us, and we
fall into darkness; something or other steals our hearts from God,
and this grieves the Holy Ghost, and the Holy Ghost leaves us to
ourselves. Let me, therefore, exhort you that have got peace with
God, to take care that you do not lose this peace. It is true, if you
are once in Christ, you cannot finally fall from God: 'There is no
condemnation to them that are in Christ Jesus;' but if you cannot
fall finally, you may fall foully, and may go with broken bones all
your days. Take care of backslidings; for Jesus Christ's sake, do not
grieve the Holy Ghost you may never recover your comfort while you
live. O take care of going a gadding and wandering from God, after
you have closed with Jesus Christ. My dear friends, I have paid dear
for backsliding. Our hearts are so cursedly wicked, that if you take
not care, if you do not keep up a constant watch, your wicked hearts
will deceive you, and draw you aside. It will be sad to be under the
scourge of a correcting Father; witness the visitation of Job, David,
and other saints in Scripture. Let me, therefore, exhort you that
have got peace to keep a close walk with Christ. I am grieved with
the loose walk of those that are Christians, that have had discoveries
of Jesus Christ; there is so little difference betwixt them and other
people, that I scarce know which is the true Christian. Christians
are afraid to speak of God — they run down with the stream; if
they come into worldly company, they will talk of the world as if
they were in their element; this you would not do when you had the
first discoveries of Christ's love; you could talk then of Christ's love
for ever, when the candle of the Lord shined upon your soul. That
time has been when you had something to say for your dear Lord;
but now you can go into company and hear others speaking about

the world bold enough, and you are afraid of being laughed at if you speak for Jesus Christ. A great many people have grown conformists now in the worst sense of the word; they will cry out against the ceremonies of the church, as they may justly do; but then you are mighty fond of ceremonies in your behavior; you will conform to the world, which is a great deal worse. Many will stay till the devil bring up new fashions. Take care, then, not to be conformed to the world. What have Christians to do with the world? Christians should be singularly good, bold for their Lord, that all who are with you may take notice that you have been with Jesus. I would exhort you to come to a settlement in Jesus Christ, so as to have a continual abiding of God in your heart. We go a-building on our faith of adherence, and lost our comfort; but we should be growing up to a faith of assurance, to know that we are God's, and so walk in the comfort of the Holy Ghost and be edified. Jesus Christ is now much wounded in the house of his friends. Excuse me in being particular; for, my friends, it grieves me more that Jesus Christ should be wounded by his friends than by his enemies. We cannot expect anything else from Deists; but for such as have felt his power, to fall away, for them not to walk agreeably to the vocation wherewith they are called — by these means we bring our Lord's religion into contempt, to be a byword among the heathen. For Christ's sake, if you know Christ keep close by him; if God have spoken peace, O keep that peace by looking up to Jesus Christ every moment. Such as have got peace with God, if you are under trials, fear not, all things shall work for your good; if you are under temptations, fear not, if he has spoken peace to your hearts, all these things shall be for your good.

But what shall I say to you that have got o peace with God? —

and these are, perhaps, the most of this congregation: it makes me
weep to think of it. Most of you, if you examine your hearts, must
confess that God never yet spoke peace to you; you are children of
the devil, if Christ is not in you, if God has not spoken peace to your
heart. Poor soul! What a cursed condition are you in. I would not be
in your case for ten thousand, thousand worlds. Why? You are just
hanging over hell. What peace can you have when God is your
enemy, when the wrath of God is abiding upon your poor soul?
Awake, then, you that are sleeping in a false peace, awake, ye carnal
professors, ye hypocrites that go to church, receive the sacrament,
read your Bibles, and never felt the power of God upon your hearts;
you that are formal professors, you that are baptized heathens;
awake, awake, and do not rest on a false bottom. Blame me not for
addressing myself to you; indeed, it is out of love to your souls. I see
you are lingering in your Sodom, and wanting to stay there; but I
come to you as the angel did to Lot, to take you by the hand. Come
away, my dear brethren — fly, fly, fly for your lives to Jesus Christ,
fly to a bleeding God, fly to a throne of grace; and beg of God to
break your hearts, beg of God to convince you of your actual sins,
beg of God to convince you of your original sin, beg of God to
convince you of your self-righteousness — beg of God to give you
faith, and to enable you to close with Jesus Christ. O you that are
secure, I must be a son of thunder to you, and O that God may
awaken you, though it be with thunder; it is out of love, indeed, that
I speak to you. I know by sad experience what it is to be lulled
asleep with a false peace; long was I lulled asleep, long did I think
myself a Christian, when I knew nothing of the Lord Jesus Christ. I
went perhaps farther than many of you do; I used to fast twice
a-week, I used to pray sometimes none times a-day, I used to receive
the sacrament constantly every Lord's-day; and yet I knew nothing

of Jesus Christ in my heart, I knew not that I must be a new
creature — I knew nothing of inward religion in my soul. And
perhaps, many of you may be deceived as I, poor creature, was; and,
therefore, it is out of love to you indeed, that I speak to you. O if
you do not take care, a form of religion will destroy your soul; you
will rest in it, and will not come to Jesus Christ at all; whereas, these
things are only the means, and not the end of religion; Christ is the
end of the law for righteousness to all that believe. O, then, awake,
you that are settled on your lees; awake you Church professors;
awake you that have got a name to live, that are rich and think you
want nothing, not considering that you are poor, and blind, and
naked; I counsel you to come and buy of Jesus Christ gold, white
raiment, and eye-salve. But I hope there are some that are a little
wounded; I hope God does not intend to let me preach in vain; I
hope God will reach some of your precious souls, and awaken some
of you out of your carnal security; I hope there are some who are
willing to come to Christ, and beginning to think that they have
been building upon a false foundation. Perhaps the devil may strike
in, and bid you despair of mercy; but fear not, what I have been
speaking to you is only out of love to you — is only to awaken you,
and let you see your danger. If any of you are willing to be
reconciled to God, God the Father, Son, and Holy Ghost, is willing
to be reconciled to you. O then, though you have no peace as yet,
come away to Jesus Christ; he is our peace, he is our peace-maker
— he has made peace betwixt God and offending man. Would you
have peace with God? Away, then, to God through Jesus Christ, who
has purchased peace; the Lord Jesus has shed his heart's blood for
this. He died for this; he rose again for this; he ascended into the
highest heaven, and is now interceding at the right hand of God.
Perhaps you think there will be no peace for you. Why so? Because

you are sinners? Because you have crucified Christ — you have put
him to open shame — you have trampled under foot the blood of the
Son of God? What of all this? Yet there is peace for you. Pray, what
did Jesus Christ say of his disciples, when he came to them the first
day of the week? The first word he said was, he showed them his
hands and his side, and said, 'Peace be unto you.' It is as much as if
he had said, Fear not, my disciples; see my hands and my feet how
they have been pierced for your sake; therefore fear not. How did
Chris speak to his disciples? 'Go tell my brethren, and tell broken-
hearted Peter in particular, that Christ is risen, that he is ascended
unto his Father and your Father, to his God and your God.' And
after Christ rose from the dead, he came preaching peace, with an
olive branch of peace, like Noah's dove; 'My peace I leave with you.'
Who were they? They were enemies of Christ as well as we, they
were deniers of Christ once as well as we. Perhaps some of you have
backslidden and lost your peace, and you think you deserve no
peace; and no more you do. But, then, God will heal your
backslidings, he will love you freely. As for you that are wounded, if
you are made willing to come to Christ, come away. Perhaps some of
you want to dress yourselves in your duties, that are but rotten rags.
No, you had better come naked as you are, for you must throw aside
your rags, and come in your blood. Some of you may say, We would
come, but we have got a hard heart. But you will never get it made
soft till ye come to Christ; he will take away the heart of stone, and
give you an heart of flesh; he will speak peace to your souls; though
ye have betrayed him, yet he will be your peace. Shall I prevail upon
any of you this morning to come to Jesus Christ? There is a great
multitude of souls here; how shortly must you all die, and go to
judgment! Even before night, or to-morrow's night, some of you may
be laid out for this kirk-yard. And how will you do if you be not at

peace with God — if the Lord Jesus Christ has not spoken peace to
your heart? If God speak not peace to you here, you will be damned
for ever. I must not flatter you, my dear friends; I will deal sincerely
with your souls. Some of you may think I carry things too far. But,
indeed, when you come to judgment, you will find what I say is true,
either to your eternal damnation or comfort. May God influence
your hearts to come to him! I am not willing to go away without
persuading you. I cannot be persuaded but God may make use of
me as a means of persuading some of you to come to the Lord Jesus
Christ. O did you but feel the peace which they have that love the
Lord Jesus Christ! 'Great peace have they,' say the psalmist, 'that
love they law; nothing shall offend them.' But there is no peace to
the wicked. I know what it is to live a life of sin; I was obliged to sin
in order to stifle conviction. And I am sure this is the way many of
you take; If you get into company, you drive off conviction. But you
had better go to the bottom at once; it must be done — your wound
must be searched, or you must be damned. If it were a matter of
indifference, I would not speak one word about it. But you will be
damned without Christ. He is the way, he is the truth, and the life. I
cannot think you should go to hell without Christ. How can you
dwell with everlasting burnings? How can you abide the thought of
living with the devil for ever? Is it not better to have some soul-
trouble here, than to be sent to hell by Jesus Christ hereafter? What
is hell, but to be absent from Christ? If there were no other hell, that
would be hell enough. It will be hell to be tormented with the devil
for ever. Get acquaintance with God, then, and be at peace. I
beseech you, as a poor worthless ambassador of Jesus Christ, that
you would be reconciled to God. My business this morning, the first
day of the week, is to tell you that Christ is willing to be reconciled
to you. Will any of you be reconciled to Jesus Christ? Then, he will

forgive you all your sins, he will blot out all your transgressions. But if you will go on and rebel against Christ, and stab him daily — if you will go on and abuse Jesus Christ, the wrath of God you must expect will fall upon you. God will not be mocked; that which a man soweth, that shall he also reap. And if you will not be at peace with God, God will not be at peace with you. Who can stand before God when he is angry? It is a dreadful thing to fall into the hands of an angry God. When the people came to apprehend Christ, they fell to the ground when Jesus said, 'I am he.' And if they could not bear the sight of Christ when clothed with the rags of mortality, how will they hear the sight of him when he is on his Father's throne? Methinks I see the poor wretches dragged out of their graves by the devil; methinks I see them trembling, crying out to the hills and rocks to cover them. But the devil will say, Come, I will take you away; and then they shall stand trembling before the judgment-seat of Christ. They shall appear before him to see him once, and hear him pronounce that irrevocable sentence, 'Depart from me, ye cursed.' Methinks I hear the poor creatures saying, Lord, if we must be damned, let some angel pronounce the sentence. No, the God of love, Jesus Christ, will pronounce it. Will ye not believe this? Do not think I am talking at random, but agreeably to the Scriptures of truth. If you do not, then show yourselves men, and this morning go away with full resolution, in the strength of God, to cleave to Christ. And may you have no rest in your souls till you rest in Jesus Christ! I could still go on, for it is sweet to talk of Christ. Do you not long for the time when you shall have new bodies — when they shall be immortal, and made like Christ's glorious body? And then they will talk of Jesus Christ for evermore. But it is time, perhaps, for you to go and prepare for your respective worship, and I would not hinder any of you. My design is, to bring poor sinners to

Jesus Christ. O that God may bring some of you to himself! May the
Lord Jesus now dismiss you with his blessing, and may the dear
Redeemer convince you that are unawakened, and turn the wicked
from the evil of their way! And may the love of God, that passeth
all understanding, fill your hearts. Grant this, O Father, for Christ's
sake; to whom, with thee and the blessed Spirit, be all honor and
glory, now and for evermore. Amen.

PATRICK HENRY

Liberty or Death

Patrick Henry, an attorney and statesman from Virginia, is perhaps best-known for his fiery oratory, sometimes compared to that of an Old Testament prophet. This is his most famous speech, given before the the Virginia House of Burgesses meeting at St. John's Church in Richmond, Virginia on March 23, 1775. He called for the Burgesses to approve and assemble a volunteer Calvary in every Virginia County. The "Give Me Liberty of Give Me Death!" speech was delivered extemporaneously, and was not transcribed until 1808.

MR. PRESIDENT: No man thinks more highly than I do of the patriotism, as well as abilities, of the very worthy gentlemen who have just addressed the House. But different men often see the same subject in different lights; and, therefore, I hope it will not be thought disrespectful to those gentlemen if, entertaining as I do, opinions of a character very opposite to theirs, I shall speak forth my sentiments freely, and without reserve. This is no time for ceremony. The question before the House is one of awful moment to this country. For my own part, I consider it as nothing less than a question of freedom or slavery; and in proportion to the magnitude of the subject ought to be the freedom of the debate. It is only in this way that we can hope to arrive at truth, and fulfil the great responsibility which we hold to God and our country. Should I keep back my opinions at such a time, through fear of giving offence, I should consider myself as guilty of treason towards my country, and of an act of disloyalty toward the majesty of heaven, which I revere above all earthly kings.

Mr. President, it is natural to man to indulge in the illusions of
hope. We are apt to shut our eyes against a painful truth, and listen
to the song of that siren till she transforms us into beasts. Is this
the part of wise men, engaged in a great and arduous struggle for
liberty? Are we disposed to be of the number of those who, having
eyes, see not, and, having ears, hear not, the things which so nearly
concern their temporal salvation? For my part, whatever anguish of
spirit it may cost, I am willing to know the whole truth; to know the
worst, and to provide for it.

I have but one lamp by which my feet are guided; and that is
the lamp of experience. I know of no way of judging of the future
but by the past. And judging by the past, I wish to know what
there has been in the conduct of the British ministry for the last
ten years, to justify those hopes with which gentlemen have been
pleased to solace themselves, and the House? Is it that insidious
smile with which our petition has been lately received? Trust it not,
sir; it will prove a snare to your feet. Suffer not yourselves to be
betrayed with a kiss. Ask yourselves how this gracious reception of
our petition comports with these war-like preparations which cover
our waters and darken our land. Are fleets and armies necessary
to a work of love and reconciliation? Have we shown ourselves so
unwilling to be reconciled, that force must be called in to win back
our love? Let us not deceive ourselves, sir. These are the implements
of war and subjugation; the last arguments to which kings resort.
I ask, gentlemen, sir, what means this martial array, if its purpose
be not to force us to submission? Can gentlemen assign any other
possible motive for it? Has Great Britain any enemy, in this quarter
of the world, to call for all this accumulation of navies and armies?

No, sir, she has none. They are meant for us; they can be meant
for no other. They are sent over to bind and rivet upon us those
chains which the British ministry have been so long forging. And
what have we to oppose to them? Shall we try argument? Sir, we
have been trying that for the last ten years. Have we anything
new to offer upon the subject? Nothing. We have held the subject
up in every light of which it is capable; but it has been all in vain.
Shall we resort to entreaty and humble supplication? What terms
shall we find which have not been already exhausted? Let us not,
I beseech you, sir, deceive ourselves. Sir, we have done everything
that could be done, to avert the storm which is now coming on.
We have petitioned; we have remonstrated; we have supplicated;
we have prostrated ourselves before the throne, and have implored
its interposition to arrest the tyrannical hands of the ministry and
Parliament. Our petitions have been slighted; our remonstrances
have produced additional violence and insult; our supplications have
been disregarded; and we have been spurned, with contempt, from
the foot of the throne. In vain, after these things, may we indulge
the fond hope of peace and reconciliation. There is no longer any
room for hope. If we wish to be free — if we mean to preserve
inviolate those inestimable privileges for which we have been so long
contending — if we mean not basely to abandon the noble struggle
in which we have been so long engaged, and which we have pledged
ourselves never to abandon until the glorious object of our contest
shall be obtained, we must fight! I repeat it, sir, we must fight! An
appeal to arms and to the God of Hosts is all that is left us!

They tell us, sir, that we are weak; unable to cope with so
formidable an adversary. But when shall we be stronger? Will it
be the next week, or the next year? Will it be when we are totally

disarmed, and when a British guard shall be stationed in every house? Shall we gather strength by irresolution and inaction? Shall we acquire the means of effectual resistance, by lying supinely on our backs, and hugging the delusive phantom of hope, until our enemies shall have bound us hand and foot? Sir, we are not weak if we make a proper use of those means which the God of nature hath placed in our power. Three millions of people, armed in the holy cause of liberty, and in such a country as that which we possess, are invincible by any force which our enemy can send against us. Besides, sir, we shall not fight our battles alone. There is a just God who presides over the destinies of nations; and who will raise up friends to fight our battles for us. The battle, sir, is not to the strong alone; it is to the vigilant, the active, the brave. Besides, sir, we have no election. If we were base enough to desire it, it is now too late to retire from the contest. There is no retreat but in submission and slavery! Our chains are forged! Their clanking may be heard on the plains of Boston! The war is inevitable — and let it come! I repeat it, sir, let it come.

It is in vain, sir, to extenuate the matter. Gentlemen may cry, Peace, Peace — but there is no peace. The war is actually begun! The next gale that sweeps from the north will bring to our ears the clash of resounding arms! Our brethren are already in the field! Why stand we here idle? What is it that gentlemen wish? What would they have? Is life so dear, or peace so sweet, as to be purchased at the price of chains and slavery? Forbid it, Almighty God! I know not what course others may take; but as for me, give me liberty or give me death!

JOHN DICKINSON

Letters from a Farmer in Pennsylvania to the Inhabitants of the British Colonies

"Moderns who make the acquaintance of John Dickinson can be forgiven
for finding him, on the whole, both irritable and irritating—hardly the
Founding Father likeliest to be singled out, from a room ablaze with talent
and inspiration, for some after-hours jollity. He would not be the man
to call for punch all around and a lively tune from the fiddler—not with
the prospect of a split from the mother country weighing heavily upon his
mind and soul . . . need we bestow on the gentleman any further thought?
Only, perhaps, if we want to understand one of the most complex and
influential figures of the entire revolutionary period, someone who was
present at all the major assemblages where thinkers and activists charted
the young nation's path. At every turn he offered counsel both eloquent
and sober. The historian Forrest McDonald has called Dickinson 'the most
underrated of all the Founders of this nation.'"—William Murchinson,
The Cost of Liberty

My dear Countrymen,

I am a Farmer, settled, after a variety of fortunes, near the
banks of the river Delaware, in the province of Pennsylvania. I
received a liberal education, and have been engaged in the busy
scenes of life; but am now convinced, that a man may be as happy
without bustle, as with it. My farm is small; my servants are few,
and good; I have a little money at interest; I wish for no more;
my employment in my own affairs is easy; and with a contented

grateful mind, undisturbed by worldly hopes or fears, relating to myself, I am completing the number of days allotted to me by divine goodness.

Being generally master of my time, I spend a good deal of it in a library, which I think the most valuable part of my small estate; and being acquainted with two or three gentlemen of abilities and learning, who honor me with their friendship, I have acquired, I believe, a greater knowledge in history, and the laws and constitution of my country, than is generally attained by men of my class, many of them not being so fortunate as I have been in the opportunities of getting information.

From my infancy I was taught to love humanity and liberty. Enquiry and experience have since confirmed my reverence for the lessons then given me, by convincing me more fully of their truth and excellence. Benevolence toward mankind, excites wishes for their welfare, and such wishes endear the means of fulfilling them. These can be found in liberty only, and therefore her sacred cause ought to be espoused by every man on every occasion, to the utmost of his power. As a charitable, but poor person does not withhold his mite, because he cannot relieve all the distresses of the miserable, so should not any honest man suppress his sentiments concerning freedom, however small their influence is likely to be. Perhaps he "may touch some wheel,"* that will have an effect greater than he could reasonably expect.

These being my sentiments, I am encouraged to offer to you, my countrymen, my thoughts on some late transactions, that appear to me to be of the utmost importance to you. Conscious of my own defects, I have waited some time, in expectation of seeing the subject treated by persons much better qualified for the task; but being therein disappointed, and apprehensive that longer delays will be injurious, I venture at length to request the attention of the public, praying, that these lines may be read with the same zeal for the happiness of British America, with which they were wrote.

With a good deal of surprise I have observed, that little notice has been taken of an act of parliament, as injurious in its principle to the liberties of these colonies, as the Stamp Act was: I mean the act for suspending the legislation of New York.

The assembly of that government complied with a former act of parliament, requiring certain provisions to be made for the troops in America, in every particular, I think, except the articles of salt, pepper and vinegar. In my opinion they acted imprudently, considering all circumstances, in not complying so far as would have given satisfaction, as several colonies did: But my dislike of their conduct in that instance, has not blinded me so much, that I cannot plainly perceive, that they have been punished in a manner pernicious to American freedom, and justly alarming to all the colonies.

If the British parliament has legal authority to issue an order, that we shall furnish a single article for the troops here, and to compel obedience to that order, they have the same right to issue an order for us to supply those troops with arms, clothes, and every necessary; and to compel obedience to that order also; in short, to lay any burthens they please upon us. What is this but taxing us at a certain sum, and leaving to us only the manner of raising it? How is this mode more tolerable than the Stamp Act? Would that act have appeared more pleasing to Americans, if being ordered thereby to raise the sum total of the taxes, the mighty privilege had been left to them, of saying how much should be paid for an instrument of writing on paper, and how much for another on parchment?

An act of parliament, commanding us to do a certain thing, if it has any validity, is a tax upon us for the expense that accrues in complying with it; and for this reason, I believe, every colony on the continent, that chose to give a mark of their respect for Great Britain, in complying with the act relating to the troops, cautiously avoided the mention of that act, lest their conduct should be attributed to its supposed obligation.

The matter being thus stated, the assembly of New York either had, or had not, a right to refuse submission to that act. If they had, and I imagine no American will say they had not, then the parliament had no right to compel them to execute it. If they had not this right, they had no right to punish them for not executing it; and therefore no right to suspend their legislation, which is a punishment. In fact, if the people of New York cannot be legally taxed but by their own representatives, they cannot be legally deprived of the privilege of legislation, only for insisting on that exclusive privilege of taxation. If they may be legally deprived in such a case, of the privilege of legislation, why may they not, with equal reason, be deprived of every other privilege? Or why may not every colony be treated in the same manner, when any of them shall dare to deny their assent to any impositions, that shall be directed? Or what signifies the repeal of the Stamp Act, if these colonies are to lose their other privileges, by not tamely surrendering that of taxation?

There is one consideration arising from this suspension, which is not generally attended to, but shows its importance very clearly. It was not necessary that this suspension should be caused by an act of parliament. The crown might have restrained the governor of New York, even from calling the assembly together, by its prerogative in the royal governments. This step, I suppose, would have been taken, if the conduct of the assembly of New York had been regarded as an act of disobedience to the crown alone; but it is regarded as an act of "disobedience to the authority of the British Legislature."* This gives the suspension a consequence vastly more affecting. It is a parliamentary assertion of the supreme authority of the British legislature over these colonies, in the point of taxation, and is intended to compel New York into a submission to that authority. It seems therefore to me as much a violation of the liberties of the people of that province, and consequently of all these colonies, as if the parliament had sent a number of regiments to be quartered upon them till they should comply. For it is evident, that the suspension is meant as a compulsion; and the method of compelling is totally indifferent. It is indeed probable, that the sight of redcoats, and the hearing of drums, would have been most alarming; because people are generally more influenced by their eyes and ears, than by their reason. But whoever seriously considers the matter, must perceive that a dreadful stroke is aimed at the liberty of these colonies. I say, of these colonies; for the cause of one is the cause of all. If the parliament may lawfully deprive New York of any of her rights, it may deprive any, or all the other colonies of their rights; and nothing can possibly so much encourage such attempts, as a mutual inattention to the interests of each other. To divide, and thus to destroy, is the first political maxim in attacking those, who are powerful by their union. He certainly is not a wise man, who folds his arms, and reposes himself at home, viewing, with unconcern, the flames that have invaded his neighbor's house, without using any endeavors to extinguish them. When Mr. Hampden's ship money case, for Three Shillings and Four-pence, was tried, all the people of England, with anxious expectation, interested themselves in the important decision; and when the slightest point, touching the freedom of one colony, is agitated, I earnestly wish, that all the rest may, with equal ardor, support their sister. Very much may be said on this subject; but I hope, more at present is unnecessary.

With concern I have observed, that two assemblies of this province have sat and adjourned, without taking any notice of this act. It may perhaps be asked, what would have been proper for them to do? I am by no means fond of inflammatory measures; I detest them. I should be sorry that anything should be done which might justly displease our sovereign, or our mother country: But a firm, modest exertion of a free spirit, should never be wanting on public occasions. It appears to me, that it would have been sufficient for the assembly to have ordered our agents to represent to the King's ministers their sense of the suspending act, and to pray for its repeal. Thus we should have borne our testimony against it; and might therefore reasonably expect that, on a like occasion, we might receive the same assistance from the other colonies.

Concordia res parvae crescunt.
Small things grow great by concord.

A Farmer

Nov. 5 [1767].

CONTINENTAL CONGRESS

The Olive Branch Petition

The Second Continental Congress presented this petition to King George in the hopes thats war could still be avoided. But the King did not even read the petition; instead, he declared the colonists to be traitors.

TO THE KING'S MOST EXCELLENT MAJESTY.

Most Gracious Sovereign: We, your Majesty's faithful subjects of the Colonies of New-Hampthire, Massachusetts-Bay, Rhode-Island and Providence Plantations, Connecticut, New-York, New-Jersey, Pennsylvania, the Counties of Newcastle, Kent, and Sussex, on Delaware, Maryland, Virginia, North Carolina, and South Carolina, in behalf of ourselves and the inhabitants of these Colonies, who have deputed us to represent them in General Congress, entreat your Majesty's gracious attention to this our humble petition.

The union between our Mother Country and these Colonies, and the energy of mild and just Government, produced benefits so remarkably important, and afforded such an assurance of their permanency and increase, that the wonder and envy of other nations were excited, while they beheld Great Britain rising to a power the most extraordinary the world had ever known.

Her rivals, observing that there was no probability of this happy connexion being broken by civil dissensions, and apprehending its future effects if left any longer undisturbed, resolved to prevent her receiving such continual and formidable accessions of wealth and strength, by checking the growth of those settlements from which they were to be derived.

In the prosecution of this attempt, events so unfavourable to the design took place, that every friend to the interest of Great Britain and these Colonies, entertained pleasing and reasonable expectations of seeing an additional force and exertion immediately given to the operations of the union hitherto experienced, by an enlargement of the dominions of the Crown, and the removal of ancient and warlike enemies to a greater distance.

At the conclusion, therefore, of the late war, the most glorious and advantageous that ever had been carried on by British arms, your loyal Colonists having contributed to its success by such repeated and strenuous exertions as frequently procured them the distinguished approbation of your Majesty, of the late King, and of Parliament, doubted not but that they should be permitted, with the rest of the Empire, to share in the blessings of peace, and the emoluments of victory and conquest.

While these recent and honourable acknowledgments of their merits remained on record in the Journals and acts of that august Legislature, the Parliament, undefaced by the imputation or even the suspicion of any offence, they were alarmed by a new system of statutes and regulations adopted for the administration of the Colonies, that filled their minds with the most painful fears and jealousies; and, to their inexpressible astonishment, perceived the danger of a foreign quarrel quickly succeeded by domestick danger, in their judgment of a more dreadful kind.

Nor were these anxieties alleviated by any tendency in this system to promote the welfare of their Mother Country. For though its effects were more immediately felt by them, yet its influence appeared to be injurious to the commerce and prosperity of Great Britain.

We shall decline the ungrateful task of describing the irksome variety of artifices practised by many of your Majesty's Ministers, the delusive pretences, fruitless terrours, and unavailing severities, that have, from time to time, been dealt out by them, in their attempts to execute this impolitick plan, or of tracing through a series of years past the progress of the unhappy differences between Great Britain and these Colonies, that have flowed from this fatal source.

Your Majesty's Ministers, persevering in their measures, and proceeding to open hostilities for enforcing them, have compelled us to arm in our own defence, and have engaged us in a controversy so peculiarly abhorrent to the affections of your still faithful Colonists, that when we consider whom we must oppose in this contest, and if it continues, what may be the consequences, our own particular misfortunes are accounted by us only as parts of our distress. Knowing to what violent resentments and incurable animosities civil discords are apt to exasperate and inflame the contending parties, we think ourselves required by indispensable obligations to Almighty God, to your Majesty, to our fellow-subjects, and to ourselves, immediately to use all the means in our power, not incompatible with our safety, for stopping the further effusion of blood, and for averting the impending calamities that threaten the British Empire.

Thus called upon to address your Majesty on affairs of such moment to America, and probably to all your Dominions, we are earnestly desirous of performing this office with the utmost deference for your Majesty; and we therefore pray, that your Majesty's royal magnanimity and benevolence may make the most favourable constructions of our expressions on so uncommon an occasion. Could we represent in their full force the sentiments that agitate the minds of us your dutiful subjects, we are

persuaded your Majesty would ascribe any seeming deviation
from reverence in our language, and even in our conduct, not to
any reprehensible intention, but to the impossibility of reconciling
the usual appearances of respect with a just attention to our own
preservation against those artful and cruel enemies who abuse your
royal confidence and authority, for the purpose of effecting our
destruction.

Attached to your Majesty's person, family, and Government,
with all devotion that principle and affection can inspire; connected
with Great Britain by the strongest ties that can unite societies, and
deploring every event that tends in any degree to weaken them,
we solemnly assure your Majesty, that we not only most ardently
desire the former harmony between her and these Colonies may be
restored, but that a concord may be established between them upon
so firm a basis as to perpetuate its blessings, uninterrupted by any
future dissensions, to succeeding generations in both countries, and
to transmit your Majesty's name to posterity, adorned with that
signal and lasting glory that has attended the memory of those
illustrious personages, whose virtues and abilities have extricated
states from dangerous convulsions, and, by securing happiness to
others, have erected the most noble and durable monuments to their
own fame.

We beg leave further to assure your Majesty, that
notwithstanding the sufferings of your loyal Colonists during the
course of this present controversy, our breasts retain too tender a
regard for the kingdom from which we derive our origin, to request
such a reconciliation as might, in any manner, be inconsistent
with her dignity or her welfare. These, related as we are to her,
honour and duty, as well as inclination, induce us to support and

advance; and the apprehensions that now oppress our hearts with unspeakable grief, being once removed, your Majesty will find your faithful subjects on this Continent ready and willing at all times, as they have ever been, with their lives and fortunes, to assert and maintain the rights and interests of your Majesty, and of our Mother Country.

We therefore beseech your Majesty, that your royal authority and influence may be graciously interposed to procure us relief from our afflicting fears and jealousies, occasioned by the system before-mentioned, and to settle peace through every part of our Dominions, with all humility submitting to your Majesty's wise consideration, whether it may not be expedient, for facilitating those important purposes, that your Majesty be pleased to direct some mode, by which the united applications of your faithful Colonists to the Throne, in pursuance of their common counsels, may be improved into a happy and permanent reconciliation; and that, in the mean time, measures may be taken for preventing the further destruction of the lives of your Majesty's subjects; and that such statutes as more immediately distress any of your Majesty's Colonies, may be repealed.

For such arrangements as your Majesty's wisdom can form for collecting the united sense of your American people, we are convinced your Majesty would receive such satisfactory proofs of the disposition of the Colonists towards their Sovereign and Parent State, that the wished for opportunity would soon be restored to them, of evincing the sincerity of their professions, by every testimony of devotion becoming the most dutiful subjects, and the most affectionate Colonists.

That your Majesty may enjoy a long and prosperous reign, and that your descendants may govern your Dominions with honour to themselves and happiness to their subjects, is our sincere prayer.

John Hancock

NEW-HAMPSHIRE	John Langdon, Thomas Cushing.
MASSACHUSETTS	Samuel Adams, John Adams, Robert Treat Paine.
RHODE-ISLAND	Stephen Hopkins, Samuel Ward, Eliphalet Dyer.
CONNECTICUT	Roger Sherman, Silas Deane.
NEW-YORK	Philip Livingston, James Duane, John Alsop, Francis Lewis, John Jay, Robert Livingston, Jr., Lewis Morris, William Floyd, Henry Wisner.
NEW JERSEY	William Livingston, John De Hart, Richard Smith.
PENNSYLVANIA	John Dickinson, Benjamin Franklin, George Ross, James Wilson, Charles Humphreys, Edward Biddle.
DELAWARE COUNTIES	Cæsar Rodney, Thomas McKean, George Read.
MARYLAND	Matthew Tilghman, Thomas Johnson, Jr., William Paca, Samuel Chase, Thomas Stone.
VIRGINIA	Patrick Henry, Jr., Richard Henry Lee, Edmund Pendleton, Benjamin Harrison, Thomas Jefferson.
NORTH-CAROLINA	William Hooper, Joseph Hewes.

SOUTH-CAROLINA   Henry Middleton, Thomas Lynch,
Christopher Gadsden, John Rutledge,
Edward Rutledge.

SECOND CONTINENTAL CONGRESS

Declaration of Independence

The Declaration of Independence set the cornerstone for the foundation of the American Republic. Thomas Jefferson was selected from the committee of five to write the document that would declare that the thirteen colonies were a free and independent people from the rule of Great Britain. Jefferson, when he penned these words, set up the foundation for our Republic. Abraham Lincoln, in the his debates with Stephen Douglas, declared that the Constitution was the frame around the golden apple of the Declaration of Independence. The language was approved on July 2, and the Declaration was ratified on July 4, 1776.

"I am well aware of the Toil and Blood and Treasure, that it will cost Us to maintain this Declaration, and support and defend these States. Yet through all the Gloom I can see the Rays of ravishing Light and Glory. I can see that the End is more than worth all the Means. And that Posterity will tryumph in that Days Transaction, even altho We should rue it, which I trust in God We shall not." — Letter from John Adams to Abigail Adams, July 3, 1776

When in the Course of human events, it becomes necessary for one people to dissolve the political bands which have connected them with another, and to assume among the powers of the earth, the separate and equal station to which the Laws of Nature and of Nature's God entitle them, a decent respect to the opinions of mankind requires that they should declare the causes which impel them to the separation.

We hold these truths to be self-evident, that all men are created equal, that they are endowed by their Creator with certain unalienable Rights, that among these are Life, Liberty and the pursuit of Happiness. --That to secure these rights, Governments are instituted among Men, deriving their just powers from the consent of the governed, --That whenever any Form of Government becomes destructive of these ends, it is the Right of the People to alter or to abolish it, and to institute new Government, laying its foundation on such principles and organizing its powers in such form, as to them shall seem most likely to effect their Safety and Happiness. Prudence, indeed, will dictate that Governments long established should not be changed for light and transient causes; and accordingly all experience hath shewn, that mankind are more disposed to suffer, while evils are sufferable, than to right themselves by abolishing the forms to which they are accustomed. But when a long train of abuses and usurpations, pursuing invariably the same Object evinces a design to reduce them under absolute Despotism, it is their right, it is their duty, to throw off such Government, and to provide new Guards for their future security. --Such has been the patient sufferance of these Colonies; and such is now the necessity which constrains them to alter their former Systems of Government. The history of the present King of Great Britain is a history of repeated injuries and usurpations, all having in direct object the establishment of an absolute Tyranny over these States. To prove this, let Facts be submitted to a candid world.

He has refused his Assent to Laws, the most wholesome and necessary for the public good.

He has forbidden his Governors to pass Laws of immediate and pressing importance, unless suspended in their operation till his Assent should be obtained; and when so suspended, he has utterly neglected to attend to them.

He has refused to pass other Laws for the accommodation of large districts of people, unless those people would relinquish the right of Representation in the Legislature, a right inestimable to them and formidable to tyrants only.

He has called together legislative bodies at places unusual, uncomfortable, and distant from the depository of their public Records, for the sole purpose of fatiguing them into compliance with his measures.

He has dissolved Representative Houses repeatedly, for opposing with manly firmness his invasions on the rights of the people.

He has refused for a long time, after such dissolutions, to cause others to be elected; whereby the Legislative powers, incapable of Annihilation, have returned to the People at large for their exercise; the State remaining in the mean time exposed to all the dangers of invasion from without, and convulsions within.

He has endeavoured to prevent the population of these States; for that purpose obstructing the Laws for Naturalization of Foreigners; refusing to pass others to encourage their migrations hither, and raising the conditions of new Appropriations of Lands.

He has obstructed the Administration of Justice, by refusing his Assent to Laws for establishing Judiciary powers.

He has made Judges dependent on his Will alone, for the tenure of their offices, and the amount and payment of their salaries.

He has erected a multitude of New Offices, and sent hither swarms of Officers to harrass our people, and eat out their substance.

He has kept among us, in times of peace, Standing Armies without the Consent of our legislatures.

He has affected to render the Military independent of and superior to the Civil power.

He has combined with others to subject us to a jurisdiction foreign to our constitution, and unacknowledged by our laws; giving his Assent to their Acts of pretended Legislation:

For Quartering large bodies of armed troops among us:

For protecting them, by a mock Trial, from punishment for any Murders which they should commit on the Inhabitants of these States:

For cutting off our Trade with all parts of the world:

For imposing Taxes on us without our Consent:

For depriving us in many cases, of the benefits of Trial by Jury:

For transporting us beyond Seas to be tried for pretended offences

For abolishing the free System of English Laws in a neighbouring Province, establishing therein an Arbitrary government, and enlarging its Boundaries so as to render it at once an example and fit instrument for introducing the same absolute rule into these Colonies:

For taking away our Charters, abolishing our most valuable Laws, and altering fundamentally the Forms of our Governments:

For suspending our own Legislatures, and declaring themselves invested with power to legislate for us in all cases whatsoever.

He has abdicated Government here, by declaring us out of his Protection and waging War against us.

He has plundered our seas, ravaged our Coasts, burnt our towns, and destroyed the lives of our people.

He is at this time transporting large Armies of foreign Mercenaries to compleat the works of death, desolation and tyranny, already begun with circumstances of Cruelty & perfidy scarcely paralleled in the most barbarous ages, and totally unworthy the Head of a civilized nation.

He has constrained our fellow Citizens taken Captive on the high Seas to bear Arms against their Country, to become the executioners of their friends and Brethren, or to fall themselves by their Hands.

He has excited domestic insurrections amongst us, and has endeavoured to bring on the inhabitants of our frontiers, the merciless Indian Savages, whose known rule of warfare, is an undistinguished destruction of all ages, sexes and conditions.

In every stage of these Oppressions We have Petitioned for Redress in the most humble terms: Our repeated Petitions have been answered only by repeated injury. A Prince whose character is thus marked by every act which may define a Tyrant, is unfit to be the ruler of a free people.

Nor have We been wanting in attentions to our Brittish brethren. We have warned them from time to time of attempts by their legislature to extend an unwarrantable jurisdiction over us. We have reminded them of the circumstances of our emigration and settlement here. We have appealed to their native justice and magnanimity, and we have conjured them by the ties of our common kindred to disavow these usurpations, which, would inevitably interrupt our connections and correspondence. They too have been deaf to the voice of justice and of consanguinity. We must, therefore, acquiesce in the necessity, which denounces our Separation, and hold them, as we hold the rest of mankind, Enemies in War, in Peace Friends.

We, therefore, the Representatives of the united States of America, in General Congress, Assembled, appealing to the Supreme Judge of the world for the rectitude of our intentions, do, in the Name, and by Authority of the good People of these Colonies, solemnly publish and declare,   That these United Colonies are, and of Right ought to be Free and Independent States; that they are Absolved from all Allegiance to the British Crown, and that all political connection between them and the State of Great Britain, is and ought to be totally dissolved; and that as Free and Independent States, they have full Power to levy War, conclude Peace, contract

Alliances, establish Commerce, and to do all other Acts and Things which Independent States may of right do. And for the support of this Declaration, with a firm reliance on the protection of divine Providence, we mutually pledge to each other our Lives, our Fortunes and our sacred Honor.

John Hancock

NEW-HAMPSHIRE	Josiah Bartlett, William Whipple, Matthew Thornton.
MASSACHUSETTS	Samuel Adams, John Adams, Robert Treat Paine, Elbridge Gerry.
RHODE-ISLAND	Stephen Hopkins, William Ellery.
CONNECTICUT	Roger Sherman, Samuel Huntington, William Williams, Oliver Wolcott.
NEW-YORK	William Floyd, Philip Livingston, Francis Lewis, Lewis Morris.
NEW JERSEY	Richard Stockton, John Witherspoon, Francis Hopkinson, John Hart, Abraham Clark.
PENNSYLVANIA	Robert Morris, Benjamin Rush, Benjamin Franklin, John Morton, George Clymer, James Smith, George Taylor, James Wilson, George Ross.
DELAWARE COUNTIES	George Read, Caesar Rodney, Thomas McKean.
MARYLAND	Samuel Chase, William Paca, Thomas Stone, Charles Carroll of Carrollton.

VIRGINIA   George Wythe, Richard Henry Lee, Thomas Jefferson, Benjamin Harrison, Thomas Nelson, Jr., Francis Lightfoot Lee, Carter Braxton.

NORTH-CAROLINA   William Hooper, Joseph Hewes, John Penn.

SOUTH-CAROLINA   Edward Rutledge, Thomas Heyward, Jr., Thomas Lynch, Jr., Arthur Middleton.

GEORGIA   Button Gwinnett, Lyman Hall, George Walton

SECOND CONTINENTAL CONGRESS

Articles of Confederation

The Articles of Confederation served as the government for the colonies following the adoption of the Declaration of Independence. It was a treaty of friendship between the states, rather than an actual government. Its weakness would lead to Shays' Rebellion and ultimately the Constitutional Convention. The Articles of Confederation were uthored by John Dickinson.

AGREED TO BY CONGRESS NOVEMBER 15, 1777; RATIFIED AND IN FORCE, MARCH 1, 1781.

PREAMBLE

To all to whom these Presents shall come, we the undersigned Delegates of the States affixed to our Names send greeting.

Whereas the Delegates of the United States of America in Congress assembled did on the fifteenth day of November in the Year of our Lord One Thousand Seven Hundred and Seventy seven, and in the Second Year of the Independence of America, agree to certain articles of Confederation and perpetual Union between the States of New Hampshire, Massachusetts-bay, Rhode Island and Providence Plantations, Connecticut, New York, New Jersey, Pennsylvania, Delaware, Maryland, Virginia, North Carolina, South Carolina and Georgia, in the words following, viz:

Articles of Confederation and perpetual Union between the States of New Hampshire, Massachusetts-bay, Rhode Island and Providence Plantations, Connecticut, New York, New Jersey, Pennsylvania,

Delaware, Maryland, Virginia, North Carolina, South Carolina and Georgia.

ARTICLE I. The Stile of this Confederacy shall be "The United States of America."

ARTICLE II. Each state retains its sovereignty, freedom, and independence, and every Power, Jurisdiction, and right, which is not by this confederation expressly delegated to the United States, in Congress assembled.

ARTICLE III. The said States hereby severally enter into a firm league of friendship with each other, for their common defense, the security of their liberties, and their mutual and general welfare, binding themselves to assist each other, against all force offered to, or attacks made upon them, or any of them, on account of religion, sovereignty, trade, or any other pretense whatever.

ARTICLE IV. The better to secure and perpetuate mutual friendship and intercourse among the people of the different States in this union, the free inhabitants of each of these States, paupers, vagabonds, and fugitives from justice excepted, shall be entitled to all privileges and immunities of free citizens in the several States; and the people of each State shall have free ingress and regress to and from any other State, and shall enjoy therein all the privileges of trade and commerce, subject to the same duties, impositions, and restrictions as the inhabitants thereof respectively, provided that such restrictions shall not extend so far as to prevent the removal of property imported into any State, to any other State, of which the owner is an inhabitant; provided also that no imposition, duties or restriction shall be laid by any State, on the property of the united States, or either of them.

ARTICLE V. For the most convenient management of the general interests of the united States, delegates shall be annually appointed in such manner as the legislatures of each State shall direct, to meet in Congress on the first Monday in November, in every year, with a power reserved to each State to recall its delegates, or any of them, at any time within the year, and to send others in their stead for the remainder of the year.

No State shall be represented in Congress by less than two, nor more than seven members; and no person shall be capable of being a delegate for more than three years in any term of six years; nor shall any person, being a delegate, be capable of holding any office under the united States, for which he, or another for his benefit, receives any salary, fees or emolument of any kind.

Each State shall maintain its own delegates in a meeting of the States, and while they act as members of the committee of the States.

In determining questions in the united States, in Congress assembled, each State shall have one vote.

Freedom of speech and debate in Congress shall not be impeached or questioned in any court or place out of Congress, and the members of Congress shall be protected in their persons from arrests or imprisonments, during the time of their going to and from, and attendance on Congress, except for treason, felony, or breach of the peace.

ARTICLE VI. No State, without the consent of the united States in Congress assembled, shall send any embassy to, or receive any embassy from, or enter into any conference, agreement, alliance or treaty with any King, Prince or State; nor shall any person holding any office of profit or trust under the united States, or any of them, accept any present, emolument, office or title of any kind whatever from any King, Prince or foreign State; nor shall the United States in congress assembled, or any of them, grant any title of nobility.

No two or more States shall enter into any treaty, confederation or alliance whatever between them, without the consent of the united States in congress assembled, specifying accurately the purposes for which the same is to be entered into, and how long it shall continue.

No State shall lay any imposts or duties, which may interfere with any stipulations in treaties, entered into by the united States in congress assembled, with any King, Prince or State, in pursuance of any treaties already proposed by congress, to the courts of France and Spain.

No vessel of war shall be kept up in time of peace by any State, except such number only, as shall be deemed necessary by the united States in congress assembled, for the defense of such State, or its trade; nor shall any body of forces be kept up by any State in time of peace, except such number only, as in the judgement of the united States, in congress assembled, shall be deemed requisite to garrison the forts necessary for the defense of such State; but every State shall always keep up a well-regulated and disciplined militia, sufficiently armed and accoutered, and shall provide and constantly have ready for use, in public stores, a due number of field pieces and tents, and a proper quantity of arms, ammunition and camp equipage.

No State shall engage in any war without the consent of the

united States in congress assembled, unless such State be actually invaded by enemies, or shall have received certain advice of a resolution being formed by some nation of Indians to invade such State, and the danger is so imminent as not to admit of a delay till the united States in congress assembled can be consulted; nor shall any State grant commissions to any ships or vessels of war, nor letters of marque or reprisal, except it be after a declaration of war by the united States in congress assembled, and then only against the kingdom or State and the subjects thereof, against which war has been so declared, and under such regulations as shall be established by the united States in congress assembled, unless such State be infested by pirates, in which case vessels of war may be fitted out for that occasion, and kept so long as the danger shall continue, or until the united States in congress assembled shall determine otherwise.

ARTICLE VII. When land forces are raised by any State for the common defense, all officers of or under the rank of colonel, shall be appointed by the legislature of each State respectively, by whom such forces shall be raised, or in such manner as such State shall direct, and all vacancies shall be filled up by the State which first made the appointment.

ARTICLE VIII. All charges of war, and all other expenses that shall be incurred for the common defense or general welfare, and allowed by the united States in congress assembled, shall be defrayed out of a common treasury, which shall be supplied by the several States in proportion to the value of all land within each State, granted or surveyed for any person, as such land and the buildings and improvements thereon shall be estimated according to such mode as the united States in congress assembled, shall from time to time direct and appoint.

The taxes for paying that proportion shall be laid and levied by the authority and direction of the legislatures of the several States within the time agreed upon by the united States in congress assembled.

ARTICLE IX. The united States in congress assembled, shall have the sole and exclusive right and power of determining on peace and war, except in the cases mentioned in the sixth article — of sending and receiving ambassadors — entering into treaties and alliances, provided that no treaty of commerce shall be made whereby the legislative power of the respective States shall be restrained from imposing such imposts and duties on foreigners, as their own people are subjected to, or from prohibiting the exportation or importation of any species of goods or commodities whatsoever — of establishing rules for deciding in all cases, what captures on land or water shall be legal, and in what manner prizes taken by land or naval forces in the service of the United States shall be divided or appropriated — of granting letters of marque and reprisal in times of peace — appointing courts for the trial of piracies and felonies committed on the high seas and establishing courts for receiving and determining finally appeals in all cases of captures, provided that no member of Congress shall be appointed a judge of any of the said courts.

The United States in Congress assembled shall also be the last resort on appeal in all disputes and differences now subsisting or that hereafter may arise between two or more States concerning boundary, jurisdiction or any other causes whatever; which authority shall always be exercised in the manner following.

Whenever the legislative or executive authority or lawful agent of
any State in controversy with another shall present a petition to
Congress stating the matter in question and praying for a hearing,
notice thereof shall be given by order of Congress to the legislative
or executive authority of the other State in controversy, and a
day assigned for the appearance of the parties by their lawful
agents, who shall then be directed to appoint by joint consent,
commissioners or judges to constitute a court for hearing and
determining the matter in question: but if they cannot agree,
Congress shall name three persons out of each of the United States,
and from the list of such persons each party shall alternately strike
out one, the petitioners beginning, until the number shall be reduced
to thirteen; and from that number not less than seven, nor more
than nine names as Congress shall direct, shall in the presence
of Congress be drawn out by lot, and the persons whose names
shall be so drawn or any five of them, shall be commissioners or
judges, to hear and finally determine the controversy, so always
as a major part of the judges who shall hear the cause shall agree
in the determination: and if either party shall neglect to attend
at the day appointed, without showing reasons, which Congress
shall judge sufficient, or being present shall refuse to strike, the
Congress shall proceed to nominate three persons out of each State,
and the secretary of Congress shall strike in behalf of such party
absent or refusing; and the judgement and sentence of the court
to be appointed, in the manner before prescribed, shall be final
and conclusive; and if any of the parties shall refuse to submit to
the authority of such court, or to appear or defend their claim or
cause, the court shall nevertheless proceed to pronounce sentence,
or judgement, which shall in like manner be final and decisive, the
judgement or sentence and other proceedings being in either case

transmitted to Congress, and lodged among the acts of Congress for the security of the parties concerned: provided that every commissioner, before he sits in judgement, shall take an oath to be administered by one of the judges of the supreme or superior court of the State, where the cause shall be tried, 'well and truly to hear and determine the matter in question, according to the best of his judgement, without favor, affection or hope of reward': provided also, that no State shall be deprived of territory for the benefit of the United States.

All controversies concerning the private right of soil claimed under different grants of two or more States, whose jurisdictions as they may respect such lands, and the States which passed such grants are adjusted, the said grants or either of them being at the same time claimed to have originated antecedent to such settlement of jurisdiction, shall on the petition of either party to the Congress of the United States, be finally determined as near as may be in the same manner as is before prescribed for deciding disputes respecting territorial jurisdiction between different States.

The United States in Congress assembled shall also have the sole and exclusive right and power of regulating the alloy and value of coin struck by their own authority, or by that of the respective States — fixing the standards of weights and measures throughout the United States — regulating the trade and managing all affairs with the Indians, not members of any of the States, provided that the legislative right of any State within its own limits be not infringed or violated — establishing or regulating post offices from one State to another, throughout all the United States, and exacting such postage on the papers passing through the same as may be requisite to defray the expenses of the said office — appointing all officers of the land forces, in the service of the United States, excepting regimental officers — appointing all the officers of the naval forces, and commissioning all officers whatever in the service of the United States — making rules for the government and regulation of the said land and naval forces, and directing their operations.

The United States in Congress assembled shall have authority to appoint a committee, to sit in the recess of Congress, to be denominated 'A Committee of the States', and to consist of one delegate from each State; and to appoint such other committees and civil officers as may be necessary for managing the general affairs of the United States under their direction — to appoint one of their members to preside, provided that no person be allowed to serve in the office of president more than one year in any term of three years; to ascertain the necessary sums of money to be raised for the service of the United States, and to appropriate and apply the same for defraying the public expenses — to borrow money, or emit bills on the credit of the United States, transmitting every half-year to the respective States an account of the sums of money so borrowed or emitted — to build and equip a navy — to agree upon the number of land forces, and to make requisitions from each State for its quota, in proportion to the number of white inhabitants in such State; which requisition shall be binding, and thereupon the legislature of each State shall appoint the regimental officers, raise the men and cloath, arm and equip them in a solid- like manner, at the expense of the United States; and the officers and men so cloathed, armed and equipped shall march to the place appointed, and within the time agreed on by the United States in Congress assembled. But if the United States in Congress assembled shall, on consideration of circumstances judge proper that any State should not raise men, or should raise a smaller number of men than the quota thereof, such extra number shall be raised, officered, cloathed, armed and equipped in the same manner as the quota of each State, unless the legislature of such State shall judge that such extra number cannot be safely spread out in the same, in which case they shall raise, officer, cloath, arm and equip as many of such extra number as they judge can be safely spared. And the officers and men so cloathed, armed, and equipped, shall march to the place appointed, and within the time agreed on by the united States in congress assembled.

The united States in congress assembled shall never engage in a war, nor grant letters of marque or reprisal in time of peace, nor enter into any treaties or alliances, nor coin money, nor regulate the value thereof, nor ascertain the sums and expenses necessary for the defense and welfare of the United States, or any of them, nor emit bills, nor borrow money on the credit of the united States, nor appropriate money, nor agree upon the number of vessels of war, to be built or purchased, or the number of land or sea forces to be raised, nor appoint a commander in chief of the army or navy, unless nine States assent to the same: nor shall a question on any other point, except for adjourning from day to day be determined, unless by the votes of the majority of the united States in congress assembled.

ARTICLE X. The committee of the States, or any nine of them, shall be authorized to execute, in the recess of congress, such of the powers of congress as the united States in congress assembled, by the consent of the nine States, shall from time to time think expedient to vest them with; provided that no power be delegated to the said Committee, for the exercise of which, by the articles of confederation, the voice of nine States in the Congress of the United States assembled be requisite.

ARTICLE XI. Canada acceding to this confederation, and adjoining in the measures of the united States, shall be admitted into, and entitled to all the advantages of this union; but no other colony shall be admitted into the same, unless such admission be agreed to by nine States.

ARTICLE XII. All bills of credit emitted, monies borrowed, and debts contracted by, or under the authority of congress, before the assembling of the united States, in pursuance of the present confederation, shall be deemed and considered as a charge against the United States, for payment and satisfaction whereof the said united States, and the public faith are hereby solemnly pledged.

ARTICLE XIII. Every State shall abide by the determination of the united States in congress assembled, on all questions which by this confederation are submitted to them. And the Articles of this confederation shall be inviolably observed by every State, and the union shall be perpetual; nor shall any alteration at any time hereafter be made in any of them; unless such alteration be agreed to in a congress of the united States, and be afterwards confirmed by the legislatures of every State.

And Whereas it hath pleased the Great Governor of the World to incline the hearts of the legislatures we respectively represent in Congress, to approve of, and to authorize us to ratify the said articles of confederation and perpetual union. Know Ye that we the undersigned delegates, by virtue of the power and authority to us given for that purpose, do by these presents, in the name and in behalf of our respective constituents, fully and entirely ratify

and confirm each and every of the said articles of confederation
and perpetual union, and all and singular the matters and things
therein contained: And we do further solemnly plight and engage
the faith of our respective constituents, that they shall abide by
the determinations of the united States in congress assembled, on
all questions, which by the said confederation are submitted to
them. And that the articles thereof shall be inviolably observed by
the States we respectively represent, and that the union shall be
perpetual.

In Witness whereof we have hereunto set our hands in Congress.
Done at Philadelphia in the State of Pennsylvania the ninth Day
of July in the Year of our Lord one thousand seven Hundred
and Seventy-eight, and in the Third Year of the independence of
America.

NEW-HAMPSHIRE	Josiah Bartlett, John Wentworth, Jr.
MASSACHUSETTS	Sᵗ John Hancock, Samuel Adams, Elbridge Gerry, Francis Dana, James Lovell, Samuel Holten.
RHODE-ISLAND	William Ellery. Henry Marchant, John Collins.
CONNECTICUT	Roger Sherman, Samuel Huntington, Oliver Wolcott, Titus Hosmer, Andrew Adams.
NEW-YORK	James Duance, Francis Lewis, William Duer, Gouverneur Morris.
NEW JERSEY	John Witherspoon, Nathaniel Scudder.
PENNSYLVANIA	Robert Morris, Daniel Roberdeau, Jonathan Bayard Smith, William Clingan, Joseph Reed.
DELAWARE COUNTIES	Thomas McKean, John Dickinson, Nicholas Van Dyke.
MARYLAND	John Hanson, Daniel Carroll

VIRGINIA	Richard Henry Lee, John Banister, Thomas Adams, John Harvie, Francis Lightfoot Lee.
NORTH-CAROLINA	John Penn, Cornelius Harnett, John Williams.
SOUTH-CAROLINA	Henry Laurens, William Henry Drayton, John Matthews, Richard Hutson, Thomas Heyward, Jr.
GEORGIA	John Walton, Edward Telfair, Edward Langworthy.

CONGRESS OF THE CONFEDERATION

Northwest Ordinance

The Northwest Ordinance was passed by the Congress of the Confederation on July 13, 1787. It outlines the means by which new states could be admitted into the Union and determines what rights they would have as part of the Union. The ordinance conatined three provisions:

(1) that the Northwest Territory be divided into "not less than three nor more than five States";

(2) that there be a three-stage method for admitting a new state to the Union—with a congressionally appointed governor, secretary, and three judges to rule in the first phase; an elected assembly and one nonvoting delegate to Congress to be elected in the second phase, when the population of the territory reached "five thousand free male inhabitants of full age;" and a state constitution to be drafted and membership to the Union to be requested in the third phase when the population reached 60,000;

(3) a bill of rights protecting religious freedom, the right to a writ of habeas corpus, *the benefit of trial by jury, and other individual rights.*

In addition the ordinance encouraged education and forbade slavery.

Section 1. Be it ordained by the United States in Congress assembled, That the said territory, for the purposes of temporary government, be one district, subject, however, to be divided into two districts, as future circumstances may, in the opinion of Congress, make it expedient.

Sec 2. Be it ordained by the authority aforesaid, That the estates, both of resident and nonresident proprietors in the said territory, dying intestate, shall descent to, and be distributed among their children, and the descendants of a deceased child, in equal parts; the descendants of a deceased child or grandchild to take the share of their deceased parent in equal parts among them: And where there shall be no children or descendants, then in equal parts to the next of kin in equal degree; and among collaterals, the children of a deceased brother or sister of the intestate shall have, in equal parts among them, their deceased parents' share; and there shall in no case be a distinction between kindred of the whole and half blood; saving, in all cases, to the widow of the intestate her third part of the real estate for life, and one third part of the personal estate; and this law relative to descents and dower, shall remain in full force until altered by the legislature of the district. And until the governor and judges shall adopt laws as hereinafter mentioned, estates in the said territory may be devised or bequeathed by wills in writing, signed and sealed by him or her in whom the estate may be (being of full age), and attested by three witnesses; and real estates may be conveyed by lease and release, or bargain and sale, signed, sealed and delivered by the person being of full age, in whom the estate may be, and attested by two witnesses, provided such wills be duly proved, and such conveyances be acknowledged, or the execution thereof duly proved, and be recorded within one year after proper magistrates, courts, and registers shall be appointed for that purpose; and personal property may be transferred by delivery; saving, however to the French and Canadian inhabitants, and other settlers of the Kaskaskies, St. Vincents and the neighboring villages who have heretofore professed themselves citizens of Virginia, their laws and customs now in force among them, relative to the descent and conveyance, of property.

Sec. 3. Be it ordained by the authority aforesaid, That there shall be appointed from time to time by Congress, a governor, whose commission shall continue in force for the term of three years, unless sooner revoked by Congress; he shall reside in the district, and have a freehold estate therein in 1,000 acres of land, while in the exercise of his office.

Sec. 4. There shall be appointed from time to time by Congress, a secretary, whose commission shall continue in force for four years unless sooner revoked; he shall reside in the district, and have a freehold estate therein in 500 acres of land, while in the exercise of his office. It shall be his duty to keep and preserve the acts and laws passed by the legislature, and the public records of the district, and the proceedings of the governor in his executive department, and transmit authentic copies of such acts and proceedings, every six months, to the Secretary of Congress: There shall also be appointed a court to consist of three judges, any two of whom to form a court, who shall have a common law jurisdiction, and reside in the district, and have each therein a freehold estate in 500 acres of land while in the exercise of their offices; and their commissions shall continue in force during good behavior.

Sec. 5. The governor and judges, or a majority of them, shall adopt and publish in the district such laws of the original States, criminal and civil, as may be necessary and best suited to the circumstances of the district, and report them to Congress from time to time: which laws shall be in force in the district until the organization of the General Assembly therein, unless disapproved of by Congress; but afterwards the Legislature shall have authority to alter them as they shall think fit.

Sec. 6. The governor, for the time being, shall be commander in chief of the militia, appoint and commission all officers in the same below the rank of general officers; all general officers shall be appointed and commissioned by Congress.

Sec. 7. Previous to the organization of the general assembly, the governor shall appoint such magistrates and other civil officers in each county or township, as he shall find necessary for the preservation of the peace and good order in the same: After the general assembly shall be organized, the powers and duties of the magistrates and other civil officers shall be regulated and defined by the said assembly; but all magistrates and other civil officers not herein otherwise directed, shall during the continuance of this temporary government, be appointed by the governor.

Sec. 8. For the prevention of crimes and injuries, the laws to be adopted or made shall have force in all parts of the district, and for the execution of process, criminal and civil, the governor shall make proper divisions thereof; and he shall proceed from time to time as circumstances may require, to lay out the parts of the district in which the Indian titles shall have been extinguished, into counties and townships, subject, however, to such alterations as may thereafter be made by the legislature.

Sec. 9. So soon as there shall be five thousand free male inhabitants of full age in the district, upon giving proof thereof to the governor, they shall receive authority, with time and place, to elect a representative from their counties or townships to represent them in the general assembly: Provided, That, for every five hundred free male inhabitants, there shall be one representative, and so on progressively with the number of free male inhabitants shall the right of representation increase, until the number of representatives shall amount to twenty five; after which, the number and proportion of representatives shall be regulated by the legislature: Provided, That no person be eligible or qualified to act as a representative unless he shall have been a citizen of one of the United States three years, and be a resident in the district, or unless he shall have resided in the district three years; and, in either case, shall likewise hold in his own right, in fee simple, two hundred acres of land within the same; Provided, also, That a freehold in fifty acres of land in the district, having been a citizen of one of the states, and being resident in the district, or the like freehold and two years residence in the district, shall be necessary to qualify a man as an elector of a representative.

Sec. 10. The representatives thus elected, shall serve for the term of two years; and, in case of the death of a representative, or removal from office, the governor shall issue a writ to the county or township for which he was a member, to elect another in his stead, to serve for the residue of the term.

Sec. 11. The general assembly or legislature shall consist of the governor, legislative council, and a house of representatives. The Legislative Council shall consist of five members, to continue in office five years, unless sooner removed by Congress; any three of whom to be a quorum: and the members of the Council shall be nominated and appointed in the following manner, to wit: As soon as representatives shall be elected, the Governor shall appoint a time and place for them to meet together; and, when met, they shall nominate ten persons, residents in the district, and each possessed of a freehold in five hundred acres of land, and return their names to Congress; five of whom Congress shall appoint and commission to serve as aforesaid; and, whenever a vacancy shall happen in the council, by death or removal from office, the house of representatives shall nominate two persons, qualified as aforesaid, for each vacancy, and return their names to Congress; one of whom congress shall appoint and commission for the residue of the term. And every five years, four months at least before the expiration of the time of service of the members of council, the said house shall nominate ten persons, qualified as aforesaid, and return their names to Congress; five of whom Congress shall appoint and commission to serve as members of the council five years, unless sooner removed. And the governor, legislative council, and house of representatives, shall have authority to make laws in all cases, for the good government of the district, not repugnant to the principles and articles in this ordinance established and declared. And all bills, having passed by a majority in the house, and by a majority in the council, shall be referred to the governor for his assent; but no bill, or legislative act whatever, shall be of any force without his assent. The governor shall have power to convene, prorogue, and dissolve the general assembly, when, in his opinion, it shall be expedient.

Sec. 12. The governor, judges, legislative council, secretary, and such other officers as Congress shall appoint in the district, shall take an oath or affirmation of fidelity and of office; the governor before the president of congress, and all other officers before the Governor. As soon as a legislature shall be formed in the district, the council and house assembled in one room, shall have authority, by joint ballot, to elect a delegate to Congress, who shall have a seat in Congress, with a right of debating but not voting during this temporary government.

Sec. 13. And, for extending the fundamental principles of civil and religious liberty, which form the basis whereon these republics, their laws and constitutions are erected; to fix and establish those principles as the basis of all laws, constitutions, and governments, which forever hereafter shall be formed in the said territory: to provide also for the establishment of States, and permanent government therein, and for their admission to a share in the federal councils on an equal footing with the original States, at as early periods as may be consistent with the general interest:

Sec. 14. It is hereby ordained and declared by the authority aforesaid, That the following articles shall be considered as articles of compact between the original States and the people and States in the said territory and forever remain unalterable, unless by common consent, to wit:

Art. 1. No person, demeaning himself in a peaceable and orderly manner, shall ever be molested on account of his mode of worship or religious sentiments, in the said territory.

Art. 2. The inhabitants of the said territory shall always be entitled to the benefits of the writ of habeas corpus, and of the trial by jury; of a proportionate representation of the people in the legislature; and of judicial proceedings according to the course of the common law. All persons shall be bailable, unless for capital offenses, where the proof shall be evident or the presumption great. All fines shall be moderate; and no cruel or unusual punishments shall be inflicted. No man shall be deprived of his liberty or property, but by the judgment of his peers or the law of the land; and, should the public exigencies make it necessary, for the common preservation, to take any person's property, or to demand his particular services, full compensation shall be made for the same. And, in the just preservation of rights and property, it is understood and declared, that no law ought ever to be made, or have force in the said territory, that shall, in any manner whatever, interfere with or affect private contracts or engagements, bona fide, and without fraud, previously formed.

Art. 3. Religion, morality, and knowledge, being necessary to good government and the happiness of mankind, schools and the means of education shall forever be encouraged. The utmost good faith shall always be observed towards the Indians; their lands and property shall never be taken from them without their consent; and, in their property, rights, and liberty, they shall never be invaded or disturbed, unless in just and lawful wars authorized by Congress; but laws founded in justice and humanity, shall from time to time be made for preventing wrongs being done to them, and for preserving peace and friendship with them.

Art. 4. The said territory, and the States which may be formed therein, shall forever remain a part of this Confederacy of the United States of America, subject to the Articles of Confederation, and to such alterations therein as shall be constitutionally made; and to all the acts and ordinances of the United States in Congress assembled, conformable thereto. The inhabitants and settlers in the said territory shall be subject to pay a part of the federal debts contracted or to be contracted, and a proportional part of the expenses of government, to be apportioned on them by Congress according to the same common rule and measure by which apportionments thereof shall be made on the other States; and the taxes for paying their proportion shall be laid and levied by the authority and direction of the legislatures of the district or districts, or new States, as in the original States, within the time agreed upon by the United States in Congress assembled. The legislatures of those districts or new States, shall never interfere with the primary disposal of the soil by the United States in Congress assembled, nor with any regulations Congress may find necessary for securing the title in such soil to the bona fide purchasers. No tax shall be imposed on lands the property of the United States; and, in no case, shall nonresident proprietors be taxed higher than residents. The navigable waters leading into the Mississippi and St. Lawrence, and the carrying places between the same, shall be common highways and forever free, as well to the inhabitants of the said territory as to the citizens of the United States, and those of any other States that may be admitted into the confederacy, without any tax, impost, or duty therefor.

Art. 5. There shall be formed in the said territory, not less than three nor more than five States; and the boundaries of the States, as soon as Virginia shall alter her act of cession, and consent to the same, shall become fixed and established as follows, to wit: The western State in the said territory, shall be bounded by the Mississippi, the Ohio, and Wabash Rivers; a direct line drawn from the Wabash and Post Vincents, due North, to the territorial line between the United States and Canada; and, by the said territorial line, to the Lake of the Woods and Mississippi. The middle State shall be bounded by the said direct line, the Wabash from Post Vincents to the Ohio, by the Ohio, by a direct line, drawn due north from the mouth of the Great Miami, to the said territorial line, and by the said territorial line. The eastern State shall be bounded by the last mentioned direct line, the Ohio, Pennsylvania, and the said territorial line: Provided, however, and it is further understood and declared, that the boundaries of these three States shall be subject so far to be altered, that, if Congress shall hereafter find it expedient, they shall have authority to form one or two States in that part of the said territory which lies north of an east and west line drawn through the southerly bend or extreme of Lake Michigan. And, whenever any of the said States shall have sixty thousand free inhabitants therein, such State shall be admitted, by its delegates, into the Congress of the United States, on an equal footing with the original States in all respects whatever, and shall be at liberty to form a permanent constitution and State government: Provided, the constitution and government so to be formed, shall be republican, and in conformity to the principles contained in these articles; and, so far as it can be consistent with the general interest of the confederacy, such admission shall be allowed at an earlier period, and when there may be a less number of free inhabitants in the State than sixty thousand.

Art. 6. There shall be neither slavery nor involuntary servitude in the said territory, otherwise than in the punishment of crimes whereof the party shall have been duly convicted: Provided, always, That any person escaping into the same, from whom labor or service is lawfully claimed in any one of the original States, such fugitive may be lawfully reclaimed and conveyed to the person claiming his or her labor or service as aforesaid.

Be it ordained by the authority aforesaid, That the resolutions of the 23rd of April, 1784, relative to the subject of this ordinance, be, and the same are hereby repealed and declared null and void.

Done by the United States, in Congress assembled, the 13th day of July, in the year of our Lord 1787, and of their soveriegnty and independence the twelfth.

CONSTITUTIONAL CONVENTION

Constitution of the United States

Calls for a Constitutional Convention began shortly after Shays' Rebellion.
The Annapolis convention of 1786 set the stage for the Constitutional
Convention in Philadelphia in 1787. The Constitutional Convention
was originally intended to simply propose amendments to the Articles of
Confederation; instead, two plans were proposed that would jettison the
Articles of Confederation—the Virginia Plan and the New Jersey Plan.
The Virginia Plan was incorporated the Constitution in its entirety, while
only certain provisions from the New Jersey plan were added. Once the
document was drafted, it went to the individual states for ratification.
By January of 1788, Delaware, Pennsylvania, New Jersey, Georgia, and
Connecticut had ratified. Massachusetts, Maryland, South Carolina,
New Hampshire, and Virgiinia delayed ratification until a Bill of Rights
was provided for; these states all ratified by July of 1788. North Carolina
and Rhode Island ratified the Constituion in 1789 and 1790 respectively,
making the Constitution the law of the land in the newly formed United
States of America.

We the People of the United States, in Order to form a
more perfect Union, establish Justice, insure domestic
Tranquility, provide for the common defence, promote
the general Welfare, and secure the Blessings of Liberty to ourselves
and our Posterity, do ordain and establish this Constitution for the
United States of America.

ARTICLE. I.

SECTION. 1.

All legislative Powers herein granted shall be vested in a
Congress of the United States, which shall consist of a Senate and
House of Representatives.

SECTION. 2.

The House of Representatives shall be composed of Members
chosen every second Year by the People of the several States, and
the Electors in each State shall have the Qualifications requisite for
Electors of the most numerous Branch of the State Legislature.

No Person shall be a Representative who shall not have attained
to the Age of twenty five Years, and been seven Years a Citizen of
the United States, and who shall not, when elected, be an Inhabitant
of that State in which he shall be chosen.

Representatives and direct Taxes shall be apportioned among the
several States which may be included within this Union, according
to their respective Numbers, which shall be determined by adding to
the whole Number of free Persons, including those bound to Service
for a Term of Years, and excluding Indians not taxed, three fifths
of all other Persons. The actual Enumeration shall be made within
three Years after the first Meeting of the Congress of the United
States, and within every subsequent Term of ten Years, in such
Manner as they shall by Law direct. The Number of Representatives
shall not exceed one for every thirty Thousand, but each State
shall have at Least one Representative; and until such enumeration
shall be made, the State of New Hampshire shall be entitled to
chuse three, Massachusetts eight, Rhode-Island and Providence
Plantations one, Connecticut five, New-York six, New Jersey four,

Pennsylvania eight, Delaware one, Maryland six, Virginia ten, North Carolina five, South Carolina five, and Georgia three.

When vacancies happen in the Representation from any State, the Executive Authority thereof shall issue Writs of Election to fill such Vacancies.

The House of Representatives shall chuse their Speaker and other Officers; and shall have the sole Power of Impeachment.

SECTION. 3.

The Senate of the United States shall be composed of two Senators from each State, chosen by the Legislature thereof, for six Years; and each Senator shall have one Vote.

Immediately after they shall be assembled in Consequence of the first Election, they shall be divided as equally as may be into three Classes. The Seats of the Senators of the first Class shall be vacated at the Expiration of the second Year, of the second Class at the Expiration of the fourth Year, and of the third Class at the Expiration of the sixth Year, so that one third may be chosen every second Year; and if Vacancies happen by Resignation, or otherwise, during the Recess of the Legislature of any State, the Executive thereof may make temporary Appointments until the next Meeting of the Legislature, which shall then fill such Vacancies.

No Person shall be a Senator who shall not have attained to the Age of thirty Years, and been nine Years a Citizen of the United States, and who shall not, when elected, be an Inhabitant of that State for which he shall be chosen.

The Vice President of the United States shall be President of the Senate, but shall have no Vote, unless they be equally divided.

The Senate shall chuse their other Officers, and also a President pro tempore, in the Absence of the Vice President, or when he shall exercise the Office of President of the United States.

The Senate shall have the sole Power to try all Impeachments. When sitting for that Purpose, they shall be on Oath or Affirmation. When the President of the United States is tried, the Chief Justice shall preside: And no Person shall be convicted without the Concurrence of two thirds of the Members present.

Judgment in Cases of Impeachment shall not extend further than to removal from Office, and disqualification to hold and enjoy any Office of honor, Trust or Profit under the United States: but the Party convicted shall nevertheless be liable and subject to Indictment, Trial, Judgment and Punishment, according to Law.

SECTION. 4.

The Times, Places and Manner of holding Elections for Senators and Representatives, shall be prescribed in each State by the Legislature thereof; but the Congress may at any time by Law make or alter such Regulations, except as to the Places of chusing Senators.

The Congress shall assemble at least once in every Year, and such Meeting shall be on the first Monday in December, unless they shall by Law appoint a different Day.

SECTION. 5.

Each House shall be the Judge of the Elections, Returns and Qualifications of its own Members, and a Majority of each shall constitute a Quorum to do Business; but a smaller Number may adjourn from day to day, and may be authorized to compel the Attendance of absent Members, in such Manner, and under such Penalties as each House may provide.

Each House may determine the Rules of its Proceedings, punish its Members for disorderly Behaviour, and, with the Concurrence of two thirds, expel a Member.

Each House shall keep a Journal of its Proceedings, and from time to time publish the same, excepting such Parts as may in their Judgment require Secrecy; and the Yeas and Nays of the Members of either House on any question shall, at the Desire of one fifth of those Present, be entered on the Journal.

Neither House, during the Session of Congress, shall, without the Consent of the other, adjourn for more than three days, nor to any other Place than that in which the two Houses shall be sitting.

SECTION. 6.

The Senators and Representatives shall receive a Compensation for their Services, to be ascertained by Law, and paid out of the Treasury of the United States. They shall in all Cases, except Treason, Felony and Breach of the Peace, be privileged from Arrest during their Attendance at the Session of their respective Houses, and in going to and returning from the same; and for any Speech or Debate in either House, they shall not be questioned in any other Place.

No Senator or Representative shall, during the Time for which he was elected, be appointed to any civil Office under the Authority of the United States, which shall have been created, or the Emoluments whereof shall have been encreased during such time; and no Person holding any Office under the United States, shall be a Member of either House during his Continuance in Office.

SECTION. 7.

All Bills for raising Revenue shall originate in the House of Representatives; but the Senate may propose or concur with Amendments as on other Bills.

Every Bill which shall have passed the House of Representatives and the Senate, shall, before it become a Law, be presented to the President of the United States; If he approve he shall sign it, but if not he shall return it, with his Objections to that House in which it shall have originated, who shall enter the Objections at large on their Journal, and proceed to reconsider it. If after such Reconsideration two thirds of that House shall agree to pass the Bill, it shall be sent, together with the Objections, to the other House, by which it shall likewise be reconsidered, and if approved by two thirds of that House, it shall become a Law. But in all such Cases the Votes of both Houses shall be determined by yeas and Nays, and the Names of the Persons voting for and against the Bill shall be entered on the Journal of each House respectively. If any Bill shall not be returned by the President within ten Days (Sundays excepted) after it shall have been presented to him, the Same shall be a Law, in like Manner as if he had signed it, unless the Congress by their Adjournment prevent its Return, in which Case it shall not be a Law.

Every Order, Resolution, or Vote to which the Concurrence of the Senate and House of Representatives may be necessary (except on a question of Adjournment) shall be presented to the President of the United States; and before the Same shall take Effect, shall be approved by him, or being disapproved by him, shall be repassed by two thirds of the Senate and House of Representatives, according to the Rules and Limitations prescribed in the Case of a Bill.

SECTION. 8.

The Congress shall have Power To lay and collect Taxes, Duties, Imposts and Excises, to pay the Debts and provide for the common Defence and general Welfare of the United States; but all Duties, Imposts and Excises shall be uniform throughout the United States;

To borrow Money on the credit of the United States;

To regulate Commerce with foreign Nations, and among the several States, and with the Indian Tribes;

To establish an uniform Rule of Naturalization, and uniform Laws on the subject of Bankruptcies throughout the United States;

To coin Money, regulate the Value thereof, and of foreign Coin, and fix the Standard of Weights and Measures;

To provide for the Punishment of counterfeiting the Securities and current Coin of the United States;

To establish Post Offices and post Roads;

To promote the Progress of Science and useful Arts, by securing for limited Times to Authors and Inventors the exclusive Right to their respective Writings and Discoveries;

To constitute Tribunals inferior to the supreme Court;

To define and punish Piracies and Felonies committed on the high Seas, and Offences against the Law of Nations;

To declare War, grant Letters of Marque and Reprisal, and make Rules concerning Captures on Land and Water;

To raise and support Armies, but no Appropriation of Money to that Use shall be for a longer Term than two Years;

To provide and maintain a Navy;

To make Rules for the Government and Regulation of the land and naval Forces;

To provide for calling forth the Militia to execute the Laws of the Union, suppress Insurrections and repel Invasions;

To provide for organizing, arming, and disciplining, the Militia, and for governing such Part of them as may be employed in the Service of the United States, reserving to the States respectively, the Appointment of the Officers, and the Authority of training the Militia according to the discipline prescribed by Congress;

To exercise exclusive Legislation in all Cases whatsoever, over such District (not exceeding ten Miles square) as may, by Cession of particular States, and the Acceptance of Congress, become the Seat of the Government of the United States, and to exercise like Authority over all Places purchased by the Consent of the Legislature of the State in which the Same shall be, for the Erection of Forts, Magazines, Arsenals, dock-Yards, and other needful Buildings;—And

To make all Laws which shall be necessary and proper for carrying into Execution the foregoing Powers, and all other Powers vested by this Constitution in the Government of the United States, or in any Department or Officer thereof.

SECTION. 9.

The Migration or Importation of such Persons as any of the States now existing shall think proper to admit, shall not be prohibited by the Congress prior to the Year one thousand eight hundred and eight, but a Tax or duty may be imposed on such Importation, not exceeding ten dollars for each Person.

The Privilege of the Writ of Habeas Corpus shall not be suspended, unless when in Cases of Rebellion or Invasion the public Safety may require it.

No Bill of Attainder or ex post facto Law shall be passed.

No Capitation, or other direct, Tax shall be laid, unless in Proportion to the Census or enumeration herein before directed to be taken.

No Tax or Duty shall be laid on Articles exported from any State.

No Preference shall be given by any Regulation of Commerce or Revenue to the Ports of one State over those of another: nor shall Vessels bound to, or from, one State, be obliged to enter, clear, or pay Duties in another.

No Money shall be drawn from the Treasury, but in Consequence of Appropriations made by Law; and a regular Statement and Account of the Receipts and Expenditures of all public Money shall be published from time to time.

No Title of Nobility shall be granted by the United States: And no Person holding any Office of Profit or Trust under them, shall, without the Consent of the Congress, accept of any present,

Emolument, Office, or Title, of any kind whatever, from any King, Prince, or foreign State.

SECTION. 10.

No State shall enter into any Treaty, Alliance, or Confederation; grant Letters of Marque and Reprisal; coin Money; emit Bills of Credit; make any Thing but gold and silver Coin a Tender in Payment of Debts; pass any Bill of Attainder, ex post facto Law, or Law impairing the Obligation of Contracts, or grant any Title of Nobility.

No State shall, without the Consent of the Congress, lay any Imposts or Duties on Imports or Exports, except what may be absolutely necessary for executing it's inspection Laws: and the net Produce of all Duties and Imposts, laid by any State on Imports or Exports, shall be for the Use of the Treasury of the United States; and all such Laws shall be subject to the Revision and Controul of the Congress.

No State shall, without the Consent of Congress, lay any Duty of Tonnage, keep Troops, or Ships of War in time of Peace, enter into any Agreement or Compact with another State, or with a foreign Power, or engage in War, unless actually invaded, or in such imminent Danger as will not admit of delay.

ARTICLE. II.

SECTION. 1.

The executive Power shall be vested in a President of the United States of America. He shall hold his Office during the Term of four Years, and, together with the Vice President, chosen for the same Term, be elected, as follows

Each State shall appoint, in such Manner as the Legislature thereof may direct, a Number of Electors, equal to the whole Number of Senators and Representatives to which the State may be entitled in the Congress: but no Senator or Representative, or Person holding an Office of Trust or Profit under the United States, shall be appointed an Elector.

The Electors shall meet in their respective States, and vote by Ballot for two Persons, of whom one at least shall not be an Inhabitant of the same State with themselves. And they shall make a List of all the Persons voted for, and of the Number of Votes for each; which List they shall sign and certify, and transmit sealed to the Seat of the Government of the United States, directed to the President of the Senate. The President of the Senate shall, in the Presence of the Senate and House of Representatives, open all the Certificates, and the Votes shall then be counted. The Person having the greatest Number of Votes shall be the President, if such Number be a Majority of the whole Number of Electors appointed; and if there be more than one who have such Majority, and have an equal Number of Votes, then the House of Representatives shall immediately chuse by Ballot one of them for President; and if no Person have a Majority, then from the five highest on the List the said House shall in like Manner chuse the President. But in chusing the President, the Votes shall be taken by States, the Representation from each State having one Vote; A quorum for this Purpose shall consist of a Member or Members from two thirds of the States, and a Majority of all the States shall be necessary to a Choice. In every Case, after the Choice of the President, the Person having the greatest Number of Votes of the Electors shall be the Vice President. But if there should remain two or more who have equal Votes, the

Senate shall chuse from them by Ballot the Vice President.

The Congress may determine the Time of chusing the Electors, and the Day on which they shall give their Votes; which Day shall be the same throughout the United States.

No Person except a natural born Citizen, or a Citizen of the United States, at the time of the Adoption of this Constitution, shall be eligible to the Office of President; neither shall any Person be eligible to that Office who shall not have attained to the Age of thirty five Years, and been fourteen Years a Resident within the United States.

In Case of the Removal of the President from Office, or of his Death, Resignation, or Inability to discharge the Powers and Duties of the said Office, the Same shall devolve on the Vice President, and the Congress may by Law provide for the Case of Removal, Death, Resignation or Inability, both of the President and Vice President, declaring what Officer shall then act as President, and such Officer shall act accordingly, until the Disability be removed, or a President shall be elected.

The President shall, at stated Times, receive for his Services, a Compensation, which shall neither be encreased nor diminished during the Period for which he shall have been elected, and he shall not receive within that Period any other Emolument from the United States, or any of them.

Before he enter on the Execution of his Office, he shall take the following Oath or Affirmation:—"I do solemnly swear (or affirm) that I will faithfully execute the Office of President of the United States, and will to the best of my Ability, preserve, protect and defend the Constitution of the United States."

SECTION. 2.

The President shall be Commander in Chief of the Army and Navy of the United States, and of the Militia of the several States, when called into the actual Service of the United States; he may require the Opinion, in writing, of the principal Officer in each of the executive Departments, upon any Subject relating to the Duties of their respective Offices, and he shall have Power to grant Reprieves and Pardons for Offences against the United States, except in Cases of Impeachment.

He shall have Power, by and with the Advice and Consent of the Senate, to make Treaties, provided two thirds of the Senators present concur; and he shall nominate, and by and with the Advice and Consent of the Senate, shall appoint Ambassadors, other public Ministers and Consuls, Judges of the supreme Court, and all other Officers of the United States, whose Appointments are not herein otherwise provided for, and which shall be established by Law: but the Congress may by Law vest the Appointment of such inferior Officers, as they think proper, in the President alone, in the Courts of Law, or in the Heads of Departments.

The President shall have Power to fill up all Vacancies that may happen during the Recess of the Senate, by granting Commissions which shall expire at the End of their next Session.

SECTION. 3.

He shall from time to time give to the Congress Information of the State of the Union, and recommend to their Consideration such Measures as he shall judge necessary and expedient; he may, on extraordinary Occasions, convene both Houses, or either of them, and in Case of Disagreement between them, with Respect to the Time of Adjournment, he may adjourn them to such Time as he shall think proper; he shall receive Ambassadors and other public Ministers; he shall take Care that the Laws be faithfully executed, and shall Commission all the Officers of the United States.

SECTION. 4.

The President, Vice President and all civil Officers of the United States, shall be removed from Office on Impeachment for, and Conviction of, Treason, Bribery, or other high Crimes and Misdemeanors.

ARTICLE III.

SECTION. 1.

The judicial Power of the United States, shall be vested in one supreme Court, and in such inferior Courts as the Congress may from time to time ordain and establish. The Judges, both of the supreme and inferior Courts, shall hold their Offices during good Behaviour, and shall, at stated Times, receive for their Services, a Compensation, which shall not be diminished during their Continuance in Office.

SECTION. 2.

The judicial Power shall extend to all Cases, in Law and Equity, arising under this Constitution, the Laws of the United States, and Treaties made, or which shall be made, under their Authority;— to all Cases affecting Ambassadors, other public Ministers and Consuls;—to all Cases of admiralty and maritime Jurisdiction;— to Controversies to which the United States shall be a Party;—to

Controversies between two or more States;— between a State and Citizens of another State,—between Citizens of different States,— between Citizens of the same State claiming Lands under Grants of different States, and between a State, or the Citizens thereof, and foreign States, Citizens or Subjects.

In all Cases affecting Ambassadors, other public Ministers and Consuls, and those in which a State shall be Party, the supreme Court shall have original Jurisdiction. In all the other Cases before mentioned, the supreme Court shall have appellate Jurisdiction, both as to Law and Fact, with such Exceptions, and under such Regulations as the Congress shall make.

The Trial of all Crimes, except in Cases of Impeachment, shall be by Jury; and such Trial shall be held in the State where the said Crimes shall have been committed; but when not committed within any State, the Trial shall be at such Place or Places as the Congress may by Law have directed.

SECTION. 3.

Treason against the United States, shall consist only in levying War against them, or in adhering to their Enemies, giving them Aid and Comfort. No Person shall be convicted of Treason unless on the Testimony of two Witnesses to the same overt Act, or on Confession in open Court.

The Congress shall have Power to declare the Punishment of Treason, but no Attainder of Treason shall work Corruption of Blood, or Forfeiture except during the Life of the Person attainted.

ARTICLE. IV.

SECTION. 1.

Full Faith and Credit shall be given in each State to the public Acts, Records, and judicial Proceedings of every other State. And the Congress may by general Laws prescribe the Manner in which such Acts, Records and Proceedings shall be proved, and the Effect thereof.

SECTION. 2.

The Citizens of each State shall be entitled to all Privileges and Immunities of Citizens in the several States.

A Person charged in any State with Treason, Felony, or other Crime, who shall flee from Justice, and be found in another State, shall on Demand of the executive Authority of the State from which he fled, be delivered up, to be removed to the State having Jurisdiction of the Crime.

No Person held to Service or Labour in one State, under the Laws thereof, escaping into another, shall, in Consequence of any Law or Regulation therein, be discharged from such Service or Labour, but shall be delivered up on Claim of the Party to whom such Service or Labour may be due.

SECTION. 3.

New States may be admitted by the Congress into this Union; but no new State shall be formed or erected within the Jurisdiction of any other State; nor any State be formed by the Junction of two or more States, or Parts of States, without the Consent of the Legislatures of the States concerned as well as of the Congress.

The Congress shall have Power to dispose of and make all needful

Rules and Regulations respecting the Territory or other Property belonging to the United States; and nothing in this Constitution shall be so construed as to Prejudice any Claims of the United States, or of any particular State.

SECTION. 4.

The United States shall guarantee to every State in this Union a Republican Form of Government, and shall protect each of them against Invasion; and on Application of the Legislature, or of the Executive (when the Legislature cannot be convened), against domestic Violence.

ARTICLE. V.

The Congress, whenever two thirds of both Houses shall deem it necessary, shall propose Amendments to this Constitution, or, on the Application of the Legislatures of two thirds of the several States, shall call a Convention for proposing Amendments, which, in either Case, shall be valid to all Intents and Purposes, as Part of this Constitution, when ratified by the Legislatures of three fourths of the several States, or by Conventions in three fourths thereof, as the one or the other Mode of Ratification may be proposed by the Congress; Provided that no Amendment which may be made prior to the Year One thousand eight hundred and eight shall in any Manner affect the first and fourth Clauses in the Ninth Section of the first Article; and that no State, without its Consent, shall be deprived of its equal Suffrage in the Senate.

ARTICLE. VI.

All Debts contracted and Engagements entered into, before the Adoption of this Constitution, shall be as valid against the United States under this Constitution, as under the Confederation.

This Constitution, and the Laws of the United States which shall be made in Pursuance thereof; and all Treaties made, or which shall be made, under the Authority of the United States, shall be the supreme Law of the Land; and the Judges in every State shall be bound thereby, any Thing in the Constitution or Laws of any State to the Contrary notwithstanding.

The Senators and Representatives before mentioned, and the Members of the several State Legislatures, and all executive and judicial Officers, both of the United States and of the several States, shall be bound by Oath or Affirmation, to support this Constitution; but no religious Test shall ever be required as a Qualification to any Office or public Trust under the United States.

ARTICLE. VII.

The Ratification of the Conventions of nine States, shall be sufficient for the Establishment of this Constitution between the States so ratifying the Same.

George Washington, President and deputy from Virginia

NEW-HAMPSHIRE	John Langdon, Nicholas Gilman.
MASSACHUSETTS	Nathaniel Gorham, Rufus King.
RHODE-ISLAND	
CONNECTICUT	Wm. Saml. Johnson, Roger Sherman.
NEW-YORK	Alexander Hamilton.
NEW JERSEY	William Livingston, David Brearley, Wm. Paterson, Jona. Dayton.
PENNSYLVANIA	Benjamin Franklin, Robert Morris, Thomas Fitzsimmons, James Wilson, Thomas Mifflin, George Clymer, Jared Ingersoll, Gouverneur Morris.

DELAWARE — George Read, John Dickinson, Jacob Broom, Gunning Bedford, Jr., Richard Bassett.

MARYLAND — James McHenry, Daniel Carroll, Daniel of St. Thos. Jenifer.

VIRGINIA — John Blair, James Madison, Jr.

NORTH-CAROLINA — William Blount, Hugh Williamson, Richard Dobbs Spaight.

SOUTH-CAROLINA — John Rutledge, Charles Pinckney, Charles Cotesworth Pinckney, Pierce Butler.

GEORGIA — George William Few, Abraham Baldwin

Attest: William Jackson, Secretary

ALEXANDER HAMILTON

Federalist 1, 2, & 84

Alexander Hamilton, John Jay, and James Madison wrote eighty-five newspaper Essays in 1787-1788, under the penname Publius, arguing for the merits of the Constitution during the ratification debate in New York. These were later pulbished for wider distribution, and becme known as the Federalist Papers.

Alexander Hamilton was born in Charlestown, Nevis (British West Indies) in 1705. He traveled to the United States as a young man after both of his parents died where he attended King's College, graduating in May, 1774. An ardent spokesman for liberty, Hamilton worked closely with George Washington during the war. As President, Washington appointed Hamilton the first Secretary of the Treasury. A proponent of strong central government for that day —which pales in comparison to what we have today—Alexander Hamilton created the national bank. He was killed in a duel with his one-time friend, Aaron Burr, in 1804.

FEDERALIST 1

To the People of the State of New York:

AFTER an unequivocal experience of the inefficiency of the subsisting federal government, you are called upon to deliberate on a new Constitution for the United States of America. The subject speaks its own importance; comprehending in its consequences nothing less than the existence of the UNION, the safety and welfare of the parts of which it is composed, the fate of an empire in many respects the most interesting in the world. It has been frequently remarked that it seems to have been reserved to the people of this country, by their conduct and example, to

decide the important question, whether societies of men are really
capable or not of establishing good government from reflection
and choice, or whether they are forever destined to depend for their
political constitutions on accident and force. If there be any truth in
the remark, the crisis at which we are arrived may with propriety
be regarded as the era in which that decision is to be made; and a
wrong election of the part we shall act may, in this view, deserve
to be considered as the general misfortune of mankind. This idea
will add the inducements of philanthropy to those of patriotism, to
heighten the solicitude which all considerate and good men must feel
for the event. Happy will it be if our choice should be directed by a
judicious estimate of our true interests, unperplexed and unbiased
by considerations not connected with the public good. But this is
a thing more ardently to be wished than seriously to be expected.
The plan offered to our deliberations affects too many particular
interests, innovates upon too many local institutions, not to involve
in its discussion a variety of objects foreign to its merits, and of
views, passions and prejudices little favorable to the discovery of
truth.

Among the most formidable of the obstacles which the new
Constitution will have to encounter may readily be distinguished
the obvious interest of a certain class of men in every State to
resist all changes which may hazard a diminution of the power,
emolument, and consequence of the offices they hold under the State
establishments; and the perverted ambition of another class of men,
who will either hope to aggrandize themselves by the confusions
of their country, or will flatter themselves with fairer prospects
of elevation from the subdivision of the empire into several partial
confederacies than from its union under one government.

It is not, however, my design to dwell upon observations of this nature. I am well aware that it would be disingenuous to resolve indiscriminately the opposition of any set of men (merely because their situations might subject them to suspicion) into interested or ambitious views. Candor will oblige us to admit that even such men may be actuated by upright intentions; and it cannot be doubted that much of the opposition which has made its appearance, or may hereafter make its appearance, will spring from sources, blameless at least, if not respectable--the honest errors of minds led astray by preconceived jealousies and fears. So numerous indeed and so powerful are the causes which serve to give a false bias to the judgment, that we, upon many occasions, see wise and good men on the wrong as well as on the right side of questions of the first magnitude to society. This circumstance, if duly attended to, would furnish a lesson of moderation to those who are ever so much persuaded of their being in the right in any controversy. And a further reason for caution, in this respect, might be drawn from the reflection that we are not always sure that those who advocate the truth are influenced by purer principles than their antagonists. Ambition, avarice, personal animosity, party opposition, and many other motives not more laudable than these, are apt to operate as well upon those who support as those who oppose the right side of a question. Were there not even these inducements to moderation, nothing could be more ill-judged than that intolerant spirit which has, at all times, characterized political parties. For in politics, as in religion, it is equally absurd to aim at making proselytes by fire and sword. Heresies in either can rarely be cured by persecution.

And yet, however just these sentiments will be allowed to be, we have already sufficient indications that it will happen in this

as in all former cases of great national discussion. A torrent of
angry and malignant passions will be let loose. To judge from the
conduct of the opposite parties, we shall be led to conclude that they
will mutually hope to evince the justness of their opinions, and
to increase the number of their converts by the loudness of their
declamations and the bitterness of their invectives. An enlightened
zeal for the energy and efficiency of government will be stigmatized
as the offspring of a temper fond of despotic power and hostile to the
principles of liberty. An over-scrupulous jealousy of danger to the
rights of the people, which is more commonly the fault of the head
than of the heart, will be represented as mere pretense and artifice,
the stale bait for popularity at the expense of the public good. It will
be forgotten, on the one hand, that jealousy is the usual concomitant
of love, and that the noble enthusiasm of liberty is apt to be infected
with a spirit of narrow and illiberal distrust. On the other hand, it
will be equally forgotten that the vigor of government is essential
to the security of liberty; that, in the contemplation of a sound and
well-informed judgment, their interest can never be separated; and
that a dangerous ambition more often lurks behind the specious
mask of zeal for the rights of the people than under the forbidden
appearance of zeal for the firmness and efficiency of government.
History will teach us that the former has been found a much more
certain road to the introduction of despotism than the latter, and
that of those men who have overturned the liberties of republics, the
greatest number have begun their career by paying an obsequious
court to the people; commencing demagogues, and ending tyrants.

In the course of the preceding observations, I have had an eye,
my fellow-citizens, to putting you upon your guard against all
attempts, from whatever quarter, to influence your decision in a

matter of the utmost moment to your welfare, by any impressions
other than those which may result from the evidence of truth. You
will, no doubt, at the same time, have collected from the general
scope of them, that they proceed from a source not unfriendly
to the new Constitution. Yes, my countrymen, I own to you that,
after having given it an attentive consideration, I am clearly of
opinion it is your interest to adopt it. I am convinced that this is the
safest course for your liberty, your dignity, and your happiness.
I affect not reserves which I do not feel. I will not amuse you with
an appearance of deliberation when I have decided. I frankly
acknowledge to you my convictions, and I will freely lay before
you the reasons on which they are founded. The consciousness of
good intentions disdains ambiguity. I shall not, however, multiply
professions on this head. My motives must remain in the depository
of my own breast. My arguments will be open to all, and may be
judged of by all. They shall at least be offered in a spirit which will
not disgrace the cause of truth.

I propose, in a series of papers, to discuss the following
interesting particulars:

THE UTILITY OF THE UNION TO YOUR POLITICAL
PROSPERITY

THE INSUFFICIENCY OF THE PRESENT CONFEDERATION
TO PRESERVE THAT UNION

THE NECESSITY OF A GOVERNMENT AT LEAST
EQUALLY ENERGETIC WITH THE ONE PROPOSED, TO
THE ATTAINMENT OF THIS OBJECT THE CONFORMITY
OF THE PROPOSED CONSTITUTION TO THE TRUE
PRINCIPLES OF REPUBLICAN GOVERNMENT ITS

ANALOGY TO YOUR OWN STATE CONSTITUTION

and lastly, THE ADDITIONAL SECURITY WHICH ITS
ADOPTION WILL AFFORD TO THE PRESERVATION OF
THAT SPECIES OF GOVERNMENT, TO LIBERTY, AND TO
PROPERTY.

In the progress of this discussion I shall endeavor to give a
satisfactory answer to all the objections which shall have made their
appearance, that may seem to have any claim to your attention.

It may perhaps be thought superfluous to offer arguments to
prove the utility of the UNION, a point, no doubt, deeply engraved
on the hearts of the great body of the people in every State, and
one, which it may be imagined, has no adversaries. But the fact is,
that we already hear it whispered in the private circles of those who
oppose the new Constitution, that the thirteen States are of too great
extent for any general system, and that we must of necessity resort
to separate confederacies of distinct portions of the whole. This
doctrine will, in all probability, be gradually propagated, till it has
votaries enough to countenance an open avowal of it. For nothing
can be more evident, to those who are able to take an enlarged
view of the subject, than the alternative of an adoption of the new
Constitution or a dismemberment of the Union. It will therefore
be of use to begin by examining the advantages of that Union, the
certain evils, and the probable dangers, to which every State will be
exposed from its dissolution. This shall accordingly constitute the
subject of my next address.

Publius

FEDERALIST 2

To the People of the State of New York:

A firm Union will be of the utmost moment to the peace and liberty of the States, as a barrier against domestic faction and insurrection. It is impossible to read the history of the petty republics of Greece and Italy without feeling sensations of horror and disgust at the distractions with which they were continually agitated, and at the rapid succession of revolutions by which they were kept in a state of perpetual vibration between the extremes of tyranny and anarchy. If they exhibit occasional calms, these only serve as short-lived contrast to the furious storms that are to succeed. If now and then intervals of felicity open to view, we behold them with a mixture of regret, arising from the reflection that the pleasing scenes before us are soon to be overwhelmed by the tempestuous waves of sedition and party rage. If momentary rays of glory break forth from the gloom, while they dazzle us with a transient and fleeting brilliancy, they at the same time admonish us to lament that the vices of government should pervert the direction and tarnish the lustre of those bright talents and exalted endowments for which the favored soils that produced them have been so justly celebrated.

From the disorders that disfigure the annals of those republics the advocates of despotism have drawn arguments, not only against the forms of republican government, but against the very principles of civil liberty. They have decried all free government as inconsistent with the order of society, and have indulged themselves in malicious exultation over its friends and partisans. Happily for mankind, stupendous fabrics reared on the basis of liberty, which have flourished for ages, have, in a few glorious instances, refuted their gloomy sophisms. And, I trust, America will be the broad and solid foundation of other edifices, not less magnificent, which will be equally permanent monuments of their errors.

But it is not to be denied that the portraits they have sketched of republican government were too just copies of the originals from which they were taken. If it had been found impracticable to have devised models of a more perfect structure, the enlightened friends to liberty would have been obliged to abandon the cause of that species of government as indefensible. The science of politics, however, like most other sciences, has received great improvement. The efficacy of various principles is now well understood, which were either not known at all, or imperfectly known to the ancients. The regular distribution of power into distinct departments; the introduction of legislative balances and checks; the institution of courts composed of judges holding their offices during good behavior; the representation of the people in the legislature by deputies of their own election: these are wholly new discoveries, or have made their principal progress towards perfection in modern times. They are means, and powerful means, by which the excellences of republican government may be retained and its imperfections lessened or avoided. To this catalogue of circumstances that tend to the amelioration of popular systems of civil government, I shall venture, however novel it may appear to some, to add one more, on a principle which has been made the foundation of an objection to the new Constitution; I mean the ENLARGEMENT of the ORBIT within which such systems are to revolve, either in respect to the dimensions of a single State or to the consolidation of several smaller States into one great Confederacy. The latter is that which immediately concerns the object under consideration. It will,

however, be of use to examine the principle in its application to a
single State, which shall be attended to in another place.

The utility of a Confederacy, as well to suppress faction and
to guard the internal tranquillity of States, as to increase their
external force and security, is in reality not a new idea. It has been
practiced upon in different countries and ages, and has received the
sanction of the most approved writers on the subject of politics. The
opponents of the plan proposed have, with great assiduity, cited
and circulated the observations of Montesquieu on the necessity
of a contracted territory for a republican government. But they
seem not to have been apprised of the sentiments of that great man
expressed in another part of his work, nor to have adverted to the
consequences of the principle to which they subscribe with such
ready acquiescence.

When Montesquieu recommends a small extent for republics,
the standards he had in view were of dimensions far short of
the limits of almost every one of these States. Neither Virginia,
Massachusetts, Pennsylvania, New York, North Carolina, nor
Georgia can by any means be compared with the models from
which he reasoned and to which the terms of his description apply.
If we therefore take his ideas on this point as the criterion of
truth, we shall be driven to the alternative either of taking refuge
at once in the arms of monarchy, or of splitting ourselves into an
infinity of little, jealous, clashing, tumultuous commonwealths, the
wretched nurseries of unceasing discord, and the miserable objects
of universal pity or contempt. Some of the writers who have come
forward on the other side of the question seem to have been aware of
the dilemma; and have even been bold enough to hint at the division
of the larger States as a desirable thing. Such an infatuated policy,

such a desperate expedient, might, by the multiplication of petty offices, answer the views of men who possess not qualifications to extend their influence beyond the narrow circles of personal intrigue, but it could never promote the greatness or happiness of the people of America.

Referring the examination of the principle itself to another place, as has been already mentioned, it will be sufficient to remark here that, in the sense of the author who has been most emphatically quoted upon the occasion, it would only dictate a reduction of the SIZE of the more considerable MEMBERS of the Union, but would not militate against their being all comprehended in one confederate government. And this is the true question, in the discussion of which we are at present interested.

So far are the suggestions of Montesquieu from standing in opposition to a general Union of the States, that he explicitly treats of a confederate republic as the expedient for extending the sphere of popular government, and reconciling the advantages of monarchy with those of republicanism.

"It is very probable," (says he(1)) "that mankind would have been obliged at length to live constantly under the government of a single person, had they not contrived a kind of constitution that has all the internal advantages of a republican, together with the external force of a monarchical government. I mean a CONFEDERATE REPUBLIC."

"This form of government is a convention by which several smaller STATES agree to become members of a larger ONE, which they intend to form. It is a kind of assemblage of societies that constitute a new one, capable of increasing, by means of new

associations, till they arrive to such a degree of power as to be able
to provide for the security of the united body."

"A republic of this kind, able to withstand an external force, may
support itself without any internal corruptions. The form of this
society prevents all manner of inconveniences."

"If a single member should attempt to usurp the supreme
authority, he could not be supposed to have an equal authority
and credit in all the confederate states. Were he to have too great
influence over one, this would alarm the rest. Were he to subdue
a part, that which would still remain free might oppose him with
forces independent of those which he had usurped and overpower
him before he could be settled in his usurpation."

"Should a popular insurrection happen in one of the confederate
states the others are able to quell it. Should abuses creep into one
part, they are reformed by those that remain sound. The state may
be destroyed on one side, and not on the other; the confederacy may
be dissolved, and the confederates preserve their sovereignty."

"As this government is composed of small republics, it enjoys the
internal happiness of each; and with respect to its external situation,
it is possessed, by means of the association, of all the advantages of
large monarchies."

I have thought it proper to quote at length these interesting
passages, because they contain a luminous abridgment of the
principal arguments in favor of the Union, and must effectually
remove the false impressions which a misapplication of other parts
of the work was calculated to make. They have, at the same time, an
intimate connection with the more immediate design of this paper;

which is, to illustrate the tendency of the Union to repress domestic
faction and insurrection.

A distinction, more subtle than accurate, has been raised
between a CONFEDERACY and a CONSOLIDATION of the States.
The essential characteristic of the first is said to be, the restriction
of its authority to the members in their collective capacities,
without reaching to the individuals of whom they are composed.
It is contended that the national council ought to have no concern
with any object of internal administration. An exact equality of
suffrage between the members has also been insisted upon as a
leading feature of a confederate government. These positions are,
in the main, arbitrary; they are supported neither by principle nor
precedent. It has indeed happened, that governments of this kind
have generally operated in the manner which the distinction taken
notice of, supposes to be inherent in their nature; but there have
been in most of them extensive exceptions to the practice, which
serve to prove, as far as example will go, that there is no absolute
rule on the subject. And it will be clearly shown in the course of this
investigation that as far as the principle contended for has prevailed,
it has been the cause of incurable disorder and imbecility in the
government.

The definition of a CONFEDERATE REPUBLIC seems simply
to be "an assemblage of societies," or an association of two or more
states into one state. The extent, modifications, and objects of the
federal authority are mere matters of discretion. So long as the
separate organization of the members be not abolished; so long as
it exists, by a constitutional necessity, for local purposes; though
it should be in perfect subordination to the general authority of
the union, it would still be, in fact and in theory, an association

of states, or a confederacy. The proposed Constitution, so far
from implying an abolition of the State governments, makes them
constituent parts of the national sovereignty, by allowing them a
direct representation in the Senate, and leaves in their possession
certain exclusive and very important portions of sovereign power.
This fully corresponds, in every rational import of the terms, with
the idea of a federal government.

In the Lycian confederacy, which consisted of twenty-three
CITIES or republics, the largest were entitled to THREE votes
in the COMMON COUNCIL, those of the middle class to TWO,
and the smallest to ONE. The COMMON COUNCIL had the
appointment of all the judges and magistrates of the respective
CITIES. This was certainly the most, delicate species of interference
in their internal administration; for if there be any thing that
seems exclusively appropriated to the local jurisdictions, it is the
appointment of their own officers. Yet Montesquieu, speaking
of this association, says: "Were I to give a model of an excellent
Confederate Republic, it would be that of Lycia." Thus we perceive
that the distinctions insisted upon were not within the contemplation
of this enlightened civilian; and we shall be led to conclude, that they
are the novel refinements of an erroneous theory.

FEDERALIST 84

To the People of the State of New York:

IN THE course of the foregoing review of the Constitution, I
have taken notice of, and endeavored to answer most of the
objections which have appeared against it. There, however,
remain a few which either did not fall naturally under any particular
head or were forgotten in their proper places. These shall now be

discussed; but as the subject has been drawn into great length, I shall so far consult brevity as to comprise all my observations on these miscellaneous points in a single paper.

The most considerable of the remaining objections is that the plan of the convention contains no bill of rights. Among other answers given to this, it has been upon different occasions remarked that the constitutions of several of the States are in a similar predicament. I add that New York is of the number. And yet the opposers of the new system, in this State, who profess an unlimited admiration for its constitution, are among the most intemperate partisans of a bill of rights. To justify their zeal in this matter, they allege two things: one is that, though the constitution of New York has no bill of rights prefixed to it, yet it contains, in the body of it, various provisions in favor of particular privileges and rights, which, in substance amount to the same thing; the other is, that the Constitution adopts, in their full extent, the common and statute law of Great Britain, by which many other rights, not expressed in it, are equally secured.

To the first I answer, that the Constitution proposed by the convention contains, as well as the constitution of this State, a number of such provisions.

Independent of those which relate to the structure of the government, we find the following: Article 1, section 3, clause 7, "Judgment in cases of impeachment shall not extend further than to removal from office, and disqualification to hold and enjoy any office of honor, trust, or profit under the United States; but the party convicted shall, nevertheless, be liable and subject to indictment, trial, judgment, and punishment according to law." Section 9, of the same article, clause 2, "The privilege of the *writ of habeas corpus*

shall not be suspended, unless when in cases of rebellion or invasion
the public safety may require it." Clause 3, "No bill of attainder or
ex-post-facto law shall be passed." Clause 7, "No title of nobility
shall be granted by the United States; and no person holding any
office of profit or trust under them, shall, without the consent of
the Congress, accept of any present, emolument, office, or title of
any kind whatever, from any king, prince, or foreign state." Article
3, section 2, clause 3, "The trial of all crimes, except in cases of
impeachment, shall be by jury; and such trial shall be held in the
State where the said crimes shall have been committed; but when
not committed within any State, the trial shall be at such place or
places as the Congress may by law have directed." Section 3, of the
same article, "Treason against the United States shall consist only
in levying war against them, or in adhering to their enemies, giving
them aid and comfort. No person shall be convicted of treason,
unless on the testimony of two witnesses to the same overt act, or on
confession in open court." And clause 3, of the same section, "The
Congress shall have power to declare the punishment of treason; but
no attainder of treason shall work corruption of blood, or forfeiture,
except during the life of the person attainted."

It may well be a question, whether these are not, upon the
whole, of equal importance with any which are to be found in the
constitution of this State. The establishment of the writ of habeas
corpus, the prohibition of ex-post-facto laws, and of TITLES OF
NOBILITY, TO WHICH WE HAVE NO CORRESPONDING
PROVISION IN OUR CONSTITUTION, are perhaps greater
securities to liberty and republicanism than any it contains. The
creation of crimes after the commission of the fact, or, in other
words, the subjecting of men to punishment for things which,

when they were done, were breaches of no law, and the practice of arbitrary imprisonments, have been, in all ages, the favorite and most formidable instruments of tyranny. The observations of the judicious Blackstone, in reference to the latter, are well worthy of recital: "To bereave a man of life, — says he, — or by violence to confiscate his estate, without accusation or trial, would be so gross and notorious an act of despotism, as must at once convey the alarm of tyranny throughout the whole nation; but confinement of the person, by secretly hurrying him to jail, where his sufferings are unknown or forgotten, is a less public, a less striking, and therefore A MORE DANGEROUS ENGINE of arbitrary government." And as a remedy for this fatal evil he is everywhere peculiarly emphatical in his encomiums on the habeas-corpus act, which in one place he calls "the BULWARK of the British Constitution."

Nothing need be said to illustrate the importance of the prohibition of titles of nobility. This may truly be denominated the corner-stone of republican government; for so long as they are excluded, there can never be serious danger that the government will be any other than that of the people.

To the second that is, to the pretended establishment of the common and state law by the Constitution, I answer, that they are expressly made subject "to such alterations and provisions as the legislature shall from time to time make concerning the same." They are therefore at any moment liable to repeal by the ordinary legislative power, and of course have no constitutional sanction. The only use of the declaration was to recognize the ancient law and to remove doubts which might have been occasioned by the Revolution. This consequently can be considered as no part of a declaration of rights, which under our constitutions must be intended as limitations of the power of the government itself.

It has been several times truly remarked that bills of rights are, in their origin, stipulations between kings and their subjects, abridgements of prerogative in favor of privilege, reservations of rights not surrendered to the prince. Such was MAGNA CHARTA, obtained by the barons, sword in hand, from King John. Such were the subsequent confirmations of that charter by succeeding princes. Such was the PETITION OF RIGHT assented to by Charles I, in the beginning of his reign. Such, also, was the Declaration of Right presented by the Lords and Commons to the Prince of Orange in 1688, and afterwards thrown into the form of an act of parliament called the Bill of Rights. It is evident, therefore, that, according to their primitive signification, they have no application to constitutions professedly founded upon the power of the people, and executed by their immediate representatives and servants. Here, in strictness, the people surrender nothing; and as they retain every thing they have no need of particular reservations. "WE, THE PEOPLE of the United States, to secure the blessings of liberty to ourselves and our posterity, do ORDAIN and ESTABLISH this Constitution for the United States of America." Here is a better recognition of popular rights, than volumes of those aphorisms which make the principal figure in several of our State bills of rights, and which would sound much better in a treatise of ethics than in a constitution of government.

But a minute detail of particular rights is certainly far less applicable to a Constitution like that under consideration, which is merely intended to regulate the general political interests of the nation, than to a constitution which has the regulation of every

species of personal and private concerns. If, therefore, the loud
clamors against the plan of the convention, on this score, are
well founded, no epithets of reprobation will be too strong for the
constitution of this State. But the truth is, that both of them contain
all which, in relation to their objects, is reasonably to be desired.

I go further, and affirm that bills of rights, in the sense and to
the extent in which they are contended for, are not only unnecessary
in the proposed Constitution, but would even be dangerous. They
would contain various exceptions to powers not granted; and, on this
very account, would afford a colorable pretext to claim more than
were granted. For why declare that things shall not be done which
there is no power to do? Why, for instance, should it be said that the
liberty of the press shall not be restrained, when no power is given
by which restrictions may be imposed? I will not contend that such
a provision would confer a regulating power; but it is evident that
it would furnish, to men disposed to usurp, a plausible pretense for
claiming that power. They might urge with a semblance of reason,
that the Constitution ought not to be charged with the absurdity
of providing against the abuse of an authority which was not
given, and that the provision against restraining the liberty of the
press afforded a clear implication, that a power to prescribe proper
regulations concerning it was intended to be vested in the national
government. This may serve as a specimen of the numerous handles
which would be given to the doctrine of constructive powers, by the
indulgence of an injudicious zeal for bills of rights.

On the subject of the liberty of the press, as much as has
been said, I cannot forbear adding a remark or two: in the first
place, I observe, that there is not a syllable concerning it in the
constitution of this State; in the next, I contend, that whatever has

been said about it in that of any other State, amounts to nothing.
What signifies a declaration, that "the liberty of the press shall be
inviolably preserved"? What is the liberty of the press? Who can
give it any definition which would not leave the utmost latitude for
evasion? I hold it to be impracticable; and from this I infer, that
its security, whatever fine declarations may be inserted in any
constitution respecting it, must altogether depend on public opinion,
and on the general spirit of the people and of the government. And
here, after all, as is intimated upon another occasion, must we seek
for the only solid basis of all our rights.

There remains but one other view of this matter to conclude
the point. The truth is, after all the declamations we have heard,
that the Constitution is itself, in every rational sense, and to every
useful purpose, A BILL OF RIGHTS. The several bills of rights in
Great Britain form its Constitution, and conversely the constitution
of each State is its bill of rights. And the proposed Constitution, if
adopted, will be the bill of rights of the Union. Is it one object of
a bill of rights to declare and specify the political privileges of the
citizens in the structure and administration of the government?
This is done in the most ample and precise manner in the plan of
the convention; comprehending various precautions for the public
security, which are not to be found in any of the State constitutions.
Is another object of a bill of rights to define certain immunities and
modes of proceeding, which are relative to personal and private
concerns? This we have seen has also been attended to, in a variety
of cases, in the same plan. Adverting therefore to the substantial
meaning of a bill of rights, it is absurd to allege that it is not to be
found in the work of the convention. It may be said that it does not
go far enough, though it will not be easy to make this appear; but

it can with no propriety be contended that there is no such thing. It certainly must be immaterial what mode is observed as to the order of declaring the rights of the citizens, if they are to be found in any part of the instrument which establishes the government. And hence it must be apparent, that much of what has been said on this subject rests merely on verbal and nominal distinctions, entirely foreign from the substance of the thing.

Another objection which has been made, and which, from the frequency of its repetition, it is to be presumed is relied on, is of this nature: "It is improper — say the objectors — to confer such large powers, as are proposed, upon the national government, because the seat of that government must of necessity be too remote from many of the States to admit of a proper knowledge on the part of the constituent, of the conduct of the representative body." This argument, if it proves any thing, proves that there ought to be no general government whatever. For the powers which, it seems to be agreed on all hands, ought to be vested in the Union, cannot be safely intrusted to a body which is not under every requisite control. But there are satisfactory reasons to show that the objection is in reality not well founded. There is in most of the arguments which relate to distance a palpable illusion of the imagination. What are the sources of information by which the people in Montgomery County must regulate their judgment of the conduct of their representatives in the State legislature? Of personal observation they can have no benefit. This is confined to the citizens on the spot. They must therefore depend on the information of intelligent men, in whom they confide; and how must these men obtain their information? Evidently from the complexion of public measures, from the public prints, from correspondences with theirrepresentatives, and with other persons who reside at the place of their deliberations. This does not apply to Montgomery County only, but to all the counties at any considerable distance from the seat of government.

It is equally evident that the same sources of information would be open to the people in relation to the conduct of their representatives in the general government, and the impediments to a prompt communication which distance may be supposed to create, will be overbalanced by the effects of the vigilance of the State governments. The executive and legislative bodies of each State will be so many sentinels over the persons employed in every department of the national administration; and as it will be in their power to adopt and pursue a regular and effectual system of intelligence, they can never be at a loss to know the behavior of those who represent their constituents in the national councils, and can readily communicate the same knowledge to the people. Their disposition to apprise the community of whatever may prejudice its interests from another quarter, may be relied upon, if it were only from the rivalship of power. And we may conclude with the fullest assurance that the people, through that channel, will be better informed of the conduct of their national representatives, than they can be by any means they now possess of that of their State representatives.

It ought also to be remembered that the citizens who inhabit the country at and near the seat of government will, in all questions that affect the general liberty and prosperity, have the same interest with those who are at a distance, and that they will stand ready to sound the alarm when necessary, and to point out the actors in any pernicious project. The public papers will be expeditious messengers of intelligence to the most remote inhabitants of the Union.

Among the many curious objections which have appeared against the proposed Constitution, the most extraordinary and the least colorable is derived from the want of some provision respecting the debts due TO the United States. This has been represented as a tacit relinquishment of those debts, and as a wicked contrivance to screen public defaulters. The newspapers have teemed with the most inflammatory railings on this head; yet there is nothing clearer than that the suggestion is entirely void of foundation, the of fspring of extreme ignorance or extreme dishonesty. In addition to the remarks I have made upon the subject in another place, I shall only observe that as it is a plain dictate of common-sense, so it is also an established doctrine of political law, that "STATES NEITHER LOSE ANY OF THEIR RIGHTS, NOR ARE DISCHARGED FROM ANY OF THEIR OBLIGATIONS, BY A CHANGE IN THE FORM OF THEIR CIVIL GOVERNMENT." The last objection of any consequence, which I at present recollect, turns upon the article of expense. If it were even true, that the adoption of the proposed government would occasion a considerable increase of expense, it would be an objection that ought to have no weight against the plan.

The great bulk of the citizens of America are with reason convinced, that Union is the basis of their political happiness. Men of sense of all parties now, with few exceptions, agree that it cannot be preserved under the present system, nor without radical alterations; that new and extensive powers ought to be granted to the national head, and that these require a different organization of the federal government a single body being an unsafe depositary of such ample authorities. In conceding all this, the question of expense must be

given up; for it is impossible, with any degree of safety, to narrow
the foundation upon which the system is to stand. The two branches
of the legislature are, in the first instance, to consist of only sixty-
five persons, which is the same number of which Congress, under
the existing Confederation, may be composed. It is true that this
number is intended to be increased; but this is to keep pace with
the progress of the population and resources of the country. It is
evident that a less number would, even in the first instance, have
been unsafe, and that a continuance of the present number would,
in a more advanced stage of population, be a very inadequate
representation of the people.

Whence is the dreaded augmentation of expense to spring?
One source indicated, is the multiplication of offices under the new
government. Let us examine this a little.

It is evident that the principal departments of the administration
under the present government, are the same which will be required
under the new. There are now a Secretary of War, a Secretary
of Foreign Affairs, a Secretary for Domestic Affairs, a Board
of Treasury, consisting of three persons, a Treasurer, assistants,
clerks, etc. These officers are indispensable under any system, and
will suffice under the new as well as the old. As to ambassadors
and other ministers and agents in foreign countries, the proposed
Constitution can make no other difference than to render their
characters, where they reside, more respectable, and their services
more useful. As to persons to be employed in the collection of
the revenues, it is unquestionably true that these will form a very
considerable addition to the number of federal officers; but it will
not follow that this will occasion an increase of public expense. It
will be in most cases nothing more than an exchange of State for

national officers. In the collection of all duties, for instance, the persons employed will be wholly of the latter description. The States individually will stand in no need of any for this purpose. What difference can it make in point of expense to pay officers of the customs appointed by the State or by the United States? There is no good reason to suppose that either the number or the salaries of the latter will be greater than those of the former.

Where then are we to seek for those additional articles of expense which are to swell the account to the enormous size that has been represented to us? The chief item which occurs to me respects the support of the judges of the United States. I do not add the President, because there is now a president of Congress, whose expenses may not be far, if any thing, short of those which will be incurred on account of the President of the United States. The support of the judges will clearly be an extra expense, but to what extent will depend on the particular plan which may be adopted in regard to this matter. But upon no reasonable plan can it amount to a sum which will be an object of material consequence.

Let us now see what there is to counterbalance any extra expense that may attend the establishment of the proposed government. The first thing which presents itself is that a great part of the business which now keeps Congress sitting through the year will be transacted by the President. Even the management of foreign negotiations will naturally devolve upon him, according to general principles concerted with the Senate, and subject to their final concurrence. Hence it is evident that a portion of the year will suffice for the session of both the Senate and the House of Representatives; we may suppose about a fourth for the latter and a third, or perhaps half, for the former. The extra business of treaties and appointments may give this extra occupation to the Senate. From this circumstance we may infer that, until the House of Representatives shall be increased greatly beyond its present number, there will be a considerable saving of expense from the difference between the constant session of the present and the temporary session of the future Congress.

But there is another circumstance of great importance in the view of economy. The business of the United States has hitherto occupied the State legislatures, as well as Congress. The latter has made requisitions which the former have had to provide for. Hence it has happened that the sessions of the State legislatures have been protracted greatly beyond what was necessary for the execution of the mere local business of the States. More than half their time has been frequently employed in matters which related to the United States. Now the members who compose the legislatures of the several States amount to two thousand and upwards, which number has hitherto performed what under the new system will be done in the first instance by sixty-five persons, and probably at no future period by above a fourth or fifth of that number. The Congress under the proposed government will do all the business of the United States themselves, without the intervention of the State legislatures, who thenceforth will have only to attend to the affairs of their particular States, and will not have to sit in any proportion as long as they have heretofore done. This difference in the time of the sessions of the State legislatures will be clear gain, and will alone form an article of saving, which may be regarded as an equivalent for any additional objects of expense that may be occasioned by the adoption of the new system.

The result from these observations is that the sources of additional expense from the establishment of the proposed Constitution are much fewer than may have been imagined; that they are counterbalanced by considerable objects of saving; and that while it is questionable on which side the scale will preponderate, it is certain that a government less expensive would be incompetent to the purposes of the Union.

Publius

JOHN JAY

Federalist 2

Founding Father John Jay (1745-1829) served as the first Chief Justice of the United States. Earlier, he had served as President of the Second Continental Congress, but having been recalled by his home state of New York in May, he was not present when the Declaration of Independence was signed in July, 1776. After the War for Independence, Jay helped to negotiate the Treaty of Paris. When his term as Chief Justice was over in 1795, he served as Governor of New York for several years.Although he was nominated for a second term by President John Adams and confirmed by the Senate, he chose instead to retire and return home to his farm.

FEDERALIST 2

To the People of the State of New York:

When the people of America reflect that they are now called upon to decide a question, which, in its consequences, must prove one of the most important that ever engaged their attention, the propriety of their taking a very comprehensive, as well as a very serious, view of it, will be evident.

Nothing is more certain than the indispensable necessity of government, and it is equally undeniable, that whenever and however it is instituted, the people must cede to it some of their natural rights in order to vest it with requisite powers. It is well worthy of consideration therefore, whether it would conduce more to the interest of the people of America that they should, to all general purposes, be one nation, under one federal government, or that they should divide themselves into separate confederacies, and give to the head of each the same kind of powers which they are advised to place in one national government.

It has until lately been a received and uncontradicted opinion that the prosperity of the people of America depended on their continuing firmly united, and the wishes, prayers, and efforts of our best and wisest citizens have been constantly directed to that object. But politicians now appear, who insist that this opinion is erroneous, and that instead of looking for safety and happiness in union, we ought to seek it in a division of the States into distinct confederacies or sovereignties. However extraordinary this new doctrine may appear, it nevertheless has its advocates; and certain characters who were much opposed to it formerly, are at present of the number. Whatever may be the arguments or inducements which have wrought this change in the sentiments and declarations of these gentlemen, it certainly would not be wise in the people at large to adopt these new political tenets without being fully convinced that they are founded in truth and sound policy.

It has often given me pleasure to observe that independent America was not composed of detached and distant territories, but that one connected, fertile, wide-spreading country was the portion of our western sons of liberty. Providence has in a particular manner blessed it with a variety of soils and productions, and watered it with innumerable streams, for the delight and accommodation of its inhabitants. A succession of navigable waters forms a kind of chain round its borders, as if to bind it together; while the most noble rivers in the world, running at convenient distances, present them with highways for the easy communication of friendly aids, and the mutual transportation and exchange of their various commodities.

With equal pleasure I have as often taken notice that Providence has been pleased to give this one connected country to one united people—a people descended from the same ancestors, speaking the same language, professing the same religion, attached to the same principles of government, very similar in their manners and customs, and who, by their joint counsels, arms, and efforts, fighting side by side throughout a long and bloody war, have nobly established general liberty and independence.

This country and this people seem to have been made for each other, and it appears as if it was the design of Providence, that an inheritance so proper and convenient for a band of brethren, united to each other by the strongest ties, should never be split into a number of unsocial, jealous, and alien sovereignties.

Similar sentiments have hitherto prevailed among all orders and denominations of men among us. To all general purposes we have uniformly been one people each individual citizen everywhere enjoying the same national rights, privileges, and protection. As a nation we have made peace and war; as a nation we have vanquished our common enemies; as a nation we have formed alliances, and made treaties, and entered into various compacts and conventions with foreign states.

A strong sense of the value and blessings of union induced the people, at a very early period, to institute a federal government to preserve and perpetuate it. They formed it almost as soon as they had a political existence; nay, at a time when their habitations were in flames, when many of their citizens were bleeding, and when the progress of hostility and desolation left little room for those calm and mature inquiries and reflections which must ever precede the formation of a wise and well-balanced government for a free people. It is not to be wondered at, that a government instituted in times so inauspicious, should on experiment be found greatly deficient and inadequate to the purpose it was intended to answer.

This intelligent people perceived and regretted these defects. Still continuing no less attached to union than enamored of liberty, they observed the danger which immediately threatened the former and more remotely the latter; and being persuaded that ample security for both could only be found in a national government more wisely framed, they as with one voice, convened the late convention at Philadelphia, to take that important subject under consideration.

This convention composed of men who possessed the confidence of the people, and many of whom had become highly distinguished by their patriotism, virtue and wisdom, in times which tried the minds and hearts of men, undertook the arduous task. In the mild season of peace, with minds unoccupied by other subjects, they passed many months in cool, uninterrupted, and daily consultation; and finally, without having been awed by power, or influenced by any passions except love for their country, they presented and recommended to the people the plan produced by their joint and very unanimous councils.

Admit, for so is the fact, that this plan is only RECOMMENDED, not imposed, yet let it be remembered that it is neither recommended to BLIND approbation, nor to BLIND reprobation; but to that sedate and candid consideration which the magnitude and importance of the subject demand, and which it certainly ought to receive. But this (as was remarked in the foregoing number of this paper) is more to be wished than expected,

that it may be so considered and examined. Experience on a former
occasion teaches us not to be too sanguine in such hopes. It is
not yet forgotten that well-grounded apprehensions of imminent
danger induced the people of America to form the memorable
Congress of 1774. That body recommended certain measures to their
constituents, and the event proved their wisdom; yet it is fresh in
our memories how soon the press began to teem with pamphlets and
weekly papers against those very measures. Not only many of the
officers of government, who obeyed the dictates of personal interest,
but others, from a mistaken estimate of consequences, or the undue
influence of former attachments, or whose ambition aimed at objects
which did not correspond with the public good, were indefatigable
in their efforts to persuade the people to reject the advice of that
patriotic Congress. Many, indeed, were deceived and deluded, but
the great majority of the people reasoned and decided judiciously;
and happy they are in reflecting that they did so.

They considered that the Congress was composed of many wise
and experienced men. That, being convened from different parts
of the country, they brought with them and communicated to each
other a variety of useful information. That, in the course of the
time they passed together in inquiring into and discussing the true
interests of their country, they must have acquired very accurate
knowledge on that head. That they were individually interested in
the public liberty and prosperity, and therefore that it was not less
their inclination than their duty to recommend only such measures
as, after the most mature deliberation, they really thought prudent
and advisable.

These and similar considerations then induced the people to
rely greatly on the judgment and integrity of the Congress; and

they took their advice, notwithstanding the various arts and
endeavors used to deter them from it. But if the people at large
had reason to confide in the men of that Congress, few of whom
had been fully tried or generally known, still greater reason have
they now to respect the judgment and advice of the convention,
for it is well known that some of the most distinguished members
of that Congress, who have been since tried and justly approved
for patriotism and abilities, and who have grown old in acquiring
political information, were also members of this convention, and
carried into it their accumulated knowledge and experience.

It is worthy of remark that not only the first, but every
succeeding Congress, as well as the late convention, have invariably
joined with the people in thinking that the prosperity of America
depended on its Union. To preserve and perpetuate it was the
great object of the people in forming that convention, and it is
also the great object of the plan which the convention has advised
them to adopt. With what propriety, therefore, or for what
good purposes, are attempts at this particular period made by
some men to depreciate the importance of the Union? Or why
is it suggested that three or four confederacies would be better
than one? I am persuaded in my own mind that the people have
always thought right on this subject, and that their universal and
uniform attachment to the cause of the Union rests on great and
weighty reasons, which I shall endeavor to develop and explain in
some ensuing papers. They who promote the idea of substituting
a number of distinct confederacies in the room of the plan of the
convention, seem clearly to foresee that the rejection of it would put
the continuance of the Union in the utmost jeopardy. That certainly
would be the case, and I sincerely wish that it may be as clearly

foreseen by every good citizen, that whenever the dissolution of the Union arrives, America will have reason to exclaim, in the words of the poet: "FAREWELL! A LONG FAREWELL TO ALL MY GREATNESS."

Publius

JAMES MADISON

Federalist 10 & 51

Virginian James Madison (1751-1836) is known as the "Father of the Consitution," so important were his contributions to both its composition and its ratification. He served in the Continental Congress, and later in the House of Representatives. He was appointed Secretary of State under President Thomas Jefferson, and elected as the fourth President of the United States in 1809.

FEDERALIST 10

To the People of the State of New York:

Among the numerous advantages promised by a well constructed Union, none deserves to be more accurately developed than its tendency to break and control the violence of faction. The friend of popular governments never finds himself so much alarmed for their character and fate, as when he contemplates their propensity to this dangerous vice. He will not fail, therefore, to set a due value on any plan which, without violating the principles to which he is attached, provides a proper cure for it. The instability, injustice, and confusion introduced into the public councils, have, in truth, been the mortal diseases under which popular governments have everywhere perished; as they continue to be the favorite and fruitful topics from which the adversaries to liberty derive their most specious declamations. The valuable improvements made by the American constitutions on the popular models, both ancient and modern, cannot certainly be too much admired; but it would be an unwarrantable partiality, to contend that they have as effectually obviated the danger on this side, as was wished and expected. Complaints are everywhere heard from our most considerate and virtuous citizens, equally the friends of public and private faith, and of public and personal liberty, that our governments are too unstable, that the public good is disregarded in the conflicts of rival parties, and that measures are too often decided, not according to the rules of justice and the rights of the minor party, but by the superior force of an interested and overbearing majority. However anxiously we may wish that these complaints had no foundation, the evidence, of known facts will not permit us to deny that they are in some degree true. It will be found, indeed, on a candid review of our situation, that some of the distresses under which we labor have been erroneously charged on the operation of our governments; but it will be found, at the same time, that other causes will not alone account for many of our heaviest misfortunes; and, particularly, for that prevailing and increasing distrust of public engagements, and alarm for private rights, which are echoed from one end of the continent to the other. These must be chiefly, if not wholly, effects of the unsteadiness and injustice with which a factious spirit has tainted our public administrations.

By a faction, I understand a number of citizens, whether amounting to a majority or a minority of the whole, who are united and actuated by some common impulse of passion, or of interest, adversed to the rights of other citizens, or to the permanent and aggregate interests of the community.

There are two methods of curing the mischiefs of faction: the ving its causes; the other, by controlling its effects.

There are again two methods of removing the causes of faction: the one, by destroying the liberty which is essential to its existence; the other, by giving to every citizen the same opinions, the same passions, and the same interests.

It could never be more truly said than of the first remedy, that it was worse than the disease. Liberty is to faction what air is to fire, an aliment without which it instantly expires. But it could not be less folly to abolish liberty, which is essential to political life, because it nourishes faction, than it would be to wish the annihilation of air, which is essential to animal life, because it imparts to fire its destructive agency.

The second expedient is as impracticable as the first would be unwise. As long as the reason of man continues fallible, and he is at liberty to exercise it, different opinions will be formed. As long as the connection subsists between his reason and his self-love, his opinions and his passions will have a reciprocal influence on each other; and the former will be objects to which the latter will attach themselves. The diversity in the faculties of men, from which the rights of property originate, is not less an insuperable obstacle to a uniformity of interests. The protection of these faculties is the first object of government. From the protection of different and unequal faculties of acquiring property, the possession of different degrees and kinds of property immediately results; and from the influence of these on the sentiments and views of the respective proprietors, ensues a division of the society into different interests and parties.

The latent causes of faction are thus sown in the nature of man; and we see them everywhere brought into different degrees of activity, according to the different circumstances of civil society.

A zeal for different opinions concerning religion, concerning government, and many other points, as well of speculation as of practice; an attachment to different leaders ambitiously contending for pre-eminence and power; or to persons of other descriptions whose fortunes have been interesting to the human passions, have, in turn, divided mankind into parties, inflamed them with mutual animosity, and rendered them much more disposed to vex and oppress each other than to co-operate for their common good. So strong is this propensity of mankind to fall into mutual animosities, that where no substantial occasion presents itself, the most frivolous and fanciful distinctions have been sufficient to kindle their unfriendly passions and excite their most violent conflicts. But the most common and durable source of factions has been the various and unequal distribution of property. Those who hold and those who are without property have ever formed distinct interests in society. Those who are creditors, and those who are debtors, fall under a like discrimination. A landed interest, a manufacturing interest, a mercantile interest, a moneyed interest, with many lesser interests, grow up of necessity in civilized nations, and divide them into different classes, actuated by different sentiments and views. The regulation of these various and interfering interests forms the principal task of modern legislation, and involves the spirit of party and faction in the necessary and ordinary operations of the government.

No man is allowed to be a judge in his own cause, because his interest would certainly bias his judgment, and, not improbably, corrupt his integrity. With equal, nay with greater reason, a body of men are unfit to be both judges and parties at the same time; yet what are many of the most important acts of legislation, but so

many judicial determinations, not indeed concerning the rights of
single persons, but concerning the rights of large bodies of citizens?
And what are the different classes of legislators but advocates
and parties to the causes which they determine? Is a law proposed
concerning private debts? It is a question to which the creditors are
parties on one side and the debtors on the other. Justice ought to
hold the balance between them. Yet the parties are, and must be,
themselves the judges; and the most numerous party, or, in other
words, the most powerful faction must be expected to prevail. Shall
domestic manufactures be encouraged, and in what degree, by
restrictions on foreign manufactures? are questions which would be
differently decided by the landed and the manufacturing classes, and
probably by neither with a sole regard to justice and the public good.
The apportionment of taxes on the various descriptions of property
is an act which seems to require the most exact impartiality; yet
there is, perhaps, no legislative act in which greater opportunity and
temptation are given to a predominant party to trample on the rules
of justice. Every shilling with which they overburden the inferior
number, is a shilling saved to their own pockets.

It is in vain to say that enlightened statesmen will be able to
adjust these clashing interests, and render them all subservient to the
public good. Enlightened statesmen will not always be at the helm.
Nor, in many cases, can such an adjustment be made at all without
taking into view indirect and remote considerations, which will
rarely prevail over the immediate interest which one party may find
in disregarding the rights of another or the good of the whole.

The inference to which we are brought is, that the CAUSES of
faction cannot be removed, and that relief is only to be sought in the
means of controlling its EFFECTS.

If a faction consists of less than a majority, relief is supplied by the republican principle, which enables the majority to defeat its sinister views by regular vote. It may clog the administration, it may convulse the society; but it will be unable to execute and mask its violence under the forms of the Constitution. When a majority is included in a faction, the form of popular government, on the other hand, enables it to sacrifice to its ruling passion or interest both the public good and the rights of other citizens. To secure the public good and private rights against the danger of such a faction, and at the same time to preserve the spirit and the form of popular government, is then the great object to which our inquiries are directed. Let me add that it is the great desideratum by which this form of government can be rescued from the opprobrium under which it has so long labored, and be recommended to the esteem and adoption of mankind.

By what means is this object attainable? Evidently by one of two only. Either the existence of the same passion or interest in a majority at the same time must be prevented, or the majority, having such coexistent passion or interest, must be rendered, by their number and local situation, unable to concert and carry into effect schemes of oppression. If the impulse and the opportunity be suffered to coincide, we well know that neither moral nor religious motives can be relied on as an adequate control. They are not found to be such on the injustice and violence of individuals, and lose their efficacy in proportion to the number combined together, that is, in proportion as their efficacy becomes needful.

From this view of the subject it may be concluded that a pure democracy, by which I mean a society consisting of a small number of citizens, who assemble and administer the government in person, can admit of no cure for the mischiefs of faction. A common passion or interest will, in almost every case, be felt by a majority of the whole; a communication and concert result from the form of government itself; and there is nothing to check the inducements to sacrifice the weaker party or an obnoxious individual. Hence it is that such democracies have ever been spectacles of turbulence and contention; have ever been found incompatible with personal security or the rights of property; and have in general been as short in their lives as they have been violent in their deaths. Theoretic politicians, who have patronized this species of government, have erroneously supposed that by reducing mankind to a perfect equality in their political rights, they would, at the same time, be perfectly equalized and assimilated in their possessions, their opinions, and their passions.

A republic, by which I mean a government in which the scheme of representation takes place, opens a different prospect, and promises the cure for which we are seeking. Let us examine the points in which it varies from pure democracy, and we shall comprehend both the nature of the cure and the efficacy which it must derive from the Union.

The two great points of difference between a democracy and a republic are: first, the delegation of the government, in the latter, to a small number of citizens elected by the rest; secondly, the greater number of citizens, and greater sphere of country, over which the latter may be extended.

The effect of the first difference is, on the one hand, to refine and enlarge the public views, by passing them through the medium of a chosen body of citizens, whose wisdom may best discern the true interest of their country, and whose patriotism and love of justice will be least likely to sacrifice it to temporary or partial considerations. Under such a regulation, it may well happen that the public voice, pronounced by the representatives of the people, will be more consonant to the public good than if pronounced by the people themselves, convened for the purpose. On the other hand, the effect may be inverted. Men of factious tempers, of local prejudices, or of sinister designs, may, by intrigue, by corruption, or by other means, first obtain the suffrages, and then betray the interests, of the people. The question resulting is, whether small or extensive republics are more favorable to the election of proper guardians of the public weal; and it is clearly decided in favor of the latter by two obvious considerations:

In the first place, it is to be remarked that, however small the republic may be, the representatives must be raised to a certain number, in order to guard against the cabals of a few; and that, however large it may be, they must be limited to a certain number, in order to guard against the confusion of a multitude. Hence, the number of representatives in the two cases not being in proportion to that of the two constituents, and being proportionally greater in the small republic, it follows that, if the proportion of fit characters be not less in the large than in the small republic, the former will present a greater option, and consequently a greater probability of a fit choice.

In the next place, as each representative will be chosen by a greater number of citizens in the large than in the small republic, it will be more difficult for unworthy candidates to practice with success the vicious arts by which elections are too often carried; and the suffrages of the people being more free, will be more likely to centre in men who possess the most attractive merit and the most diffusive and established characters.

It must be confessed that in this, as in most other cases, there is a mean, on both sides of which inconveniences will be found to lie. By enlarging too much the number of electors, you render the representatives too little acquainted with all their local circumstances and lesser interests; as by reducing it too much, you render him unduly attached to these, and too little fit to comprehend and pursue great and national objects. The federal Constitution forms a happy combination in this respect; the great and aggregate interests being referred to the national, the local and particular to the State legislatures.

The other point of difference is, the greater number of citizens and extent of territory which may be brought within the compass of republican than of democratic government; and it is this circumstance principally which renders factious combinations less to be dreaded in the former than in the latter. The smaller the society, the fewer probably will be the distinct parties and interests composing it; the fewer the distinct parties and interests, the more frequently will a majority be found of the same party; and the smaller the number of individuals composing a majority, and the smaller the compass within which they are placed, the more easily will they concert and execute their plans of oppression. Extend the sphere, and you take in a greater variety of parties and interests; you make it less probable that a majority of the whole will have a common motive to invade the rights of other citizens; or if such a common motive exists, it will be more difficult for all who feel it to discover their own strength, and to act in unison with each other. Besides other impediments, it may be remarked that, where there is

a consciousness of unjust or dishonorable purposes, communication
is always checked by distrust in proportion to the number whose
concurrence is necessary.

Hence, it clearly appears, that the same advantage which a
republic has over a democracy, in controlling the effects of faction,
is enjoyed by a large over a small republic,—is enjoyed by the Union
over the States composing it. Does the advantage consist in the
substitution of representatives whose enlightened views and virtuous
sentiments render them superior to local prejudices and schemes of
injustice? It will not be denied that the representation of the Union
will be most likely to possess these requisite endowments. Does
it consist in the greater security afforded by a greater variety of
parties, against the event of any one party being able to outnumber
and oppress the rest? In an equal degree does the increased variety
of parties comprised within the Union, increase this security. Does
it, in fine, consist in the greater obstacles opposed to the concert
and accomplishment of the secret wishes of an unjust and interested
majority? Here, again, the extent of the Union gives it the most
palpable advantage.

The influence of factious leaders may kindle a flame within
their particular States, but will be unable to spread a general
conflagration through the other States. A religious sect may
degenerate into a political faction in a part of the Confederacy; but
the variety of sects dispersed over the entire face of it must secure
the national councils against any danger from that source. A rage
for paper money, for an abolition of debts, for an equal division
of property, or for any other improper or wicked project, will be
less apt to pervade the whole body of the Union than a particular
member of it; in the same proportion as such a malady is more likely

to taint a particular county or district, than an entire State.

In the extent and proper structure of the Union, therefore, we behold a republican remedy for the diseases most incident to republican government. And according to the degree of pleasure and pride we feel in being republicans, ought to be our zeal in cherishing the spirit and supporting the character of Federalists.

FEDERALIST 51

TO WHAT expedient, then, shall we finally resort, for maintaining in practice the necessary partition of power among the several departments, as laid down in the Constitution? The only answer that can be given is, that as all these exterior provisions are found to be inadequate, the defect must be supplied, by so contriving the interior structure of the government as that its several constituent parts may, by their mutual relations, be the means of keeping each other in their proper places. Without presuming to undertake a full development of this important idea, I will hazard a few general observations, which may perhaps place it in a clearer light, and enable us to form a more correct judgment of the principles and structure of the government planned by the convention. In order to lay a due foundation for that separate and distinct exercise of the different powers of government, which to a certain extent is admitted on all hands to be essential to the preservation of liberty, it is evident that each department should have a will of its own; and consequently should be so constituted that the members of each should have as little agency as possible in the appointment of the members of the others. Were this principle rigorously adhered to, it would require that all the appointments for the supreme executive, legislative, and judiciary magistracies should be drawn from the same fountain of authority, the people, through

channels having no communication whatever with one another.
Perhaps such a plan of constructing the several departments would
be less difficult in practice than it may in contemplation appear.
Some difficulties, however, and some additional expense would
attend the execution of it. Some deviations, therefore, from the
principle must be admitted. In the constitution of the judiciary
department in particular, it might be inexpedient to insist rigorously
on the principle: first, because peculiar qualifications being essential
in the members, the primary consideration ought to be to select that
mode of choice which best secures these qualifications; secondly,
because the permanent tenure by which the appointments are held in
that department, must soon destroy all sense of dependence on the
authority conferring them. It is equally evident, that the members of
each department should be as little dependent as possible on those of
the others, for the emoluments annexed to their offices. Were the
executive magistrate, or the judges, not independent of the
legislature in this particular, their independence in every other
would be merely nominal. But the great security against a gradual
concentration of the several powers in the same department, consists
in giving to those who administer each department the necessary
constitutional means and personal motives to resist encroachments of
the others. The provision for defense must in this, as in all other
cases, be made commensurate to the danger of attack. Ambition
must be made to counteract ambition. The interest of the man must
be connected with the constitutional rights of the place. It may be a
reflection on human nature, that such devices should be necessary to
control the abuses of government. But what is government itself, but
the greatest of all reflections on human nature? If men were angels,
no government would be necessary. If angels were to govern men,
neither external nor internal controls on government would be

necessary. In framing a government which is to be administered by
men over men, the great difficulty lies in this: you must first enable
the government to control the governed; and in the next place oblige
it to control itself. A dependence on the people is, no doubt, the
primary control on the government; but experience has taught
mankind the necessity of auxiliary precautions. This policy of
supplying, by opposite and rival interests, the defect of better
motives, might be traced through the whole system of human
affairs, private as well as public. We see it particularly displayed in
all the subordinate distributions of power, where the constant aim is
to divide and arrange the several offices in such a manner as that
each may be a check on the other that the private interest of every
individual may be a sentinel over the public rights. These inventions
of prudence cannot be less requisite in the distribution of the
supreme powers of the State. But it is not possible to give to each
department an equal power of self-defense. In republican
government, the legislative authority necessarily predominates. The
remedy for this inconveniency is to divide the legislature into
different branches; and to render them, by different modes of
election and different principles of action, as little connected with
each other as the nature of their common functions and their
common dependence on the society will admit. It may even be
necessary to guard against dangerous encroachments by still
further precautions. As the weight of the legislative authority
requires that it should be thus divided, the weakness of the executive
may require, on the other hand, that it should be fortified. An
absolute negative on the legislature appears, at first view, to be the
natural defense with which the executive magistrate should be
armed. But perhaps it would be neither altogether safe nor alone
sufficient. On ordinary occasions it might not be exerted with the

requisite firmness, and on extraordinary occasions it might be
perfidiously abused. May not this defect of an absolute negative be
supplied by some qualified connection between this weaker
department and the weaker branch of the stronger department, by
which the latter may be led to support the constitutional rights of the
former, without being too much detached from the rights of its own
department? If the principles on which these observations are
founded be just, as I persuade myself they are, and they be applied
as a criterion to the several State constitutions, and to the federal
Constitution it will be found that if the latter does not perfectly
correspond with them, the former are infinitely less able to bear such
a test. There are, moreover, two considerations particularly
applicable to the federal system of America, which place that system
in a very interesting point of view. First. In a single republic, all the
power surrendered by the people is submitted to the administration
of a single government; and the usurpations are guarded against by
a division of the government into distinct and separate departments.
In the compound republic of America, the power surrendered by the
people is first divided between two distinct governments, and then
the portion allotted to each subdivided among distinct and separate
departments. Hence a double security arises to the rights of the
people. The different governments will control each other, at the
same time that each will be controlled by itself. Second. It is of
great importance in a republic not only to guard the society against
the oppression of its rulers, but to guard one part of the society
against the injustice of the other part. Different interests necessarily
exist in different classes of citizens. If a majority be united by a
common interest, the rights of the minority will be insecure. There
are but two methods of providing against this evil: the one by
creating a will in the community independent of the majority that is,

of the society itself; the other, by comprehending in the society so many separate descriptions of citizens as will render an unjust combination of a majority of the whole very improbable, if not impracticable. The first method prevails in all governments possessing an hereditary or self-appointed authority. This, at best, is but a precarious security; because a power independent of the society may as well espouse the unjust views of the major, as the rightful interests of the minor party, and may possibly be turned against both parties. The second method will be exemplified in the federal republic of the United States. Whilst all authority in it will be derived from and dependent on the society, the society itself will be broken into so many parts, interests, and classes of citizens, that the rights of individuals, or of the minority, will be in little danger from interested combinations of the majority. In a free government the security for civil rights must be the same as that for religious rights. It consists in the one case in the multiplicity of interests, and in the other in the multiplicity of sects. The degree of security in both cases will depend on the number of interests and sects; and this may be presumed to depend on the extent of country and number of people comprehended under the same government. This view of the subject must particularly recommend a proper federal system to all the sincere and considerate friends of republican government, since it shows that in exact proportion as the territory of the Union may be formed into more circumscribed Confederacies, or States oppressive combinations of a majority will be facilitated: the best security, under the republican forms, for the rights of every class of citizens, will be diminished: and consequently the stability and independence of some member of the government, the only other security, must be proportionately increased. Justice is the end of government. It is the end of civil society. It ever has been and ever will be pursued until it be obtained, or until liberty be lost in the pursuit. In a society under the forms of which the stronger faction can readily unite and oppress the weaker, anarchy may as truly be said to reign as in a state of nature, where the weaker individual is not secured against the violence of the stronger; and as, in the latter state, even the stronger individuals are prompted, by the uncertainty of their condition, to submit to a government which may protect the weak as well as themselves; so, in the former state, will the more powerful factions or parties be gradnally induced, by a like motive, to wish for a government which will protect all parties, the weaker as well as the more powerful. It can be little doubted that if the State of Rhode Island was separated from the Confederacy and left to itself, the insecurity of rights under the popular form of government within such narrow limits would be displayed by such reiterated oppressions of factious majorities that some power altogether independent of the people would soon be called for by the voice of the very factions whose misrule had proved the necessity of it. In the extended republic of the United States, and among the great variety of interests, parties, and sects which it embraces, a coalition of a majority of the whole society could seldom take place on any other principles than those of justice and the general good; whilst there being thus less danger to a minor from the will of a major party, there must be less pretext, also, to provide for the security of the former, by introducing into the government a will not dependent on the latter, or, in other words, a will independent of the society itself. It is no less certain than it is important, notwithstanding the contrary opinions which have been entertained, that the larger the society, provided it lie within a practical sphere, the more duly capable it will be of self-government. And happily for the REPUBLICAN CAUSE, the practicable sphere may be carried to a

very great extent, by a judicious modification and mixture of the
FEDERAL PRINCIPLE.

Publius

PATRICK HENRY

Anti-Federalist Writings

*The Anti-Federalists included James Monroe, John Hancock, Sam
Adams, George Mason, and Patrick Henry among others, many of whom
were prominent in state and local politics. These men raised concerns
about the tendency of any government toward overreach and tyranny.
Not surprisingly, where the Federalists mounted a well-organized and
coordinated argument for their position, the Anti-Federalists were often at
odds with one another in terms of solutions. The concerns that they raised,
however, about the proposed Constitution's lack of protection for personal
liberties and property rights were conceded by even the Federalists.
Thus, the Anti-Federalists provided the invaluable service of provoking
discussion and solutions that utlimately resulted in the Bill of Rights. The
following is a speech given before the Virginia Ratifying Convention.*

SPEECH OF PATRICK HENRY, 5 JUNE, 1788

Mr. Chairman ... — When I asked that question, I
thought the meaning of my interrogation was obvious:
The fate of this question and of America may depend
on this: Have they said, we, the States? Have they made a proposal
of a compact between states? If they had, this would be a
confederation: It is otherwise most clearly a consolidated
government. The question turns, Sir, on that poor little thing-the
expression, We, the people, instead of the States, of America. I need
not take much pains to show that the principles of this system are
extremely pernicious, impolitic, and dangerous. Is this a monarchy,
like England-a compact between prince and people, with checks on
the former to secure the liberty of the latter? Is this a Confederacy,

like Holland-an association of a number of independent states, each
of which retains its individual sovereignty? It is not a democracy,
wherein the people retain all their rights securely. Had these
principles been adhered to, we should not have been brought to this
alarming transition, from a Confederacy to a consolidated
Government. We have no detail of these great consideration, which,
in my opinion, ought to have abounded before we should recur to a
government of this kind. Here is a revolution as radical as that
which separated us from Great Britain. It is radical in this
transition; our rights and privileges are endangered, and the
sovereignty of the states will be relinquished: And cannot we plainly
see that this is actually the case? The rights of conscience, trial by
jury, liberty of the press, all your immunities and franchises, all
pretensions to human rights and privileges, are rendered insecure, if
not lost, by this change, so loudly talked of by some, and
inconsiderately by others. Is this tame relinquishment of rights
worthy of freemen? Is it worthy of that manly fortitude that ought
to characterize republicans? It is said eight States have adopted this
plan. I declare that if twelve States and a half had adopted it, I
would, with manly firmness, and in spite of an erring world, reject
it. You are not to inquire how your trade may be increased, nor how
you are to become a great and powerful people, but how your
liberties can be secured; for liberty ought to be the direct end of
your Government. Having premised these things, I shall, with the
aid of my judgment and information, which, I confess, are not
extensive, go into the discussion of this system more minutely. Is it
necessary for your liberty that you should abandon those great
rights by the adoption of this system? Is the relinquishment of the
trial by jury and the liberty of the press necessary for your liberty?
Will the abandonment of your most sacred rights tend to the

security of your liberty? Liberty, the greatest of all earthly
blessings—give us that precious jewel, and you may take every thing
else: But I am fearful I have lived long enough to become an fellow:
Perhaps an invincible attachment to the dearest rights of man, may,
in these refined, enlightened days, be deemed old fashioned: If so, I
am contented to be so: I say, the time has been when every pore of
my heart beat for American liberty, and which, I believe, had a
counterpart in the breast of every true American: But suspicions
have gone forth—suspicions of my integrity—publicly reported that
my professions are not real. Twenty-three years ago was I supposed
a traitor to my country; I was then said to be the bane of sedition,
because I supported the rights of my country: I may be thought
suspicious when I say our privileges and rights are in danger. But,
Sir, a number of the people of this country are weak enough to think
these things are too true: I am happy to find that the Honorable
Gentleman on the other side declares they are groundless: But, Sir,
suspicion is a virtue, as long as its object is the preservation of the
public good, and as long as it stays within proper bounds: Should it
fall on me, I am contented: Conscious rectitude is a powerful
consolation: I trust there are many who think my professions for the
public good to be real. Let your suspicion look to both sides: There
are many on the other side, who possibly may have been persuaded
of the necessity of these measures, which I conceive to be dangerous
to your liberty. Guard with jealous attention the public liberty.
Suspect every one who approaches that jewel. Unfortunately,
nothing will preserve it but downright force: Whenever you give up
that force, you are inevitably ruined. I am answered by gentlemen,
that though I might speak of terrors, yet the fact was, that we were
surrounded by none of the dangers apprehended. I conceive this new
Government to be one of those dangers: It has produced those

horrors which distress many of our best citizens. We are come hither to preserve the poor commonwealth of Virginia, if it can be possibly done: Something must be done to preserve your liberty and mine: The Confederation; this same despised Government, merits, in my opinion, the highest encomium: It carried us through a long and dangerous war: It rendered us victorious in that bloody conflict with a powerful nation: It has secured us a territory greater than any European monarch possesses: And shall a Government which has been thus strong and vigorous, be accused of imbecility and abandoned for want of energy? Consider what you are about to do before you part with this Government. Take longer time in reckoning things: Revolutions like this have happened in almost every country in Europe: Similar examples are to be found in ancient Greece and ancient Rome: Instances of the people losing their liberty by their carelessness and the ambition of a few. We are cautioned by the Honorable Gentleman who presides, against faction and turbulence: I acknowledge that licentiousness is dangerous, and that it ought to be provided against: I acknowledge also the new form of Government may effectually prevent it: Yet, there is another thing it will as effectually do: it will oppress and ruin the people. There are sufficient guards placed against sedition and licentiousness: For when power is given to this Government to suppress these, or, for any other purpose, the language it assumes is clear, express, and unequivocal; but when this Constitution speaks of privileges, there is an ambiguity, Sir, a fatal ambiguity—an ambiguity which is very astonishing: In the clause under consideration, there is the strangest language that I can conceive. I mean, when it says that there shall not be more Representatives than one for every 30,000. Now, Sir, how easy is it to evade this privilege? "The number shall not exceed one for every 30,000." This may be

satisfied by one Representative from each State. Let our numbers be
ever so great, this immense continent, may, by this artful
expression, be reduced to have but 13 Representatives: I confess this
construction is not natural; but the ambiguity of the expression lays
a good ground for a quarrel. Why was it not clearly and
unequivocally expressed, that they should be entitled, to have one
for every 30,000? This would have obviated all disputes; and was this
difficult to be done? What is the inference? When population
increases, and a state shall send Representatives in this proportion,
Congress may remand them, because the right of having one for
every 30,000 is not clearly expressed: this possibility of reducing the
number to one for each state approximates to probability by that
other expression, "but each state shall at least have one
Representative." Now, is it not clear that, from the first expression,
the number might be reduced so much that some States should have
no Representatives at all, were it not for the insertion of this last
expression? And as this is the only restriction upon them, we may
fairly conclude that they may restrain the number to one from each
State: Perhaps the same horrors may hang over my mind again. I
shall be told I am continually afraid: But, Sir, I have strong cause of
apprehension: In some parts of the plan before you, the great rights
of freemen are endangered, in other parts absolutely taken away.
How does your trial by jury stand? In civil cases gone-not
sufficiently secured in criminal-this best privilege is gone: But we are
told that we need not fear; because those in power, being our
Representatives, will not abuse the power we put in their hands: I
am not well versed in history, but I will submit to your recollection,
whether liberty has been destroyed most often by the licentiousness
of the people, or by the tyranny of rulers? I imagine, sir, you will
find the balance on the side of tyranny: Happy will you be if you

miss the fate of those nations, who, omitting to resist their
oppressors, or negligently suffering their liberty to be wrested from
them, have groaned under intolerable despotism. Most of the human
race are now in this deplorable condition: And those nations who
have gone in search of grandeur, power, and splendor, have also
fallen a sacrifice, and been the victims of their own folly: While they
acquired those visionary blessings, they lost their freedom. My great
objection to this Government is, that it does not leave us the means
of defending our rights, or of waging war against tyrants: It is
urged by some gentlemen, that this new plan will bring us an
acquisition of strength, an army, and the militia of the States: This
is an idea extremely ridiculous: Gentlemen cannot be earnest. This
acquisition will trample on our fallen liberty: Let my beloved
Americans guard against that fatal lethargy that has pervaded the
universe: Have we the means of resisting disciplined armies, when
our only defence, the militia, is put into the hands of Congress?

. . . Let no Gentlemen be told, that it is not safe to reject this
Government. Wherefore is it not safe? We are told there are
dangers; but those dangers are ideal; they cannot be demonstrated:
To encourage us to adopt it, they tell us that there is a plain, easy
way of getting amendments: When I come to contemplate this part,
I suppose that I am mad, or that my countrymen are so: The way to
amendment is, in my conception, shut. Let us consider this plain,
easy way: "The Congress, whenever two thirds of both Houses shall
deem it necessary, shall propose amendments to this Constitution,
or, on the application of the Legislatures of two thirds of the several
states, shall call a Convention for proposing amendments, which, in
either case, shall be valid to all intents and purposes, as part of this
Constitution, when ratified by the Legislatures of three-fourths of

the several States, or by the Conventions in three-fourths thereof, as the one or the other mode of ratification may be proposed by the Congress. Provided, that no amendment which may be made prior to the year 1808, shall in any manner affect the first and fourth clauses in the ninth section of the first article; and that no State, without its consent, shall be deprived of its equal suffrage in the Senate." Hence it appears that three-fourths of the States must ultimately agree to any amendments that may be necessary. Let us consider the consequence of this: However uncharitable it may appear, yet I must tell my opinion, that the most unworthy character may get into power, and prevent the introduction of amendments: Let us suppose (for the case is supposable, possible, and probable) that you happen to deal those powers to unworthy hands; will they relinquish powers already in their possession, or agree to amendments? Two-thirds of the Congress, or, of the State Legislatures, are necessary even to propose amendments: If one-third of these be unworthy men, they may prevent the application for amendments; but what is destructive and mischievous, is, that three-fourths of the State Legislatures, or of the State Conventions, must concur in the amendments when proposed: In such numerous bodies, there must necessarily be some designing bad men: To suppose that so large a number as three-fourths of the States will concur, is to suppose that they will possess genius, intelligence, and integrity, approaching to miraculous. It would indeed be miraculous that they should concur in the same amendments, or even in such as would bear some likeness to one another. For four of the smallest States, that do not collectively contain one-tenth part of the population of the United States, may obstruct the most salutary and necessary amendments: Nay, in these four States, six tenths of the people may reject these amendments; and suppose, that amendments shall be opposed to amendments (which is highly probable) is it possible, that three-fourths can ever agree to the same amendments? A bare majority in these four small States may hinder the adoption of amendments . . . A trifling minority may reject the most salutary amendments. Is this an easy mode of securing the public liberty? It is, Sir, a most fearful situation, when the most contemptible minority can prevent the alteration of the most oppressive Government; for it may, in many respects, prove to be such. Is this the spirit of republicanism? What, Sir, is the genius of democracy? . . .that a majority of the community have a right to alter their Government when found to be oppressive: But how different is the genius of your new Constitution from this? How different from the sentiments of freemen, that a contemptible minority can prevent the good of the majority? If then Gentlemen standing on this ground, are come to that point, that they are willing to bind themselves and their posterity to be oppressed, I am amazed and inexpressibly astonished. If this be the opinion of the majority, I must submit; but to me, Sir, it appears perilous and destructive: I cannot help thinking so: Perhaps it may be the result of my age; these may be feelings natural to a man of my years, when the American spirit has left him, and his mental powers, like the members of the body, are decayed. If, Sir, amendments are left to the twentieth or tenth part of the people of America, your liberty is gone forever. We have heard that there is a great deal of bribery practiced in the House of Commons in England; and that many of the members raised themselves to preferments, by selling the rights of the people: But, Sir, the tenth part of that body cannot continue oppressions on the rest of the people. English liberty is in this case, on a firmer foundation than American liberty. It will be easily contrived to procure the

opposition of one tenth of the people to any alteration, however
judicious. The Honorable Gentleman who presides, told us, that to
prevent abuses in our Government, we will assemble in Convention,
recall our delegated powers, and punish our servants for abusing the
trust reposed in them. Oh, Sir, we should have fine times indeed, if
to punish tyrants, it were only sufficient to assemble the people.
Your arms wherewith you could defend yourselves, are gone; and
you have no longer an aristocratical; no longer democratical spirit.
Did you ever read of any revolution in a nation, brought about by
the punishment of those in power, inflicted by those who had no
power at all? You read of a riot act in a country which is called one
of the freest in the world, where a few neighbors cannot assemble
without the risk of being shot by a hired soldiery, the engines of
despotism. We may see such an act in America. A standing army
we shall have also, to execute the execrable commands of tyranny:
And how are you to punish them? Will you order them to be
punished? Who shall obey these orders? Will your Mace-bearer be a
match for a disciplined regiment? In what situation are we to be?
The clause before you gives a power of direct taxation, unbounded
and unlimited: Exclusive power of Legislation in all cases
whatsoever, for ten miles square; and over all places purchased for
the erection of forts, magazines, arsenals, dockyards, etc. What
resistance could be made? The attempt would be madness. You will
find all the strength of this country in the hands of your enemies:
Those garrisons will naturally be the strongest places in the
country. Your militia is given up to Congress also in another part of
this plan: They will therefore act as they think proper: All power
will be in their own possession: You cannot force them to receive
their punishment: Of what service would militia be to you, when
most probably you will not have a single musket in the State; for as

arms are to be provided by Congress, they may or may not furnish them. Let me here call your attention to that part which gives the Congress power, "To provide for organizing, arming, and disciplining the militia, and for governing such part of them as may be employed in the service of the United States, reserving to the States respectively, the appointment of the officers, and the authority of training the militia, according to the discipline prescribed by Congress." By this, Sir, you see that their control over our last and best defence is unlimitted. If they neglect or refuse to discipline or arm our militia, they will be useless: the States can do neither, this power being exclusively given to Congress: The power of appointing officers over men not disciplined or armed is ridiculous: So that this pretended little remains of power left to the States may, at the pleasure of Congress, be rendered nugatory. Our situation will be deplorable indeed: Nor can we ever expect to get this government amended, since I have already shewn, that a very small minority may prevent it; and that small minority interested in the continuance of the oppression: Will the oppressor let go the oppressed? Was there even an instance? Can the annals of mankind exhibit one single example, where rulers overcharged with power willingly let go the oppressed, though solicited and requested most earnestly? The application for amendments will therefore be fruitless. Sometimes the oppressed have got loose by one of those bloody struggles that desolate a country. A willing relinquishment of power is one of those things which human nature never was, nor ever will be capable of: The Honorable Gentleman's observations respecting the people's right of being the agents in the formation of this Government, are not accurate in my humble conception. The distinction between a National Government and a Confederacy is not sufficiently discerned. Had the delegates who were sent to

Philadelphia a power to propose a Consolidated Government instead
of a Confederacy? Were they not deputed by States, and not by the
people? The assent of the people in their collective capacity is not
necessary to the formation of a Federal Government. The people
have no right to enter into leagues, alliances, or confederations: They
are not the proper agents for this purpose: States and sovereign
powers are the only proper agents for this kind of Government:
Shew me an instance where the people have exercised this business:
Has it not always gone through the Legislatures? I refer you to the
treaties with France, Holland, and other nations: How were they
made? Were they not made by the States? Are the people therefore
in their aggregate capacity, the proper persons to form a
Confederacy? This, therefore, ought to depend on the consent of the
Legislatures; the people having never sent delegates to make any
proposition for changing the Government. Yet I must say, at the
same time, that it was made on grounds the most pure, and perhaps
I might have been brought to consent to it so far as to the change of
Government; but there is one thing in it which I never would
acquiesce in. I mean the changing it into a Consolidated
Government; which is so abhorrent in my mind. The Honorable
Gentleman then went on to the figure we make with foreign nations;
the contemptible one we make in France and Holland; which,
according to the substance of my notes, he attributes to the present
feeble Government. An opinion has gone forth, we find, that we are
a contemptible people: The time has been when we were thought
otherwise: Under the same despised Government, we commanded
the respect of all Europe: Wherefore are we now reckoned
otherwise? The American spirit has fled from hence: It has gone to
regions, where it has never been expected: It has gone to the people
of France in search of a splendid Government-a strong energetic

Government. Shall we imitate the example of those nations who have gone from a simple to a splendid Government? Are those nations more worthy of our imitation? What can make an adequate satisfaction to them for the loss they have suffered in attaining such a Government for the loss of their liberty? If we admit this Consolidated Government it will be because we like a great splendid one. Some way or other we must be a great and mighty empire; we must have an army, and a navy, and a number of things: When the American spirit was in its youth, the language of America was different: Liberty, Sir, was then the primary object. We are descended from a people whose Government was founded on liberty: Our glorious forefathers of Great-Britain, made liberty the foundation of every thing. That country is become a great, mighty, and splendid nation; not because their Government is strong and energetic; but, Sir, because liberty is its direct end and foundation: We drew the spirit of liberty from our British ancestors; by that spirit we have triumphed over every difficulty: But now, Sir, the American spirit, assisted by the ropes and chains of consolidation, is about to convert this country to a powerful and mighty empire: If you make the citizens of this country agree to become the subjects of one great consolidated empire of America, your Government will not have sufficient energy to keep them together: Such a Government is incompatible with the genius of republicanism: There will be no checks, no real balances, in this Government: What can avail your specious imaginary balances, your rope-dancing, chain-rattling, ridiculous ideal checks and contrivances? But, Sir, we are not feared by foreigners: we do not make nations tremble: Would this, Sir, constitute happiness, or secure liberty? I trust, Sir, our political hemisphere will ever direct their operations to the security of those objects. Consider our situation, Sir: Go to the poor man, ask him what he does; he will inform you, that he enjoys the fruits of his labour, under his own fig-tree, with his wife and children around him, in peace and security. Go to every other member of society, you will find the same tranquil ease and content; you will find no alarms or disturbances: Why then tell us of dangers to terrify us into an adoption of this new Government? And yet who knows the dangers that this new system may produce; they are out of the sight of the common people: They cannot foresee latent consequences: I dread the operation of it on the middling and lower classes of people: It is for them I fear the adoption of this system. I fear I tire the patience of the Committee, but I beg to be indulged with a few more observations: When I thus profess myself an advocate for the liberty of the people, I shall be told, I am a designing man, that I am to be a great man, that I am to be a demagogue; and many similar illiberal insinuations will be thrown out; but, Sir, conscious rectitude, out-weighs those things with me: I see great jeopardy in this new Government. I see none from our present one: I hope some Gentleman or other will bring forth, in full array, those dangers, if there be any, that we may see and touch them.

JAMES MADISON

Bill of Rights

The Bill of Rights comprises the first ten Amendments to the Consttituion of the United States. Federalist James Madison drafted these amendments to address the concerns raised by the Anti-Federalists. The Bill of Rights was ratified by the states by the end of 1791, thus becoming a part of the Constitution.

AMENDMENT I

Congress shall make no law respecting an establishment of religion, or prohibiting the free exercise thereof; or abridging the freedom of speech, or of the press; or the right of the people peaceably to assemble, and to petition the government for a redress of grievances.

AMENDMENT II

A well regulated militia, being necessary to the security of a free state, the right of the people to keep and bear arms, shall not be infringed.

AMENDMENT III

No soldier shall, in time of peace be quartered in any house, without the consent of the owner, nor in time of war, but in a manner to be prescribed by law.

AMENDMENT IV

The right of the people to be secure in their persons, houses, papers, and effects, against unreasonable searches and seizures, shall not be violated, and no warrants shall issue, but upon probable cause, supported by oath or affirmation, and particularly describing the place to be searched, and the persons or things to be seized.

AMENDMENT V

No person shall be held to answer for a capital, or otherwise infamous crime, unless on a presentment or indictment of a grand jury, except in cases arising in the land or naval forces, or in the militia, when in actual service in time of war or public danger; nor shall any person be subject for the same offense to be twice put in jeopardy of life or limb; nor shall be compelled in any criminal case to be a witness against himself, nor be deprived of life, liberty, or property, without due process of law; nor shall private property be taken for public use, without just compensation.

AMENDMENT VI

In all criminal prosecutions, the accused shall enjoy the right to a speedy and public trial, by an impartial jury of the state and district wherein the crime shall have been committed, which district shall have been previously ascertained by law, and to be informed of the nature and cause of the accusation; to be confronted with the witnesses against him; to have compulsory process for obtaining witnesses in his favor, and to have the assistance of counsel for his defense.

AMENDMENT VII

In suits at common law, where the value in controversy shall exceed twenty dollars, the right of trial by jury shall be preserved, and no fact tried by a jury, shall be otherwise reexamined in any court of the United States, than according to the rules of the common law.

AMENDMENT VIII

Excessive bail shall not be required, nor excessive fines imposed, nor cruel and unusual punishments inflicted.

AMENDMENT IX

The enumeration in the Constitution, of certain rights, shall not be construed to deny or disparage others retained by the people.

AMENDMENT X

The powers not delegated to the United States by the Constitution, nor prohibited by it to the states, are reserved to the states respectively, or to the people.

UNITED STATES CONGRESS

Amendments to the Constitution

The Founding Fathers knew that the Constitution they had created was not an infallible document. They therefore put processes in place by which it could be amended. Amendments to the Constitution require a two-thirds majority in both the House and Senate or the calling of a Constitutional convention with at least two-thirds of the state legislatures present. To the present day, only the former has been used to amend the Constitution.

AMENDMENT XI (1795)

The Judicial power of the United States shall not be construed to extend to any suit in law or equity, commenced or prosecuted against one of the United States by Citizens of another State, or by Citizens or Subjects of any Foreign State.

AMENDMENT XII (1804)

The Electors shall meet in their respective states and vote by ballot for President and Vice-President, one of whom, at least, shall not be an inhabitant of the same state with themselves; they shall name in their ballots the person voted for as President, and in distinct ballots the person voted for as Vice-President, and they shall make distinct lists of all persons voted for as President, and of all persons voted for as Vice-President, and of the number of votes for each, which lists they shall sign and certify, and transmit sealed to the seat of the government of the United States, directed to the President of the Senate;-The President of the Senate shall, in the presence of the Senate and House of Representatives, open all the certificates and the votes shall then be counted;-The person having the greatest Number of votes for President, shall be the President, if such number be a majority of the whole number of Electors appointed; and if no person have such majority, then from the persons having the highest numbers not exceeding three on the list of those voted for as President, the House of Representatives shall choose immediately, by ballot, the President. But in choosing the President, the votes shall be taken by states, the representation from each state having one vote; a quorum for this purpose shall consist of a member or members from two-thirds of the states, and a majority of all the states shall be necessary to a choice. And if the House of Representatives shall not choose a President whenever the right of choice shall devolve upon them, before the fourth day of March next following, then the Vice-President shall act as President, as in the case of the death or other constitutional disability of the President-The person having the greatest number of votes as Vice-President, shall be the Vice-President, if such number be a majority of the whole number of Electors appointed, and if no person have a majority, then from the two highest numbers on the list, the Senate shall choose the Vice-President; a quorum for the purpose shall consist of two-thirds of the whole number of Senators, and a majority of the whole number shall be necessary to a choice. But no person constitutionally ineligible to the office of President shall be eligible to that of Vice-President of the United States.

AMENDMENT XIII (1865)

SECTION 1

Neither slavery nor involuntary servitude, except as a punishment for crime whereof the party shall have been duly convicted, shall exist within the United States, or any place subject to their jurisdiction.

SECTION 2

Congress shall have power to enforce this article by appropriate legislation.

AMENDMENT XIV (1868)

SECTION 1

All persons born or naturalized in the United States and subject to the jurisdiction thereof, are citizens of the United States and of the State wherein they reside. No State shall make or enforce any law which shall abridge the privileges or immunities of citizens of the United States; nor shall any State deprive any person of life, liberty, or property, without due process of law; nor deny to any person within its jurisdiction the equal protection of the laws.

SECTION 2

Representatives shall be apportioned among the several States according to their respective numbers, counting the whole number of persons in each State, excluding Indians not taxed. But when the right to vote at any election for the choice of electors for President and Vice President of the United States, Representatives in Congress, the Executive and Judicial officers of a State, or the members of the Legislature thereof, is denied to any of the male inhabitants of such State, being twenty-one years of age, and citizens of the United States, or in any way abridged, except for participation in rebellion, or other crime, the basis of representation therein shall be reduced in the proportion which the number of such male citizens shall bear to the whole number of male citizens twenty-one years of age in such State.

SECTION 3

No person shall be a Senator or Representative in Congress, or elector of President and Vice President, or hold any office, civil or military, under the United States, or under any State, who, having previously taken an oath, as a member of Congress, or as an officer of the United States, or as a member of any State legislature, or as an executive or judicial officer of any State, to support the Constitution of the United States, shall have engaged in insurrection or rebellion against the same, or given aid or comfort to the enemies thereof. But Congress may by a vote of two-thirds of each House, remove such disability.

SECTION 4

The validity of the public debt of the United States, authorized by law, including debts incurred for payment of pensions and bounties for services in suppressing insurrection or rebellion, shall not be questioned. But neither the United States nor any State shall assume or pay any debt or obligation incurred in aid of insurrection or rebellion against the United States, or any claim for the loss or emancipation of any slave; but all such debts, obligations and claims shall be held illegal and void.

SECTION 5

The Congress shall have power to enforce, by appropriate legislation, the provisions of this article.

AMENDMENT XV (1870)

SECTION 1

The right of citizens of the United States to vote shall not be denied or abridged by the United States or by any State on account of race, color, or previous condition of servitude.

SECTION 2

The Congress shall have power to enforce this article by appropriate legislation.

AMENDMENT XVI (1913)

The Congress shall have power to lay and collect taxes on incomes, from whatever source derived, without apportionment among the several States, and without regard to any census or enumeration.

AMENDMENT XVII (1913)

The Senate of the United States shall be composed of two Senators from each State, elected by the people thereof, for six years; and each Senator shall have one vote. The electors in each State shall have the qualifications requisite for electors of the most numerous branch of the State legislatures.

When vacancies happen in the representation of any State in the Senate, the executive authority of such State shall issue writs of election to fill such vacancies: Provided, That the legislature of any State may empower the executive thereof to make temporary appointments until the people fill the vacancies by election as the legislature may direct.

This amendment shall not be so construed as to affect the election or term of any Senator chosen before it becomes valid as part of the Constitution.

AMENDMENT XVIII (1919)

SECTION 1

After one year from the ratification of this article the manufacture, sale, or transportation of intoxicating liquors within, the importation thereof into, or the exportation thereof from the United States and all territory subject to the jurisdiction thereof for beverage purposes is hereby prohibited.

SECTION 2

The Congress and the several States shall have concurrent power to enforce this article by appropriate legislation.

SECTION 3

This article shall be inoperative unless it shall have been ratified as an amendment to the Constitution by the legislatures of the several States, as provided in the Constitution, within seven years from the date of the submission hereof to the States by the Congress.

AMENDMENT XIX (1920)

The right of citizens of the United States to vote shall not be denied or abridged by the United States or by any State on account of sex.

Congress shall have power to enforce this article by appropriate legislation.

AMENDMENT XX (1933)
SECTION 1

The terms of the President and Vice President shall end at noon on the 20th day of January, and the terms of Senators and Representatives at noon on the 3d day of January, of the years in which such terms would have ended if this article had not been ratified; and the terms of their successors shall then begin.

SECTION 2

The Congress shall assemble at least once in every year, and such meeting shall begin at noon on the 3d day of January, unless they shall by law appoint a different day.

SECTION 3

If, at the time fixed for the beginning of the term of the President, the President elect shall have died, the Vice President elect shall become President. If a President shall not have been chosen before the time fixed for the beginning of his term, or if the President elect shall have failed to qualify, then the Vice President elect shall act as President until a President shall have qualified; and the Congress may by law provide for the case wherein neither a President elect nor a Vice President elect shall have qualified, declaring who shall then act as President, or the manner in which one who is to act shall be selected, and such person shall act accordingly until a President or Vice President shall have qualified.

SECTION 4

The Congress may by law provide for the case of the death of any of the persons from whom the House of Representatives may choose a President whenever the right of choice shall have devolved upon them, and for the case of the death of any of the persons from whom the Senate may choose a Vice President whenever the right of choice shall have devolved upon them.

SECTION 5

Sections 1 and 2 shall take effect on the 15th day of October following the ratification of this article.

SECTION 6

This article shall be inoperative unless it shall have been ratified as an amendment to the Constitution by the legislatures of three-fourths of the several States within seven years from the date of its submission.

AMENDMENT XXI (1933)
SECTION 1

The eighteenth article of amendment to the Constitution of the United States is hereby repealed.

SECTION 2

The transportation or importation into any State, Territory, or possession of the United States for delivery or use therein of intoxicating liquors, in violation of the laws thereof, is hereby prohibited.

SECTION 3

This article shall be inoperative unless it shall have been ratified as an amendment to the Constitution by conventions in the several States, as provided in the Constitution, within seven years from the date of the submission hereof to the States by the Congress.

AMENDMENT XXII (1951)
SECTION 1

No person shall be elected to the office of the President more than twice, and no person who has held the office of President, or acted as President, for more than two years of a term to which some other person was elected President shall be elected to the office of the President more than once. But this Article shall not apply to any person holding the office of President, when this Article was proposed by the Congress, and shall not prevent any person who may be holding the office of President, or acting as President, during the term within which this Article becomes operative from holding the office of President or acting as President during the remainder of such term.

SECTION 2

This article shall be inoperative unless it shall have been ratified as an amendment to the Constitution by the legislatures of three-fourths of the several States within seven years from the date of its submission to the States by the Congress.

AMENDMENT XXIII (1961)
SECTION 1

The District constituting the seat of Government of the United States shall appoint in such manner as the Congress may direct:

A number of electors of President and Vice President equal to the whole number of Senators and Representatives in Congress to which the District would be entitled if it were a State, but in no event more than the least populous State; they shall be in addition to those appointed by the States, but they shall be considered, for the purposes of the election of President and Vice President, to be electors appointed by a State; and they shall meet in the District and perform such duties as provided by the twelfth article of amendment.

SECTION 2

The Congress shall have power to enforce this article by appropriate legislation.

AMENDMENT XXIV (1964)

SECTION 1

The right of citizens of the United States to vote in any primary or other election for President or Vice President for electors for President or Vice President, or for Senator or Representative in Congress, shall not be denied or abridged by the United States or any State by reason of failure to pay any poll tax or other tax.

SECTION 2

The Congress shall have power to enforce this article by appropriate legislation.

AMENDMENT XXV (1967)

SECTION 1

In case of the removal of the President from office or of his death or resignation, the Vice President shall become President.

SECTION 2

Whenever there is a vacancy in the office of the Vice President, the President shall nominate a Vice President who shall take office upon confirmation by a majority vote of both Houses of Congress.

SECTION 3

Whenever the President transmits to the President pro tempore of the Senate and the Speaker of the House of Representatives his written declaration that he is unable to discharge the powers and duties of his office, and until he transmits to them a written declaration to the contrary, such powers and duties shall be discharged by the Vice President as Acting President.

SECTION 4

Whenever the Vice President and a majority of either the principal officers of the executive departments or of such other body as Congress may by law provide, transmit to the President pro tempore of the Senate and the Speaker of the House of Representatives their written declaration that the President is unable to discharge the powers and duties of his office, the Vice President shall immediately assume the powers and duties of the office as Acting President.

Thereafter, when the President transmits to the President pro tempore of the Senate and the Speaker of the House of Representatives his written declaration that no inability exists, he shall resume the powers and duties of his office unless the Vice President and a majority of either the principal officers of the executive department or of such other body as Congress may by law provide, transmit within four days to the President pro tempore of the Senate and the Speaker of the House of Representatives their written declaration that the President is unable to discharge the powers and duties of his office. Thereupon Congress shall decide the issue, assembling within forty-eight hours for that purpose if not in session. If the Congress, within twenty-one days after receipt of the latter written declaration, or, if Congress is not in session, within twenty-one days after Congress is required to assemble, determines by two-thirds vote of both Houses that the President is unable to discharge the powers and duties of his office, the Vice President shall continue to discharge the same as Acting President; otherwise, the President shall resume the powers and duties of his office.

AMENDMENT XXVI (1971)

SECTION 1

The right of citizens of the United States, who are eighteen years of age or older, to vote shall not be denied or abridged by the United States or by any State on account of age.

SECTION 2

The Congress shall have power to enforce this article by appropriate legislation.

AMENDMENT XXVII (1992)

No law varying the compensation for the services of the Senators and Representatives shall take effect, until an election of Representatives shall have intervened.

FRANCIS HOPKINSON

Hail, Columbia!

Francis Hopkinson was a congressman from Pennsylvania whose father was one of the signers of the Declaration of Independance. Hopkinson wrote this song in 1798 for Washington's first inauguration. It was an unofficial National Anthem until 1931, and is still used today ceremonially for the entrance of the Vice President at a public state occasion.

Hail! Columbia, happy land!
Hail! ye heroes, heav'n-born band,
Who fought and bled in freedom's cause,
Who fo't and bled in freedom's cause,
And when the storm of war was gone,
Enjoyed the peace your valor won;
Let Independence be your boast,
Ever mindful what it cost,
Ever grateful for the prize,
Let is altar reach the skies.

Refrain:
Firm, united let us be,
Rallying round our liberty,
As a band of brothers joined,
Peace and safety we shall find.

Immortal Patriots, rise once more!
Defend your rights, defend your shore;
Let no rude foe with impious hand,
Let no rude foe with impious hand,

Invade the shrine where sacred lies,
Of toil and blood the well-earned prize;
While off'ring peace sincere and just,
In heav'n we place a manly trust,
That truth and justice may prevail,
And ev'ry scheme of bondage fail! [Refrain]

Sound, sound the trump of fame!
Let Washington's great name
Ring thro' the world with loud applause,
Ring thro' the world with loud applause!
Let ev'ry clime to freedom dear,
Listen with a joyful ear;
With equal skill with steady pow'r
He governs in the fearful hour
Of horid war or guides with ease,
The happier time of honest peace. [Refrain]

GEORGE WASHINGTON

Farewell Address

"First in war, first in peace, and first in the hearts of his countrymen."
This fitting tribute to George Washington, offered at his death by fellow
soldier and statesman Henry Lee, captures the essence of the man. As
Commanding General of the Continental Army, Washington led hd
the troops to victory in the American War for Independence. Turning
down a popular call to be crowned as king of the new country, this
new Cincinnatus resigned his commission, relinquished his sword, and
returned to his beloved estate, Mount Vernon, where he planned to live
out the remainder of his life. This was not to be, for in 1789, he answered
the call of the fledgling country to serve as the first Commander in Chief.
George Washington served two terms as President of the United States,
then once more refused the clamor of those who would make him President
for life. To this day, the peaceful transfer of power first modeled by George
Washington, and carried out by every president since, is one of the greatest
—and most unique—accomplishments of the American experiment in
liberty. His Farewell Address, drafted by James Madison and revised by
Washington himself along with Alexander Hamilton, was first published
in September 1792 in the American Daily Advertiser. *In it, Washington*
first tenders his resignation, and then proceeds to offer sage advice to the
citizens of his country regarding the preservation of their dearly bought
liberty.

FRIENDS AND CITIZENS:

The period for a new election of a citizen to administer the
executive government of the United States being not far
distant, and the time actually arrived when your thoughts
must be employed in designating the person who is to be clothed

with that important trust, it appears to me proper, especially as it may conduce to a more distinct expression of the public voice, that I should now apprise you of the resolution I have formed, to decline being considered among the number of those out of whom a choice is to be made.

I beg you, at the same time, to do me the justice to be assured that this resolution has not been taken without a strict regard to all the considerations appertaining to the relation which binds a dutiful citizen to his country; and that in withdrawing the tender of service, which silence in my situation might imply, I am influenced by no diminution of zeal for your future interest, no deficiency of grateful respect for your past kindness, but am supported by a full conviction that the step is compatible with both.

The acceptance of, and continuance hitherto in, the office to which your suffrages have twice called me have been a uniform sacrifice of inclination to the opinion of duty and to a deference for what appeared to be your desire. I constantly hoped that it would have been much earlier in my power, consistently with motives which I was not at liberty to disregard, to return to that retirement from which I had been reluctantly drawn. The strength of my inclination to do this, previous to the last election, had even led to the preparation of an address to declare it to you; but mature reflection on the then perplexed and critical posture of our affairs with foreign nations, and the unanimous advice of persons entitled to my confidence, impelled me to abandon the idea.

I rejoice that the state of your concerns, external as well as internal, no longer renders the pursuit of inclination incompatible with the sentiment of duty or propriety, and am persuaded, whatever partiality may be retained for my services, that, in the present circumstances of our country, you will not disapprove my determination to retire.

The impressions with which I first undertook the arduous trust were explained on the proper occasion. In the discharge of this trust, I will only say that I have, with good intentions, contributed towards the organization and administration of the government the best exertions of which a very fallible judgment was capable. Not unconscious in the outset of the inferiority of my qualifications, experience in my own eyes, perhaps still more in the eyes of others, has strengthened the motives to diffidence of myself; and every day the increasing weight of years admonishes me more and more that the shade of retirement is as necessary to me as it will be welcome. Satisfied that if any circumstances have given peculiar value to my services, they were temporary, I have the consolation to believe that, while choice and prudence invite me to quit the political scene, patriotism does not forbid it.

In looking forward to the moment which is intended to terminate the career of my public life, my feelings do not permit me to suspend the deep acknowledgment of that debt of gratitude which I owe to my beloved country for the many honors it has conferred upon me; still more for the steadfast confidence with which it has supported me; and for the opportunities I have thence enjoyed of manifesting my inviolable attachment, by services faithful and persevering, though in usefulness unequal to my zeal. If benefits have resulted to our country from these services, let it always be remembered to your praise, and as an instructive example in our annals, that under circumstances in which the passions, agitated in every direction, were liable to mislead, amidst appearances sometimes dubious, vicissitudes of fortune often discouraging, in situations in which not unfrequently want of success has countenanced the spirit of criticism, the constancy of your support was the essential prop of the efforts, and a guarantee of the plans by which they were effected. Profoundly penetrated with this idea, I shall carry it with me to my grave, as a strong incitement to unceasing vows that heaven may continue to you the choicest tokens of its beneficence; that your union and brotherly affection may be perpetual; that the free Constitution, which is the work of your hands, may be sacredly maintained; that its administration in every department may be stamped with wisdom and virtue; that, in fine, the happiness of the people of these States, under the auspices of liberty, may be made complete by so careful a preservation and so prudent a use of this blessing as will acquire to them the glory of recommending it to the applause, the affection, and adoption of every nation which is yet a stranger to it.

Here, perhaps, I ought to stop. But a solicitude for your welfare, which cannot end but with my life, and the apprehension of danger, natural to that solicitude, urge me, on an occasion like the present, to offer to your solemn contemplation, and to recommend to your frequent review, some sentiments which are the result of much reflection, of no inconsiderable observation, and which appear to me all-important to the permanency of your felicity as a people. These will be offered to you with the more freedom, as you can only see in them the disinterested warnings of a parting friend, who can possibly have no personal motive to bias his counsel. Nor can I forget, as an encouragement to it, your indulgent reception of my sentiments on a former and not dissimilar occasion.

Interwoven as is the love of liberty with every ligament of your hearts, no recommendation of mine is necessary to fortify or confirm the attachment.

The unity of government which constitutes you one people is also now dear to you. It is justly so, for it is a main pillar in the edifice of your real independence, the support of your tranquility at home, your peace abroad; of your safety; of your prosperity; of that very liberty which you so highly prize. But as it is easy to foresee that, from different causes and from different quarters, much pains will be taken, many artifices employed to weaken in your minds the conviction of this truth; as this is the point in your political fortress against which the batteries of internal and external enemies will be most constantly and actively (though often covertly and insidiously) directed, it is of infinite moment that you should properly estimate the immense value of your national union to your collective and individual happiness; that you should cherish a cordial, habitual, and immovable attachment to it; accustoming yourselves to think and speak of it as of the palladium of your political safety and prosperity; watching for its preservation with jealous anxiety; discountenancing whatever may suggest even a suspicion that it can in any event be abandoned; and indignantly frowning upon the first dawning of every attempt to alienate any portion of our country from the rest, or to enfeeble the sacred ties which now link together the various parts.

For this you have every inducement of sympathy and interest. Citizens, by birth or choice, of a common country, that country has a right to concentrate your affections. The name of American, which belongs to you in your national capacity, must always exalt the just pride of patriotism more than any appellation derived from local discriminations. With slight shades of difference, you have the same religion, manners, habits, and political principles. You have in a common cause fought and triumphed together; the independence and liberty you possess are the work of joint counsels, and joint efforts of common dangers, sufferings, and successes.

But these considerations, however powerfully they address themselves to your sensibility, are greatly outweighed by those which apply more immediately to your interest. Here every portion of our country finds the most commanding motives for carefully guarding and preserving the union of the whole.

The North, in an unrestrained intercourse with the South, protected by the equal laws of a common government, finds in the productions of the latter great additional resources of maritime and commercial enterprise and precious materials of manufacturing industry. The South, in the same intercourse, benefiting by the agency of the North, sees its agriculture grow and its commerce expand. Turning partly into its own channels the seamen of the North, it finds its particular navigation invigorated; and, while it contributes, in different ways, to nourish and increase the general mass of the national navigation, it looks forward to the protection of a maritime strength, to which itself is unequally adapted. The East, in a like intercourse with the West, already finds, and in the progressive improvement of interior communications by land and water, will more and more find a valuable vent for the commodities which it brings from abroad, or manufactures at home. The West derives from the East supplies requisite to its growth and comfort, and, what is perhaps of still greater consequence, it must of necessity owe the secure enjoyment of indispensable outlets for its own productions to the weight, influence, and the future maritime strength of the Atlantic side of the Union, directed by an indissoluble community of interest as one nation. Any other tenure by which the West can hold this essential advantage, whether derived from its own separate strength, or from an apostate and unnatural connection with any foreign power, must be intrinsically precarious.

While, then, every part of our country thus feels an immediate and particular interest in union, all the parts combined cannot fail to find in the united mass of means and efforts greater strength, greater resource, proportionably greater security from external danger, a less frequent interruption of their peace by foreign nations; and, what is of inestimable value, they must derive from union an exemption from those broils and wars between themselves, which so frequently afflict neighboring countries not tied together by the same governments, which their own rival ships alone would be sufficient to produce, but which opposite foreign alliances, attachments, and intrigues would stimulate and embitter. Hence, likewise, they will avoid the necessity of those overgrown military establishments which, under any form of government, are inauspicious to liberty, and which are to be regarded as particularly hostile to republican liberty. In this sense it is that your union ought to be considered as a main prop of your liberty, and that the love of the one ought to endear to you the preservation of the other.

These considerations speak a persuasive language to every reflecting and virtuous mind, and exhibit the continuance of the Union as a primary object of patriotic desire. Is there a doubt whether a common government can embrace so large a sphere? Let experience solve it. To listen to mere speculation in such a case were criminal. We are authorized to hope that a proper organization of the whole with the auxiliary agency of governments for the respective subdivisions, will afford a happy issue to the experiment. It is well worth a fair and full experiment. With such powerful and obvious motives to union, affecting all parts of our country, while experience shall not have demonstrated its impracticability, there will always be reason to distrust the patriotism of those who in any quarter may endeavor to weaken its bands.

In contemplating the causes which may disturb our Union, it occurs as matter of serious concern that any ground should have been furnished for characterizing parties by geographical discriminations, Northern and Southern, Atlantic and Western; whence designing men may endeavor to excite a belief that there is a real difference of local interests and views. One of the expedients of party to acquire influence within particular districts is to misrepresent the opinions and aims of other districts. You cannot shield yourselves too much against the jealousies and heartburnings which spring from these misrepresentations; they tend to render alien to each other those who ought to be bound together by fraternal affection. The inhabitants of our Western country have lately had a useful lesson on this head; they have seen, in the negotiation by the Executive, and in the unanimous ratification by the Senate, of the treaty with Spain, and in the universal satisfaction at that event, throughout the United States, a decisive proof how unfounded were the suspicions propagated among them of a policy in the General Government and in the Atlantic States unfriendly to their interests in regard to the Mississippi; they have been witnesses to the formation of two treaties, that with Great Britain, and that with Spain, which secure to them everything they could desire, in respect to our foreign relations, towards confirming their prosperity. Will it not be their wisdom to rely for the preservation of these advantages on the Union by which they were procured ? Will they not henceforth be deaf to those advisers, if such there are, who would sever them from their brethren and connect them with aliens?

To the efficacy and permanency of your Union, a government for the whole is indispensable. No alliance, however strict, between the parts can be an adequate substitute; they must inevitably experience the infractions and interruptions which all alliances in all times have experienced. Sensible of this momentous truth, you have improved upon your first essay, by the adoption of a constitution of government better calculated than your former for an intimate union, and for the efficacious management of your common concerns. This government, the offspring of our own choice, uninfluenced and unawed, adopted upon full investigation and mature deliberation, completely free in its principles, in the distribution of its powers, uniting security with energy, and containing within itself a provision for its own amendment, has a just claim to your confidence and your support. Respect for its authority, compliance with its laws, acquiescence in its measures, are duties enjoined by the fundamental maxims of true liberty. The basis of our political systems is the right of the people to make and to alter their constitutions of government. But the Constitution which at any time exists, till changed by an explicit and authentic act of the whole people, is sacredly obligatory upon all. The very idea of the power and the right of the people to establish government presupposes the duty of every individual to obey the established government.

All obstructions to the execution of the laws, all combinations and associations, under whatever plausible character, with the real design to direct, control, counteract, or awe the regular deliberation and action of the constituted authorities, are destructive of this fundamental principle, and of fatal tendency. They serve to organize faction, to give it an artificial and extraordinary force; to put, in the place of the delegated will of the nation the will of a party, often a small but artful and enterprising minority of the community; and, according to the alternate triumphs of different parties, to make the public administration the mirror of the ill-concerted and incongruous projects of faction, rather than the organ of consistent and wholesome plans digested by common counsels and modified by mutual interests.

However combinations or associations of the above description may now and then answer popular ends, they are likely, in the course of time and things, to become potent engines, by which cunning, ambitious, and unprincipled men will be enabled to subvert the power of the people and to usurp for themselves the reins of government, destroying afterwards the very engines which have lifted them to unjust dominion.

Towards the preservation of your government, and the permanency of your present happy state, it is requisite, not only that you steadily discountenance irregular oppositions to its acknowledged authority, but also that you resist with care the spirit of innovation upon its principles, however specious the pretexts. One method of assault may be to effect, in the forms of the Constitution, alterations which will impair the energy of the system, and thus to undermine what cannot be directly overthrown. In all the changes to which you may be invited, remember that time and habit are at least as necessary to fix the true character of governments as of other human institutions; that experience is the surest standard by which to test the real tendency of the existing constitution of a country; that facility in changes, upon the credit of mere hypothesis and opinion, exposes to perpetual change, from the endless variety of hypothesis and opinion; and remember, especially, that for the efficient management of your common interests, in a country so extensive as ours, a government of as much vigor as is consistent with the perfect security of liberty is indispensable. Liberty itself will find in such a government, with powers properly distributed and adjusted, its surest guardian. It is, indeed, little else than a name, where the government is too feeble to withstand the enterprises of faction, to confine each member of the society within the limits prescribed by the laws, and to maintain all in the secure and tranquil enjoyment of the rights of person and property.

I have already intimated to you the danger of parties in the State, with particular reference to the founding of them on geographical discriminations. Let me now take a more comprehensive view, and warn you in the most solemn manner against the baneful effects of the spirit of party generally.

This spirit, unfortunately, is inseparable from our nature, having its root in the strongest passions of the human mind. It exists under different shapes in all governments, more or less stifled, controlled, or repressed; but, in those of the popular form, it is seen in its greatest rankness, and is truly their worst enemy.

The alternate domination of one faction over another, sharpened by the spirit of revenge, natural to party dissension, which in different ages and countries has perpetrated the most horrid enormities, is itself a frightful despotism. But this leads at length to a more formal and permanent despotism. The disorders and miseries which result gradually incline the minds of men to seek security and repose in the absolute power of an individual; and sooner or later the chief of some prevailing faction, more able or more fortunate than his competitors, turns this disposition to the purposes of his own elevation, on the ruins of public liberty.

Without looking forward to an extremity of this kind (which nevertheless ought not to be entirely out of sight), the common and continual mischiefs of the spirit of party are sufficient to make it the interest and duty of a wise people to discourage and restrain it.

It serves always to distract the public councils and enfeeble the public administration. It agitates the community with ill-founded jealousies and false alarms, kindles the animosity of one part against another, foments occasionally riot and insurrection. It opens the door to foreign influence and corruption, which finds a facilitated access to the government itself through the channels of party passions. Thus the policy and the will of one country are subjected to the policy and will of another.

There is an opinion that parties in free countries are useful checks upon the administration of the government and serve to keep alive the spirit of liberty. This within certain limits is probably true; and in governments of a monarchical cast, patriotism may look with indulgence, if not with favor, upon the spirit of party. But in those of the popular character, in governments purely elective, it is a spirit not to be encouraged. From their natural tendency, it is certain there will always be enough of that spirit for every salutary purpose. And there being constant danger of excess, the effort ought to be by force of public opinion, to mitigate and assuage it. A fire not to be quenched, it demands a uniform vigilance to prevent its bursting into a flame, lest, instead of warming, it should consume.

It is important, likewise, that the habits of thinking in a free country should inspire caution in those entrusted with its administration, to confine themselves within their respective constitutional spheres, avoiding in the exercise of the powers of one department to encroach upon another. The spirit of encroachment tends to consolidate the powers of all the departments in one, and thus to create, whatever the form of government, a real despotism. A just estimate of that love of power, and proneness to abuse it, which predominates in the human heart, is sufficient to satisfy us of the truth of this position. The necessity of reciprocal checks in the exercise of political power, by dividing and distributing it into different depositaries, and constituting each the guardian of the public weal against invasions by the others, has been evinced by experiments ancient and modern; some of them in our country and under our own eyes. To preserve them must be as necessary as to institute them. If, in the opinion of the people, the distribution or modification of the constitutional powers be in any particular wrong, let it be corrected by an amendment in the way which the Constitution designates. But let there be no change by usurpation; for though this, in one instance, may be the instrument of good, it is the customary weapon by which free governments are destroyed. The precedent must always greatly overbalance in permanent evil any partial or transient benefit, which the use can at any time yield.

Of all the dispositions and habits which lead to political prosperity, religion and morality are indispensable supports. In vain would that man claim the tribute of patriotism, who should labor to subvert these great pillars of human happiness, these firmest props of the duties of men and citizens. The mere politician, equally with the pious man, ought to respect and to cherish them. A volume could not trace all their connections with private and public felicity. Let it simply be asked: Where is the security for property, for reputation, for life, if the sense of religious obligation desert the oaths which are the instruments of investigation in courts of justice ? And let us with caution indulge the supposition that morality can be maintained without religion. Whatever may be conceded to the influence of refined education on minds of peculiar structure, reason and experience both forbid us to expect that national morality can prevail in exclusion of religious principle.

It is substantially true that virtue or morality is a necessary spring of popular government. The rule, indeed, extends with more or less force to every species of free government. Who that is a sincere friend to it can look with indifference upon attempts to shake the foundation of the fabric?

Promote then, as an object of primary importance, institutions for the general diffusion of knowledge. In proportion as the structure of a government gives force to public opinion, it is essential that public opinion should be enlightened.

As a very important source of strength and security, cherish public credit. One method of preserving it is to use it as sparingly as possible, avoiding occasions of expense by cultivating peace, but remembering also that timely disbursements to prepare for danger frequently prevent much greater disbursements to repel it, avoiding likewise the accumulation of debt, not only by shunning occasions of expense, but by vigorous exertion in time of peace to discharge the debts which unavoidable wars may have occasioned, not ungenerously throwing upon posterity the burden which we ourselves ought to bear. The execution of these maxims belongs to your representatives, but it is necessary that public opinion should co-operate. To facilitate to them the performance of their duty, it is essential that you should practically bear in mind that towards the payment of debts there must be revenue; that to have revenue there must be taxes; that no taxes can be devised which are not more or less inconvenient and unpleasant; that the intrinsic embarrassment, inseparable from the selection of the proper objects (which is always a choice of difficulties), ought to be a decisive motive for a candid construction of the conduct of the government in making it, and for a spirit of acquiescence in the measures for obtaining revenue, which the public exigencies may at any time dictate.

Observe good faith and justice towards all nations; cultivate peace and harmony with all. Religion and morality enjoin this conduct; and can it be, that good policy does not equally enjoin it - It will be worthy of a free, enlightened, and at no distant period, a great nation, to give to mankind the magnanimous and too novel example of a people always guided by an exalted justice and benevolence. Who can doubt that, in the course of time and things, the fruits of such a plan would richly repay any temporary advantages which might be lost by a steady adherence to it ? Can it be that Providence has not connected the permanent felicity of a nation with its virtue ? The experiment, at least, is recommended by every sentiment which ennobles human nature. Alas! is it rendered impossible by its vices?

In the execution of such a plan, nothing is more essential than that permanent, inveterate antipathies against particular nations, and passionate attachments for others, should be excluded; and that, in place of them, just and amicable feelings towards all should be cultivated. The nation which indulges towards another

a habitual hatred or a habitual fondness is in some degree a slave.
It is a slave to its animosity or to its affection, either of which is
sufficient to lead it astray from its duty and its interest. Antipathy
in one nation against another disposes each more readily to offer
insult and injury, to lay hold of slight causes of umbrage, and to be
haughty and intractable, when accidental or trifling occasions of
dispute occur. Hence, frequent collisions, obstinate, envenomed, and
bloody contests. The nation, prompted by ill-will and resentment,
sometimes impels to war the government, contrary to the best
calculations of policy. The government sometimes participates in
the national propensity, and adopts through passion what reason
would reject; at other times it makes the animosity of the nation
subservient to projects of hostility instigated by pride, ambition, and
other sinister and pernicious motives. The peace often, sometimes
perhaps the liberty, of nations, has been the victim.

So likewise, a passionate attachment of one nation for another
produces a variety of evils. Sympathy for the favorite nation,
facilitating the illusion of an imaginary common interest in cases
where no real common interest exists, and infusing into one the
enmities of the other, betrays the former into a participation in
the quarrels and wars of the latter without adequate inducement
or justification. It leads also to concessions to the favorite nation of
privileges denied to others which is apt doubly to injure the nation
making the concessions; by unnecessarily parting with what ought
to have been retained, and by exciting jealousy, ill-will, and a
disposition to retaliate, in the parties from whom equal privileges are
withheld. And it gives to ambitious, corrupted, or deluded citizens
(who devote themselves to the favorite nation), facility to betray
or sacrifice the interests of their own country, without odium,

sometimes even with popularity; gilding, with the appearances of
a virtuous sense of obligation, a commendable deference for public
opinion, or a laudable zeal for public good, the base or foolish
compliances of ambition, corruption, or infatuation.

As avenues to foreign influence in innumerable ways, such
attachments are particularly alarming to the truly enlightened and
independent patriot. How many opportunities do they afford to
tamper with domestic factions, to practice the arts of seduction, to
mislead public opinion, to influence or awe the public councils. Such
an attachment of a small or weak towards a great and powerful
nation dooms the former to be the satellite of the latter.

Against the insidious wiles of foreign influence (I conjure you to
believe me, fellow-citizens) the jealousy of a free people ought to be
constantly awake, since history and experience prove that foreign
influence is one of the most baneful foes of republican government.
But that jealousy to be useful must be impartial; else it becomes the
instrument of the very influence to be avoided, instead of a defense
against it. Excessive partiality for one foreign nation and excessive
dislike of another cause those whom they actuate to see danger only
on one side, and serve to veil and even second the arts of influence
on the other. Real patriots who may resist the intrigues of the
favorite are liable to become suspected and odious, while its tools and
dupes usurp the applause and confidence of the people, to surrender
their interests.

The great rule of conduct for us in regard to foreign nations is
in extending our commercial relations, to have with them as little
political connection as possible. So far as we have already formed
engagements, let them be fulfilled with perfect good faith. Here

let us stop. Europe has a set of primary interests which to us have none; or a very remote relation. Hence she must be engaged in frequent controversies, the causes of which are essentially foreign to our concerns. Hence, therefore, it must be unwise in us to implicate ourselves by artificial ties in the ordinary vicissitudes of her politics, or the ordinary combinations and collisions of her friendships or enmities.

Our detached and distant situation invites and enables us to pursue a different course. If we remain one people under an efficient government. the period is not far off when we may defy material injury from external annoyance; when we may take such an attitude as will cause the neutrality we may at any time resolve upon to be scrupulously respected; when belligerent nations, under the impossibility of making acquisitions upon us, will not lightly hazard the giving us provocation; when we may choose peace or war, as our interest, guided by justice, shall counsel.

Why forego the advantages of so peculiar a situation? Why quit our own to stand upon foreign ground? Why, by interweaving our destiny with that of any part of Europe, entangle our peace and prosperity in the toils of European ambition, rivalship, interest, humor or caprice?

It is our true policy to steer clear of permanent alliances with any portion of the foreign world; so far, I mean, as we are now at liberty to do it; for let me not be understood as capable of patronizing infidelity to existing engagements. I hold the maxim no less applicable to public than to private affairs, that honesty is always the best policy. I repeat it, therefore, let those engagements be observed in their genuine sense. But, in my opinion, it is unnecessary and would be unwise to extend them.

Taking care always to keep ourselves by suitable establishments on a respectable defensive posture, we may safely trust to temporary alliances for extraordinary emergencies.

Harmony, liberal intercourse with all nations, are recommended by policy, humanity, and interest. But even our commercial policy should hold an equal and impartial hand; neither seeking nor granting exclusive favors or preferences; consulting the natural course of things; diffusing and diversifying by gentle means the streams of commerce, but forcing nothing; establishing (with powers so disposed, in order to give trade a stable course, to define the rights of our merchants, and to enable the government to support them) conventional rules of intercourse, the best that present circumstances and mutual opinion will permit, but temporary, and liable to be from time to time abandoned or varied, as experience and circumstances shall dictate; constantly keeping in view that it is folly in one nation to look for disinterested favors from another; that it must pay with a portion of its independence for whatever it may accept under that character; that, by such acceptance, it may place itself in the condition of having given equivalents for nominal favors, and yet of being reproached with ingratitude for not giving more. There can be no greater error than to expect or calculate upon real favors from nation to nation. It is an illusion, which experience must cure, which a just pride ought to discard.

In offering to you, my countrymen, these counsels of an old and affectionate friend, I dare not hope they will make the strong and lasting impression I could wish; that they will control the usual current of the passions, or prevent our nation from running the course which has hitherto marked the destiny of nations. But, if I may even flatter myself that they may be productive of some partial benefit, some occasional good; that they may now and then recur to moderate the fury of party spirit, to warn against the mischiefs of foreign intrigue, to guard against the impostures of pretended patriotism; this hope will be a full recompense for the solicitude for your welfare, by which they have been dictated.

How far in the discharge of my official duties I have been guided by the principles which have been delineated, the public records and other evidences of my conduct must witness to you and to the world. To myself, the assurance of my own conscience is, that I have at least believed myself to be guided by them.

In relation to the still subsisting war in Europe, my proclamation of the twenty-second of April, 1793, is the index of my plan. Sanctioned by your approving voice, and by that of your representatives in both houses of Congress, the spirit of that measure has continually governed me, uninfluenced by any attempts to deter or divert me from it.

After deliberate examination, with the aid of the best lights I could obtain, I was well satisfied that our country, under all the circumstances of the case, had a right to take, and was bound in duty and interest to take, a neutral position. Having taken it, I determined, as far as should depend upon me, to maintain it, with moderation, perseverance, and firmness.

The considerations which respect the right to hold this conduct, it is not necessary on this occasion to detail. I will only observe that, according to my understanding of the matter, that right, so far from being denied by any of the belligerent powers, has been virtually admitted by all.

The duty of holding a neutral conduct may be inferred, without anything more, from the obligation which justice and humanity impose on every nation, in cases in which it is free to act, to maintain inviolate the relations of peace and amity towards other nations.

The inducements of interest for observing that conduct will best be referred to your own reflections and experience. With me a predominant motive has been to endeavor to gain time to our country to settle and mature its yet recent institutions, and to progress without interruption to that degree of strength and consistency which is necessary to give it, humanly speaking, the command of its own fortunes.

Though, in reviewing the incidents of my administration, I am unconscious of intentional error, I am nevertheless too sensible of my defects not to think it probable that I may have committed many errors. Whatever they may be, I fervently beseech the Almighty to avert or mitigate the evils to which they may tend. I shall also carry with me the hope that my country will never cease to view them with indulgence; and that, after forty five years of my life dedicated to its service with an upright zeal, the faults of incompetent abilities will be consigned to oblivion, as myself must soon be to the mansions of rest.

Relying on its kindness in this as in other things, and actuated by that fervent love towards it, which is so natural to a man who views in it the native soil of himself and his progenitors for several generations, I anticipate with pleasing expectation that retreat in which I promise myself to realize, without alloy, the sweet enjoyment of partaking, in the midst of my fellow-citizens, the benign influence of good laws under a free government, the ever-favorite object of my heart, and the happy reward, as I trust, of our mutual cares, labors, and dangers.

Geo. Washington.

PRESBYTERIAN UNITED SYNOD

Revisions to the Westminster Confession

Church historian Dr. D. G. Hart[1] explains, "The substance of the revision was to reformulate the Westminster Divines' teaching on the civil magistrate. The Westminster Assembly had been called by Parliament, and its affirmations about the role and function of the government, especially in ecclesiastical matters, reflected a situation in which the state exerted control over the church as part of the price of religious establishment. The American revision of 1787-1789 took into account the new situation in the United States, where the state had no authority over the church."

The text below is excerpted from church historian Philip Schaff's 1876 text Creeds of Christendom, Volume I, Chapter 7.

After the Revolutionary War the united Synod of Philadelphia and New York, which met at Philadelphia, May 28, 1787, appointed a committee to prepare an alteration in the Confession of Faith, Chapter XX (closing paragraph), Chapter XXII., 3 and Ch. XXXI., 1, 2 in consequence of the new relation of Church and State. The changes proposed were adopted by the joint Synod at a subsequent meeting in Philadelphia, May 28, 1788, in the following action:

'The Synod having fully considered the draught of the form of government and discipline, did, on a review of the whole, and hereby do ratify and adopt the same, as now altered and amended, as the Constitution of the Presbyterian Church in America, and order the same to be considered and strictly observed as the rule of

1 "New Horizons." The Orthodox Presbyterian Church. Accessed August 11, 2017. https://tinyurl.com/yd3cx9n3.

their proceedings by all the inferior judicatories belonging to the body. And they order that a correct copy be printed, and that the Westminster Confession of faith, as now altered, be printed in full along with it, as making a part of the Constitution.

'Resolved, That the true intent and meaning of the above ratification by the Synod is, that the Form of Government and Discipline, and the Confession of Faith, as now ratified, is to continue to be our constitution and the confession of our faith and practice unalterable, unless two thirds of the Presbyteries under the care of the General Assembly shall propose alterations or amendments, and such alterations or amendments shall be agreed to and enacted by the General Assembly.'

On the day following (May 29) the Synod 'took into consideration the Westminster Larger and Shorter Catechisms, and having made a small amendment of the Larger, did approve, and do hereby approve and ratify the said Catechisms, as now agreed on, as the Catechisms of the Presbyterian Church in the said United States.' At the same time it was ordered that all these standards, as altered and adapted to the wants of the American churches, be printed and bound up in one volume.

The changes consist in the omission of those sentences which imply the union of Church and State, or the principle of ecclesiastical establishments, making it the duty of the civil magistrate not only to protect, but also to support religion, and giving to the magistrate power to call and ratify ecclesiastical synods and councils, and to punish heretics. Instead of this, the American revision confines the duty of the civil magistrate to the legal protection of religion in its public exercise, without distinction of Christian creeds or organizations. It thus professes the principle of religious liberty and equality of all denominations before the law. This principle has been faithfully and consistently adhered to by the large body of the Presbyterian Church in America, and has become the common law of the land. To facilitate the comparison we present the respective sections in parallel columns:

Original

Ch. XXIII. 3.—Of the Civil Magistrate.

The civil magistrate, may not assume to himself the administration of the Word and Sacraments, or the power of the keys of the kingdom of heaven;yet he hath authority, and it is his duty to take order, that unity and peace be preserved in the Church, that the truth of God be kept pure and entire, that all blasphemies and heresies be suppressed, all corruptions and abuses in worship and discipline prevented or reformed; and all the ordinances of God duly settled, administered, and observed.For the better effecting whereof he hath power to call synods, to be present at them, and to provide that whatsoever is transacted in them be according to the mind of God.

Revision

XXIII. 3.—Of the Civil Magistrate.

Civil magistrates may not assume to themselves the administration of the Word and Sacraments;or the power of the keys of the kingdom of heaven; or, in the least, interfere in matters of faith. Yet, as nursing fathers, it is the duty of civil magistrates to protect the Church of our common Lord, without giving the preference to any denomination of Christians above the rest, in such a manner that all ecclesiastical persons whatever shall enjoy the full, free, and unquestioned liberty of discharging every part of their sacred functions without violence or danger. And as Jesus Christ hath appointed a regular government and discipline in his Church, no law of any commonwealth should interfere with, let, or hinder the due exercise thereof among the voluntary members of any denomination of Christians, according to their own profession and belief. It is the duty of civil magistrates to protect the person and good name of all their people, in such an effectual manner as that no person be suffered, either upon pretense of religion or infidelity, to offer any indignity, violence, abuse, or injury to any other person whatsoever; and to take order that all religious and ecclesiastical assemblies be held without molestation or disturbance.

Original	Revision
Ch. XXXI.—Of Synods and Councils.	Ch. XXXI.—Of Synods and Councils.
For the better government and further edification of the Church, there ought to be such assemblies as are commonly called synods or councils. II. As magistrates may lawfully call a synod of ministers and other fit persons to consult and advise with about matters of religion:1570 so, if magistrates be open enemies to the Church, the ministers of Christ, of themselves, by virtue of their office; or they, with other fit persons, upon delegation from their churches, may meet together in such assemblies.	For the better government and further edification of the Church, there ought to be such assemblies as are commonly called synods or councils. And it belongeth to the overseers and other rulers of the particular churches, by virtue of their office, and the power which Christ hath given them for edification, and not for destruction, to appoint such assemblies; and to convene together in them, as often as they shall judge it expedient for the good of the Church.

In Ch. XX., § 4, the last sentence, 'and by the power of the civil magistrate,' was omitted, so as to read, 'they [the offenders] may lawfully be called to account, and proceeded against by the censures of the Church.'[2]

The only change made in the Larger Catechism was the striking out of the words 'tolerating a false religion,' among the sins forbidden in the Second Commandment (Quest. 109).

The example set by the Presbyterian Church in the United States was afterwards (1801) followed by the Protestant Episcopal Church in the revision of the political sections of the Thirty-nine Articles of Religion.

EPISCOPAL CHURCH IN AMERICA

Revisions to the Thirty-Nine Articles

Church historian Philip Schaff writes that "the General Convention held at Trenton, New Jersey, Sept. 3–12, 1801, [adopted] the Thirty-nine Articles in the form which they have since retained in the American Episcopal Church, and are incorporated in its editions of the Prayer-Book. The only doctrinal difference is the omission of the Athanasian Creed from Art. VIII.; the remaining changes are political, and adapted to the separation of Church and State. Otherwise even 'the obsolete diction' is retained . . . The only change in the Prayer-Book which has a doctrinal bearing, besides the omission of the Athanasian Creed, is the insertion of the Prayer of Oblation and Invocation from the Scotch (and the First Edwardine) Prayer-Book, through the influence of Bishop Seabury, who had been consecrated in the Scotch Episcopal Church." — 1876, Creeds of Christendom, Volume 1, Chapter 7.

Below are the revisions resulting from the newly formed and adopted republican form of government in the United States of America. For reference, the original 37th article (1571, 1662) reads thus:

> "The King's Majesty hath the chief power in this Realm of England, and other his Dominions, unto whom the chief Government of all Estates of this Realm, whether they be Ecclesiastical or Civil, in all causes doth appertain, and is not, nor ought to be, subject to any foreign Jurisdiction. Where we attribute to the King's Majesty the chief government, by which Titles we understand the minds of some

slanderous folks to be offended; we give not our Princes the ministering either of God's Word, or of the Sacraments, the which thing the Injunctions also lately set forth by Elizabeth our Queen do most plainly testify; but that only prerogative, which we see to have been given always to all godly Princes in holy Scriptures by God himself; that is, that they should rule all estates and degrees committed to their charge by God, whether they be Ecclesiastical or Temporal, and restrain with the civil sword the stubborn and evil-doers.

The Bishop of Rome hath no jurisdiction in this Realm of England.

The Laws of the Realm may punish Christian men with death, for heinous and grievous offences.

It is lawful for Christian men, at the commandment of the Magistrate, to wear weapons, and serve in the wars.

Resolutions of the Bishops, the Clergy, and the Laity of the Protestant Episcopal Church in the United States of America, in Convention, in the city of Trenton, the 12th day of September, in the year of our Lord 1801, respecting the Articles of Religion.

'The Articles of Religion are hereby ordered to be set forth with the following directions, to be observed in all future editions of the same; that is to say --

'The following to be the title, viz.:

"Articles of Religion, as established by the Bishops, the Clergy, and the Laity of the Protestant Episcopal Church in the United

States of America, in Convention, on the 12th day of September, in the year of our Lord 1801."

'The Articles to stand as in the Book of Common Prayer of the Church of England, with the following alterations and omissions, viz.:

. . .

'Under the title "Article 21," the following note to be inserted, namely, '"The 21st of the former Articles is omitted, because it is partly of a local and civil nature, and is provided for, as to the remaining parts of it, in other Articles."

'The 35th Article to be inserted with the following note, namely,

'"This Article is received in this Church, so far as it declares the Books of Homilies to be an explication of Christian doctrine, and instructive in piety and morals. But all references to the constitution and laws of England are considered as inapplicable to the circumstances of this Church: which also suspends the order for the reading of said homilies in churches until a revision of them may conveniently be made, for the clearing of them, as well from obsolete words and phrases, as from the local references."

. . .

'The 37th Article to be omitted, and the following substituted in its place:

'"Art. XXXVII. Of the Power of the Civil Magistrate.

'"The power of the civil magistrate extendeth to all men, as well Clergy as Laity, in all things temporal; but hath no authority in things purely spiritual. And we hold it to be the duty of all men who are professors of the gospel, to pay respectful obedience to the civil authority, regularly and legitimately constituted."

'Adopted by the House of Bishops.

WILLIAM WHITE, D.D., Presiding Bishop.

'Adopted by the House of Clerical and Lay Deputies.

ABRAHAM BEACH, D.D., President.

FRANCIS SCOTT KEY

The Star-Spangled Banner

Francis Scott Key, an attorney from Washington, D.C., was held prisoner aboard a British naval ship in 1814 awaiting the end of the attack on Balitmore. During a heavy bombardment one night, Key watched in agony as the battered Stars and Stripes were lowered over Fort McHenry. Shortly, he saw with some relief that that grand old flag was replaced by a smaller American flag. In the morning, the full-size flag was once again raised signalling victory for the Americans. In an overflow of emotion and relief, he wrote a poem titled "Defence of Fort M'Henry" to commemorate the events of that night. In a grand irony, his lyrics were eventually put to a popular British tune. The song was eventually renamed "The Star-Spangled Banne," and in 1931, it was formally made the National Anthem of the United States by congressional resolution.

O say can you see, by the dawn's early light,
What so proudly we hail'd at the twilight's last gleaming,
Whose broad stripes and bright stars through
 the perilous fight
O'er the ramparts we watch'd were so gallantly streaming?
And the rocket's red glare, the bombs bursting in air,
Gave proof through the night that our flag was still there,
O say does that star-spangled banner yet wave
O'er the land of the free and the home of the brave?

On the shore dimly seen through the mists of the deep
Where the foe's haughty host in dread silence reposes,
What is that which the breeze, o'er the towering steep,

As it fitfully blows, half conceals, half discloses?
Now it catches the gleam of the morning's first beam,
In full glory reflected now shines in the stream,
'Tis the star-spangled banner - O long may it wave
O'er the land of the free and the home of the brave!

And where is that band who so vauntingly swore,
That the havoc of war and the battle's confusion
A home and a Country should leave us no more?
Their blood has wash'd out their foul footstep's pollution.
No refuge could save the hireling and slave
From the terror of flight or the gloom of the grave,
And the star-spangled banner in triumph doth wave
O'er the land of the free and the home of the brave.

O thus be it ever when freemen shall stand
Between their lov'd home and the war's desolation!
Blest with vict'ry and peace may the heav'n rescued land
Praise the power that hath made and preserv'd us a nation!
Then conquer we must, when our cause it is just,
And this be our motto - "In God is our trust,"
And the star-spangled banner in triumph shall wave
O'er the land of the free and the home of the brave.

Missouri Compromise

The Missouri Compromise was an attempt to preserve the balance of power in the United States Congress between slave states and free states and to defuse the growing tensions between North and South. It was passed in 1820 after much bitter debate, admitting Maine, a free state, and Missouri, a slave state, to the Union. A further provision of the Missouri Compromise stipulated that slavery was to be prohibited in the Louisiana Territory north of the 36° 30' latitude line. Many southerners were concerned that it would set a precedent for the authority of Congress to override state soveregnty. Nevertheless, this provision was the law of the land until it was repealed by the Kansas-Nebraska Act in 1854. The Supreme Court ruled the Missouri Compromise unconstitutional three years later in the Dred Scott decision when it declared that Congress did not have the authority to prohibit slavery in United States territories.

An Act to authorize the people of the Missouri territory to form a constitution and state government, and for the admission of such state into the Union on an equal footing with the original states, and to prohibit slavery in certain territories.

Be it enacted by the Senate and House of Representatives of the United States of America, in Congress assembled, That the inhabitants of that portion of the Missouri territory included within the boundaries herein after designated, be, and they are hereby, authorized to form for themselves a constitution and state government, and to assume such name as they shall deem proper; and the said state, when formed, shall be admitted into the Union, upon an equal footing with the original states, in all respects whatsoever.

SEC. 2. And be it further enacted, That the said state shall consist of all the territory included within the following boundaries, to wit: Beginning in the middle of the Mississippi river, on the parallel of thirty-six degrees of north latitude; thence west, along that parallel of latitude, to the St. Francois river; thence up, and following the course of that river, in the middle of the main channel thereof, to the parallel of latitude of thirty-six degrees and thirty minutes; thence west, along the same, to a point where the said parallel is intersected by a meridian line passing through the middle of the mouth of the Kansas river, where the same empties into the Missouri river, thence, from the point aforesaid north, along the said meridian line, to the intersection of the parallel of latitude which passes through the rapids of the river Des Moines, making the said line to correspond with the Indian boundary line; thence east, from the point of intersection last aforesaid, along the said parallel of latitude, to the middle of the channel of the main fork of the said river Des Moines ; thence down arid along the middle of the main channel of the said river Des Moines, to the mouth of the same, where it empties into the Mississippi river; thence, due east, to the middle of the main channel of the Mississippi river; thence down, and following the course of the Mississippi river, in the middle of the main channel thereof, to the place of beginning : Provided, The said state shall ratify the boundaries aforesaid . And provided also, That the said state shall have concurrent jurisdiction on the river Mississippi, and every other river bordering on the said state so far as the said rivers shall form a common boundary to the said state; and any other state or states, now or hereafter to be formed and bounded by the same, such rivers to be common to both; and that the river Mississippi, and the navigable rivers and waters leading into the same, shall be common highways, and for ever free, as well to the inhabitants of the said state as to other citizens of the United States, without any tax, duty impost, or toll, therefor, imposed by the said state.

SEC. 3. And be it further enacted, That all free white male citizens of the United States, who shall have arrived at the age of twenty-one years, and have resided in said territory: three months previous to the day of election, and all other persons qualified to vote for representatives to the general assembly of the said territory, shall be qualified to be elected and they are hereby qualified and authorized to vote, and choose representatives to form a convention, who shall be apportioned amongst the several counties as follows:

From the county of Howard, five representatives. From the county of Cooper, three representatives. From the county of Montgomery, two representatives. From the county of Pike, one representative. From the county of Lincoln, one representative. From the county of St. Charles, three representatives. From the county of Franklin, one representative. From the county of St. Louis, eight representatives. From the county of Jefferson, one representative. From the county of Washington, three representatives. From the county of St. Genevieve, four representatives. From the county of Madison, one representative. From the county of Cape Girardeau, five representatives. From the county of New Madrid, two representatives. From the county of Wayne, and that portion of the county of Lawrence which falls within the boundaries herein designated, one representative.

And the election for the representatives aforesaid shall be holden on the first Monday, and two succeeding days of May next, throughout the several counties aforesaid in the said territory, and shall be, in every respect, held and conducted in the same manner, and under the same regulations as is prescribed by the laws of the said territory regulating elections therein for members of the general assembly, except that the returns of the election in that portion of Lawrence county included in the boundaries aforesaid, shall be made to the county of Wayne, as is provided in other cases under the laws of said territory.

SEC. 4. And be it further enacted, That the members of the conven tion thus duly elected, shall be, and they are hereby authorized to meet at the seat of government of said territory on the second Monday of the month of June next; and the said convention, when so assembled, shall have power and authority to adjourn to any other place in the said territory, which to them shall seem best for the convenient transaction of their business; and which convention, when so met, shall first determine by a majority of the whole number elected, whether it be, or be not, expedient at that time to form a constitution and state government for the people within the said territory, as included within the boundaries above designated; and if it be deemed expedient, the convention shall be, and hereby is, authorized to form a constitution and state government; or, if it be deemed more expedient, the said convention shall provide by ordinance for electing representatives to form a constitution or frame of government; which said representatives shall be chosen in such manner, and in such proportion as they shall designate; and shall meet at such time and place as shall be prescribed by the said ordinance; and shall then form for the people of said territory, within the boundaries aforesaid, a constitution and state government: Provided, That the same, whenever formed, shall be republican, and not repugnant to the constitution of the United States; and that the legislature of said state shall never interfere with the primary disposal of the soil by the United States, nor with any regulations Congress may find necessary for securing the title in such soil to the bona fide purchasers ; and that no tax shall be imposed on lands the property of the United States ; and in no case shall non-resident proprietors be taxed higher than residents.

SEC. 5. And be it further enacted, That until the next general census shall be taken, the said state shall be entitled to one representative in the House of Representatives of the United States.

SEC. 6. And be it further enacted, That the following propositions be, and the same are hereby, offered to the convention of the said territory of Missouri, when formed, for their free acceptance or rejection, which, if accepted by the convention, shall be obligatory upon the United States:

First. That section numbered sixteen in every township, and when such section has been sold, or otherwise disposed of, other lands equivalent thereto, and as contiguous as may be, shall be granted to the state for the use of the inhabitants of such township, for the use of schools.

Second. That all salt springs, not exceeding twelve in number, with six sections of land adjoining to each, shall be granted to the said state for the use of said state, the same to be selected by the legislature of the said state, on or before the first day of January, in the year one thousand eight hundred and twenty-five ; and the same, when so selected, to be used under such terms, conditions, and regulations, as the legislature of said state shall direct: Provided, That no salt spring, the right whereof now is, or hereafter shall be, confirmed or adjudged to any individual or individuals, shall, by this section, be granted to the said state: And provided also, That the legislature shall never sell or lease the same, at anyone time, for a longer period than ten years, without the consent of Congress.

Third. That five per cent. of the net proceeds of the sale of lands lying within the said territory or state, and which shall be sold by Congress, from and after the first day of January next, after deducting all expenses incident to the same, shall be reserved for making public roads and canals, of which three fifths shall be applied to those objects within the state, under the direction of the legislature thereof; and the other two fifths in defraying, under the direction of Congress, the expenses to be incurred in making of a road or roads, canal or canals, leading to the said state.

Fourth. That four entire sections of land be, and the same are hereby, granted to the said state, for the purpose of fixing their seat of government thereon; which said sections shall, under the direction of the legislature of said state, be located, as near as may be, in one body, at any time, in such townships and ranges as the legislature aforesaid may select, on any of the public lands of the United States: Provided, That such locations shall be made prior to the public sale of the lands of the United States surrounding such location.

Fifth. That thirty-six sections, or one entire township, which shall be designated by the President of the United States, together with the other lands heretofore reserved for that purpose, shall be reserved for the use of a seminary of learning, and vested in the legislature of said state, to be appropriated solely to the use of such seminary by the said legislature: Provided, That the five foregoing propositions herein offered, are on the condition that the convention of the said state shall provide, by an ordinance, irrevocable without the consent or the United States, that every and each tract of land sold by the United States, from and after the firsl day of January next, shall remain exempt from any tax laid by order or under the authority of the state, whether for state, county, or township, or any other purpose whatever, for the term of five years from and after the day of sale; And further, That the bounty lands granted, or hereafter to be granted, for military services during the late war, shall, while they continue to be held by the patentees, or their heirs remain exempt as aforesaid from taxation for the term of three year; from and after the date of the patents respectively.

SEC. 7. And be it further enacted, That in case a constitution and state government shall be formed for the people of the said territory of Missouri, the said convention or representatives, as soon thereafter as may be, shall cause a true and attested copy of such constitution or frame of state government, as shall be formed or provided, to be transmitted to Congress.

SEC. 8. And be it further enacted. That in all that territory ceded by France to the United States, under the name of Louisiana, which lies north of thirty-six degrees and thirty minutes north latitude, not included within the limits of the state, contemplated by this act, slavery and involuntary servitude, otherwise than in the punishment of crimes, whereof the parties shall have been duly convicted, shall be, and is hereby, forever prohibited: Provided always, That any person escaping into the same, from whom labour or service is lawfully claimed, in any state or territory of the United States, such fugitive may be lawfully reclaimed and conveyed to the person claiming his or her labour or service as aforesaid.

JOHN QUINCY ADAMS

Monroe Doctrine

The Monroe Doctrine was set forth during President Monroe's seventh annual message to Congress, December 2, 1823. This established a key principle of American sovereignty, that "the American continents, by the free and independent condition which they have assumed and maintain, are henceforth not to be considered as subjects for future colonization by any European powers. . ." This doctrine was actually penned by James Monroe's Secretary of State, John Quincy Adams, yet its attribution to Monroe shows the growing influence of the American Presidency, even during the early years of the American Republic.

A t the proposal of the Russian Imperial Government, made through the minister of the Emperor residing here, a full power and instructions have been transmitted to the minister of the United States at St. Petersburg to arrange by amicable negotiation the respective rights and interests of the two nations on the northwest coast of this continent. A similar proposal has been made by His Imperial Majesty to the Government of Great Britain, which has likewise been acceded to. The Government of the United States has been desirous by this friendly proceeding of manifesting the great value which they have invariably attached to the friendship of the Emperor and their solicitude to cultivate the best understanding with his Government. In the discussions to which this interest has given rise and in the arrangements by which they may terminate the occasion has been judged proper for asserting, as a principle in which the rights and interests of the United States are involved, that the American continents, by the free and independent

condition which they have assumed and maintain, are henceforth not
to be considered as subjects for future colonization by any European
powers. . .

It was stated at the commencement of the last session that a
great effort was then making in Spain and Portugal to improve the
condition of the people of those countries, and that it appeared to
be conducted with extraordinary moderation. It need scarcely be
remarked that the results have been so far very different from what
was then anticipated. Of events in that quarter of the globe, with
which we have so much intercourse and from which we derive our
origin, we have always been anxious and interested spectators. The
citizens of the United States cherish sentiments the most friendly in
favor of the liberty and happiness of their fellow-men on that side of
the Atlantic. In the wars of the European powers in matters relating
to themselves we have never taken any part, nor does it comport
with our policy to do so. It is only when our rights are invaded or
seriously menaced that we resent injuries or make preparation for
our defense. With the movements in this hemisphere we are of
necessity more immediately connected, and by causes which must
be obvious to all enlightened and impartial observers. The political
system of the allied powers is essentially different in this respect
from that of America. This difference proceeds from that which
exists in their respective Governments; and to the defense of our
own, which has been achieved by the loss of so much blood and
treasure, and matured by the wisdom of their most enlightened
citizens, and under which we have enjoyed unexampled felicity,
this whole nation is devoted. We owe it, therefore, to candor and
to the amicable relations existing between the United States and
those powers to declare that we should consider any attempt on
their part to extend their system to any portion of this hemisphere

as dangerous to our peace and safety. With the existing colonies
or dependencies of any European power we have not interfered and
shall not interfere. But with the Governments who have declared
their independence and maintain it, and whose independence we
have, on great consideration and on just principles, acknowledged,
we could not view any interposition for the purpose of oppressing
them, or controlling in any other manner their destiny, by any
European power in any other light than as the manifestation of an
unfriendly disposition toward the United States. In the war between
those new Governments and Spain we declared our neutrality at
the time of their recognition, and to this we have adhered, and
shall continue to adhere, provided no change shall occur which, in
the judgement of the competent authorities of this Government,
shall make a corresponding change on the part of the United States
indispensable to their security.

The late events in Spain and Portugal shew that Europe is still
unsettled. Of this important fact no stronger proof can be adduced
than that the allied powers should have thought it proper, on any
principle satisfactory to themselves, to have interposed by force in
the internal concerns of Spain. To what extent such interposition
may be carried, on the same principle, is a question in which all
independent powers whose governments differ from theirs are
interested, even those most remote, and surely none of them more so
than the United States. Our policy in regard to Europe, which was
adopted at an early stage of the wars which have so long agitated
that quarter of the globe, nevertheless remains the same, which
is, not to interfere in the internal concerns of any of its powers;
to consider the government de facto as the legitimate government
for us; to cultivate friendly relations with it, and to preserve those

relations by a frank, firm, and manly policy, meeting in all instances the just claims of every power, submitting to injuries from none. But in regard to those continents circumstances are eminently and conspicuously different.

It is impossible that the allied powers should extend their political system to any portion of either continent without endangering our peace and happiness; nor can anyone believe that our southern brethren, if left to themselves, would adopt it of their own accord. It is equally impossible, therefore, that we should behold such interposition in any form with indifference. If we look to the comparative strength and resources of Spain and those new Governments, and their distance from each other, it must be obvious that she can never subdue them. It is still the true policy of the United States to leave the parties to themselves, in hope that other powers will pursue the same course. . . .

CONGRESS OF THE UNITED STATES

Indian Removal Act

On March 28, 1830, Congress passed the Indian Removal Act, which began the forced relocation of thousands of Native Americans, becoming what is now known as the Trail of Tears. The Act freed up huge swaths of valuable farmland. There were some opposing voices in Congress, most notably Tennesean Davey Crockett. Eventually, nearly 50,000 Native Americans were forcibly relocated to the new Indian Territory, now part of the state of Oklahoma. It has been estimated that 4000 died along the way.

AN ACT TO PROVIDE FOR AN EXCHANGE OF LANDS WITH THE INDIANS RESIDING IN ANY OF THE STATES OR TERRITORIES, AND FOR THEIR REMOVAL WEST OF THE RIVER MISSISSIPPI.

Be it enacted by the Senate and House of Representatives of the United States of America, in Congress assembled, That it shall and may be lawful for the President of the United States to cause so much of any territory belonging to the United States, west of the river Mississippi, not included in any state or organized territory, and to which the Indian title has been extinguished, as he may judge necessary, to be divided into a suitable number of districts, for the reception of such tribes or nations of Indians as may choose to exchange the lands where they now reside, and remove there; and to cause each of said districts to be so described by natural or artificial marks, as to be easily distinguished from every other.

And be it further enacted, That it shall and may be lawful for the President to exchange any or all of such districts, so to be laid off and described, with any tribe or nation of Indians now residing within the limits of any of the states or territories, and with which the United States have existing treaties, for the whole or any part or portion of the territory claimed and occupied by such tribe or nation, within the bounds of any one or more of the states or territories, where the land claimed and occupied by the Indians, is owned by the United States, or the United States are bound to the state within which it lies to extinguish the Indian claim thereto.

And be it further enacted, That in the making of any such exchange or exchanges, it shall and may be lawful for the President solemnly to assure the tribe or nation with which the exchange is made, that the United States will forever secure and guaranty to them, and their heirs or successors, the country so exchanged with them; and if they prefer it, that the United States will cause a patent or grant to be made and executed to them for the same: Provided always, That such lands shall revert to the United States, if the Indians become extinct, or abandon the same.

And be it further enacted, That if, upon any of the lands now occupied by the Indians, and to be exchanged for, there should be such improvements as add value to the land claimed by any individual or individuals of such tribes or nations, it shall and may be lawful for the President to cause such value to be ascertained by appraisement or otherwise, and to cause such ascertained value to be paid to the person or persons rightfully claiming such improvements. And upon the payment of such valuation, the improvements so valued and paid for, shall pass to the United States, and possession shall not afterwards be permitted to any of the same tribe.

And be it further enacted, That upon the making of any such exchange as is contemplated by this act, it shall and may be lawful for the President to cause such aid and assistance to be furnished to the emigrants as may be necessary and proper to enable them to remove to, and settle in, the country for which they may have exchanged; and also, to give them such aid and assistance as may be necessary for their support and subsistence for the first year after their removal.

And be it further enacted, That it shall and may be lawful for the President to cause such tribe or nation to be protected, at their new residence, against all interruption or disturbance from any other tribe or nation of Indians, or from any other person or persons whatever.

And be it further enacted, That it shall and may be lawful for the President to have the same superintendence and care over any tribe or nation in the country to which they may remove, as contemplated by this act, that he is now authorized to have over them at their present places of residence: Provided, That nothing in this act contained shall be construed as authorizing or directing the violation of any existing treaty between the United States and any of the Indian tribes.

And be it further enacted, That for the purpose of giving effect to the Provisions of this act, the sum of five hundred thousand dollars is hereby appropriated, to be paid out of any money in the treasury, not otherwise appropriated.

SAMUEL FRANCIS SMITH

My Country, 'Tis of Thee

*Samuel Francis Smith, a seminary student at Andover Theological
Seminary, wrote this song for an Independence Day celebration in 1831. Set
to the British tune "God Save the Queen," it so well-known that it is almost
considered a national anthem along with "The Star-Spangled Banner."*

My country, 'tis of thee,
Sweet land of liberty,
Of thee I sing;
Land where my fathers died,
Land of the pilgrims' pride,
From ev'ry mountainside
Let freedom ring!

My native country, thee,
Land of the noble free,
Thy name I love;
I love thy rocks and rills,
Thy woods and templed hills;
My heart with rapture thrills,
Like that above.
Let music swell the breeze,

And ring from all the trees
Sweet freedom's song;
Let mortal tongues awake;
Let all that breathe partake;
Let rocks their silence break,
The sound prolong.

My fathers' God to Thee,
Author of liberty,
To Thee we sing.
Long may our land be bright,
With freedom's holy light,
Protect us by Thy might,
Great God our King.

ALEXIS DE TOQUEVILLE

Democracy in America

Sometimes, the best way to truly understand ourselves is to listen to what an "outsider" has to say about us. French diplomat Alexis de Tocqueville visited America in 1831, and published his philosophical treatise detailing both his researches and his impressions in 1835. Following his understanding of the course of liberty in America, he landed on the shores of New England and made his way inland. He particularly commends the men who landed in New England and their noble aim of freedom to live and worship according to the dictates of conscience. In response to a memoir written by one of those early settlers, the Roman Catholic Tocqueville describes the Protestant Puritans as no mere adventurers, but "the seed of a great people that God comes to deposit from his hands onto a predestined land."[1] Because of this, Tocqueville notes that "Democracy such as antiquity had not dared to dream of sprang full-grown and fully armed from the midst of the old feudal society."[2] He goes on to describe how this old Puritan New England mindset manifested itself in the township model, which provides the best example of—and the best hope for—democracy in America. Though he predicts an inevitable downfall of democracy accompanied by an inevitable coming of the tyrant, Tocqueville holds out hope that liberty will have a long run before that day, largely owing to its noble birth on the tiny New England coast.

I.ii. ORIGIN OF THE ANGLO-AMERICANS, AND ITS
IMPORTANCE IN RELATION TO THEIR FUTURE
CONDITION.

A fter the birth of a human being his early years are
obscurely spent in the toils or pleasures of childhood. As
he grows up the world receives him, when his manhood
begins, and he enters into contact with his fellows. He is then studied
for the first time, and it is imagined that the germ of the vices and
the virtues of his maturer years is then formed.

This, if I am not mistaken, is a great error. We must begin
higher up; we must watch the infant in his mother's arms; we must
see the first images which the external world casts upon the dark
mirror of his mind; the first occurrences which he witnesses; we
must hear the first words which awaken the sleeping powers of
thought, and stand by his earliest efforts, if we would understand the
prejudices, the habits, and the passions which will rule his life. The
entire man is, so to speak, to be seen in the cradle of the child.

The growth of nations presents something analogous to this: they
all bear some marks of their origin; and the circumstances which
accompanied their birth and contributed to their rise affect the
whole term of their being.

If we were able to go back to the elements of states, and to
examine the oldest monuments of their history, I doubt not that
we should discover the primal cause of the prejudices, the habits,
the ruling passions, and, in short, of all that constitutes what is
called the national character: we should then find the explanation
of certain customs which now seem at variance with the prevailing
manners; of such laws as conflict with established principles; and

of such incoherent opinions as are here and there to be met with in society, like those fragments of broken chains which we sometimes see hanging from the vault of an edifice, and supporting nothing. This might explain the destinies of certain nations which seem borne on by an unknown force to ends of which they themselves are ignorant. But hitherto facts have been wanting to researches of this kind: the spirit of inquiry has only come upon communities in their latter days; and when they at length contemplated their origin, time had already obscured it, or ignorance and pride adorned it with truth-concealing fables.

America is the only country in which it has been possible to witness the natural and tranquil growth of society, and where the influence exercised on the future condition of states by their origin is clearly distinguishable.

At the period when the peoples of Europe landed in the New World their national characteristics were already completely formed; each of them had a physiognomy of its own; and as they had already attained that stage of civilization at which men are led to study themselves, they have transmitted to us a faithful picture of their opinions, their manners, and their laws. The men of the sixteenth century are almost as well known to us as our contemporaries. America consequently exhibits in the broad light of day the phænomena which the ignorance or rudeness of earlier ages conceals from our researches. Near enough to the time when the states of America were founded to be accurately acquainted with their elements, and sufficiently removed from that period to judge of some of their results, the men of our own day seem destined to see further than their predecessors into the series of human events. Providence has given us a torch which our forefathers did not possess, and has allowed us to discern fundamental causes in the history of the world which the obscurity of the past concealed from them.

If we carefully examine the social and political state of America after having studied its history, we shall remain perfectly convinced that not an opinion, not a custom, not a law, I may even say not an event, is upon record which the origin of that people will not explain. The readers of this book will find the germ of all that is to follow in the present chapter, and the key to almost the whole work.

The emigrants who came at different periods to occupy the territory now covered by the American Union, differed from each other in many respects; their aim was not the same, and they governed themselves on different principles.

These men had, however, certain features in common, and they were all placed in an analogous situation. The tie of language is perhaps the strongest and the most durable that can unite mankind. All the emigrants spoke the same tongue; they were all offsets from the same people. Born in a country which had been agitated for centuries by the struggles of faction, and in which all parties had been obliged in their turn to place themselves under the protection of the laws, their political education had been perfected in this rude school, and they were more conversant with the notions of right, and the principles of true freedom, than the greater part of their European contemporaries. At the period of the first emigrations, the parish system, that fruitful germ of free institutions, was deeply rooted in the habits of the English; and with it the doctrine of the sovereignty of the people had been introduced into the bosom of the monarchy of the House of Tudor.

. . . The two or three main ideas which constitute the basis of the social theory of the United States were first combined in the Northern English colonies, more generally denominated the States of New England. The principles of New England spread at first to the neighbouring states; they then passed successively to the more distant ones; and at length they imbued the whole Confederation. They now extend their influence beyond its limits over the whole American world. The civilization of New England has been like a beacon lit upon a hill, which after it has diffused its warmth around, tinges the distant horizon with its glow.

The foundation of New England was a novel spectacle, and all the circumstances attending it were singular and original. The large majority of colonies have been first inhabited either by men without education and without resources, driven by their poverty and their misconduct from the land which gave them birth, or by speculators and adventurers greedy of gain. Some settlements cannot even boast so honourable an origin; St. Domingo was founded by buccaneers; and, at the present day, the criminal courts of England supply the population of Australia.

The settlers who established themselves on the shores of New England all belonged to the more independent classes of their native country. Their union on the soil of America at once presented the singular phænomenon of a society containing neither lords nor common people, neither rich nor poor. These men possessed, in proportion to their number, a greater mass of intelligence than is to be found in any European nation of our own time. All, without a single exception, had received a good education, and many of them were known in Europe for their talents and their acquirements. The other colonies had been founded by adventurers without family; the emigrants of New England brought with them the best elements of order and morality, they landed in the desert accompanied by their wives and children. But what most especially distinguished them was the aim of their undertaking. They had not been obliged by necessity to leave their country, the social position they abandoned was one to be regretted, and their means of subsistence were certain. Nor did they cross the Atlantic to improve their situation or to increase their wealth; the call which summoned them from the comforts of their homes was purely intellectual; and in facing the inevitable suffering of exile their object was the triumph of an idea.

The emigrants, or, as they deservedly styled themselves, the Pilgrims, belonged to that English sect, the austerity of whose principles had acquired for them the name of Puritans. Puritanism was not merely a religious doctrine, but it corresponded in many points with the most absolute democratic and republican theories. It was this tendency which had aroused its most dangerous adversaries. Persecuted by the Government of the mother-country, and disgusted by the habits of a society opposed to the rigour of their own principles, the Puritans went forth to seek some rude and unfrequented part of the world, where they could live according to their own opinions, and worship God in freedom.

A few quotations will throw more light upon the spirit of these pious adventurers than all we can say of them. Nathaniel Morton, the historian of the first years of the settlement, thus opens his subject:

Gentle Reader,
I have for some length of time looked upon it as
a duty incumbent, especially on the immediate
successors of those that have had so large experience

of those many memorable and signall demonstrations
of God's goodness, viz., the first beginners of this
Plantation in New England, to commit to writing his
gracious dispensations on that behalf; having so many
inducements thereunto, not onely otherwise, but so
plentifully in the Sacred Scriptures: that so, what we
have seen, and what our fathers have told us, (Psalm
lxxviii. 3, 4,) we may not hide from our children,
shewing to the generations to come the praises of the
Lord; that especially the seed of Abraham his servant,
and the children of Jacob his chosen (Psalm cv. 5, 6,)
may remember his marvellous works in the beginning
and progress of the planting of New England, his
wonders and the judgements of his mouth; how that
God brought a vine into this wilderness; that He cast
out the heathen, and planted it; that He made room
for it and caused it to take deep root; and it filled the
land (Psalm Ixxx. 8, 9.). And not onely so, but also
that He hath guided his people by his strength to his
holy habitation, and planted them in the mountain
of his inheritance in respect of precious Gospel-
enjoyments: and that as especially God may have the
glory of all unto whom it is most due; so also some
rays of glory may reach the names of those blessed
Saints, that were the main instruments and the
beginning of this happy enterprize.

It is impossible to read this opening paragraph without an
involuntary feeling of religious awe; it breathes the very savour of
Gospel antiquity. The sincerity of the author heightens his power
of language. The band which to his eyes was a mere party of

adventurers gone forth to seek their fortune beyond seas, appears to the reader as the germ of a great nation wafted by Providence to a predestined shore.

The author thus continues his narrative of the departure of the first pilgrims.

> So they left that goodly and pleasant city of Leyden, which had been their resting-place for above eleven years; but they knew that they were pilgrims and strangers here below, and looked not much on these things, but lifted up their eyes to Heaven, their dearest country, where God hath prepared for them a city (Heb. xi. 16.), and therein quieted their spirits. When they came to Delfs-Haven they found the ship and all things ready; and such of their friends as could not come with them, followed after them, and sundry came from Amsterdam to see them shipt, and to take their leaves of them. One night was spent with little sleep with the most, but with friendly entertainment and Christian discourse, and other real expressions of true Christian love. The next day they went on board, and their friends with them, where truly doleful was the sight of that sad and mournful parting, to hear what sighs and sobs and prayers did sound amongst them; what tears did gush from every eye, and pithy speeches pierced each other's heart, that sundry of the Dutch strangers that stood on the Key as spectators could not refrain from tears. But the tide (which stays for no man) calling them away, that were thus loth to depart, their Reverend Pastor falling down on his

knees, and they all with him, with watery cheeks
commended them with most fervent prayers unto the
Lord and his blessing; and then with mutual embraces
and many tears, they took their leaves one of another,
which proved to be the last leave to many of them."

The emigrants were about 150 in number, including the women
and the children. Their object was to plant a colony on the shores of
the Hudson; but after having been driven about for some time in the
Atlantic Ocean, they were forced to land on that arid coast of New
England which is now the site of the town of Plymouth. The rock is
still shown on which the pilgrims disembarked.

But before we pass on . . . let the reader with
me make a pause and seriously consider this poor
people's present condition, the more to be raised up to
admiration of God's goodness towards them in their
preservation: for being now passed the vast ocean,
and a sea of troubles before them in expectation,
they had now no friends to welcome them, no inns
to entertain or refresh them, no houses, or much less
towns to repair unto to seek for succour: and for the
season it was winter, and they that know the winters
of the country, know them to be sharp and violent,
subject to cruel and fierce storms, dangerous to travel
to known places, much more to search unknown
coasts. Besides, what could they see but a hideous and
desolate wilderness, full of wilde beasts, and wilde
men? and what multitudes of them there were, they
then knew not: for which way soever they turned their
eyes (save upward to Heaven) they could have but little

solace or content in respect of any outward object; for
summer being ended, all things stand in appearance
with a weather-beaten face, and the whole country
full of woods and thickets, represented a wild and
savage hew; if they looked behind them, there was the
mighty ocean which they had passed, and was now as
a main bar or gulph to separate them from all the civil
parts of the world.

It must not be imagined that the piety of the Puritans was of a
merely speculative kind, or that it took no cognizance of the course
of worldly affairs. Puritanism, as I have already remarked, was
scarcely less a political than a religious doctrine. No sooner had
the emigrants landed on the barren coast, described by Nathaniel
Morton, than it was their first care to constitute a society, by
passing the following Act:

In the name of God, Amen. We, whose names
are underwritten, the loyal subjects of our dread
Sovereign Lord King James, &c. &c., Having
undertaken for the glory of God, and advancement
of the Christian Faith, and the honour of our King
and country, a voyage to plant the first colony in
the northern parts of Virginia; Do by these presents
solemnly and mutually, in the presence of God and
one another, covenant and combine ourselves together
into a civil body politick, for our better ordering
and preservation, and furtherance of the ends
aforesaid: and by virtue hereof do enact, constitute
and frame such just and equal laws, ordinances, acts,
constitutions, and officers, from time to time, as shall

be thought most meet and convenient for the general
good of the Colony: unto which we promise all due
submission and obedience," &c.

This happened in 1620, and from that time forwards the
emigration went on. The religious and political passions which
ravaged the British Empire during the whole reign of Charles
I., drove fresh crowds of sectarians every year to the shores of
America. In England the stronghold of Puritanism was in the
middle classes, and it was from the middle classes that the majority
of the emigrants came. The population of New England increased
rapidly; and whilst the hierarchy of rank despotically classed the
inhabitants of the mother-country, the colony continued to present
the novel spectacle of a community homogeneous in all its parts. A
democracy, more perfect than any which antiquity had dreamt of,
started in full size and panoply from the midst of an ancient feudal
society.

. . . In New England, townships were completely and definitively
constituted as early as 1650. The independence of the township
was the nucleus round which the local interests, passions, rights,
and duties collected and clung. It gave scope to the activity of a
real political life, most thoroughly democratic and republican. The
colonies still recognised the supremacy of the mother-country;
monarchy was still the law of the State; but the republic was already
established in every township.

The towns named their own magistrates of every kind, rated
themselves, and levied their own taxes. In the parish of New
England the law of representation was not adopted, but the affairs
of the community were discussed, as at Athens, in the marketplace,
by a general assembly of the citizens.

In studying the laws which were promulgated at this first era of the American republics, it is impossible not to be struck by the remarkable acquaintance with the science of government, and the advanced theory of legislation which they display. The ideas there formed of the duties of society towards its members are evidently much loftier and more comprehensive than those of the European legislators at that time: obligations were there imposed which were elsewhere slighted. In the States of New England, from the first, the condition of the poor was provided for; strict measures were taken for the maintenance of roads, and surveyors were appointed to attend to them; registers were established in every parish, in which the results of public deliberations, and the births, deaths, and marriages of the citizens were entered; clerks were directed to keep these registers; officers were charged with the administration of vacant inheritances, and with the arbitration of litigated landmarks; and many others were created whose chief functions were the maintenance of public order in the community. The law enters into a thousand useful provisions for a number of social wants which are at present very inadequately felt in France.

But it is by the attention it pays to Public Education that the original character of American civilization is at once placed in the clearest light. "It being," says the law, "one chief project of Satan to keep men from the knowledge of the Scripture by persuading from the use of tongues, to the end that learning may not be buried in the graves of our forefathers, in church and commonwealth, the Lord assisting our endeavours,. . . . " Here follow clauses establishing schools in every township, and obliging the inhabitants, under pain of heavy fines, to support them. Schools of a superior kind were founded in the same manner in the more populous districts. The

municipal authorities were bound to enforce the sending of children
to school by their parents; they were empowered to inflict fines upon
all who refused compliance; and in cases of continued resistance
society assumed the place of the parent, took possession of the child,
and deprived the father of those natural rights which he used to
so bad a purpose. The reader will undoubtedly have remarked the
preamble of these enactments: in America, religion is the road to
knowledge, and the observance of the Divine laws leads man to civil
freedom.

If, after having cast a rapid glance over the state of American
society in 1650, we turn to the condition of Europe, and more
especially to that of the Continent, at the same period, we cannot
fail to be struck with astonishment. On the continent of Europe,
at the beginning of the seventeenth century, absolute monarchy
had everywhere triumphed over the ruins of the oligarchical and
feudal liberties of the Middle Ages. Never were the notions of right
more completely confounded than in the midst of the splendour and
literature of Europe; never was there less political activity among
the people; never were the principles of true freedom less widely
circulated; and at that very time, those principles, which were
scorned or unknown by the nations of Europe, were proclaimed in
the deserts of the New World, and were accepted as the future creed
of a great people. The boldest theories of the human reason were
put into practice by a community so humble, that not a statesman
condescended to attend to it; and a legislation without a precedent
was produced offhand by the imagination of the citizens. In the
bosom of this obscure democracy, which had as yet brought forth
neither generals, nor philosophers, nor authors, a man might stand
up in the face of a free people and pronounce the following fine
definition of liberty.

"Nor would I have you to mistake in the point of your own
liberty. There is a liberty of corrupt nature, which is affected
both by men and beasts to do what they list; and this liberty is
inconsistent with authority, impatient of all restraint; by this liberty
'sumus omnes deteriores:' 't is the grand enemy of truth and peace,
and all the ordinances of God are bent against it. But there is a
civil, a moral, a federal liberty which is the proper end and object
of authority; it is a Uberty for that only which is just and good: for
this liberty you are to stand with the hazard of your very lives, and
whatsoever crosses it, is not authority, but a distemper thereof. This
liberty is maintained in a way of subjection to authority; and the
authority set over you will, in all administrations for your good, be
quietly submitted unto by all but such as have a disposition to shake
off the yoke and lose their true liberty, by their murmuring at the
honour and power of authority."

The remarks I have made will suffice to display the character of
Anglo-American civilization in its true light. It is the result (and this
should be constantly present to the mind) of two distinct elements,
which in other places have been in frequent hostility, but which in
America have been admirably incorporated and combined with one
another. I allude to the spirit of Religion, and the spirit of Liberty.

The settlers of New England were at the same time ardent
sectarians and daring innovators. Narrow as the limits of some of
their religious opinions were, they were entirely free from political
prejudices.

Hence arose two tendencies, distinct but not opposite, which are
constantly discernible in the manners as well as in the laws of the
country.

It might be imagined that men who sacrificed their friends, their family, and their native land to a religious conviction, were absorbed in the pursuit of the intellectual advantages which they purchased at so dear a rate. The energy, however, with which they strove for the acquirement of wealth, moral enjoyment, and the comforts as well as liberties of the world, is scarcely inferior to that with which they devoted themselves to Heaven.

Political principles, and all human laws and institutions were moulded and altered at their pleasure; the barriers of the society in which they were born were broken down before them; the old principles which had governed the world for ages were no more; a path without a term, and a field without an horizon were opened to the exploring and ardent curiosity of man: but at the limits of the political world he checks his researches, he discreetly lays aside the use of his most formidable faculties, he no longer consents to doubt or to innovate, but carefully abstaining from raising the curtain of the sanctuary, he yields with submissive respect to truths which he will not discuss.

Thus in the moral world, everything is classed, adapted, decided, and foreseen; in the political world everything is agitated, uncertain, and disputed: in the one is a passive, though a voluntary, obedience; in the other an independence, scornful of experience, and jealous of authority.

These two tendencies, apparently so discrepant, are far from conflicting; they advance together, and mutually support each other.

Religion perceives that civil liberty affords a noble exercise to the faculties of man, and that the political world is a field prepared

by the Creator for the efforts of the intelligence. Contented with
the freedom and the power which it enjoys in its own sphere, and
with the place which it occupies, the empire of religion is never
more surely established than when it reigns in the hearts of men
unsupported by aught beside its native strength.

Religion is no less the companion of liberty in all its battles and
its triumphs; the cradle of its infancy, and the divine source of its
claims. The safeguard of morality is religion, and morality is the
best security of law, and the surest pledge of freedom.

I.I.5 EXISTENCE OF THE TOWNSHIP

I have already observed, that the principle of the sovereignty
of the people governs the whole political system of the Anglo-
Americans. Every page of this book will afford new instances
of the same doctrine. In the nations by which the sovereignty of
the people is recognised, every individual possesses an equal share
of power, and participates alike in the government of the State.
Every individual is, therefore, supposed to be as well informed,
as virtuous, and as strong as any of his fellow-citizens. He obeys
the government, not because he is inferior to the authorities which
conduct it, or that he is less capable than his neighbour of governing
himself, but because he acknowledges the utility of an association
with his fellow-men, and because he knows that no such association
can exist without a regulating force. If he be a subject in all that
concerns the mutual relations of citizens, he is free, and responsible
to God alone for all that concerns himself. Hence arises the maxim
that every one is the best and the sole judge of his own private
interest, and that society has no right to control a man's actions,
unless they are prejudicial to the common weal, or unless the
common weal demands his cooperation. This doctrine is universally

admitted in the United States. I shall hereafter examine the general influence which it exercises on the ordinary actions of life: I am now speaking of the nature of municipal bodies.

The township, taken as a whole, and in relation to the government of the country, may be looked upon as an individual to whom the theory I have just alluded to is applied. Municipal independence is therefore a natural consequence of the principle of the sovereignty of the people in the United States: all the American republics recognise it more or less; but circumstances have peculiarly favoured its growth in New England.

In this part of the Union the impulsion of political activity was given in the townships; and it may almost be said that each of them originally formed an independent nation. When the kings of England asserted their supremacy, they were contented to assume the central power of the State. The townships of New England remained as they were before; and although they are now subject to the State, they were at first scarcely dependent upon it. It is important to remember that they have not been invested with privileges, but that they have, on the contrary, forfeited a portion of their independence to the State. The townships are only subordinate to the State in those interests which I shall term social, as they are common to all the citizens. They are independent in all that concerns themselves; and amongst the inhabitants of New England I believe that not a man is to be found who would acknowledge that the State has any right to interfere in their local interests. The towns of New England buy and sell, prosecute or are indicted, augment or diminish their rates, without the slightest opposition on the part of the administrative authority of the State.

They are bound, however, to comply with the demands of the community. If the State is in need of money, a town can neither give nor withhold the supplies. If the State projects a road, the township cannot refuse to let it cross its territory; if a police regulation is made by the State, it must be enforced by the town. A uniform system of instruction is organized all over the country, and every town is bound to establish the schools which the law ordains. In speaking of the administration of the United States, I shall have occasion to point out the means by which the townships are compelled to obey in these different cases: I here merely show the existence of the obligation. Strict as this obligation is, the government of the State imposes it in principle only, and in its performance the township resumes all its independent rights. Thus, taxes are voted by the State, but they are levied and collected by the township; the existence of a school is obligatory, but the township builds, pays, and superintends it. In France the State-collector receives the local imposts; in America the town-collector receives the taxes of the State. Thus the French Government lends its agents to the commune; in America, the township is the agent of the Government. This fact alone shows the extent of the differences which exist between the two nations.

II.i.5 PUBLIC SPIRIT OF THE TOWNSHIPS OF NEW ENGLAND.

In America, not only do municipal bodies exist, but they are kept alive and supported, by public spirit. The township of New England possesses two advantages which infallibly secure the attentive interest of mankind, namely, independence and authority. Its sphere is indeed small and limited, but within that

sphere its action is unrestrained; and its independence gives to it a
real importance, which its extent and population may not always
ensure.

It is to be remembered that the affections of men generally lie on
the side of authority. Patriotism is not durable in a conquered nation.
The New Englander is attached to his township, not only because
he was born in it, but because it constitutes a social body of which
he is a member, and whose government claims and deserves the
exercise of his sagacity. In Europe the absence of local public spirit
is a frequent subject of regret to those who are in power; everyone
agrees that there is no surer guarantee of order and tranquillity,
and yet nothing is more difficult to create. If the municipal bodies
were made powerful and independent, the authorities of the nation
might be disunited, and the peace of the country endangered. Yet,
without power and independence, a town may contain good subjects,
but it can have no active citizens. Another important fact is that the
township of New England is so constituted as to excite the warmest
of human affections, without arousing the ambitious passions of
the heart of man. The officers of the county are not elected, and
their authority is very limited. Even the State is only a second-rate
community, whose tranquil and obscure administration offers no
inducement sufficient to draw men away from the circle of their
interests into the turmoil of public affairs. The federal government
confers power and honour on the men who conduct it; but these
individuals can never be very numerous. The high station of the
Presidency can only be reached at an advanced period of life; and
the other federal functionaries are generally men who have been
favoured by fortune, or distinguished in some other career. Such
cannot be the permanent aim of the ambitious. But the township

serves as a centre for the desire of public esteem, the want of exciting interests, and the taste for authority and popularity, in the midst of the ordinary relations of life; and the passions which commonly embroil society, change their character when they find a vent so near the domestic hearth and the family circle.

In the American States power has been disseminated with admirable skill, for the purpose of interesting the greatest possible number of persons in the common weal. Independently of the electors who are from time to time called into action, the body politic is divided into innumerable functionaries and officers, who all, in their several spheres, represent the same powerful whole in whose name they act. The local administration thus affords an unfailing source of profit and interest to a vast number of individuals.

The American system, which divides the local authority among so many citizens, does not scruple to multiply the functions of the town officers. For in the United States it is believed, and with truth, that patriotism is a kind of devotion which is strengthened by ritual observance. In this manner the activity of the township is continually perceptible; it is daily manifested in the fulfilment of a duty, or the exercise of a right; and a constant though gentle motion is thus kept up in society, which animates without disturbing it.

The American attaches himself to his home, as the mountaineer clings to his hills, because the characteristic features of his country are there more distinctly marked than elsewhere. The existence of the townships of New England is in general a happy one. Their government is suited to their tastes, and chosen by themselves. In the midst of the profound peace and general comfort which reign in America, the commotions of municipal discord are unfrequent.

The conduct of local business is easy. The political education of the people has long been complete; say rather that it was complete when the people first set foot upon the soil. In New England no tradition exists of a distinction of ranks; no portion of the community is tempted to oppress the remainder; and the abuses which may injure isolated individuals are forgotten in the general contentment which prevails. If the government is defective, (and it would no doubt be easy to point out its deficiences,) the fact that it really emanates from those it governs, and that it acts, either ill or well, casts the protecting spell of a parental pride over its faults. No term of comparison disturbs the satisfaction of the citizen: England formerly governed the mass of the colonies, but the people was always sovereign in the township, where its rule is not only an ancient, but a primitive state.

The native of New England is attached to his township because it is independent and free: his cooperation in its affairs ensures his attachment to its interest; the well-being it affords him secures his affection; and its welfare is the aim of his ambition and of his future exertions: he takes a part in every occurrence in the place; he practises the art of government in the small sphere within his reach; he accustoms himself to those forms which can alone ensure the steady progress of liberty; he imbibes their spirit; he acquires a taste for order, comprehends the union or the balance of powers, and collects clear practical notions on the nature of his duties and the extent of his rights.

DANIEL WEBSTER

Second Reply to Hayne

*The South Carolina Nullification Crisis of 1828-1832 tested the old
Constitutional Theory of Nullification, which said that states could nullify
federal laws within their borders. When the Federal Government passed
the Tariffs of 1828-1832, the state of South Carolina passed an ordinance
of nullification declaring the tariffs unconstitutional and therefore null
and void in the state. The state's case for nullification was made by Senator
Robert Y. Hayne and Senator John C. Calhoun, who had been Andrew
Jackson's Vice President. Senator Daniel Webster of Massachusetts
responded to Senator Hayne on January 26-27th 1830.*

Mr. President — When the mariner has been tossed
for many days in thick weather, and on an unknown
sea, he naturally avails himself of the first pause in
the storm, the earliest glance of the sun, to take his latitude, and
ascertain how far the elements have driven him from his true
course. Let us imitate this prudence, and, before we float farther on
the waves of this debate, refer to the point from which we departed,
that we may at least be able to conjecture where we now are. I ask
for the reading of the resolution before the Senate. . . We have thus
heard, Sir, what the resolution is which is actually before us for
consideration; and it will readily occur to every one, that it is almost
the only subject about which something has not been said in the
speech, running through two days, by which the Senate has been
entertained by the gentleman from South Carolina. Every topic in
the wide range of our public affairs, whether past or present, - every
thing, general or local, whether belonging to national politics or
party politics, - seems to have attracted more or less of the honorable

member's attention, save only the resolution before the Senate. He
has spoken of every thing but the public lands; they have escaped his
notice. To that subject, in all his excursions, he has not paid even the
cold respect of a passing glance...

Sir, let me recur to pleasing recollections; let me indulge in
refreshing rememberance of the past; let me remind you that, in
early times, no States cherished greater harmony, both of principle
and feeling, than Massachusetts and South Carolina. Would to
God that harmony might again return! Shoulder to shoulder they
went through the Revolution, hand in hand they stood round the
administration of Washington, and felt his own great arm lean on
them for support. Unkind feeling, if it exist, alienation, and distrust
are the growth, unnatural to such soils, of false principles since
sown. They are weeds, the seeds of which that same great arm
never scattered.

Mr. President,I shall enter on no encomium upon Massachusetts;
she needs none. There she is. Behold her, and judge for yourselves.
There is her history; the world knows it by heart. The past, at
least, is secure. There is Boston, and Concord, and Lexington, and
Bunker Hill; and there they will remain for ever. The bones of her
sons, falling in the great struggle for Independence, now lie mingled
with the soil of every State from New England to Georgia; and there
they will lie for ever. And Sir, where American Liberty raised its
first voice, and where its youth was nurtured and sustained, there
it still lives, in the strength of its manhood, and full of its original
spirit. If discord and disunion shall wound it, if party strife and
blind ambition shall hawk at and tear it, if folly and madness, if
uneasiness under salutary and necessary restraint, shall suceed in
seperating it from that Union, by which alone its existence is made

sure, it will stand, in the end, by the side of that cradle in which its infancy was rocked; over the friends who gather round it; and it will fall at last, if fall it must, amidst the proudest monuments of its own glory, and on the very spot of its origin.

There yet remains to be performed, Mr. President, by far the most grave and important duty, which I feel to be devolved on me by this occasion. It is to state, and to defend, what I conceive to be the true principles of the Constitution under which we are here assembled. I might well have desired that so weighty a task should have fallen into other and abler hands. I could have wished that it should have been executed by those whose character and experience give weight and influence to their opinions, such as cannot possibly belong to mine. But, Sir, I have met the occasion, not sought it; and I shall proceed to state my own sentiments, without challenging for them any particular regard, with studied plainness, and as much precision as possible.

I understand the honorable gentleman from South Carolina to maintain, that it is a right of the State legislatures to interfere, whenever, in their judgment, this government transcends its constitutional limits, and to arrest the operation of its laws.

I understand him to maintain this right, as a right existing under the Constitution, not as a right to overthrow it on the ground of extreme nexessity, such as would justify violent revolution.

I understand him to maintain an authority, on the part of the States, thus to interfere, for the purpose of correcting the exercise of power by the general government, of checking it, and of compelling it to conform to their opinion of the extend of its powers.

I understand him to maintain that the ultimate power of judging of the constitutional extent of its own authority is not lodged exclusively in the general government, or any branch of it: but that, on the contrary, the States may lawfully decide for themselves, and each State for itself, whether, in a given case, the act of the general government transcends its power.

I understand him to insist, that, if the exigency of the case, in the opinion of any State government, require it, such State government may, by its own sovereign authority, annul an act of the general government which it deems plainly and palpably unconstitutional.

This is the sum of what I understand from him to be the South Carolina doctrine, and the doctrine which he maintains. I propose to consider it, and compare it with the Constitution. Allow me to say, as a preliminary remark, that I call this the South Carolina doctrive only because the gentleman himself has so denominated it. I do not feel at liberty to say that South Carolina, as a State, has ever advanced these sentiments. I hope she has not, and never may. That a great majority of her people are opposed to the tariff laws, is doubtless true. That a majority, somewhat less than that just mentioned, conscientiously believe that these laws are unconstitutional, may probably also be true. But that any majority holds the right of direct State interference at State discretion, the right of nullifying acts of Congress by acts of State legislation, is more than I know, and what I shall be slow to believe...

This leads us to inquire into the origin of this government and the source of its power. Whose agent is it? Is it the creature of the State legislatures, or the creature of the people? If the government of the United States be the agent of the State governments, then they may control it, provided they can agree in the manner of controlling it; if it be the agent of the people, then the people alone can control it, restrain it, modify, or reform it. It is observable enough, that the doctrine for which the honorable gentleman contends leads him to the necessity of maintaining, not only that this general government is the creature of the States, but that it is the creature of each of the States severally, so that each may assert the power for itself of determining whether it acts whithin the limits of its authority. It is the servant of four-and-twenty masters, of different will and different purposes and yet bound to obey all. This absurdity (for it seems no less) arises from a misconception as to the origin of this government and its true character. It is, Sir, the people's Constitution, the people's government, made for the people, made by the people, and answerable to the people. The people of the United States have declared that the Constitution shall be the supreme law. We must either admit the proposition, or dispute their authority. The States are, unquestionably, sovereign, so far as their sovereignty is not affected by this supreme law. But the State legislatures, as political bodies, however sovereign, are yet not sovereign over the people. So far as the people have given the power to the general government, so far the grant is unquestionably good, and the government holds of the people, and not of the State governments. We are all agents of the same supreme power, the people. The general government and the State governments derive their authority from the same source. Neither can, in relation to the other, be called primary, though one is definite and restricted, and the other general and residuary. The national government possesses those powers which it will be shown the people have conferred upon it, and no more. All the rest belongs to the State governments, or to the people themselves. So far as the people have restrained State sovereignty, by the expression of their will, in the Constitution of the United States, so far, it must be admitted. State sovereignty is effectually controlled. I do not contend that it is, or ought to be, controlled farther. The sentiment to which I have referred propounds that State sovereignty is only to be controlled by its own "feeling of justice": that is to say, it is not to be controlled at all, for one who is to follow his own feelings is under no legal control. Now, however men may think this ought to be, the fact is, that the people of the United States have chosen to impose control on State sovereignties. There are those, doubtless, who wish they had been left without restraing; but the Constitution has ordered the matter differently. To make war, for instance, is an exercise of sovereignty; but the Constitution declares that no State shall make war. To coin money is another exercise of sovereign power, but no State is at liberty to coin money. Again, the Constitution says that no sovereign State shall be so sovereign as to make a treaty. These prohibitions, it must be confessed, are a control on the State sovereignty of South Carolina, as well as of the other States, which does not arise "from her own feelings of honorable justice." The opinion referred to, therefore, is in defiance of the plainest provsions of the Constitution...

I must now beg to ask, Sir, Whence is this supposed right of the States derived? Where do they find the power to interfere with the laws of the Union? Sir the opinion which the honorable gentleman maintains is a notion founded in a total misapprehension, in my judgment, of the origin of this governemnt, and of the foundation on which it stands. I hold it to be a popular government, erected by the people; those who administer it, responsible to the people; and itself capable of being amended and modified, just as the people may choose it should be. It is as popular, just as truly emanating

from the people, as the State governments. It is created for one
purpuse; the State governments for another. It has its own powers;
they have theirs. There is no more authority with them to arrest the
operation of a law of Congress, than with Congress to arrest the
operation of their laws. We are here to administer a Constitution
emanating immediately from the people, and trusted by them to
our administration. It is not the creature of the State governments.
It is of no moment to the argument, that certain acts of the State
legislatures are necessary to fill our seats in this body. That is not
one of their original State powers, a part of the sovereignty of the
State. It is a duty which the people, by the Constitution itself, have
imposed on the State legislatures; and which they might have left
toe performed elsewhere, if they had seen fit. So they have left
the choice of President with electors; but all this does not affect
the proposition that this whole government, President, Senate, and
House of Representatives, is a popular government. It leaves it still
all its popular character. The governor of a State (in some of the
States) is chosen, not directly by the people, but by those who are
chosen by the people, for the purpose of performing, among other
duties, that of electing a governor. Is the government of the State,
on that account, not a popular government? This government, Sir, is
the independent offspring of the popular will. It is not the creature
of State legislatures; nay, more, if the whole truth must be told, the
people brought it into existence, established it, and have hitherto
supported it, for the very purpose, amongst others, of imposing
certain salutary restraints on State sovereignties. The States cannot
now make war; they cannot contract alliances; they cannot make,
each for itself, separate regulations of commerce; they cannot
lay imposts; they cannot coin money. If this Constitution, Sir, be
the creature of State legislatures, it must be admitted that it has

obtained a strange control over the volitions of its creators.

The people, then, Sir, erected this government. They gave it
a Constitution, and in that Constitution they have enumerated
the powers which they bestow on it.. They have made it a limited
government. They have defined its authority. They have restrained
it to the exercise of such powers as are granted; and all others, they
declare, are reserved to the States or the people. But, Sir, they have
not stopped here. If they had, they would have accomplished but half
their work. No definition can be so clear, as to avoid possibility of
doubt; no limitation so precise, as to exclude all uncertainty. Who,
then, shall construe this grant of the people? Who shall interpret
their will, where it may be supposed they have left it doubtful? With
whom do they repose this ultimate right of deciding on the powers
of government? Sir, they have settled all this in the fullest manner.
They have left it with the government itself, in its appropriate
branches. Sir, the very chief end, the main design, for which the
whole Constitution was framed and adopted, was to establish a
government that should not be obliged to act through State agency,
or depend on State opinion and State discretion. The people had had
quite enough of that kind of government under the Confederation.
Under that system, the legal action, the application of law to
individuals, belonged exclusively to the States. Congress could only
recommend; their acts were not of binding force, till the States had
adopted and sanctioned them. Are we in that condition still? Are we
yet at the mercy of State discretion and State construction? Sir, if
we are, then vain will be our attempt to maintain the Constitution
under which we sit.

But, Sir, the people have wisely provided, in the Constitution
itself, a proper, suitable mode and tribunal for settling questions

of Constitutional law. There are in the Constitution grants of powers to Congress, and restrictions on these powers. There are, also, prohibitions on the States. Some authority must, therefore, necessarily exist, having the ultimate jurisdiction to fix and ascertain the interpretation of these grants, restrictions, and prohibitions. The Constitution has itself pointed out, ordaned, and established that authority. How has it accomplished this great and essential end? By declaring, Sir, that "the Constitution, and the laws of the United States made in pursuance thereof, shall be the supreme law of the land, any thing in the constitution or laws of any State to the contrary notwithstanding."

This, Sir, was the first great step. By this the supremacy of the Constitution and laws of the United States is declared. The people so will it. No State law is to be valid which comes in conflict with the Constitution, or any law of the United States passed in pursuance of it. But who shall decide this question of intereference? To whom lies the last appeal? This, Sir, the Constitution itself decides also, by declaring, "That the judicial power shall extend to all cases arising under the Constitution and laws of the United States." These two provisions cover the whole ground. They are, in truth, the keystone of the arch! With these it is a government; without them it is a confederation. In pursuance of these clear and express provisions, Congress established, at its very first session, in the judicial act, a mode for carrying them into full effect, and for bringing all questions of constitutional power to the final decision of the Supreme Court. It then, Sir, became a government. It then had the means of self-protection; and but for this, it would, in all probability, have been now among things which are past. Having constituted the government, and declared its powers, the people have further said, that, since somebody must decide on the extent of these powers, the government shall itself decide; subject always, like other popular governments, to its responsibility to the people...

I have not allowed myself, Sir, to look beyond the Union, to see what might lie hidden in the dark recess behind. I have not cooly weighed the chances of preserving liberty when the bonds that unite us together shall be broken asunder. I have not accustomed myself to hang over the precipice of disunion, to see whether, with my short sight, I can fathom the depth of the abyss below; nor could I regard him as a safe counsellor in the affairs of this government, whose thoughts should be mainly bent on considering, not how the Union may be best preserved, but how tolerable might be the condition of the people when it should be broken up and destroyed. While the Union lasts, we have high, exciting, gratifiying prospects spread out before us and our children. Beyond that I seek not to penetrate the veil. God grant that in my day, at least, that curtain may not rise! God grant that on my vision never may be opened what lies behind! When my eyes shall be turned to behold for the last time the sun in heaven, may I not see him shing on the broken and dishonored fragments of a once glorious Union; on States dissevered, discordant, belligerent; on a land rent with civil feuds, or drenched, it may be, in fraternal blood! Let their last feeble and lingering glance rather behold the gorgeous ensign of the republic, now known and honored throughout the earth, still full high advanced, its arms and trophies streaming in their original lustre, not a stripe erased or polluteddd, not a single star obscured, bearing for its motto, no such miserable interrogatory as "What is all this worth?" nor those other words of delusion and folly, "Liberty first and Union afterwards"; but everywhere, spread all over in characters of living light, plazing on all it sample folds, as they float over the sea and over the land, and in every wind under the whole heavens, that other sentiment, dear to every true American heart, - Liberty and Union, now and for ever, one and inseperable!

ROGER B. TANEY

Dred Scott v. Sanford

In the 1830s, a slave from Missouri named Dred Scott spent several years with his master in states that prohibited slavery. He subsequently sued in the Missouri courts for his freedom arguing that his sojourn in free states had legally freed him. His case eventually made its way to the Supreme Court, and resulted in this ruling. The Dred Scott ruling remained the law of the land concerning citizenship of black slaves until the ratification of the 14th Amendment.

TANEY, C.J., Opinion of the Court

Mr. Chief Justice TANEY delivered the opinion of the court.

This case has been twice argued. After the argument at the last term, differences of opinion were found to exist among the members of the court, and as the questions in controversy are of the highest importance, and the court was at that time much pressed by the ordinary business of the term, it was deemed advisable to continue the case and direct a re-argument on some of the points in order that we might have an opportunity of giving to the whole subject a more deliberate consideration. It has accordingly been again argued by counsel, and considered by the court; and I now proceed to deliver its opinion.

1. Had the Circuit Court of the United States jurisdiction to hear and determine the case between these parties? And

2. If it had jurisdiction, is the judgment it has given erroneous or not?

. . . The defendant pleaded in abatement to the jurisdiction of the court, that the plaintiff was not a citizen of the State of Missouri, as alleged in his declaration, being a negro of African descent, whose ancestors were of pure African blood and who were brought into this country and sold as slaves.

To this plea the plaintiff demurred, and the defendant joined in demurrer. The court overruled the plea, and gave judgment that the defendant should answer over. And he thereupon put in sundry pleas in bar, upon which issues were joined, and at the trial the verdict and judgment were in his favor. Whereupon the plaintiff brought this writ of error.

Before we speak of the pleas in bar, it will be proper to dispose of the questions which have arisen on the plea in abatement.

That plea denies the right of the plaintiff to sue in a court of the United States, for the reasons therein stated.

. . . The question is simply this: can a negro whose ancestors were imported into this country and sold as slaves become a member of the political community formed and brought into existence by the Constitution of the United States, and as such become entitled to all the rights, and privileges, and immunities, guarantied by that instrument to the citizen, one of which rights is the privilege of suing in a court of the United States in the cases specified in the Constitution?

It will be observed that the plea applies to that class of persons only whose ancestors were negroes of the African race, and imported into this country and sold and held as slaves. The only matter in issue before the court, therefore, is, whether the descendants of such slaves, when they shall be emancipated, or who are born of parents who had become free before their birth, are citizens of a State in the sense in which the word "citizen" is used in the Constitution of the United States. And this being the only matter in dispute on the pleadings, the court must be understood as speaking in this opinion of that class only, that is, of those persons who are the descendants of Africans who were imported into this country and sold as slaves.

The situation of this population was altogether unlike that of the Indian race. The latter, it is true, formed no part of the colonial communities, and never amalgamated with them in social connections or in government. But although they were uncivilized, they were yet a free and independent people, associated together in nations or tribes and governed by their own laws. Many of these political communities were situated in territories to which the white race claimed the ultimate right of dominion. But that claim was acknowledged to be subject to the right of the Indians to occupy it as long as they thought proper, and neither the English nor colonial Governments claimed or exercised any dominion over the tribe or nation by whom it was occupied, nor claimed the right to the possession of the territory, until the tribe or nation consented to cede it. These Indian Governments were regarded and treated as foreign Governments as much so as if an ocean had separated the red man from the white, and their freedom has constantly been acknowledged, from the time of the first emigration to the English colonies to the present day, by the different Governments which succeeded each other. Treaties have been negotiated with them, and their alliance sought for in war, and the people who compose these Indian political communities have always been treated as foreigners not living under our Government. It is true that the course of events has brought the Indian tribes within the limits of the United States under subjection to the white race, and it has been found necessary, for their sake as well as our own, to regard them as in a state of pupilage, and to legislate to a certain extent over them and the territory they occupy. But they may, without doubt, like the subjects of any other foreign Government, be naturalized by the authority of Congress, and become citizens of a State, and of the United States, and if an individual should leave his nation or tribe and take up his abode among the white population, he would be entitled to all the rights and privileges which would belong to an emigrant from any other foreign people.

We proceed to examine the case as presented by the pleadings. The words "people of the United States" and "citizens" are synonymous terms, and mean the same thing. They both describe the political body who, according to our republican institutions, form the sovereignty and who hold the power and conduct the Government through their representatives. They are what we familiarly call the "sovereign people," and every citizen is one of this people, and a constituent member of this sovereignty. The question before us is whether the class of persons described in the plea in abatement compose a portion of this people, and are constituent members of this sovereignty? We think they are not, and that they are not included, and were not intended to be included, under the word "citizens" in the Constitution, and can therefore claim none of the rights and privileges which that instrument provides for and secures to citizens of the United States. On the contrary, they were at that time considered as a subordinate and inferior class of beings who had been subjugated by the dominant race, and, whether emancipated or not, yet remained subject to their authority, and had no rights or privileges but such as those who held the power and the

Government might choose to grant them.

The duty of the court is to interpret the instrument they have framed with the best lights we can obtain on the subject, and to administer it as we find it, according to its true intent and meaning when it was adopted.

In discussing this question, we must not confound the rights of citizenship which a State may confer within its own limits and the rights of citizenship as a member of the Union. It does not by any means follow, because he has all the rights and privileges of a citizen of a State, that he must be a citizen of the United States. He may have all of the rights and privileges of the citizen of a State and yet not be entitled to the rights and privileges of a citizen in any other State. For, previous to the adoption of the Constitution of the United States, every State had the undoubted right to confer on whomsoever it pleased the character of citizen, and to endow him with all its rights. But this character, of course, was confined to the boundaries of the State, and gave him no rights or privileges in other States beyond those secured to him by the laws of nations and the comity of States. Nor have the several States surrendered the power of conferring these rights and privileges by adopting the Constitution of the United States. Each State may still confer them upon an alien, or anyone it thinks proper, or upon any class or description of persons, yet he would not be a citizen in the sense in which that word is used in the Constitution of the United States, nor entitled to sue as such in one of its courts, nor to the privileges and immunities of a citizen in the other States. The rights which he would acquire would be restricted to the State which gave them. The Constitution has conferred on Congress the right to establish an uniform rule of naturalization, and this right is evidently exclusive, and has always been held by this court to be so. Consequently, no

State, since the adoption of the Constitution, can, by naturalizing an alien, invest him with the rights and privileges secured to a citizen of a State under the Federal Government, although, so far as the State alone was concerned, he would undoubtedly be entitled to the rights of a citizen and clothed with all the rights and immunities which the Constitution and laws of the State attached to that character.

It is very clear, therefore, that no State can, by any act or law of its own, passed since the adoption of the Constitution, introduce a new member into the political community created by the Constitution of the United States. It cannot make him a member of this community by making him a member of its own. And, for the same reason, it cannot introduce any person or description of persons who were not intended to be embraced in this new political family which the Constitution brought into existence, but were intended to be excluded from it.

The question then arises, whether the provisions of the Constitution, in relation to the personal rights and privileges to which the citizen of a State should be entitled, embraced the negro African race, at that time in this country or who might afterwards be imported, who had then or should afterwards be made free in any State, and to put it in the power of a single State to make him a citizen of the United States and endue him with the full rights of citizenship in every other State without their consent? Does the Constitution of the United States act upon him whenever he shall be made free under the laws of a State, and raised there to the rank of a citizen, and immediately clothe him with all the privileges of a citizen in every other State, and in its own courts?

The court think the affirmative of these propositions cannot be maintained. And if it cannot, the plaintiff in error could not

be a citizen of the State of Missouri within the meaning of the
Constitution of the United States, and, consequently, was not
entitled to sue in its courts.

. . . And while the case is yet open and pending in the inferior
State court, the plaintiff goes into the Circuit Court of the United
States, upon the same case and the same evidence and against
the same party, and proceeds to judgment, and then brings here
the same case from the Circuit Court, which the law would not
have permitted him to bring directly from the State court. And
if this court takes jurisdiction in this form, the result, so far as
the rights of the respective parties are concerned, is in every
respect substantially the same as if it had, in open violation of law,
entertained jurisdiction over the judgment of the State court upon
a writ of error, and revised and reversed its judgment upon the
ground that its opinion upon the question of law was erroneous. It
would ill become this court to sanction such an attempt to evade the
law, or to exercise an appellate power in this circuitous way which
it is forbidden to exercise in the direct and regular and invariable
forms of judicial proceedings.

Upon the whole, therefore, it is the judgment of this court that
it appears by the record before us that the plaintiff in error is not
a citizen of Missouri in the sense in which that word is used in
the Constitution, and that the Circuit Court of the United States,
for that reason, had no jurisdiction in the case, and could give no
judgment in it. Its judgment for the defendant must, consequently,
be reversed, and a mandate issued directing the suit to be dismissed
for want of jurisdiction.

AFRICAN-AMERICAN SLAVES

Negro Spirituals

These were the faith-filled songs of the Afircan slaves, who often sang as they worked. The remarkable lyrics of these spirituals shine a spotlight on the enduring gsopel hope of Jesus Christ in even the most difficult and degrading circumstances imaginable.

SWING LOW, SWEET CHARIOT

I looked over Jordan, and what did I see,
Coming for to carry me home;
A band of angels coming after me,
Coming for to carry me home.

If you get there before I do,
Coming for to carry me home;
Tell all my friends I'm coming too,
Coming for to carry me home.

Chorus
Swing Low, sweet chariot,
Coming for to carry me home,
Swing low, sweet chariot,
Coming for to carry me home.

GO DOWN, MOSES

When Israel was in Egypt's land,
Let my people go;
Oppressed so hard they could not stand,
Let my people go.

Thus Saith the Lord, bold Moses said,
Let my people go;
If not I'll smite your fist born dead,
Let my people go.

The Lord told Moses what to do,
Let my people go;
To lead the children of Israel through,
Let my people go.

Chorus
Go down, Moses,
'Way doen in Egypt's land.
Tell ole Pharaoh,
Let my people go.

IT'S A ME, O LORD STANDIN' IN THE NEED OF PRAYER

Not my brother, it's a me, O Lord.
Not my sister, it's a me, O Lord,

Not my father, it's a me, O Lord.
Not my mother, it's a me , O Lord,

Chorus
It's a me It's a me O Lord standin' in the need of prayer.
It's a me It's a me O Lord standin' in the need of prayer. 1

NOBODY KNOWS THE TROUBLE I'VE HAD

Sometimes I'm up, sometimes I'm down,
Oh, yes, Lord.
Sometimes I'm almost to the ground,
Oh, yes, Lord

Oh,

I never shall forget that day,
Oh, yes, Lord.
When Jesus washed my sins away,
Oh, yes, Lord
Oh,

Chorus
Nobody knows the trouble I've had,
Nobody knows but Jesus.
Nobody knows the trouble I've had,
Glory Hallelujah!

WAIT 'TILL I PUT ON MY CROWN

I came this night for to sing and pray,
Oh yes! Oh yes!
To drive old Satan far away,
Oh yes! Oh yes!
That heav'nly home is bright and fair,
Oh yes! Oh yes!
But very few can enter there,
Oh yes! Oh wait 'till I put on my crown
Wait 'till I put on my crown
Wait 'till I put on my crown
Oh yes, Oh yes.

If you want to catch that heav'nly breeze,
Oh yes! Oh yes!
Go down in the valley on your knees,
Oh yes! Oh yes!
Go bow your knees upon the ground,

Oh yes! Oh yes!
And ask your Lord to turn you 'round
Oh yes! Oh wait 'till I put on my robe
Wait 'till I put on my robe
Wait 'till I put on my robe
Oh yes, Oh, yes.

ALEXANDER STEPHENS

Cornerstone Speech

Alexander Stephens was a congressman from Georgia , and a member of the Whig and Democratic Parties. Small in stature and weighing less than a hundred pounds, Stephens enjoyed a friendship with the 6'4" Abraham Lincoln, first formed when both were serving in Congress. During debate over the Mexican War, which both men opposed, Lincoln said of Stephens, "A slim, pale-faced, consumptive man . . . has just concluded the very best speech, of an hour's length, I ever heard." Later, Stephens said of Lincoln, "Mr. Lincoln was careful as to his manners, awkward in his speech, but was possessed of a very strong, clear and vigorous mind. He always attracted the riveted attention of the House when he spoke; his manner of speech as well as thought was original...his anecdotes were always exceedingly apt and pointed, and socially he always kept his company in a roar of laughter." In January 1865, both men participated in an unsuccessful attempt to broker a peaceful end to the war. After seeing the diminutive Stephens remove his several layers of cloaks and coats, Lincoln exclaimed, "Never have I seen so small a nubbin come out of so much husk."

Following the formation of the Confederacy, Stephens was elected Vice President. The Cornerstone speech was delivered extemporaneously in Savannah; Georgia, on March 21, 1861, and was transcribed by a local journalist. Below is a condensed version of the speech.

I was remarking, that we are passing through one of the greatest revolutions in the annals of the world. Seven States have within the last three months thrown off an old government and formed a new. This revolution has been signally marked, up to this time, by the fact of its having been accomplished without the loss of a single drop of blood. [Applause.]

This new constitution, or form of government, constitutes the subject to which your attention will be partly invited. In reference to it, I make this first general remark. It amply secures all our ancient rights, franchises, and liberties. All the great principles of Magna Charta are retained in it. No citizen is deprived of life, liberty, or property, but by the judgment of his peers under the laws of the land. The great principle of religious liberty, which was the honor and pride of the old constitution, is still maintained and secured. All the essentials of the old constitution, which have endeared it to the hearts of the American people, have been preserved and perpetuated. [Applause.] Some changes have been made. Of these I shall speak presently. Some of these I should have preferred not to have seen made; but these, perhaps, meet the cordial approbation of a majority of this audience, if not an overwhelming majority of the people of the Confederacy. Of them, therefore, I will not speak. But other important changes do meet my cordial approbation. They form great improvements upon the old constitution. So, taking the whole new constitution, I have no hesitancy in giving it as my judgment that it is decidedly better than the old. [Applause.]

Allow me briefly to allude to some of these improvements. The question of building up class interests, or fostering one branch of industry to the prejudice of another under the exercise of the revenue power, which gave us so much trouble under the old constitution, is put at rest forever under the new. We allow the imposition of no duty with a view of giving advantage to one class of persons, in any trade or business, over those of another ... This old thorn of the tariff, which was the cause of so much irritation in the old body politic, is removed forever from the new. [Applause.]

Again, the subject of internal improvements, under the power
of Congress to regulate commerce, is put at rest under our system
. . . Our opposition sprang from no hostility to commerce, or all
necessary aids for facilitating it. With us it was simply a question,
upon whom the burden should fall. . . What justice was there in
taking this money, which our people paid into the common treasury
on the importation of our iron, and applying it to the improvement
of rivers and harbors elsewhere?

The true principle is to subject the commerce of every locality,
to whatever burdens may be necessary to facilitate it. If Charleston
harbor needs improvement, let the commerce of Charleston bear the
burden. . . This is again the broad principle of perfect equality and
justice. [Applause.] And it is especially set forth and established in
our new constitution.

Another feature to which I will allude, is that the new
constitution provides that cabinet ministers and heads of
departments may have the privilege of seats upon the floor of
the Senate and House of Representatives—may have the right
to participate in the debates and discussions upon the various
subjects of administration. I should have preferred that this
provision should have gone further, and required the President
to select his constitutional advisers from the Senate and House of
Representatives. That would have conformed entirely to the practice
in the British Parliament, which, in my judgment, is one of the
wisest provisions in the British constitution. It is the only feature
that saves that government. It is that which gives it stability in
its facility to change its administration. Ours, as it is, is a great
approximation to the right principle.

Another change in the constitution relates to the length of the tenure of the presidential office. In the new constitution it is six years instead of four, and the President rendered ineligible for a re-election. This is certainly a decidedly conservative change. It will remove from the incumbent all temptation to use his office or exert the powers confided to him for any objects of personal ambition. The only incentive to that higher ambition which should move and actuate one holding such high trusts in his hands, will be the good of the people, the advancement, prosperity, happiness, safety, honor, and true glory of the confederacy. [Applause.]

But not to be tedious in enumerating the numerous changes for the better, allow me to allude to one other—though last, not least. The new constitution has put at rest, forever, all the agitating questions relating to our peculiar institution—African slavery as it exists amongst us—the proper status of the negro in our form of civilization. This was the immediate cause of the late rupture and present revolution. Jefferson in his forecast, had anticipated this, as the "rock upon which the old Union would split." He was right. What was conjecture with him, is now a realized fact. But whether he fully comprehended the great truth upon which that rock stood and stands, may be doubted. The prevailing ideas entertained by him and most of the leading statesmen at the time of the formation of the old constitution, were that the enslavement of the African was in violation of the laws of nature; that it was wrong in principle, socially, morally, and politically. It was an evil they knew not well how to deal with, but the general opinion of the men of that day was that, somehow or other in the order of Providence, the institution would be evanescent and pass away. This idea, though not incorporated in the constitution, was the prevailing idea at that

time. The constitution, it is true, secured every essential guarantee
to the institution while it should last, and hence no argument can
be justly urged against the constitutional guarantees thus secured,
because of the common sentiment of the day. Those ideas, however,
were fundamentally wrong. They rested upon the assumption of
the equality of races. This was an error. It was a sandy foundation,
and the government built upon it fell when the "storm came and the
wind blew."

Our new government is founded upon exactly the opposite
idea; its foundations are laid, its cornerstone rests upon the great
truth, that the negro is not equal to the white man; that slavery—
subordination to the superior race—is his natural and normal
condition. [Applause.] This, our new government, is the first, in the
history of the world, based upon this great physical, philosophical,
and moral truth. This truth has been slow in the process of its
development, like all other truths in the various departments of
science. It has been so even amongst us. Many who hear me,
perhaps, can recollect well, that this truth was not generally
admitted, even within their day. The errors of the past generation
still clung to many as late as twenty years ago. Those at the North,
who still cling to these errors, with a zeal above knowledge, we justly
denominate fanatics. All fanaticism springs from an aberration of
the mind—from a defect in reasoning. It is a species of insanity.
One of the most striking characteristics of insanity, in many
instances, is forming correct conclusions from fancied or erroneous
premises; so with the anti-slavery fanatics; their conclusions are
right if their premises were. They assume that the negro is equal,
and hence conclude that he is entitled to equal privileges and rights
with the white man. If their premises were correct, their conclusions
would be logical and just—but their premise being wrong, their

whole argument fails. I recollect once of having heard a gentleman
from one of the northern States, of great power and ability,
announce in the House of Representatives, with imposing effect,
that we of the South would be compelled, ultimately, to yield upon
this subject of slavery, that it was as impossible to war successfully
against a principle in politics, as it was in physics or mechanics.
That the principle would ultimately prevail. That we, in maintaining
slavery as it exists with us, were warring against a principle, a
principle founded in nature, the principle of the equality of men.
The reply I made to him was, that upon his own grounds, we should,
ultimately, succeed, and that he and his associates, in this crusade
against our institutions, would ultimately fail. The truth announced,
that it was as impossible to war successfully against a principle in
politics as it was in physics and mechanics, I admitted; but told him
that it was he, and those acting with him, who were warring against
a principle. They were attempting to make things equal which the
Creator had made unequal.

In the conflict thus far, success has been on our side, complete
throughout the length and breadth of the Confederate States. It
is upon this, as I have stated, our social fabric is firmly planted;
and I cannot permit myself to doubt the ultimate success of a full
recognition of this principle throughout the civilized and enlightened
world.

As I have stated, the truth of this principle may be slow in
development, as all truths are and ever have been, in the various
branches of science. It was so with the principles announced by
Galileo—it was so with Adam Smith and his principles of political
economy. It was so with Harvey, and his theory of the circulation of
the blood. It is stated that not a single one of the medical profession,
living at the time of the announcement of the truths made by him,

admitted them. Now, they are universally acknowledged. May
we not, therefore, look with confidence to the ultimate universal
acknowledgment of the truths upon which our system rests?
It is the first government ever instituted upon the principles in
strict conformity to nature, and the ordination of Providence, in
furnishing the materials of human society. Many governments have
been founded upon the principle of the subordination and serfdom
of certain classes of the same race; such were and are in violation
of the laws of nature. Our system commits no such violation of
nature's laws. With us, all of the white race, however high or low,
rich or poor, are equal in the eye of the law. Not so with the negro.
Subordination is his place. He, by nature, or by the curse against
Canaan, is fitted for that condition which he occupies in our system.
The architect, in the construction of buildings, lays the foundation
with the proper material-the granite; then comes the brick or the
marble. . . It is, indeed, in conformity with the ordinance of the
Creator. It is not for us to inquire into the wisdom of his ordinances,
or to question them. For his own purposes, he has made one race to
differ from another, as he has made "one star to differ from another
star in glory."

The great objects of humanity are best attained when there is
conformity to his laws and decrees, in the formation of governments
as well as in all things else. Our confederacy is founded upon
principles in strict conformity with these laws. This stone which was
rejected by the first builders "is become the chief of the corner"—the
real "corner-stone"—in our new edifice. [Applause.]

I have been asked, what of the future? It has been apprehended
by some that we would have arrayed against us the civilized world.
I care not who or how many they may be against us, when we stand

upon the eternal principles of truth, if we are true to ourselves and the principles for which we contend, we are obliged to, and must triumph. [Immense applause.]

Thousands of people who begin to understand these truths are not yet completely out of the shell; they do not see them in their length and breadth. We hear much of the civilization and christianization of the barbarous tribes of Africa. In my judgment, those ends will never be attained, but by first teaching them the lesson taught to Adam, that "in the sweat of his brow he should eat his bread," [applause,] and teaching them to work, and feed, and clothe themselves.

But to pass on: Some have propounded the inquiry whether it is practicable for us to go on with the confederacy without further accessions? Have we the means and ability to maintain nationality among the powers of the earth? On this point I would barely say, that as anxiously as we all have been, and are, for the border States, with institutions similar to ours, to join us, still we are abundantly able to maintain our position, even if they should ultimately make up their minds not to cast their destiny with us. That they ultimately will join us—be compelled to do it—is my confident belief; but we can get on very well without them, even if they should not.

We have all the essential elements of a high national career. The idea has been given out at the North, and even in the border States, that we are too small and too weak to maintain a separate nationality. This is a great mistake. In extent of territory we embrace five hundred and sixty-four thousand square miles and upward. This is upward of two hundred thousand square miles more than was included within the limits of the original thirteen

States. It is an area of country more than double the territory of
France or the Austrian empire. France, in round numbers, has but
two hundred and twelve thousand square miles. Austria, in round
numbers, has two hundred and forty-eight thousand square miles.
Ours is greater than both combined. It is greater than all France,
Spain, Portugal, and Great Britain, including England, Ireland, and
Scotland, together. In population we have upward of five millions,
according to the census of 1860; this includes white and black. The
entire population, including white and black, of the original thirteen
States, was less than four millions in 1790, and still less in '76, when
the independence of our fathers was achieved. If they, with a less
population, dared maintain their independence against the greatest
power on earth, shall we have any apprehension of maintaining ours
now?

. . . It is true, I believe I state but the common sentiment, when I
declare my earnest desire that the border States should join us. The
differences of opinion that existed among us anterior to secession,
related more to the policy in securing that result by co-operation
than from any difference upon the ultimate security we all looked to
in common.

These differences of opinion were more in reference to policy
than principle, and as Mr. Jefferson said in his inaugural, in 1801,
after the heated contest preceding his election, there might be
differences of opinion without differences on principle, and that all,
to some extent, had been federalists and all republicans; so it may
now be said of us, that whatever differences of opinion as to the best
policy in having a co-operation with our border sister slave States, if
the worst came to the worst, that as we were all co-co-operationists,
we are now all for independence, whether they come or not.

[Continued applause.]

In this connection I take this occasion to state, that I was not
without grave and serious apprehensions, that if the worst came
to the worst, and cutting loose from the old government should be
the only remedy for our safety and security, it would be attended
with much more serious ills than it has been as yet. Thus far we
have seen none of those incidents which usually attend revolutions.
No such material as such convulsions usually throw up has been
seen. Wisdom, prudence, and patriotism, have marked every step
of our progress thus far. This augurs well for the future, and it is
a matter of sincere gratification to me, that I am enabled to make
the declaration. Of the men I met in the Congress at Montgomery,
I may be pardoned for saying this, an abler, wiser, a more
conservative, deliberate, determined, resolute, and patriotic body of
men, I never met in my life. [Great applause.] Their works speak for
them; the provisional government speaks for them; the constitution
of the permanent government will be a lasting monument of their
worth, merit, and statesmanship. [Applause.]

But to return to the question of the future. What is to be the
result of this revolution?

Will every thing, commenced so well, continue as it has begun?
In reply to this anxious inquiry, I can only say it all depends upon
ourselves. A young man starting out in life on his majority, with
health, talent, and ability, under a favoring Providence, may be
said to be the architect of his own fortunes. His destinies are in his
own hands. He may make for himself a name, of honor or dishonor,
according to his own acts. If he plants himself upon truth, integrity,
honor and uprightness, with industry, patience and energy, he

cannot fail of success. So it is with us. We are a young republic, just
entering upon the arena of nations; we will be the architects of our
own fortunes. Our destiny, under Providence, is in our own hands.
With wisdom, prudence, and statesmanship on the part of our
public men, and intelligence, virtue and patriotism on the part of
the people, success, to the full measures of our most sanguine hopes,
may be looked for. But if unwise counsels prevail—if we become
divided—if schisms arise—if dissensions spring up—if factions are
engendered—if party spirit, nourished by unholy personal ambition
shall rear its hydra head, I have no good to prophesy for you.
Without intelligence, virtue, integrity, and patriotism on the part of
the people, no republic or representative government can be durable
or stable.

We have intelligence, and virtue, and patriotism. All that is
required is to cultivate and perpetuate these. Intelligence will not
do without virtue. France was a nation of philosophers. These
philosophers become Jacobins. They lacked that virtue, that
devotion to moral principle, and that patriotism which is essential
to good government Organized upon principles of perfect justice
and right-seeking amity and friendship with all other powers—I
see no obstacle in the way of our upward and onward progress.
Our growth, by accessions from other States, will depend greatly
upon whether we present to the world, as I trust we shall, a better
government than that to which neighboring States belong. If we do
this, North Carolina, Tennessee, and Arkansas cannot hesitate long;
neither can Virginia, Kentucky, and Missouri. They will necessarily
gravitate to us by an imperious law. We made ample provision in our
constitution for the admission of other States; it is more guarded,
and wisely so, I think, than the old constitution on the same subject,

but not too guarded to receive them as fast as it may be proper. Looking to the distant future, and, perhaps, not very far distant either, it is not beyond the range of possibility, and even probability, that all the great States of the north-west will gravitate this way, as well as Tennessee, Kentucky, Missouri, Arkansas, etc. Should they do so, our doors are wide enough to receive them, but not until they are ready to assimilate with us in principle.

The process of disintegration in the old Union may be expected to go on with almost absolute certainty if we pursue the right course. We are now the nucleus of a growing power which, if we are true to ourselves, our destiny, and high mission, will become the controlling power on this continent. To what extent accessions will go on in the process of time, or where it will end, the future will determine. So far as it concerns States of the old Union, this process will be upon no such principles of reconstruction as now spoken of, but upon reorganization and new assimilation. [Loud applause.] Such are some of the glimpses of the future as I catch them.

But at first we must necessarily meet with the inconveniences and difficulties and embarrassments incident to all changes of government. These will be felt in our postal affairs and changes in the channel of trade. These inconveniences, it is to be hoped, will be but temporary, and must be borne with patience and forbearance.

As to whether we shall have war with our late confederates, or whether all matters of differences between us shall be amicably settled, I can only say that the prospect for a peaceful adjustment is better, so far as I am informed, than it has been.

The prospect of war is, at least, not so threatening as it has been. The idea of coercion, shadowed forth in President Lincoln's inaugural, seems not to be followed up thus far so vigorously as was

expected. Fort Sumter, it is believed, will soon be evacuated. What
course will be pursued toward Fort Pickens, and the other forts on
the gulf, is not so well understood. It is to be greatly desired that all
of them should be surrendered. Our object is peace, not only with
the North, but with the world. All matters relating to the public
property, public liabilities of the Union when we were members of it,
we are ready and willing to adjust and settle upon the principles of
right, equity, and good faith. War can be of no more benefit to the
North than to us. Whether the intention of evacuating Fort Sumter
is to be received as an evidence of a desire for a peaceful solution of
our difficulties with the United States, or the result of necessity, I
will not undertake to say. I would fain hope the former. Rumors are
afloat, however, that it is the result of necessity. All I can say to you,
therefore, on that point is, keep your armor bright and your powder
dry. [Enthusiastic cheering.]

    The surest way to secure peace, is to show your ability to
maintain your rights. The principles and position of the present
administration of the United States—the republican party—present
some puzzling questions. While it is a fixed principle with them
never to allow the increase of a foot of slave territory, they seem
to be equally determined not to part with an inch "of the accursed
soil." Notwithstanding their clamor against the institution, they
seemed to be equally opposed to getting more, or letting go what
they have got. They were ready to fight on the accession of Texas,
and are equally ready to fight now on her secession. Why is this?
How can this strange paradox be accounted for? There seems to
be but one rational solution—and that is, notwithstanding their
professions of humanity, they are disinclined to give up the benefits
they derive from slave labor. Their philanthropy yields to their

interest The idea of enforcing the laws, has but one object, and that is a collection of the taxes, raised by slave labor to swell the fund, necessary to meet their heavy appropriations. The spoils is what they are after—though they come from the labor of the slave. [Continued applause.]

Mr. Stephens reviewed at some length, the extravagance and profligacy of appropriations by the Congress of the United States for several years past, and in this connection took occasion to allude to another one of the great improvements in our new constitution, which is a clause prohibiting Congress from appropriating any money from the treasury, except by a two-third vote, unless it be for some object which the executive may say is necessary to carry on the government.

When it is thus asked for, and estimated for, he continued, the majority may appropriate. This was a new feature.

Our fathers had guarded the assessment of taxes by insisting that representation and taxation should go together. This was inherited from the mother country, England. It was one of the principles upon which the revolution had been fought. Our fathers also provided in the old constitution, that all appropriation bills should originate in the representative branch of Congress, but our new constitution went a step further, and guarded not only the pockets of the people, but also the public money, after it was taken from their pockets.

He alluded to the difficulties and embarrassments which seemed to surround the question of a peaceful solution of the controversy with the old government. How can it be done? is perplexing many minds. The President seems to think that he cannot recognize our independence, nor can he, with and by the advice of the Senate, do so. The constitution makes no such provision. A general convention of all the States has been suggested by some.

Without proposing to solve the difficulty, he barely made the following suggestion:

"That as the admission of States by Congress under the constitution was an act of legislation, and in the nature of a contract or compact between the States admitted and the others admitting, why should not this contract or compact be regarded as of like character with all other civil contracts—liable to be rescinded by mutual agreement of both parties? The seceding States have rescinded it on their part, they have resumed their sovereignty. Why cannot the whole question be settled, if the north desire peace, simply by the Congress, in both branches, with the concurrence of the President, giving their consent to the separation, and a recognition of our independence?" This he merely offered as a suggestion, as one of the ways in which it might be done with much less violence by constructions to the constitution than many other acts of that government. [Applause.] The difficulty has to be solved in some way or other—this may be regarded as a fixed fact.

JEFFERSON DAVIS

Secession Speech

*Following the election of 1860, the South began to respond to the what
she perceived as the impending violation of her sovereignty by the North.
The first state to secede was South Carolina. On January 21st 1861, in the
Senate Chamber, Senator Jefferson Davis of Mississippi, future president
of the Confederate States of America, rose to announce to the Congress the
decision of his state on the question of loyalties.*

I rise, Mr. President, for the purpose of announcing to the
Senate that I have satisfactory evidence that the State of
Mississippi, by a solemn ordinance of her people in convention
assembled, has declared her separation from the United States.
Under these circumstances, of course my functions are terminated
here. It has seemed to me proper, however, that I should appear
in the Senate to announce that fact to my associates, and I will
say but very little more. The occasion does not invite me to go into
argument; and my physical condition would not permit me to do so
if it were otherwise; and yet it seems to become me to say something
on the part of the State I here represent, on an occasion as solemn as
this.

It is known to Senators who have served with me here, that
I have for many years advocated, as an essential attribute of
State sovereignty, the right of a State to secede from the Union.
Therefore, if I had thought that Mississippi was acting without
sufficient provocation, or without an existing necessity, I should still,
under my theory of the Government, because of my allegiance to the
State of which   I am a citizen, have been bound by her action. I,
however, may be permitted to say that I do think she has justifiable

cause, and I approve of her act. I conferred with her people before
that act was taken, counseled them then that if the state of things
which they apprehended should exist when the convention met, they
should take the action which they have now adopted.

I hope none who hear me will confound this expression of mine
with the advocacy of the right of a State to remain in the Union,
and to disregard its constitutional obligation by the nullification of
the law. Such is not my theory. Nullification and secession, so often
confounded, are indeed antagonistic principles. Nullification is a
remedy which it is sought to apply within the Union, and against
the agent of the States. It is only to be justified when the agent has
violated his constitutional obligation, and a State, assuming to judge
for itself, denies the right of the agent thus to act, and appeals to
the other States of the Union for a decision; but when the States
themselves, and when the people of the States, have so acted as to
convince us that they will not regard our constitutional rights, then,
and then for the first time, arises the doctrine of secession in its
practical application.

A great man who now reposes with his fathers, and who has
often been arraigned for want of fealty to the Union, advocated
the doctrine of nullification, because it preserved the Union.
It was because of his deep-seated attachment to the Union, his
determination to find some remedy for existing ills short of a
severance of the ties which bound South Carolina to the other States,
that Mr. Calhoun advocated the doctrine of nullification, which he
proclaimed to be peaceful, to be within the limits of State power, not
to disturb the Union, but only to be a means of bringing the agent
before the tribunal of the States for their judgement.

Secession belongs to a different class of remedies. It is to be

justified upon the basis that the States are sovereign. There was a
time when none denied it. I hope the time may come again, when
a better comprehension of the theory of our Government, and the
inalienable rights of the people of the States, will prevent any one
from denying that each State is a sovereign, and thus may reclaim
the grants which it has made to any agent whomsoever.

I therefore say I concur in the action of the people of Mississippi,
believing it to be necessary and proper, and should have been bound
by their action if my belief had been otherwise; and this brings me
to the important point which I wish on this last occasion to present
to the Senate. It is by this confounding of nullification and secession
that the name of a great man, whose ashes now mingle with his
mother earth, has been invoked to justify coercion against a seceded
State. The phrase, "to execute the laws," was an expression which
General Jackson applied to the case of a State refusing to obey the
laws while yet a member of the Union. That is not the case which is
now presented. The laws are to be executed over the United States,
and upon the people of the United States. They have no relation
to any foreign country. It is a perversion of terms, at least it is a
great mis-apprehension of the case, which cites that expression for
application to a State which has withdrawn from the Union. You
may make war on a foreign State. If it be the purpose of gentlemen,
they may make war against a State which has withdrawn from the
Union; but there are no laws of the United States to be executed
within the limits of a seceded State. A State finding herself in the
condition in which Mississippi has judged she is, in which her safety
requires that she should provide for the maintenance of her rights
out of the Union, surrenders all the benefits, (and they are known
to be many,) deprives herself of the advantages, (and they are

known to be great,) severs all the ties of affection, (and they are close and enduring,) which have bound her to the Union; and thus divesting herself of every benefit, taking upon herself every burden, she claims to be exempt from any power to execute the laws of the United States within her limits.

I well remember an occasion when Massachusetts was arraigned before the bar of the Senate, and when the doctrine of coercion was rife and to be applied against her because of the rescue of a fugitive slave in Boston. My opinion then was the same that it is now. Not in a spirit of egotism, but to show that I am not influenced in my opinion because the case is my own, I refer to that time and that occasion as containing the opinion which I then entertained, and on which my present conduct is based. I then said, if Massachusetts, following her through a stated line of conduct, chose to take the last step, which separates her from the Union, it is her right to go, and I will neither vote one dollar nor one man to coerce her back; but I will say to her, God speed, in memory of the kind associations which once existed between her and the other States.

It has been a conviction of pressing necessity, it has been a belief that we are to be deprived in the Union of the rights which our fathers bequeathed to us, which has brought Mississippi to her present decision. She has heard proclaimed the theory that all men are created free and equal, and this made the basis of an attack upon her social institutions; and the sacred Declaration of Independence has been invoked to maintain the position of the equality of the races. That Declaration of Independence is to be construed by the circumstances and purposes for which it was made. The communities were declaring their independence; the people of those communities were asserting that no man was born—to use

the language of Mr. Jefferson—booted and spurred to ride over
the rest of mankind; that men were created equal—meaning the
men of the political community; that there was no divine right to
rule; that no man inherited the right to govern; that there were no
classes by which power and place descended to families, but that
all stations were equally within the grasp of each member of the
body politic. These were the great principles they announced; these
were the purposes for which they made their declaration; these were
the ends to which their enunciation was directed. They have no
reference to the slave; else, how happened it that among the items of
arraignment made against George III was that he endeavored to do
just what the North has been endeavoring of late to do – to stir up
insurrection among our slaves?   Had the Declaration announced
that the negroes were free and equal, how was the Prince to be
arraigned for stirring up insurrection among them? And how was
this to be enumerated among the high crimes which caused the
colonies to sever their connection with the mother country? When
our Constitution was formed, the same idea was rendered more
palpable, for there we find provision made for that very class of
persons as property; they were not put upon the footing of equality
with white men—not even upon that of paupers and convicts; but, so
far as representation was concerned, were discriminated against as
a lower caste, only to be represented in the numerical proportion of
three-fifths.

Then, Senators, we recur to the compact which binds us together;
we recur to the principles upon which our Government was founded;
and when you deny them, and when you deny us the right to
withdraw from a Government which thus perverted threatens to
be destructive of our rights, we but tread in the path of our fathers
when we proclaim our independence, and take the hazard. This

is done, not in hostility to others; not to injure any section of the country, not even for our own pecuniary benefit, but from the high and solemn motive of defending and protecting the rights we inherited, and which it is our duty to transmit unshorn to our children.

I find in myself, perhaps, a type of the general feeling of my constituents towards yours. I am sure I feel no hostility to you, Senators from the North. I am sure there is not one of you, whatever sharp discussion there may have been between us, to whom I cannot now say, in the presence of my God, I wish you well; and such, I am sure, is the feeling of the people whom I represent towards those whom you represent. I therefore feel that I but express their desire when I say I hope, and they hope, for peaceful relations with you, though we must part. They may be mutually beneficial to us in the future, as they have been in the past, if you so will it. The reverse may bring disaster on every portion of the country; and if you will have it thus, we will invoke the God of our fathers, who delivered them from the power of the lion, to protect us from the ravages of the bear; and thus, putting our trust in God, and in our firm hearts and strong arms, we will vindicate the right as best we may.

In the course of my service here, associated at different times with a variety of Senators, I see now around me some with whom I have served long; there have been points of collision; but whatever of offense there has been to me, I leave here; I carry with me no hostile remembrance. Whatever offense I have given which has not been redressed, or for which satisfaction has not been demanded, I have, Senators, in this hour of our parting, to offer you my apology for any pain which, in the heat of discussion, I have inflicted. I go hence unencumbered by the remembrance of any injury received, and having discharged the duty of making the only reparation in my power for any injury offered.

Mr. President, and Senators, having made the announcement which the occasion seemed to me to require, it only remains for me to bid you a final adieu.

CONFEDERATE STATES

Confederate Constitution

The Confederacy was originally composed of seven states, South Carolina, Mississippi, Florida, Alabama, Georgia, Louisiana, and Texas. These states came together in Montgomery, Alabama and created the Constitution of the Confederacy on March 11th, 1861.

PREAMBLE

We, the people of the Confederate States, each State acting in its sovereign and independent character, in order to form a permanent federal government, establish justice, insure domestic tranquillity, and secure the blessings of liberty to ourselves and our posterity invoking the favor and guidance of Almighty God do ordain and establish this Constitution for the Confederate States of America.

ARTICLE I

SECTION I. All legislative powers herein delegated shall be vested in a Congress of the Confederate States, which shall consist of a Senate and House of Representatives.

SEC. 2. (I) The House of Representatives shall be composed of members chosen every second year by the people of the several States; and the electors in each State shall be citizens of the Confederate States, and have the qualifications requisite for electors of the most numerous branch of the State Legislature; but no person of foreign birth, not a citizen of the Confederate States, shall be allowed to vote for any officer, civil or political, State or Federal.

(2) No person shall be a Representative who shall not have

attained the age of twenty-five years, and be a citizen of the Confederate States, and who shall not when elected, be an inhabitant of that State in which he shall be chosen.

(3) Representatives and direct taxes shall be apportioned among the several States, which may be included within this Confederacy, according to their respective numbers, which shall be determined by adding to the whole number of free persons, including those bound to service for a term of years, and excluding Indians not taxed, three-fifths of all slaves. ,The actual enumeration shall be made within three years after the first meeting of the Congress of the Confederate States, and within every subsequent term of ten years, in such manner as they shall by law direct. The number of Representatives shall not exceed one for every fifty thousand, but each State shall have at least one Representative; and until such enumeration shall be made, the State of South Carolina shall be entitled to choose six; the State of Georgia ten; the State of Alabama nine; the State of Florida two; the State of Mississippi seven; the State of Louisiana six; and the State of Texas six.

(4) When vacancies happen in the representation from any State the executive authority thereof shall issue writs of election to fill such vacancies.

(5) The House of Representatives shall choose their Speaker and other officers; and shall have the sole power of impeachment; except that any judicial or other Federal officer, resident and acting solely within the limits of any State, may be impeached by a vote of two-thirds of both branches of the Legislature thereof.

SEC. 3. (I) The Senate of the Confederate States shall be composed of two Senators from each State, chosen for six years by the

Legislature thereof, at the regular session next immediately
preceding the commencement of the term of service; and each
Senator shall have one vote.

(2) Immediately after they shall be assembled, in consequence
of the first election, they shall be divided as equally as may be into
three classes. The seats of the Senators of the first class shall be
vacated at the expiration of the second year; of the second class
at the expiration of the fourth year; and of the third class at the
expiration of the sixth year; so that one-third may be chosen every
second year; and if vacancies happen by resignation, or other wise,
during the recess of the Legislature of any State, the Executive
thereof may make temporary appointments until the next meeting
of the Legislature, which shall then fill such vacancies.

(3) No person shall be a Senator who shall not have attained the
age of thirty years, and be a citizen of the Confederate States; and
who shall not, then elected, be an inhabitant of the State for which
he shall be chosen.

(4) The Vice President of the Confederate States shall be president
of the Senate, but shall have no vote unless they be equally divided.

(5) The Senate shall choose their other officers; and also a
president pro tempore in the absence of the Vice President, or when
he shall exercise the office of President of the Confederate states.

(6) The Senate shall have the sole power to try all impeachments.
When sitting for that purpose, they shall be on oath or affirmation.
When the President of the Confederate States is tried, the Chief
Justice shall preside; and no person shall be convicted without the
concurrence of two-thirds of the members present.

(7) Judgment in cases of impeachment shall not extend further than to removal from office, and disqualification to hold any office of honor, trust, or profit under the Confederate States; but the party convicted shall, nevertheless, be liable and subject to indictment, trial, judgment, and punishment according to law.

SEC. 4. (I) The times, places, and manner of holding elections for Senators and Representatives shall be prescribed in each State by the Legislature thereof, subject to the provisions of this Constitution; but the Congress may, at any time, by law, make or alter such regulations, except as to the times and places of choosing Senators.

(2) The Congress shall assemble at least once in every year; and such meeting shall be on the first Monday in December, unless they shall, by law, appoint a different day.

SEC. 5. (I) Each House shall be the judge of the elections, returns, and qualifications of its own members, and a majority of each shall constitute a quorum to do business; but a smaller number may adjourn from day to day, and may be authorized to compel the attendance of absent members, in such manner and under such penalties as each House may provide.

(2) Each House may determine the rules of its proceedings, punish its members for disorderly behavior, and, with the concurrence of two-thirds of the whole number, expel a member.

(3) Each House shall keep a journal of its proceedings, and from time to time publish the same, excepting such parts as may in their judgment require secrecy; and the yeas and nays of the members of either House, on any question, shall, at the desire of one-fifth of those present, be entered on the journal.

(4) Neither House, during the session of Congress, shall, without the consent of the other, adjourn for more than three days, nor to any other place than that in which the two Houses shall be sitting.

SEC. 6. (I) The Senators and Representatives shall receive a compensation for their services, to be ascertained by law, and paid out of the Treasury of the Confederate States. They shall, in all cases, except treason, felony, and breach of the peace, be privileged from arrest during their attendance at the session of their respective Houses, and in going to and returning from the same; and for any speech or debate in either House, they shall not be questioned in any other place. 'o Senator or Representative shall, during the time for which he was elected, be appointed to any civil office under the authority of the Confederate States, which shall have been created, or the emoluments whereof shall have been increased during such time; and no person holding any office under the Confederate States shall be a member of either House during his continuance in office. But Congress may, by law, grant to the principal officer in each of the Executive Departments a seat upon the floor of either House, with the privilege of discussing any measures appertaining to his department.

SEC. 7. (I) All bills for raising revenue shall originate in the House of Representatives; but the Senate may propose or concur with amendments, as on other bills.

(2) Every bill which shall have passed both Houses, shall, before it becomes a law, be presented to the President of the Confederate States; if he approve, he shall sign it; but if not, he shall return it, with his objections, to that House in which it shall have originated, who shall enter the objections at large on their journal, and proceed

to reconsider it. If, after such reconsideration, two-thirds of that House shall agree to pass the bill, it shall be sent, together with the objections, to the other House, by which it shall likewise be reconsidered, and if approved by two-thirds of that House, it shall become a law. But in all such cases, the votes of both Houses shall be determined by yeas and nays, and the names of the persons voting for and against the bill shall be entered on the journal of each House respectively. If any bill shall not be returned by the President within ten days (Sundays excepted) after it shall have been presented to him, the same shall be a law, in like manner as if he had signed it, unless the Congress, by their adjournment, prevent its return; in which case it shall not be a law. The President may approve any appropriation and disapprove any other appropriation in the same bill. In such case he shall, in signing the bill, designate the appropriations disapproved; and shall return a copy of such appropriations, with his objections, to the House in which the bill shall have originated; and the same proceedings shall then be had as in case of other bills disapproved by the President.

(3) Every order, resolution, or vote, to which the concurrence of both Houses may be necessary (except on a question of adjournment) shall be presented to the President of the Confederate States; and before the same shall take effect, shall be approved by him; or, being disapproved by him, shall be repassed by two-thirds of both Houses, according to the rules and limitations prescribed in case of a bill.

SEC. 8. The Congress shall have power —

(I) To lay and collect taxes, duties, imposts, and excises for revenue, necessary to pay the debts, provide for the common defense,

and carry on the Government of the Confederate States; but no
bounties shall be granted from the Treasury; nor shall any duties
or taxes on importations from foreign nations be laid to promote or
foster any branch of industry; and all duties, imposts, and excises
shall be uniform throughout the Confederate States.

(2) To borrow money on the credit of the Confederate States.

(3) To regulate commerce with foreign nations, and among the
several States, and with the Indian tribes; but neither this, nor any
other clause contained in the Constitution, shall ever be construed
to delegate the power to Congress to appropriate money for any
internal improvement intended to facilitate commerce; except for the
purpose of furnishing lights, beacons, and buoys, and other aids to
navigation upon the coasts, and the improvement of harbors and the
removing of obstructions in river navigation; in all which cases such
duties shall be laid on the navigation facilitated thereby as may be
necessary to pay the costs and expenses thereof.

(4) To establish uniform laws of naturalization, and uniform laws
on the subject of bankruptcies, throughout the Confederate States;
but no law of Congress shall discharge any debt contracted before
the passage of the same.

(5) To coin money, regulate the value thereof, and of foreign coin,
and fix the standard of weights and measures.

(6) To provide for the punishment of counterfeiting the securities
and current coin of the Confederate States.

(7) To establish post offices and post routes; but the expenses of
the Post Office Department, after the Ist day of March in the year
of our Lord eighteen hundred and sixty-three, shall be paid out of

its own revenues.

(8) To promote the progress of science and useful arts, by securing for limited times to authors and inventors the exclusive right to their respective writings and discoveries.

(9) To constitute tribunals inferior to the Supreme Court.

(10) To define and punish piracies and felonies committed on the high seas, and offenses against the law of nations.

(11) To declare war, grant letters of marque and reprisal, and make rules concerning captures on land and water.

(12) To raise and support armies; but no appropriation of money to that use shall be for a longer term than two years.

(13) To provide and maintain a navy.

(14) To make rules for the government and regulation of the land and naval forces.

(15) To provide for calling forth the militia to execute the laws of the Confederate States, suppress insurrections, and repel invasions.

(16) To provide for organizing, arming, and disciplining the militia, and for governing such part of them as may be employed in the service of the Confederate States; reserving to the States, respectively, the appointment of the officers, and the authority of training the militia according to the discipline prescribed by Congress.

(17) To exercise exclusive legislation, in all cases whatsoever, over such district (not exceeding ten miles square) as may, by cession of one or more States and the acceptance of Congress, become the seat

of the Government of the Confederate States; and to exercise like authority over all places purchased by the consent of the Legislature of the State in which the same shall be, for the . erection of forts, magazines, arsenals, dockyards, and other needful buildings; and

(18) To make all laws which shall be necessary and proper for carrying into execution the foregoing powers, and all other powers vested by this Constitution in the Government of the Confederate States, or in any department or officer thereof.

SEC. 9. (I) The importation of negroes of the African race from any foreign country other than the slaveholding States or Territories of the United States of America, is hereby forbidden; and Congress is required to pass such laws as shall effectually prevent the same.

(2) Congress shall also have power to prohibit the introduction of slaves from any State not a member of, or Territory not belonging to, this Confederacy.

(3) The privilege of the writ of habeas corpus shall not be suspended, unless when in cases of rebellion or invasion the public safety may require it.

(4) No bill of attainder, ex post facto law, or law denying or impairing the right of property in negro slaves shall be passed.

(5) No capitation or other direct tax shall be laid, unless in proportion to the census or enumeration hereinbefore directed to be taken.

(6) No tax or duty shall be laid on articles exported from any State, except by a vote of two-thirds of both Houses.

(7) No preference shall be given by any regulation of commerce or revenue to the ports of one State over those of another.

(8) No money shall be drawn from the Treasury, but in consequence of appropriations made by law; and a regular statement and account of the receipts and expenditures of all public money shall be published from time to time.

(9) Congress shall appropriate no money from the Treasury except by a vote of two-thirds of both Houses, taken by yeas and nays, unless it be asked and estimated for by some one of the heads of departments and submitted to Congress by the President; or for the purpose of paying its own expenses and contingencies; or for the payment of claims against the Confederate States, the justice of which shall have been judicially declared by a tribunal for the investigation of claims against the Government, which it is hereby made the duty of Congress to establish.

(10) All bills appropriating money shall specify in Federal currency the exact amount of each appropriation and the purposes for which it is made; and Congress shall grant no extra compensation to any public contractor, officer, agent, or servant, after such contract shall have been made or such service rendered.

(11) No title of nobility shall be granted by the Confederate States; and no person holding any office of profit or trust under them shall, without the consent of the Congress, accept of any present, emolument, office, or title of any kind whatever, from any king, prince, or foreign state.

(12) Congress shall make no law respecting an establishment of religion, or prohibiting the free exercise thereof; or abridging

CONFEDERATE STATES

the freedom of speech, or of the press; or the right of the people peaceably to assemble and petition the Government for a redress of grievances.

(13) A well-regulated militia being necessary to the security of a free State, the right of the people to keep and bear arms shall not be infringed.

(14) No soldier shall, in time of peace, be quartered in any house without the consent of the owner; nor in time of war, but in a manner to be prescribed by law.

(15) The right of the people to be secure in their persons, houses, papers, and effects, against unreasonable searches and seizures, shall not be violated; and no warrants shall issue but upon probable cause, supported by oath or affirmation, and particularly describing the place to be searched and the persons or things to be seized.

(16) No person shall be held to answer for a capital or otherwise infamous crime, unless on a presentment or indictment of a grand jury, except in cases arising in the land or naval forces, or in the militia, when in actual service in time of war or public danger; nor shall any person be subject for the same offense to be twice put in jeopardy of life or limb; nor be compelled, in any criminal case, to be a witness against himself; nor be deprived of life, liberty, or property without due process of law; nor shall private property be taken for public use, without just compensation.

(17) In all criminal prosecutions the accused shall enjoy the right to a speedy and public trial, by an impartial jury of the State and district wherein the crime shall have been committed, which district shall have been previously ascertained by law, and to be informed

of the nature and cause of the accusation; to be confronted with the witnesses against him; to have compulsory process for obtaining witnesses in his favor; and to have the assistance of counsel for his defense.

(18) In suits at common law, where the value in controversy shall exceed twenty dollars, the right of trial by jury shall be preserved; and no fact so tried by a jury shall be otherwise reexamined in any court of the Confederacy, than according to the rules of common law.

(19) Excessive bail shall not be required, nor excessive fines imposed, nor cruel and unusual punishments inflicted.

(20) Every law, or resolution having the force of law, shall relate to but one subject, and that shall be expressed in the title.

SEC. 10. (I) No State shall enter into any treaty, alliance, or confederation; grant letters of marque and reprisal; coin money; make anything but gold and silver coin a tender in payment of debts; pass any bill of attainder, or ex post facto law, or law impairing the obligation of contracts; or grant any title of nobility.

(2) No State shall, without the consent of the Congress, lay any imposts or duties on imports or exports, except what may be absolutely necessary for executing its inspection laws; and the net produce of all duties and imposts, laid by any State on imports, or exports, shall be for the use of the Treasury of the Confederate States; and all such laws shall be subject to the revision and control of Congress.

(3) No State shall, without the consent of Congress, lay any duty on tonnage, except on seagoing vessels, for the improvement of its

rivers and harbors navigated by the said vessels; but such duties shall not conflict with any treaties of the Confederate States with foreign nations; and any surplus revenue thus derived shall, after making such improvement, be paid into the common treasury. Nor shall any State keep troops or ships of war in time of peace, enter into any agreement or compact with another State, or with a foreign power, or engage in war, unless actually invaded, or in such imminent danger as will not admit of delay. But when any river divides or flows through two or more States they may enter into compacts with each other to improve the navigation thereof.

ARTICLE II

SECTION I. (I) The executive power shall be vested in a President of the Confederate States of America. He and the Vice President shall hold their offices for the term of six years; but the President shall not be reeligible. The President and Vice President shall be elected as follows:

(2) Each State shall appoint, in such manner as the Legislature thereof may direct, a number of electors equal to the whole number of Senators and Representatives to which the State may be entitled in the Congress; but no Senator or Representative or person holding an office of trust or profit under the Confederate States shall be appointed an elector.

(3) The electors shall meet in their respective States and vote by ballot for President and Vice President, one of whom, at least, shall not be an inhabitant of the same State with themselves; they shall name in their ballots the person voted for as President, and in distinct ballots the person voted for as Vice President, and they shall make distinct lists of all persons voted for as President, and

of all persons voted for as Vice President, and of the number of votes for each, which lists they shall sign and certify, and transmit, sealed, to the seat of the Government of. the Confederate States, directed to the President of the Senate; the President of the Senate shall, in the presence of the Senate and House of Representatives, open all the certificates, and the votes shall then be counted; the person having the greatest number of votes for President shall be the President, if such number be a majority of the whole number of electors appointed; and if no person have such majority, then from the persons having the highest numbers, not exceeding three, on the list of those voted for as President, the House of Representatives shall choose immediately, by ballot, the President. But in choosing the President the votes shall be taken by States, the representation from each State having one vote; a quorum for this purpose shall consist of a member or members from two-thirds of the States, and a majority of all the States shall be necessary to a choice. And if the House of Representatives shall not choose a President, whenever the right of choice shall devolve upon them, before the 4th day of March next following, then the Vice President shall act as President, as in case of the death, or other constitutional disability of the President.

(4) The person having the greatest number of votes as Vice President shall be the Vice President, if such number be a majority of the whole number of electors appointed; and if no person have a majority, then, from the two highest numbers on the list, the Senate shall choose the Vice President; a quorum for the purpose shall consist of two-thirds of the whole number of Senators, and a majority of the whole number shall be necessary to a choice.

(5) But no person constitutionally ineligible to the office of President shall be eligible to that of Vice President of the Confederate

States.

(6) The Congress may determine the time of choosing the electors, and the day on which they shall give their votes; which day shall be the same throughout the Confederate States.

(7) No person except a natural-born citizen of the Confederate States, or a citizen thereof at the time of the adoption of this Constitution, or a citizen thereof born in the United States prior to the 20th of December, 1860, shall be eligible to the office of President; neither shall any person be eligible to that office who shall not have attained the age of thirty-five years, and been fourteen years a resident within the limits of the Confederate States, as they may exist at the time of his election.

(8) In case of the removal of the President from office, or of his death, resignation, or inability to discharge the powers and duties of said office, the same shall devolve on the Vice President; and the Congress may, by law, provide for the case of removal, death, resignation, or inability, both of the President and Vice President, declaring what officer shall then act as President; and such officer shall act accordingly until the disability be removed or a President shall be elected.

(9) The President shall, at stated times, receive for his services a compensation, which shall neither be increased nor diminished during the period for which he shall have been elected; and he shall not receive within that period any other emolument from the Confederate States, or any of them.

(10) Before he enters on the execution of his office he shall take the following oath or affirmation:

SEC. 2. (I) The President shall be Commander-in-Chief of the Army and Navy of the Confederate States, and of the militia of the several States, when called into the actual service of the Confederate States; he may require the opinion, in writing, of the principal officer in each of the Executive Departments, upon any subject relating to the duties of their respective offices; and he shall have power to grant reprieves and pardons for offenses against the Confederate States, except in cases of impeachment.

(2) He shall have power, by and with the advice and consent of the Senate, to make treaties; provided two-thirds of the Senators present concur; and he shall nominate, and by and with the advice and consent of the Senate shall appoint, ambassadors, other public ministers and consuls, judges of the Supreme Court, and all other officers of the Confederate States whose appointments are not herein otherwise provided for, and which shall be established by law; but the Congress may, by law, vest the appointment of such inferior officers, as they think proper, in the President alone, in the courts of law, or in the heads of departments.

(3) The principal officer in each of the Executive Departments, and all persons connected with the diplomatic service, may be removed from office at the pleasure of the President. All other civil officers of the Executive Departments may be removed at any time by the President, or other appointing power, when their services are unnecessary, or for dishonesty, incapacity. inefficiency, misconduct, or neglect of duty; and when so removed, the removal shall be reported to the Senate, together with the reasons therefor.

(4) The President shall have power to fill all vacancies that may happen during the recess of the Senate, by granting commissions

which shall expire at the end of their next session; but no person rejected by the Senate shall be reappointed to the same office during their ensuing recess.

SEC. 3. (I) The President shall, from time to time, give to the Congress information of the state of the Confederacy, and recommend to their consideration such measures as he shall judge necessary and expedient; he may, on extraordinary occasions, convene both Houses, or either of them; and in case of disagreement between them, with respect to the time of adjournment, he may adjourn them to such time as he shall think proper; he shall receive ambassadors and other public ministers; he shall take care that the laws be faithfully executed, and shall commission all the officers of the Confederate States.

SEC. 4. (I) The President, Vice President, and all civil officers of the Confederate States, shall be removed from office on impeachment for and conviction of treason, bribery, or other high crimes and misdemeanors.

ARTICLE III

SECTION I. (I) The judicial power of the Confederate States shall be vested in one Supreme Court, and in such inferior courts as the Congress may, from time to time, ordain and establish. The judges, both of the Supreme and inferior courts, shall hold their offices during good behavior, and shall, at stated times, receive for their services a compensation which shall not be diminished during their continuance in office.

SEC. 2. (I) The judicial power shall extend to all cases arising under this Constitution, the laws of the Confederate States, and treaties made, or which shall be made, under their authority; to all cases affecting ambassadors, other public ministers and consuls; to all cases of admiralty and maritime jurisdiction; to controversies to which the Confederate States shall be a party; to controversies between two or more States; between a State and citizens of another State, where the State is plaintiff; between citizens claiming lands under grants of different States; and between a State or the citizens thereof, and foreign states, citizens, or subjects; but no State shall be sued by a citizen or subject of any foreign state.

(2) In all cases affecting ambassadors, other public ministers and consuls, and those in which a State shall be a party, the Supreme Court shall have original jurisdiction. In all the other cases before mentioned, the Supreme Court shall have appellate jurisdiction both as to law and fact, with such exceptions and under such regulations as the Congress shall make.

(3) The trial of all crimes, except in cases of impeachment, shall be by jury, and such trial shall be held in the State where the said crimes shall have been committed; but when not committed within any State, the trial shall be at such place or places as the Congress may by law have directed.

SEC. 3. (I) Treason against the Confederate States shall consist only in levying war against.them, or in adhering to their enemies, giving them aid and comfort. No person shall be convicted of treason unless on the testimony of two witnesses to the same overt act, or on confession in open court.

(2) The Congress shall have power to declare the punishment of treason; but no attainder of treason shall work corruption of blood, or forfeiture, except during the life of the person attainted.

ARTICLE IV

SECTION I. (I) Full faith and credit shall be given in each State to the public acts, records, and judicial proceedings of every other State; and the Congress may, by general laws, prescribe the manner in which such acts, records, and proceedings shall be proved, and the effect thereof.

SEC. 2. (I) The citizens of each State shall be entitled to all the privileges and immunities of citizens in the several States; and shall have the right of transit and sojourn in any State of this Confederacy, with their slaves and other property; and the right of property in said slaves shall not be thereby impaired.

(2) A person charged in any State with treason, felony, or other crime against the laws of such State, who shall flee from justice, and be found in another State, shall, on demand of the executive authority of the State from which he fled, be delivered up, to be removed to the State having jurisdiction of the crime.

(3) No slave or other person held to service or labor in any State or Territory of the Confederate States, under the laws thereof, escaping or lawfully carried into another, shall, in consequence of any law or regulation therein, be discharged from such service or labor; but shall be delivered up on claim of the party to whom such slave belongs,. or to whom such service or labor may be due.

SEC. 3. (I) Other States may be admitted into this Confederacy by a vote of two-thirds of the whole House of Representatives and two-thirds of the Senate, the Senate voting by States; but no new State shall be formed or erected within the jurisdiction of any other State, nor any State be formed by the junction of two or more States, or parts of States, without the consent of the Legislatures of the States concerned, as well as of the Congress.

(2) The Congress shall have power to dispose of and make allneedful rules and regulations concerning the property of the Confederate States, including the lands thereof.

(3) The Confederate States may acquire new territory; and Congress shall have power to legislate and provide governments for the inhabitants of all territory belonging to the Confederate States, lying without the limits of the several Sates; and may permit them, at such times, and in such manner as it may by law provide, to form States to be admitted into the Confederacy. In all such territory the institution of negro slavery, as it now exists in the Confederate States, shall be recognized and protected be Congress and by the Territorial government; and the inhabitants of the several Confederate States and Territories shall have the right to take to such Territory any slaves lawfully held by them in any of the States or Territories of the Confederate States.

(4) The Confederate States shall guarantee to every State that now is, or hereafter may become, a member of this Confederacy, a republican form of government; and shall protect each of them against invasion; and on application of the Legislature or of the Executive when the Legislature is not in session) against domestic violence.

ARTICLE V

SECTION I. (I) Upon the demand of any three States, legally assembled in their several conventions, the Congress shall summon a convention of all the States, to take into consideration such amendments to the Constitution as the said States shall concur in suggesting at the time when the said demand is made; and should

any of the proposed amendments to the Constitution be agreed on
by the said convention, voting by States, and the same be ratified
by the Legislatures of two- thirds of the several States, or by
conventions in two-thirds thereof, as the one or the other mode of
ratification may be proposed by the general convention, they shall
thenceforward form a part of this Constitution. But no State shall,
without its consent, be deprived of its equal representation in the
Senate.

ARTICLE VI

SECTION I. The Government established by this Constitution is the
successor of the Provisional Government of the Confederate States of
America, and all the laws passed by the latter shall continue in force
until the same shall be repealed or modified; and all the officers
appointed by the same shall remain in office until their successors
are appointed and qualified, or the offices abolished.

2. All debts contracted and engagements entered into before
the adoption of this Constitution shall be as valid against the
Confederate States under this Constitution, as under the Provisional
Government.

3. This Constitution, and the laws of the Confederate States
made in pursuance thereof, and all treaties made, or which shall
be made, under the authority of the Confederate States, shall be
the supreme law of the land; and the judges in every State shall be
bound thereby, anything in the constitution or laws of any State to
the contrary notwithstanding.

4. The Senators and Representatives before mentioned, and
the members of the several State Legislatures, and all executive
and judicial officers, both of the Confederate States and of the

several States, shall be bound by oath or affirmation to support this Constitution; but no religious test shall ever be required as a qualification to any office or public trust under the Confederate States.

5. The enumeration, in the Constitution, of certain rights shall not be construed to deny or disparage others retained by the people of the several States.

6. The powers not delegated to the Confederate States by the Constitution, nor prohibited by it to the States, are reserved to the States, respectively, or to the people thereof.

ARTICLE VII

I. The ratification of the conventions of five States shall be sufficient for the establishment of this Constitution between the States so ratifying the same.

2. When five States shall have ratified this Constitution, in the manner before specified, the Congress under the Provisional Constitution shall prescribe the time for holding the election of President and Vice President; and for the meeting of the Electoral College; and for counting the votes, and inaugurating the President. They shall, also, prescribe the time for holding the first election of members of Congress under this Constitution, and the time for assembling the same. Until the assembling of such Congress, the Congress under the Provisional Constitution shall continue to exercise the legislative powers granted them; not extending beyond the time limited by the Constitution of the Provisional Government.

Adopted unanimously by the Congress of the Confederate States of South Carolina, Georgia, Florida, Alabama, Mississippi,

Louisiana, and Texas, sitting in convention at the capitol, the city of Montgomery, Ala., on the eleventh day of March, in the year eighteen hundred and Sixty-one.

Howell Cobb, President of the Congress.

SOUTH CAROLINA — R. Barnwell Rhett, C. G. Memminger, Wm. Porcher Miles, James Chesnut, Jr., R. W. Barnwell, William W. Boyce, Lawrence M. Keitt, T. J. Withers.

GEORGIA — Francis S. Bartow, Martin J. Crawford, Benjamin H. Hill, Thos. R. R. Cobb.

FLORIDA — Jackson Morton, J. Patton Anderson, Jas. B. Owens.

ALABAMA — Richard W. Walker, Robt. H. Smith, Colin J. McRae, William P. Chilton, Stephen F. Hale, David P. Lewis, Tho. Fearn, Jno. Gill Shorter, J. L. M. Curry.

MISSISSIPPI — Alex. M. Clayton, James T. Harrison, William S. Barry, W. S. Wilson, Walker Brooke, W. P. Harris, J. A. P. Campbell.

LOUISIANA — Alex. de Clouet, C. M. Conrad, Duncan F. Kenner, Henry Marshall.

TEXAS — John Hemphill, Thomas N. Waul, John H. Reagan, Williamson S. Oldham, Louis T. Wigfall, John Gregg, William Beck Ochiltree.

ROBERT E. LEE
Personal Correspondence

In February, 1861, after the secession of Texas, my father was ordered to report to General Scott, the Commander-in-Chief of the United States Army. He immediately relinquished the command of his regiment, and departed from Fort Mason, Texas, for Washington. He reached Arlington March ist. April lyth, Virginia seceded. On the i8th Colonel Lee had a long interview with General Scott. On April 2oth he tendered his resignation of his commission in the United States Army. The same day he wrote to General Scott the following letter :

ARLINGTON, VIRGINIA, APRIL 20, 1861.

General: Since my interview with you on the 18th inst. I have felt that I ought no longer to retain my commission in the Army. I therefore tender my resignation, which I request you will recommend for acceptance. It would have been presented at once but for the struggle it has cost me to separate myself from a service to which I have devoted the best years of my life, and all the ability I possessed.

During the whole of that time more than a quarter of a century I have experienced nothing but kindness from my superiors and a most cordial friendship from my comrades. To no one, General, have I been as much indebted as to yourself for uniform kindness and consideration, and it has always been my ardent desire to merit your approbation. I shall carry to the grave the most grateful recollections of your kind consideration, and your name and fame shall always be dear to me.

Save in the defense of my native State, I never desire again to draw my sword.

Be pleased to accept my most earnest wishes for the continuance of your happiness and prosperity, and believe me most truly yours,

Robert E. Lee

His resignation was written the same day.

ARLINGTON, Washington City P. O., April 20, 1861.

HONOURABLE SIMON CAMERON, SECRETARY OF WAR.

Sir: I have the honour to tender the resignation of my command as Colonel of the First Regiment of Cavalry.

Very respectfully your obedient servant,

Robert E. Lee
Colonel First Cavalry

ARLINGTON, VIRGINIA, APRIL 20, 1861.

My Dear Sister: I am grieved at my inability to see you. ... I have been waiting for a 'more convenient season,' which has brought to many before me deep and lasting regret. Now we are in a state of war which will yield to nothing. The whole South is in a state of revolution, into which Virginia, after a long struggle, has been drawn; and though I recognise no necessity for this state of things, and would have forborne and pleaded to the end for redress of grievances, real or supposed, yet in my own person I had to meet the question whether I should take part against my native State.

With all my devotion to the Union and the feeling of loyalty and duty of an American citizen, I have not been able to make up my mind to raise my hand against my relatives, my children, my home. I have therefore resigned my commission in the Army, and save in defense of my native State, with the sincere hope that my poor services may never be needed, I hope I may never be called on to draw my sword. I know you will blame me; but you must think as kindly of me as you can, and believe that I have endeavoured to do what I thought right.

To show you the feeling and struggle it has cost me, I send you a copy of my letter of resignation. I have no time for more. May God guard and protect you and yours, and shower upon you everlasting blessings, is the prayer of your devoted brother,

Robert E. Lee

JOSHUA CHAMBERLAIN

Gettysburg Account

Joshua Chamberlain (1828-1914)

From the Encyclopedia Americana (1920)/Chamberlain, Joshua Lawrence

CHAMBERLAIN, Joshua Lawrence, American soldier and educator: b. Brewer, Me., 8 Sept 1828; d. 24 Feb. 1914; graduated Bowdoin College 1852 and Bangor Theological Seminary 1855; received the honorary degree of LL.D., Pennsylvania College, 1866, and from Bowdoin College 1869; professor of rhetoric and oratory, Bowdoin, 1856, and in 1861 professor of modern languages of Europe. On 8 Aug. 1862 he entered the army as lieutenant-colonel of volunteers and served through the Civil War in the Army of the Potomac in every campaign and nearly every great battle from Antietam to Appomattox, and was several times wounded, twice severely. He received the Congressional Medal of Honor for his remarkable conduct in the defense of Round Top, Gettysburg, 2 July 1863, and was advanced to the command of a brigade. On 18 June 1864 he was promoted brigadier-general on the field by General Grant for distinguished gallantry in leading a desperate charge, and early the following spring he received a special promotion as brevet major-general, "for conspicuous gallantry in action." In the campaign of 1865 he commanded two brigades of the first division, fifth corps. In the order disbanding that army he was retained in the service and was offered a colonelcy in the regular army, but the condition of his wounds induced him to decline the service, and in January 1866 he returned to Maine.

In the autumn of that year he was elected governor of Maine, and served in that office for four terms. In 1871 he was chosen president of Bowdoin College, and continued in that position for 12 years, his

administration being marked by a broadening of the course and a large
increase in the resources of the college. During this time he was elected
major-general of Maine, to command the militia of the State. In 1880 when
for a time there was no active or legal State government, he was called to
the capital "to preserve the peace and institutions of the State." This he
accomplished without the use or show of military force. In 1883 he retired
from the presidency of Bowdoin and settled in New York to practise law. In
1885 he went to Florida and engaged in the work of railroad building and
public improvements on the West Coast. He was much sought for as writer
and orator. He published 'Maine, Her Place in History' (1877); 'Ethics
and Politics of the Spanish War' (1898); 'Property: Its Office and Sanction'
(1900); 'De Monts and Acadia' (1904); 'Ruling Powers in History' (1905).
He also edited 'Universities and Their Sons' (1898).

GENERAL CHAMBERLAIN'S ADDRESS FOR THE TWENTIETH MAINE MONUMENT AT GETTYSBURG, OCTOBER 3, 1889

A quarter of a century ago on this rugged crest you were doing what you deemed your duty. To-day you come with modest mein, with care more for truth than for priase, to retrace and record the simple facts - the outward form - of your movements and action. But far more than this entered into your thought and motive, and far greater was the result of the action taken than any statistical descrition of it could import.

You were making history. The world has recorded for you more than you have written. The centuries to come will share and recognize the victory won here, with growing gratitude. The country has ackowledged your service. Your State is proud of it. The well-earned and unsought name has moved you already to ackowledge your deserts. Your own loyal and loving zeal for justice has indeed anticipated the State's recognition. At your own cost you set your monument here to mark the ground where failthful service and devotion wrought a result to momentous.

Today your historians have recalled the facts. On that line which has been so patiently and candidly investigated and as far as possible freed from doubt and unclearness, your admirable record leaves little to be desired. But as this is a suitable, if not final, opportunity for accurate and complete statement of these facts, I may be indulged in a remark or two germane to this matter, which recent visits and this occasion itself suggests.

I am certain that the position of this monument is quite to the left of the center of our regimental line when the final charge was ordered. Our original left did not extend quite to the great rock which now supports this memorial of honor. When we changed front with our left wing and extended it by the flank and rear, the color was brought to mark the new centre, which was to become the salient of our formation; and it was placed, I was sorry to do it, on the smooth and open slope, and in a position completely exposed. Beyond this the left was refused and extended in single rank. When the charge was made I was beside the color-bearer, and I know well that we struck the enemy where their line was open to view, and the ground comparatively unobstructed. The color advanced in the direction of the proper front of the right wing, and passed the rock altogether to our left. I am not at all criticising the judgement of our comrades who selected the great boulder for the base of the monument. It was entirely fitting to mark it with that honor, as it became so conspicuous an object during the terrible struggle - the centre and pivot of the whirlpool that raged around.

I take note also of the surprise of several officers to hear that
it was some other than a single one of them who came to me in
the course of the fight with information of the enemy's extended
movements to envelop our left. Now, as might well be believed of
such gentlemen and soldiers, they are all right; no one of them is
wrong.

It was quite early in the action, and while as yet only our right
wing was hotly engaged, that an officer from that centre reported to
me that a large body of the enemy could be seen in his front,

moving along the bottom of the valley below us, deliberately toward
our extreme left and rear. I sprang upon a rock in our line, which
allowed me to see over the heads of those with whom we were then
engaged, and the movement and intent of the enemy was plain to
be seen. It was this timely knowledge that enabled me to plan the
prompt movement which you so admirably executed - that rapid
change of front, doubling back upon ourselves, and the single rank
formation, which proved so effectual for our stubborn resistance.

Sometime after this, while we were hard pressed all upon sides,
an officer from the extreme left reported to me, with great anxiety,
that the enemy were outflanking our left, thrown back as it was.
I found the situation critical, and immediately ordered the right
company to repair to the extreme left in support, and sent to eh
commanding officer of the 83rd Penn. regiment, asking him to
extend his left to cover the ground vacated on our right. But as a
found this movement produced much confusion, and this withdrawal
was likely to be misconstrued into a retreat, I was obliged to
countermand the order, and let the left wing hold on as best it could,
and as best it did.

One more matter. In the third fierce onsent of the enemy, through a rift in the rolling smoke I saw with consternation that our centre was nearly shot away, and the color guarded by only a little group, who seemed to be checking the enmy by their heroic bearing and not by numbers, and I sent the adjutant to the commanding officer of the color company, to ask him to hold on if he possibly could, till I could reinforce him from some other regiment. So little expectation had I that the adjutant could live to reach the spot, I pressed into my service a trusted sergeant and dispatched him with the same message. Meantime the crash had come, and out of the flame and smoke emerged that center, bearing the color still aloft, forced back, pressed in upon itself, but solid and firm, and impregnable front, face to the foe. The enemy on their part had also recoiled, and were gathering in the low shrubbery for a new assault. Our ammunition was gone. It was manifest that we could not stand before the wave that was ready to roll upon us. Knowing all this I resolved upon the desperate chances of counter-charge with the bayonet. I at once sent to the left wing to give them notice and time for the required change of front. Just then the brave and thoughtful Lieutenant, commanding the color company, came up to me and said, "I think I could press forward with my company, if you will permit me, and cover the ground where our dead and wounded are." "You shall have the chance," was my answer, "I am about to order a charge. We are to make a great right wheel." What he did, you who know him know. What you did, the world knows.

I am sorry to have heard it intimated that any hesitated when that order was given. That was not so. No man hesitated. There might be the appearance of it to those who did no understand the whole situation. The left wing bent back like an ox-bow, or sharp lunette, hand to take some little time to come up into the line of our general front, so as to form the close, continuous edge which was to strike like a sword-cut upon the enemy's ranks. By the time they ad got up and straightened the line, the centre and salient, you may be sure, was already in motion. Nobody hesitated to obey the order. In fact, to tell the truth, the order was never given, or but imperfectly. The enemy were already pressing up the slope. There was only time or need for the words, "Bayonet! Forward to the right!" The quick-witted and tense-nerved men caught the words out of my lips, and almost the action out of my hands.

So much elucidation of facts. You see there may be stories, apparently not consistent with each other, yet all of them true in their time and place, and so far as each actor is concerned.

And while every one here, officer and soldier, did more than his duty, and acted with utmost intelligence and spirit, you must permit me to add the remark that I commanded my regiment that day.

Words elsewhere spoken by me to-day in our State's behalf strive to express the motive and purpose of this great struggle, and the character and consequence of the victory vouchsafed us. It is there I speak of country; here it needs only that I speak of you, and of ground made glorious by you and yours.

The lesson imporessed on me as I stand here and my heart and mind traverse your faces, and the years that are gone, is that in a great, momentous struggle like this commemorated here, it is character that tells. I do not mean simply or chiefly bravery. Many a man has that, who may become surprised or idsconcerted at a sudden change in the posture of affairs. What I mean by character is a firm and seasoned substance of soul. I mean such qualities or acquirements as intelligence, thoughtfulness, consicentiousness, right-mindedness, patience, fortitude, long-suffering and unconquerable resolve.

I could see all this on your faces when you were coming into position here for the desperate encounter; man by man, file by file, on the right into line. I knew that you all knew that was staked on your endurance and heroism. Some of you heard Vincent say to me, with such earnest and prophetic eyes, pointing to the right of our position and the front of the oncoming attack, "You understand, Colonel, this ground must be held at all costs!" I did understand; with a heavy weight on my mind and spirit. You understood; and it was done. Held, and at what cost! Held, and for what effect!

There is no need that I should recount to the friends who stand around us here, what would have happened had this little line - this thin, keen edge of Damascus stell - been broken down from its guard. All can see what would have become of our Brigade swallowed up; of Weed's, struck in the rear of Hazlitt's guns, taken in the flank and turned to launch their thunder-bolts upon our troops, already sore pressed in the gorge at our feet, and the fields upon the great front and right. Round Top lost - the day lost - Gettysburg lost - who can tell or dream what for loss thence would follow!

I do not know whether any friends who now stand here on this calm and sunny day, comprehend how the weight of such a responsibility presses upon the spirit. We were young then. We do not count ourselves old yet; and these things were done more than twenty-six years ago/. We believe we could do them now; but we wonder how we could have done them then. Doubtless the spring and elasticity of youth helped us to bear the burden and recover from the shock. But something more than youthful ardor and dash was demended for such a test. And that was yours. In thought, in habit, in experience, in discipline, you were veterans. It was a matter, as I have said, of character. It was the soul of youth suddenly springing into the flush and flower of manhood. It was the force of the characters you had formed in the silent and peaceful years by the mother's knee and by the father's side, which stood you in such stead in the day of trial. And so it is. We know not of the future, and cannot plan for it much. But we can hold our spirits and our bodies so pure and high, we may cherish such thoughts and such ideals, and dream such dreams of lofty purpose, that we can determine and know what manner of men we will be whenever and wherever the hour strikes, that calls to noble action. This predestination God has given us in charge. No man becomes suddenly different from his habit and cherished thought. We carry our accostumed manners with us. And it was the boyhood you brought from your homes which made you men; which braced your hearts, which shone upon your foreheads, which held you steadfast in mind and body, and lifted these heights of Gettysburg to immortal glory.

This Round Top spur, as it is easy to see to-day, was a commanding position in that battle, and confessedly the key of the field for that day's fight. It is deliberately so pronounced in official papersby the leaders of both sides. I stood on that summit not long ago with Longstreet and officers of ourown army, not so much disposed as he by the events of that day's fighting, to praise the Fifth Corps,and they one and all acknowledged that this was by nature and in fact the supreme position. One ofthe ablest of the southern historians, describing in his impassioned style the fight which circled andflamed around this crast, says, "That was the glittering coronet we longed to clutch." The glitteringcoronet was won, but not by them. All honor to those who seeing it, seized it in thought; who gainedit, who held it, who glorified it. All honor to Warren, first and last, and now forever, of the Fifth Corps; to Vincent, to Rice, to Hazlitt, to Weed, to Ayres, - chief commanders here. Peace be to their spirits where they have gone. Honor and sacred remembrance to those who fell here, and buried part of our hearts with them. Honor to the memory of those who fought here with us and for us, and who fell elsewhere, or have died since, heart-broken at the harshness or injustice of a political government. Honor to you, who have wrought and endured so much and so well. And so, farewell.

ABRAHAM LINCOLN

Gettysburg Address

President Abraham Lincoln was invited to the dedication of the Gettysburg memorial as an afterthought. He had been asked to give brief remarks after the main speaker of the day was done—more than a small slight to his office. He agreed to do so, and penned what is arguably the most famous speech in American history enroute to the ceremony. Lincoln was laconic, compressing his powerful remarks into a mere 272 words. The first speaker, Edward Everett, considered the greatest orator of his day, spoke for two hours, Lincoln for three minutes. In a letter to Lincoln written the day after the dedication, Everett praised the President for his eloquent and concise speech, saying, "I should be glad if I could flatter myself that I came as near to the central idea of the occasion, in two hours, as you did in two minutes." But the Chicago Times observed, "The cheek of every American must tingle with shame as he reads the silly, flat and dishwatery utterances of the man who has to be pointed out to intelligent foreigners as the President of the United States." The movers and shakers of the day may have disdained Lincoln's rhetorical ability, and Lincoln himself dismissed the entire day's speeches with the words, "the world will little note, nor long remember what we say here . . ." History, however, has not judged his words so; instead, the Gettysburg Address is a perennial inclusion wherever the great speeches of the world are collected.

Four score and seven years ago our fathers brought forth on this continent, a new nation, conceived in Liberty, and dedicated to the proposition that all men are created equal.

Now we are engaged in a great civil war, testing whether that nation, or any nation so conceived and so dedicated, can long endure. We are met on a great battle-field of that war. We have come to dedicate a portion of that field, as a final resting place for those who here gave their lives that that nation might live. It is altogether fitting and proper that we should do this.

But, in a larger sense, we can not dedicate -- we can not consecrate -- we can not hallow -- this ground. The brave men, living and dead, who struggled here, have consecrated it, far above our poor power to add or detract. The world will little note, nor long remember what we say here, but it can never forget what they did here. It is for us the living, rather, to be dedicated here to the unfinished work which they who fought here have thus far so nobly advanced. It is rather for us to be here dedicated to the great task remaining before us -- that from these honored dead we take increased devotion to that cause for which they gave the last full measure of devotion -- that we here highly resolve that these dead shall not have died in vain -- that this nation, under God, shall have a new birth of freedom -- and that government of the people, by the people, for the people, shall not perish from the earth.

Abraham Lincoln
November 19, 1863

ABRAHAM LINCOLN

Emancipation Proclamation

On January 1, 1863, two years into the bloody and devastating war,
President Abraham Lincoln issued the Emancipation Proclamation, which
called for an end to slavery only in the Confederate States that had left the
Union. The Proclamation excluded slaveholding border states which had
not seceded, thus slavery remained legal in parts of the North. This largely
symbolic gesture did not immediately free any slaves, as the Confederacy
did not recognize the authority of the United States government. But the
Emancipation Proclamation did shape perceptions of the war's purpose,
connecting Union victories to expansion of freedom for the slaves. It
also allowed black Americans to join the Union Army and Navy, which
provided another 200,000 soldiers and sailors by the end of the war.

January 1, 1863

A Transcription

By the President of the United States of America:
A Proclamation.

Whereas, on the twenty-second day of September, in
the year of our Lord one thousand eight hundred and
sixty-two, a proclamation was issued by the President
of the United States, containing, among other things, the following,
to wit:

"That on the first day of January, in the year of our Lord one
thousand eight hundred and sixty-three, all persons held as slaves
within any State or designated part of a State, the people whereof
shall then be in rebellion against the United States, shall be then,
thenceforward, and forever free; and the Executive Government

of the United States, including the military and naval authority thereof, will recognize and maintain the freedom of such persons, and will do no act or acts to repress such persons, or any of them, in any efforts they may make for their actual freedom.

"That the Executive will, on the first day of January aforesaid, by proclamation, designate the States and parts of States, if any, in which the people thereof, respectively, shall then be in rebellion against the United States; and the fact that any State, or the people thereof, shall on that day be, in good faith, represented in the Congress of the United States by members chosen thereto at elections wherein a majority of the qualified voters of such State shall have participated, shall, in the absence of strong countervailing testimony, be deemed conclusive evidence that such State, and the people thereof, are not then in rebellion against the United States."

Now, therefore I, Abraham Lincoln, President of the United States, by virtue of the power in me vested as Commander-in-Chief, of the Army and Navy of the United States in time of actual armed rebellion against the authority and government of the United States, and as a fit and necessary war measure for suppressing said rebellion, do, on this first day of January, in the year of our Lord one thousand eight hundred and sixty-three, and in accordance with my purpose so to do publicly proclaimed for the full period of one hundred days, from the day first above mentioned, order and designate as the States and parts of States wherein the people thereof respectively, are this day in rebellion against the United States, the following, to wit:

Arkansas, Texas, Louisiana, (except the Parishes of St. Bernard, Plaquemines, Jefferson, St. John, St. Charles, St. James Ascension,

Assumption, Terrebonne, Lafourche, St. Mary, St. Martin, and
Orleans, including the City of New Orleans) Mississippi, Alabama,
Florida, Georgia, South Carolina, North Carolina, and Virginia,
(except the forty-eight counties designated as West Virginia, and
also the counties of Berkley, Accomac, Northampton, Elizabeth
City, York, Princess Ann, and Norfolk, including the cities of
Norfolk and Portsmouth[)], and which excepted parts, are for the
present, left precisely as if this proclamation were not issued.

And by virtue of the power, and for the purpose aforesaid,
I do order and declare that all persons held as slaves within said
designated States, and parts of States, are, and henceforward shall
be free; and that the Executive government of the United States,
including the military and naval authorities thereof, will recognize
and maintain the freedom of said persons.

And I hereby enjoin upon the people so declared to be free to
abstain from all violence, unless in necessary self-defence; and I
recommend to them that, in all cases when allowed, they labor
faithfully for reasonable wages.

And I further declare and make known, that such persons of
suitable condition, will be received into the armed service of the
United States to garrison forts, positions, stations, and other places,
and to man vessels of all sorts in said service.

And upon this act, sincerely believed to be an act of justice,
warranted by the Constitution, upon military necessity, I invoke
the considerate judgment of mankind, and the gracious favor of
Almighty God.

In witness whereof, I have hereunto set my hand and caused the
seal of the United States to be affixed.

Done at the City of Washington, this first day of January, in the year of our Lord one thousand eight hundred and sixty three, and of the Independence of the United States of America the eighty-seventh.

By the President: Abraham Lincoln
William Seward, Secretary of State.

ABRAHAM LINCOLN

Second Inaugural Address

*This was the shortest Presidential Inaugural Address in history, at just
701 words and no more than six or seven minutes long. However, like the
even shorter Gettysburg Address, Lincoln packed much into few words,
Considered to be one of the most memorable of all inaugural addresses, it
was striking for its heavy biblical content. Historian Ronald White notes,
"Within 701 words Lincoln mentions God fourteen times, quotes the Bible
four times and invokes prayer three times." The address is also noted for
the somber tone, reflecting on the "scourge of war," which Lincoln believed
to be a judgement on America—both North and South—for the sin of
slavery, the "bondsmen's 250 years of unrequited toil." Just forty-one days
after delivering the address, Lincoln was killed by an assassin's bullet..*

Fellow-Countrymen:

At this second appearing to take the oath of the
Presidential office there is less occasion for an extended
address than there was at the first. Then a statement
somewhat in detail of a course to be pursued seemed fitting and
proper. Now, at the expiration of four years, during which public
declarations have been constantly called forth on every point and
phase of the great contest which still absorbs the attention and
engrosses the energies of the nation, little that is new could be
presented. The progress of our arms, upon which all else chiefly
depends, is as well known to the public as to myself, and it is, I trust,
reasonably satisfactory and encouraging to all. With high hope for
the future, no prediction in regard to it is ventured.

On the occasion corresponding to this four years ago all thoughts
were anxiously directed to an impending civil war. All dreaded

it, all sought to avert it. While the inaugural address was being delivered from this place, devoted altogether to saving the Union without war, insurgent agents were in the city seeking to destroy it without war--seeking to dissolve the Union and divide effects by negotiation. Both parties deprecated war, but one of them would make war rather than let the nation survive, and the other would accept war rather than let it perish, and the war came.

One-eighth of the whole population were colored slaves, not distributed generally over the Union, but localized in the southern part of it. These slaves constituted a peculiar and powerful interest. All knew that this interest was somehow the cause of the war. To strengthen, perpetuate, and extend this interest was the object for which the insurgents would rend the Union even by war, while the Government claimed no right to do more than to restrict the territorial enlargement of it. Neither party expected for the war the magnitude or the duration which it has already attained. Neither anticipated that the cause of the conflict might cease with or even before the conflict itself should cease. Each looked for an easier triumph, and a result less fundamental and astounding. Both read the same Bible and pray to the same God, and each invokes His aid against the other. It may seem strange that any men should dare to ask a just God's assistance in wringing their bread from the sweat of other men's faces, but let us judge not, that we be not judged. The prayers of both could not be answered. That of neither has been answered fully. The Almighty has His own purposes. "Woe unto the world because of offenses; for it must needs be that offenses come, but woe to that man by whom the offense cometh." If we shall suppose that American slavery is one of those offenses which, in the providence of God, must needs come, but which, having continued through His appointed time, He now wills to remove, and that He gives to both North and South this terrible war as the woe due to those by whom the offense came, shall we discern therein any departure from those divine attributes which the believers in a living God always ascribe to Him? Fondly do we hope, fervently do we pray, that this mighty scourge of war may speedily pass away. Yet, if God wills that it continue until all the wealth piled by the bondsman's two hundred and fifty years of unrequited toil shall be sunk, and until every drop of blood drawn with the lash shall be paid by another drawn with the sword, as was said three thousand years ago, so still it must be said "the judgments of the Lord are true and righteous altogether."

With malice toward none, with charity for all, with firmness in the right as God gives us to see the right, let us strive on to finish the work we are in, to bind up the nation's wounds, to care for him who shall have borne the battle and for his widow and his orphan, to do all which may achieve and cherish a just and lasting peace among ourselves and with all nations.

PHILIP BLISS

Man of Sorrows

Philip Bliss (1838-1876) was a farmboy from Pennsylvania. His father had cultivated in him a love for the gospel and for music. Bliss was ten years old when he first heard a piano. From that day, in his spare time from farm work and lumber camps, he pursued his passion, and eventually became a music teacher. Later, Bliss set out as a traveling musician and began writing hymns. His fame quickly spread. Over the course of about twelve years, he produced at least twenty hymns per year. In 1876, on their way to sing at D.L Moody's Tabernacle in Chicago, Bliss and his wife died when their train derailed and caught fire. Crawling to save his wife pinned in the wreckage, Bliss, age thirty-eight, said he would perish with her if he could not save her. His efforts did not avail, and both did indeed perish that day. In his trunk was found the beautiful hymn, "I Will Sing of My Redeemer."

Man of sorrows what a name
For the Son of God, who came
Ruined sinners to reclaim:
Hallelujah, what a Savior!

Bearing shame and scoffing rude,
In my place condemned he stood,
Sealed my pardon with his blood:
Hallelujah, what a Savior!

Guilty, helpless, lost were we;
Blameless Lamb of God was he,
Sacrificed to set us free:
Hallelujah, what a Savior!

He was lifted up to die;
"It is finished" was his cry;
Now in heaven exalted high:
Hallelujah, what a Savior!

When he comes, our glorious King,
All his ransomed home to bring,
Then anew this song we'll sing:
Hallelujah, what a Savior!

HORATIO SPAFFORD

It Is Well

*Horatio Spafford (1828-1888) was a successful Chicago businessman and
a Presbyterian church elder. The story of this hymn is as beloved as the
hymn itself. Spafford and his wife had lost their young son from scarlet
fever, and soon after had suffered devastating business losses in the Great
Chicago Fire of 1871. The family decided to go abroad together in 1873 as
a respite from their sorrows, sailing on the* Ville du Havre *to England. At
the last minute, business concerns delayed Spafford, but he sent his family
on ahead, intending to join them as soon as he could settle his affairs. The*
Ville du Havre *never made it to England; it sunk in the frigid black waters
of the Atlantic after colliding with an iron vessel. Two hundred thirty-three
souls perished that night, among them, all four of the Spaffords' daughters.
Upon arriving in England, his wife sent a telegram with only the words
"Saved alone." Spafford sailed immediately to join his wife. As he crossed
over the wreck site, he calmed his soul by saying, "It is well; the will of God
be done." The hymn then flowed freely over the tip of his pen.*

When peace, like a river, attendeth my way,
When sorrows like sea billows roll;
Whatever my lot, Thou has taught me to say,
It is well, it is well, with my soul.

Refrain
It is well, with my soul,
It is well, with my soul,
It is well, it is well, with my soul.

Though Satan should buffet, though trials should come,
Let this blest assurance control,

That Christ has regarded my helpless estate,
And hath shed His own blood for my soul.

Refrain

My sin, oh, the bliss of this glorious thought!
My sin, not in part but the whole,
Is nailed to the cross, and I bear it no more,
Praise the Lord, praise the Lord, O my soul!

Refrain

For me, be it Christ, be it Christ hence to live:
If Jordan above me shall roll,
No pang shall be mine, for in death as in life
Thou wilt whisper Thy peace to my soul.

Refrain

But, Lord, 'tis for Thee, for Thy coming we wait,
The sky, not the grave, is our goal;
Oh trump of the angel! Oh voice of the Lord!
Blessèd hope, blessèd rest of my soul!

Refrain

And Lord, haste the day when my faith shall be sight,
The clouds be rolled back as a scroll;
The trump shall resound, and the Lord shall descend,
Even so, it is well with my soul.

FANNY CROSBY

Blessed Assurance

The most prolific hymn-writer in America, Frances Jane Crosby (1820-1915), became blind at just six weeks of age due to the error of a poorly trained doctor. She lived for ninety-five years in blindness, but not in darkness. At just nine years of age, she wrote:

O what a happy soul am I,
Although I cannot see,
I am resolved that in this world
Contented I will be.
How many blessings I enjoy
That other people don't.
To weep and sigh because I'm blind,
I cannot, and I won't.

Fanny composed over 8,000 hymns in her long lifetime; many are among the most beloved hymns sung in Christian churches to this day. "Blessed Assurance," written in 1873, is one such.

Blessèd assurance, Jesus is mine!
O what a foretaste of glory divine!
Heir of salvation, purchase of God,
Born of His Spirit, washed in His blood.

Refrain

This is my story, this is my song,
Praising my Savior, all the day long;
This is my story, this is my song,

Praising my Savior, all the day long.

Refrain

Perfect submission, perfect delight,
Visions of rapture now burst on my sight;
Angels descending bring from above
Echoes of mercy, whispers of love.

Refrain

Perfect submission, all is at rest
I in my Savior am happy and blest,
Watching and waiting, looking above,
Filled with His goodness, lost in His love.

Refrain

ELIZABETH CADY STANTON

Declaration of Sentiments

Elizabeth Cady Stanton (1815-1902) organized a meeting in Seneca Falls, New York in 1848, thus launching the women's rights movement in America. Stanton, mother of seven, wrote and presented the Declaration of Sentiments, a document fashioned after the American Declaration of Independence, demanding equal rights for women in law, education, employment, and property. She also made a fierce argument for a woman's right to vote—a radical idea in 1848. Of the 300 male and female attendees, only 100 (32 male and 68 female) signed the Declaration of Sentiments, including abolitionist Frederick Douglass. Most attendees had been active in the anti-slavery abolitionist movement of the 1830s and 1840s. In 1865, Amendment XIII to the United States Constitution abolished slavery and involuntary servitude. In 1920, 18 years after Stanton's death and 72 years after the Declaration of Sentiments, Amendment XIX to the United States Constitution granted American women the right to vote.

When, in the course of human events, it becomes necessary for one portion of the family of man to assume among the people of the earth a position different from that which they have hitherto occupied, but one to which the laws of nature and of nature's God entitle them, a decent respect to the opinions of mankind requires that they should declare the causes that impel them to such a course.

We hold these truths to be self-evident; that all men and women are created equal; that they are endowed by their Creator with certain inalienable rights; that among these are life, liberty, and the pursuit of happiness; that to secure these rights governments are instituted, deriving their just powers from the consent of the governed. Whenever any form of Government becomes destructive of these ends, it is the right of those who suffer from it to refuse allegiance to it, and to insist upon the institution of a new government, laying its foundation on such principles, and organizing its powers in such form as to them shall seem most likely to effect their safety and happiness. Prudence, indeed, will dictate that governments long established should not be changed for light and transient causes; and accordingly, all experience hath shown that mankind are more disposed to suffer, while evils are sufferable, than to right themselves, by abolishing the forms to which they are accustomed. But when a long train of abuses and usurpations, pursuing invariably the same object, evinces a design to reduce them under absolute despotism, it is their duty to throw off such government, and to provide new guards for their future security. Such has been the patient sufferance of the women under this government, and such is now the necessity which constrains them to demand the equal station to which they are entitled.

The history of mankind is a history of repeated injuries and usurpations on the part of man toward woman, having in direct object the establishment of an absolute tyranny over her. To prove this, let facts be submitted to a candid world.

He has never permitted her to exercise her inalienable right to the elective franchise.

He has compelled her to submit to laws, in the formation of which she had no voice.

He has withheld from her rights which are given to the most

ignorant and degraded men - both natives and foreigners.

Having deprived her of this first right of a citizen, the elective franchise, thereby leaving her without representation in the halls of legislation, he has oppressed her on all sides.

He has made her, if married, in the eye of the law, civilly dead.

He has taken from her all right in property, even to the wages she earns.

He has made her, morally, an irresponsible being, as she can commit many crimes, with impunity, provided they be done in the presence of her husband. In the covenant of marriage, she is compelled to promise obedience to her husband, he becoming, to all intents and purposes, her master - the law giving him power to deprive her of her liberty, and to administer chastisement.

He has so framed the laws of divorce, as to what shall be the proper causes of divorce; in case of separation, to whom the guardianship of the children shall be given, as to be wholly regardless of the happiness of women - the law, in all cases, going upon the false supposition of the supremacy of man, and giving all power into his hands.

After depriving her of all rights as a married woman, if single and the owner of property, he has taxed her to support a government which recognizes her only when her property can be made profitable to it.

He has monopolized nearly all the profitable employments, and from those she is permitted to follow, she receives but a scanty remuneration.

He closes against her all the avenues to wealth and distinction, which he considers most honorable to himself. As a teacher of theology, medicine, or law, she is not known.

He has denied her the facilities for obtaining a thorough education - all colleges being closed against her.

He allows her in Church as well as State, but a subordinate position, claiming Apostolic authority for her exclusion from the ministry, and with some exceptions, from any public participation in the affairs of the Church.

He has created a false public sentiment, by giving to the world a different code of morals for men and women, by which moral delinquencies which exclude women from society, are not only tolerated but deemed of little account in man.

He has usurped the prerogative of Jehovah himself, claiming it as his right to assign for her a sphere of action, when that belongs to her conscience and her God.

He has endeavored, in every way that he could to destroy her confidence in her own powers, to lessen her self-respect, and to make her willing to lead a dependent and abject life.

Now, in view of this entire disfranchisement of one-half the people of this country, their social and religious degradation, - in view of the unjust laws above mentioned, and because women do feel themselves aggrieved, oppressed, and fraudulently deprived of their most sacred rights, we insist that they have immediate admission to all the rights and privileges which belong to them as citizens of these United States.

In entering upon the great work before us, we anticipate no small amount of misconception, misrepresentation, and ridicule; but we shall use every instrumentality within our power to effect our object. We shall employ agents, circulate tracts, petition the State and national Legislatures, and endeavor to enlist the pulpit and the press in our behalf. We hope this Convention will be followed by a series of Conventions, embracing every part of the country.

Firmly relying upon the final triumph of the Right and the True, we do this day affix our signatures to this declaration.

WILLIAM JENNINGS BRYAN

Cross of Gold Speech

From 1868 up to 1892, with the exception of 1880, the Democratic Party had always nominated a man from New York, since New York was the swing state needed to win. At the 1896 Democratic National Convention in Chicago former Congressman William Jennings Bryan of Nebraska electrified the audience with his "Cross of Gold" speech, which advocated in favor of expanding the money supply through silver coinage in place of the fixed money supply provided by the gold standard in effect at that time. Bryan's argument did not prevail, but the gold standard did not survive the Great Depression of the twentieth century.

I would be presumptuous, indeed, to present myself against the distinguished gentlemen to whom you have listened if this were but a measuring of ability; but this is not a contest among persons. The humblest citizen in all the land when clad in the armor of a righteous cause is stronger than all the whole hosts of error that they can bring. I come to speak to you in defense of a cause as holy as the cause of liberty—the cause of humanity. When this debate is concluded, a motion will be made to lay upon the table the resolution offered in commendation of the administration and also the resolution in condemnation of the administration. I shall object to bringing this question down to a level of persons. The individual is but an atom; he is born, he acts, he dies; but principles are eternal; and this has been a contest of principle.

Never before in the history of this country has there been witnessed such a contest as that through which we have passed. Never before in the history of American politics has a great issue been fought out as this issue has been by the voters themselves.

On the 4th of March, 1895, a few Democrats, most of them members of Congress, issued an address to the Democrats of the nation asserting that the money question was the paramount issue of the hour; asserting also the right of a majority of the Democratic Party to control the position of the party on this paramount issue; concluding with the request that all believers in free coinage of silver in the Democratic Party should organize and take charge of and control the policy of the Democratic Party. Three months later, at Memphis, an organization was perfected, and the silver Democrats went forth openly and boldly and courageously proclaiming their belief and declaring that if successful they would crystallize in a platform the declaration which they had made; and then began the conflict with a zeal approaching the zeal which inspired the crusaders who followed Peter the Hermit. Our silver Democrats went forth from victory unto victory, until they are assembled now, not to discuss, not to debate, but to enter up the judgment rendered by the plain people of this country.

But in this contest, brother has been arrayed against brother, and father against son. The warmest ties of love and acquaintance and association have been disregarded. Old leaders have been cast aside when they refused to give expression to the sentiments of those whom they would lead, and new leaders have sprung up to give direction to this cause of freedom. Thus has the contest been waged, and we have assembled here under as binding and solemn instructions as were ever fastened upon the representatives of a people.

We do not come as individuals. Why, as individuals we might have been glad to compliment the gentleman from New York

[Senator Hill], but we knew that the people for whom we speak would never be willing to put him in a position where he could thwart the will of the Democratic Party. I say it was not a question of persons; it was a question of principle; and it is not with gladness, my friends, that we find ourselves brought into conflict with those who are now arrayed on the other side. The gentleman who just preceded me [Governor Russell] spoke of the old state of Massachusetts. Let me assure him that not one person in all this convention entertains the least hostility to the people of the state of Massachusetts.

But we stand here representing people who are the equals before the law of the largest cities in the state of Massachusetts. When you come before us and tell us that we shall disturb your business interests, we reply that you have disturbed our business interests by your action. We say to you that you have made too limited in its application the definition of a businessman. The man who is employed for wages is as much a businessman as his employer. The attorney in a country town is as much a businessman as the corporation counsel in a great metropolis. The merchant at the crossroads store is as much a businessman as the merchant of New York. The farmer who goes forth in the morning and toils all day, begins in the spring and toils all summer, and by the application of brain and muscle to the natural resources of this country creates wealth, is as much a businessman as the man who goes upon the Board of Trade and bets upon the price of grain. The miners who go 1,000 feet into the earth or climb 2,000 feet upon the cliffs and bring forth from their hiding places the precious metals to be poured in the channels of trade are as much businessmen as the few financial magnates who in a backroom corner the money of the world.

We come to speak for this broader class of businessmen. Ah.
my friends, we say not one word against those who live upon the
Atlantic Coast; but those hardy pioneers who braved all the dangers
of the wilderness, who have made the desert to blossom as the
rose—those pioneers away out there, rearing their children near to
nature's heart, where they can mingle their voices with the voices
of the birds—out there where they have erected schoolhouses for
the education of their children and churches where they praise their
Creator, and the cemeteries where sleep the ashes of their dead—are
as deserving of the consideration of this party as any people in this
country.

It is for these that we speak. We do not come as aggressors. Our
war is not a war of conquest. We are fighting in the defense of our
homes, our families, and posterity. We have petitioned, and our
petitions have been scorned. We have entreated, and our entreaties
have been disregarded. We have begged, and they have mocked
when our calamity came.

We beg no longer; we entreat no more; we petition no more. We defy
them!

The gentleman from Wisconsin has said he fears a Robespierre.
My friend, in this land of the free you need fear no tyrant who will
spring up from among the people. What we need is an Andrew
Jackson to stand as Jackson stood, against the encroachments of
aggregated wealth.

They tell us that this platform was made to catch votes. We
reply to them that changing conditions make new issues; that
the principles upon which rest Democracy are as everlasting as
the hills; but that they must be applied to new conditions as they

arise. Conditions have arisen and we are attempting to meet those conditions. They tell us that the income tax ought not to be brought in here; that is not a new idea. They criticize us for our criticism of the Supreme Court of the United States. My friends, we have made no criticism. We have simply called attention to what you know. If you want criticisms, read the dissenting opinions of the Court. That will give you criticisms.

They say we passed an unconstitutional law. I deny it. The income tax was not unconstitutional when it was passed. It was not unconstitutional when it went before the Supreme Court for the first time. It did not become unconstitutional until one judge changed his mind; and we cannot be expected to know when a judge will change his mind.

The income tax is a just law. It simply intends to put the burdens of government justly upon the backs of the people. I am in favor of an income tax. When I find a man who is not willing to pay his share of the burden of the government which protects him, I find a man who is unworthy to enjoy the blessings of a government like ours.

He says that we are opposing the national bank currency. It is true. If you will read what Thomas Benton said, you will find that he said that in searching history he could find but one parallel to Andrew Jackson. That was Cicero, who destroyed the conspiracies of Cataline and saved Rome. He did for Rome what Jackson did when he destroyed the bank conspiracy and saved America.

We say in our platform that we believe that the right to coin money and issue money is a function of government. We believe it. We believe it is a part of sovereignty and can no more with safety be delegated to private individuals than can the power to make penal statutes or levy laws for taxation.

Mr. Jefferson, who was once regarded as good Democratic authority, seems to have a different opinion from the gentleman who has addressed us on the part of the minority. Those who are opposed to this proposition tell us that the issue of paper money is a function of the bank and that the government ought to go out of the banking business. I stand with Jefferson rather than with them, and tell them, as he did, that the issue of money is a function of the government and that the banks should go out of the governing business.

They complain about the plank which declares against the life tenure in office. They have tried to strain it to mean that which it does not mean. What we oppose in that plank is the life tenure that is being built up in Washington which establishes an office-holding class and excludes from participation in the benefits the humbler members of our society. . . .

Let me call attention to two or three great things. The gentleman from New York says that he will propose an amendment providing that this change in our law shall not affect contracts which, according to the present laws, are made payable in gold. But if he means to say that we cannot change our monetary system without protecting those who have loaned money before the change was made, I want to ask him where, in law or in morals, he can find authority for not protecting the debtors when the act of 1873 was passed when he now insists that we must protect the creditor. He says he also wants to amend this platform so as to provide that if we fail to maintain the parity within a year that we will then suspend the coinage of silver. We reply that when we advocate a thing which we believe will be successful we are not compelled to raise a doubt as to our own sincerity by trying to show what we will do if we are wrong.

I ask him, if he will apply his logic to us, why he does not apply it to himself. He says that he wants this country to try to secure an international agreement. Why doesn't he tell us what he is going to do if they fail to secure an international agreement. There is more reason for him to do that than for us to expect to fail to maintain the parity. They have tried for thirty years—thirty years—to secure an international agreement, and those are waiting for it most patiently who don't want it at all.

Now, my friends, let me come to the great paramount issue. If they ask us here why it is we say more on the money question than we say upon the tariff question, I reply that if protection has slain its thousands the gold standard has slain its tens of thousands. If they ask us why we did not embody all these things in our platform which we believe, we reply to them that when we have restored the money of the Constitution, all other necessary reforms will be possible, and that until that is done there is no reform that can be accomplished.

Why is it that within three months such a change has come over the sentiments of the country? Three months ago, when it was confidently asserted that those who believed in the gold standard would frame our platforms and nominate our candidates, even the advocates of the gold standard did not think that we could elect a President; but they had good reasons for the suspicion, because there is scarcely a state here today asking for the gold standard that is not within the absolute control of the Republican Party.

But note the change. Mr. McKinley was nominated at St. Louis upon a platform that declared for the maintenance of the gold standard until it should be changed into bimetallism by an international agreement. Mr. McKinley was the most popular man among the Republicans ; and everybody three months ago in the Republican Party prophesied his election. How is it today? Why, that man who used to boast that he looked like Napoleon, that man shudders today when he thinks that he was nominated on the anniversary of the Battle of Waterloo. Not only that, but as he listens he can hear with ever increasing distinctness the sound of the waves as they beat upon the lonely shores of St. Helena.

Why this change? Ah, my friends. is not the change evident to anyone who will look at the matter? It is because no private character, however pure, no personal popularity, however great, can protect from the avenging wrath of an indignant people the man who will either declare that he is in favor of fastening the gold standard upon this people, or who is willing to surrender the right of self-government and place legislative control in the hands of foreign potentates and powers. . . .

We go forth confident that we shall win. Why? Because upon the paramount issue in this campaign there is not a spot of ground upon which the enemy will dare to challenge battle. Why, if they tell us that the gold standard is a good thing, we point to their platform and tell them that their platform pledges the party to get rid of a gold standard and substitute bimetallism. If the gold standard is a good thing, why try to get rid of it? If the gold standard, and I might call your attention to the fact that some of the very people who are in this convention today and who tell you that we ought to declare in favor of international bimetallism and thereby declare that the gold standard is wrong and that the principles of bimetallism are better—these very people four months ago were open and avowed advocates of the gold standard and telling us that we could not legislate two metals together even with all the world.

I want to suggest this truth, that if the gold standard is a good thing we ought to declare in favor of its retention and not in favor of abandoning it; and if the gold standard is a bad thing, why should we wait until some other nations are willing to help us to let it go?

Here is the line of battle. We care not upon which issue they force the fight. We are prepared to meet them on either issue or on both. If they tell us that the gold standard is the standard of civilization, we reply to them that this, the most enlightened of all nations of the earth, has never declared for a gold standard, and both the parties this year are declaring against it. If the gold standard is the standard of civilization, why, my friends, should we not have it? So if they come to meet us on that, we can present the history of our nation. More than that, we can tell them this, that they will search the pages of history in vain to find a single instance in which the common people of any land ever declared themselves in favor of a gold standard. They can find where the holders of fixed investments have.

Mr. Carlisle said in 1878 that this was a struggle between the idle holders of idle capital and the struggling masses who produce the wealth and pay the taxes of the country; and my friends, it is simply a question that we shall decide upon which side shall the Democratic Party fight. Upon the side of the idle holders of idle capital, or upon the side of the struggling masses? That is the question that the party must answer first; and then it must be answered by each individual hereafter. The sympathies of the Democratic Party, as described by the platform, are on the side of the struggling masses, who have ever been the foundation of the Democratic Party.

There are two ideas of government. There are those who believe that if you just legislate to make the well-to-do prosperous, that their prosperity will leak through on those below. The Democratic idea has been that if you legislate to make the masses prosperous their prosperity will find its way up and through every class that rests upon it.

You come to us and tell us that the great cities are in favor of the gold standard. I tell you that the great cities rest upon these broad and fertile prairies. Burn down your cities and leave our farms, and your cities will spring up again as if by magic. But destroy our farms and the grass will grow in the streets of every city in the country.

My friends, we shall declare that this nation is able to legislate for its own people on every question without waiting for the aid or consent of any other nation on earth, and upon that issue we expect to carry every single state in the Union.

I shall not slander the fair state of Massachusetts nor the state of New York by saying that when citizens are confronted with the proposition, "Is this nation able to attend to its own business?"—I will not slander either one by saying that the people of those states will declare our helpless impotency as a nation to attend to our own business. It is the issue of 1776 over again. Our ancestors, when but 3 million, had the courage to declare their political independence of every other nation upon earth. Shall we, their descendants, when we have grown to 70 million, declare that we are less independent than our forefathers? No, my friends, it will never be the judgment of this people. Therefore, we care not upon what lines the battle is fought. If they say bimetallism is good but we cannot have it till some nation helps us, we reply that, instead of having a gold standard because England has, we shall restore bimetallism, and then let England have bimetallism because the United States have.

If they dare to come out in the open field and defend the gold standard as a good thing, we shall fight them to the uttermost, having behind us the producing masses of the nation and the world. Having behind us the commercial interests and the laboring interests and all the toiling masses, we shall answer their demands for a gold standard by saying to them, you shall not press down upon the brow of labor this crown of thorns. You shall not crucify mankind upon a cross of gold.

KATHARINE LEE BATES

America, The Beautiful

Katharine Lee Bates (1859-1929) was born on the coast of New Englad in Falmouth, Massachusetts. In 1893 as a professor of English Literature at Wellesley College, Bates travelled to Colorado to teach a summer course. While on an end-of-session celebratory excursion to Pike's Peak in the Rocky Mountains, she penned the words to one of America's best-loved patriotic songs. She later wrote, "It was then and there, as I was looking out over the sea-like expanse of fertile country spreading away so far under those ample skies, that the opening lines of the hymn floated into my mind." Bates' poem first appeared in The Congregationalist *on July 4, 1895. After several revisions, the hymn was set to music composed by Samuel A. Ward.*

O beautiful for halcyon skies,
For amber waves of grain,
For purple mountain majesties
Above the enameled plain!
America! America!
God shed His grace on thee,
Till souls wax fair as earth and air
And music-hearted sea!

O beautiful for pilgrim feet
Whose stern, impassioned stress
A thoroughfare for freedom beat
Across the wilderness!
America! America!
God shed His grace on thee

Till paths be wrought through wilds of thought
By pilgrim foot and knee!

O beautiful for glory-tale
Of liberating strife,
When once or twice, for man's avail,
Men lavished precious life!
America! America!
God shed His grace on thee
Till selfish gain no longer stain, The banner of the free!

O beautiful for patriot dream
That sees beyond the years
Thine alabaster cities gleam
Undimmed by human tears!
America! America!
God shed His grace on thee
Till nobler men keep once again
Thy whiter jubilee!

THEODORE ROOSEVELT
The Man with the Muck Rake

In 1901, Vice President Theodore Roosevelt was propelled into the
presidency by the bullet of President William McKinley's assassin. At the
age of forty-three, "Teddy" became the youngest president in American
history. This hero of the Spanish American War and the former Governor
of New York brought his progressive vigor to the White House in affairs
both foreign and domestic. He championed the Sherman Antitrust Act,
broke up the railroad monopolies, and advocated for fair labor and food
safety laws. A nature conservationist, Teddy Roosevelt significantly
enlarged National Park lands in the western states. He strengthened the
United States as a global military power and oversaw the construction of
the Panama Canal. In every way, he lived up to his motto "Speak softly,
and carry a big stick."

Teddy Roosevelt is also remembered today for coining the term
"muckraker," to describe the investigative journalists of the early 20th
century. In 1906, Upton Sinclair The Jungle, a novel which exposed
horrific practices in the meatpacking industry. This helped spur many
"muckrakers" to expose other practices in labor and industry, leading to
changes in labor and food safety laws. In this speech, Roosevelt reproves
muckrakers for their tendency toward character assasination.

Over a century ago Washington laid the corner stone of
the Capitol in what was then little more than a tract of
wooded wilderness here beside the Potomac. We now find
it necessary to provide by great additional buildings for the business
of the government.

This growth in the need for the housing of the government is but a proof and example of the way in which the nation has grown and the sphere of action of the national government has grown. We now administer the affairs of a nation in which the extraordinary growth of population has been outstripped by the growth of wealth in complex interests. The material problems that face us today are not such as they were in Washington's time, but the underlying facts of human nature are the same now as they were then. Under altered external form we war with the same tendencies toward evil that were evident in Washington's time, and are helped by the same tendencies for good. It is about some of these that I wish to say a word today.

In Bunyan's "Pilgrim's Progress" you may recall the description of the Man with the Muck Rake, the man who could look no way but downward, with the muck rake in his hand; who was offered a celestial crown for his muck rake, but who would neither look up nor regard the crown he was offered, but continued to rake to himself the filth of the floor.

In "Pilgrim's Progress" the Man with the Muck Rake is set forth as the example of him whose vision is fixed on carnal instead of spiritual things. Yet he also typifies the man who in this life consistently refuses to see aught that is lofty, and fixes his eyes with solemn intentness only on that which is vile and debasing.

Now, it is very necessary that we should not flinch from seeing what is vile and debasing. There is filth on the floor, and it must be scraped up with the muck rake; and there are times and places where this service is the most needed of all the services that can be performed. But the man who never does anything else, who never thinks or speaks or writes, save of his feats with the muck rake, speedily becomes, not a help but one of the most potent forces for evil.

There are in the body politic, economic and social, many and grave evils, and there is urgent necessity for the sternest war upon them. There should be relentless exposure of and attack upon every evil man, whether politician or business man, every evil practice, whether in politics, business, or social life. I hail as a benefactor every writer or speaker, every man who, on the platform or in a book, magazine, or newspaper, with merciless severity makes such attack, provided always that he in his turn remembers that the attack is of use only if it is absolutely truthful.

The liar is no whit better than the thief, and if his mendacity takes the form of slander he may be worse than most thieves. It puts a premium upon knavery untruthfully to attack an honest man, or even with hysterical exaggeration to assail a bad man with untruth.

An epidemic of indiscriminate assault upon character does no good, but very great harm. The soul of every scoundrel is gladdened whenever an honest man is assailed, or even when a scoundrel is untruthfully assailed.

Now, it is easy to twist out of shape what I have just said, easy to affect to misunderstand it, and if it is slurred over in repetition not difficult really to misunderstand it. Some persons are sincerely incapable of understanding that to denounce mud slinging does not mean the endorsement of whitewashing; and both the interested individuals who need whitewashing and those others who practice mud slinging like to encourage such confusion of ideas.

One of the chief counts against those who make indiscriminate assault upon men in business or men in public life is that they invite a reaction which is sure to tell powerfully in favor of the unscrupulous scoundrel who really ought to be attacked, who ought to be exposed, who ought, if possible, to be put in the penitentiary. If Aristides is praised overmuch as just, people get tired of hearing it; and over-censure of the unjust finally and from similar reasons results in their favor.

Any excess is almost sure to invite a reaction; and, unfortunately, the reactions instead of taking the form of punishment of those guilty of the excess, is apt to take the form either of punishment of the unoffending or of giving immunity, and even strength, to offenders. The effort to make financial or political profit out of the destruction of character can only result in public calamity. Gross and reckless assaults on character, whether on the stump or in newspaper, magazine, or book, create a morbid and vicious public sentiment, and at the same time act as a profound deterrent to able men of normal sensitiveness and tend to prevent them from entering the public service at any price.

As an instance in point, I may mention that one serious difficulty encountered in getting the right type of men to dig the Panama canal is the certainty that they will be exposed, both without, and, I am sorry to say, sometimes within, Congress, to utterly reckless assaults on their character and capacity.

At the risk of repetition let me say again that my plea is not for immunity to, but for the most unsparing exposure of, the politician who betrays his trust, of the big business man who makes or spends his fortune in illegitimate or corrupt ways. There should be a resolute effort to hunt every such man out of the position he has disgraced. Expose the crime, and hunt down the criminal;

but remember that even in the case of crime, if it is attacked in sensational, lurid, and untruthful fashion, the attack may do more damage to the public mind than the crime itself.

It is because I feel that there should be no rest in the endless war against the forces of evil that I ask the war be conducted with sanity as well as with resolution. The men with the muck rakes are often indispensable to the well being of society; but only if they know when to stop raking the muck, and to look upward to the celestial crown above them, to the crown of worthy endeavor. There are beautiful things above and round about them; and if they gradually grow to feel that the whole world is nothing but muck, their power of usefulness is gone.

If the whole picture is painted black there remains no hue whereby to single out the rascals for distinction from their fellows. Such painting finally induces a kind of moral color blindness; and people affected by it come to the conclusion that no man is really black, and no man really white, but they are all gray.

In other words, they neither believe in the truth of the attack, nor in the honesty of the man who is attacked; they grow as suspicious of the accusation as of the offense; it becomes well nigh hopeless to stir them either to wrath against wrongdoing or to enthusiasm for what is right; and such a mental attitude in the public gives hope to every knave, and is the despair of honest men. To assail the great and admitted evils of our political and industrial life with such crude and sweeping generalizations as to include decent men in the general condemnation means the searing of the public conscience. There results a general attitude either of cynical belief in and indifference to public corruption or else of a distrustful inability to discriminate between the good and the bad. Either attitude is fraught with untold damage to the country as a whole.

The fool who has not sense to discriminate between what is good and what is bad is well nigh as dangerous as the man who does discriminate and yet chooses the bad. There is nothing more distressing to every good patriot, to every good American, than the hard, scoffing spirit which treats the allegation of dishonesty in a public man as a cause for laughter. Such laughter is worse than the crackling of thorns under a pot, for it denotes not merely the vacant mind, but the heart in which high emotions have been choked before they could grow to fruition. There is any amount of good in the world, and there never was a time when loftier and more disinterested work for the betterment of mankind was being done than now. The forces that tend for evil are great and terrible, but the forces of truth and love and courage and honesty and generosity and sympathy are also stronger than ever before. It is a foolish and timid, no less than a wicked thing, to blink the fact that the forces of evil are strong, but it is even worse to fail to take into account the strength of the forces that tell for good.

Hysterical sensationalism is the poorest weapon wherewith to fight for lasting righteousness. The men who with stern sobriety and truth assail the many evils of our time, whether in the public press, or in magazines, or in books, are the leaders and allies of all engaged in the work for social and political betterment. But if they give good reason for distrust of what they say, if they chill the ardor of those who demand truth as a primary virtue, they thereby betray the good cause and play into the hands of the very men against whom they are nominally at war.

In his Ecclesiastical Polity that fine old Elizabethan divine, Bishop Hooker, wrote:

He that goeth about to persuade a multitude that they are not so well governed as they ought to be shall never want attentive and favorable hearers, because they know the manifold defects whereunto every kind of regimen is subject, but the secret lets and difficulties, which in public proceedings are innumerable and inevitable, they have not ordinarily the judgment to consider.

This truth should be kept constantly in mind by every free people desiring to preserve the sanity and poise indispensable to the permanent success of self-government. Yet, on the other hand, it is vital not to permit this spirit of sanity and self-command to degenerate into mere mental stagnation. Bad though a state of hysterical excitement is, and evil though the results are which come from the violent oscillations such excitement invariably produces, yet a sodden acquiescence in evil is even worse.

At this moment we are passing through a period of great unrest-social, political, and industrial unrest. It is of the utmost importance for our future that this should prove to be not the unrest of mere rebelliousness against life, of mere dissatisfaction with the inevitable inequality of conditions, but the unrest of a resolute and eager ambition to secure the betterment of the individual and the nation.

So far as this movement of agitation throughout the country takes the form of a fierce discontent with evil, of a determination to punish the authors of evil, whether in industry or politics, the feeling is to be heartily welcomed as a sign of healthy life.

If, on the other hand, it turns into a mere crusade of appetite against appetite, of a contest between the brutal greed of the "have nots" and the brutal greed of the "haves," then it has no significance for good, but only for evil. If it seeks to establish a line of cleavage, not along the line which divides good men from bad, but along that other line, running at right angles thereto, which divides those who are well off from those who are less well off, then it will be fraught with immeasurable harm to the body politic.

We can no more and no less afford to condone evil in the man of capital than evil in the man of no capital. The wealthy man who exults because there is a failure of justice in the effort to bring some trust magnate to account for his misdeeds is as bad as, and no worse than, the so-called labor leader who clamorously strives to excite a foul class feeling on behalf of some other labor leader who is implicated in murder. One attitude is as bad as the other, and no worse; in each case the accused is entitled to exact justice; and in neither case is there need of action by others which can be construed into an expression of sympathy for crime.

It is a prime necessity that if the present unrest is to result in permanent good the emotion shall be translated into action, and that the action shall be marked by honesty, sanity, and self-restraint. There is mighty little good in a mere spasm of reform. The reform that counts is that which comes through steady, continuous growth; violent emotionalism leads to exhaustion.

It is important to this people to grapple with the problems connected with the amassing of enormous fortunes, and the use of those fortunes, both corporate and individual, in business. We should discriminate in the sharpest way between fortunes well won and fortunes ill won; between those gained as an incident to performing great services to the community as a whole and those gained in evil fashion by keeping just within the limits of mere law honesty. Of course, no amount of charity in spending such fortunes in any way compensates for misconduct in making them.

As a matter of personal conviction, and without pretending to discuss the details or formulate the system, I feel that we shall ultimately have to consider the adoption of some such scheme as that of a progressive tax on all fortunes, beyond a certain amount, either given in life or devised or bequeathed upon death to any individual-a tax so framed as to put it out of the power of the owner of one of these enormous fortunes to hand on more than a certain amount to any one individual; the tax of course, to be imposed by the national and not the state government. Such taxation should, of course, be aimed merely at the inheritance or transmission in their entirety of those fortunes swollen beyond all healthy limits. Again, the national government must in some form exercise supervision over corporations engaged in interstate business-and all large corporations engaged in interstate business-whether by license or otherwise, so as to permit us to deal with the far reaching evils of overcapitalization.

This year we are making a beginning in the direction of serious effort to settle some of these economic problems by the railway rate legislation. Such legislation, if so framed, as I am sure it will be, as to secure definite and tangible results, will amount to something of itself; and it will amount to a great deal more in so far as it is taken as a first step in the direction of a policy of superintendence and control over corporate wealth engaged in interstate commerce; this superintendence and control not to be exercised in a spirit of malevolence toward the men who have created the wealth, but with

the firm purpose both to do justice to them and to see that they in
their turn do justice to the public at large.

The first requisite in the public servants who are to deal in this
shape with corporations, whether as legislators or as executives, is
honesty. This honesty can be no respecter of persons. There can be
no such thing as unilateral honesty. The danger is not really from
corrupt corporations; it springs from the corruption itself, whether
exercised for or against corporations.

The eighth commandment reads, "Thou shalt not steal." It does
not read, "Thou shalt not steal from the rich man." It does not
read, "Thou shalt not steal from the poor man." It reads simply and
plainly, "Thou shalt not steal."

No good whatever will come from that warped and mock
morality which denounces the misdeeds of men of wealth and forgets
the misdeeds practiced at their expense; which denounces bribery,
but blinds itself to blackmail; which foams with rage if a corporation
secures favors by improper methods, and merely leers with hideous
mirth if the corporation is itself wronged.

The only public servant who can be trusted honestly to protect
the rights of the public against the misdeeds of a corporation is that
public man who will just as surely protect the corporation itself from
wrongful aggression.

If a public man is willing to yield to popular clamor and do
wrong to the men of wealth or to rich corporations, it may be set
down as certain that if the opportunity comes he will secretly and
furtively do wrong to the public in the interest of a corporation.

But in addition to honesty, we need sanity. No honesty will make a public man useful if that man is timid or foolish, if he is a hot-headed zealot or an impracticable visionary. As we strive for reform we find that it is not at all merely the case of a long uphill pull. On the contrary, there is almost as much of breeching work as of collar work. To depend only on traces means that there will soon be a runaway and an upset.

The men of wealth who today are trying to prevent the regulation and control of their business in the interest of the public by the proper government authorities will not succeed, in my judgment, in checking the progress of the movement. But if they did succeed they would find that they had sown the wind and would surely reap the whirlwind, for they would ultimately provoke the violent excesses which accompany a reform coming by convulsion instead of by steady and natural growth.

On the other hand, the wild preachers of unrest and discontent, the wild agitators against the entire existing order, the men who act crookedly, whether because of sinister design or from mere puzzle headedness, the men who preach destruction without proposing any substitute for what they intend to destroy, or who propose a substitute which would be far worse than the existing evils-all these men are the most dangerous opponents of real reform. If they get their way they will lead the people into a deeper pit than any into which they could fall under the present system. If they fail to get their way they will still do incalculable harm by provoking the kind of reaction which in its revolt against the senseless evil of their teaching would enthrone more securely than ever the evils which their misguided followers believe they are attacking.

More important than aught else is the development of the

broadest sympathy of man for man. The welfare of the wage worker, the welfare of the tiller of the soil, upon these depend the welfare of the entire country; their good is not to be sought in pulling down others; but their good must be the prime object of all our statesmanship.

Materially we must strive to secure a broader economic opportunity for all men, so that each shall have a better chance to show the stuff of which he is made. Spiritually and ethically we must strive to bring about clean living and right thinking. We appreciate that the things of the body are important; but we appreciate also that the things of the soul are immeasurably more important.

The foundation stone of national life is, and ever must be, the high individual character of the average citizen.

BIBLIOGRAPHY

This Bibliography lists works that we have used in researching and creating these *Primary Source Readers*. Some are cited by short footnotes throughout the text. The texts, poems, hymns and biographical sketch excerpts are in the public domain unless otherwise noted.

Oxford English Dictionary Online. Oxford University Press. http://www.oed.com (accessed May 30, 2020).

Merriam-Webster.com Dictionary. Merriam-Webster, https://www.merriam-webster.com.

Made in the USA
Middletown, DE
13 August 2020